INTERNATIONAL FINANCIAL REPORTING STANDARDS: CONTEXT, ANALYSIS AND COMMENT

INTERNATIONAL FINANCIAL REPORTING STANDARDS: CONTEXT, ANALYSIS AND COMMENT

Critical Perspectives in Business and Management

Edited by
David Alexander and
Christopher Nobes

Volume II
The early years of the International Accounting Standards Committee

Routledge
Taylor & Francis Group

LONDON AND NEW YORK

First published 2008
by Routledge
2 Park Square, Milton Park, Abingdon, Oxon, OX14 4RN, UK

Simultaneously published in the USA and Canada
by Routledge
270 Madison Avenue, New York, NY 10016

Routledge is an imprint of the Taylor & Francis Group, an informa business

Typeset in 10/12pt Times NR MT by Graphicraft Limited, Hong Kong
Printed and bound in Great Britain by
MPG Books Ltd, Bodmin, Cornwall

British Library Cataloguing in Publication Data
A catalogue record for this book is available from the British Library

Library of Congress Cataloging in Publication Data

International financial reporting standards : context, analysis and comment /
edited by David Alexander and Christopher Nobes.
p. cm. – (Critical perspectives on business and management)
Includes bibliographical references and index.
ISBN 978-0-415-38097-3 (set) – ISBN 978-0-415-38098-0 (cloth : alk. paper)
1. International Accounting Standards Board.   2. International Accounting Standards
Committee.   3. Financial statements – Standards.   4. Accounting –
Standards.   I. Alexander, David, 1941–   II. Nobes, Christopher.
HF5626.I58376   2007
657′.30218–dc22   2007045142

ISBN10: 0-415-38097-9 (Set)
ISBN10: 0-415-38099-5 (Volume II)

ISBN13: 978-0-415-38097-3 (Set)
ISBN13: 978-0-415-38099-7 (Volume II)

Publisher's Note

References within each chapter are as they appear in the original
complete work.

CONTENTS

CONTENTS

vi

CONTENTS

ACKNOWLEDGEMENTS

The publishers would like to thank the following for permission to reprint their material:

Peter Walton for permission to reprint P. Walton, 'Accountancy – the Most Exciting Profession in the World' (an 'Interview with Lord Benson'), *Accounting and Business*, June 1996, pp. 12–13. Reprinted with permission.

AICPA for permission to reprint W. E. Olson, 'The Establishment of International Organizations', in *The Accounting Profession – Years of Trial: 1969–1980* (New York: AICPA, 1982), pp. 223–243.

Canadian Institute of Chartered Accountants CICA for kind permission to reproduce J. A. Hepworth, 'International Accounting Standards Committee – The Future', in W. J. Brennan, ed., *The Internationalization of the Accountancy Profession* (Toronto: CICA, 1979) pp. 40–57.

American Institute of Certified Public Accountants for permission to reprint J. A. Burggraaff, 'IASC Developments: An Update', *Journal of Accountancy*, September 1982, pp. 104–110. Copyright © 1982 from *The Journal of Accountancy* by the AICPA. Opinions of the authors are their own and do not necessarily reflect policies of the AICPA. Reprinted with permission.

International Accounting Standards Committee Foundation for kind permission to reprint ICAEW (and others), An Agreement to Establish an International Accounting Standards Committee, (London: ICAEW, etc., 1973). Reproduced by kind permission of the International Accounting Standards Committee Foundation.

International Accounting Standards Committee Foundation for kind permission to reprint IASC, Preface to Statements of International Accounting Standards (London: IASC, 1983). Reproduced by kind permission of the International Accounting Standards Committee Foundation.

International Accounting Standards Committee Foundation for kind permission to reprint IASC, Constitution of the International Accounting

Standards Committee, (London: IASC, 1992). Reproduced by kind permission of the International Accounting Standards Committee Foundation.

Elsevier for permission to reprint William J. Violet, 'The Development of International Accounting Standards: An Anthropological Perspective'. This article was published in *International Journal of Accounting*, Education and Research, Spring 1983, pp. 1–12. Copyright Elsevier 1983. Reprinted with permission.

Elsevier for permission to reprint Juan M. Rivera, 'The Internationalization of Accounting Standards: Past Problems and Current Prospects'. This article was published in *International Journal of Accounting*, 24, 4, 1989, pp. 320–341. Copyright Elsevier 1989. Reprinted with permission.

American Accounting Association for permission to reprint R. S. Olusegun Wallace, 'Survival Strategies of a Global Organization: The Case of the International Accounting Standards Committee', *Accounting Horizons*, 4, 2, June 1990, pp. 1–22. Reproduced by kind permission of the American Accounting Association.

American Accounting Association for permission to reprint R. K. Goeltz, 'International Accounting Harmonization: The Impossible (and Unnecessary?) Dream', *Accounting Horizons*, March 1991, pp. 85–88. Reproduced by kind permission of the American Accounting Association.

American Accounting Association for permission to reprint S. E. C. Purvis, H. Gernon and M. A. Diamond, 'The IASC and its Comparability Project: Prerequisites for Success', *Accounting Horizons*, June 1991, pp. 25–44. Reproduced by kind permission of the American Accounting Association and the authors.

S. E. C. Purvis for permission to reprint S. E. C. Purvis, H. Gernon and M. A. Diamond, 'The IASC and its Comparability Project: Prerequisites for Success', *Accounting Horizons*, June 1991, pp. 25–44.

Taylor & Francis for permission to reprint Sara York Kenny and Robert K. Larson, 'Lobbying Behaviour and the Development of International Accounting Standards: The Case of the IASC's Joint Venture Project', *European Accounting Review*, 3, December 1993, pp. 531–554. (Taylor & Francis Ltd, http://www.informaworld.com) reprinted by permission of the publisher and authors.

Elsevier for permission to reprint R. D. Nair and Werner G. Frank, 'The Harmonization of International Accounting Standards, 1973–1979'. This article was published in *International Journal of Accounting*, Education and Research, Fall 1981, pp. 61–77. Copyright Elsevier 1981. Reprinted with permission.

Elsevier for permission to reprint S. M. McKinnon and Paul Janell, 'The International Accounting Standards Committee: A Performance Evaluation'. This article was published in *International Journal of Accounting*, Education and Research, Spring 1984, pp. 19–34. Copyright Elsevier 1984. Reprinted with permission.

Elsevier for permission to reprint Thomas G. Evans and Martin E. Taylor, '"Bottom Line Compliance" with the IASC: A Comparative Analysis'. This article was published in *International Journal of Accounting*, Education and Research, Fall 1982, pp. 115–128. Copyright Elsevier 1982. Reprinted with permission.

Blackwell for permission to reprint R. Brunovs and R. J. Kirsh, 'Goodwill Accounting in Selected Countries and the Harmonization of International Accounting Standards', *Abacus*, 27, 2, 1991, pp. 135–161. Reprinted by permission of Blackwell Publishing.

Accounting and Business Research for permission to reprint P. Weetman, E. A. E. Jones, C. A. Adams and S. J. Gray, 'Profit Measurement and UK Accounting Standards: A Case of Increasing Disharmony in Relation to US GAAP and IASs', *Accounting and Business Research*, 28, 3, Summer 1998, pp. 189–208. Reprinted by permission of CCH Magazines.

Disclaimer

INTRODUCTION

This is the second of four volumes in this series of published papers concerning the International Accounting Standards Committee (IASC) and its successor, the International Accounting Standards Board (IASB). The first volume looked at the context and background to these bodies. This volume deals with the first part of the life of IASC. Volume III deals with the second part; Volume IV looks at the IASB.

Although several of the papers in Volume I mention the IASC or the IASB, those bodies were not the specific subject of the papers. By contrast, the IASC/B or its standards are the specific subject of the papers in this and the other two volumes. The papers in this volume are divided into three parts, as detailed below.

Foundation of the IASC

In Volume I of this series, accounting diversity was examined. However, diversity does not automatically lead to work on standardisation. There must be a demand for standardisation and people with power, ability and incentive to drive it forward. The first part of this present volume (part 5) deals with antecedents to the creation of the IASC, and with its foundation. We begin with a brief summary of the antecedents.

The first World Congress of Accountants was held in St Louis (USA) in 1904 (see Table 1). At the Ninth Congress in Paris in 1967, a working party

Table 1 World congresses of accountants.

1904	St. Louis	1972	Sydney
1926	Amsterdam	1977	Munich
1929	New York	1982	Mexico City
1933	London	1987	Tokyo
1937	Berlin	1992	Washington
1952	London	1997	Paris
1957	Amsterdam	2002	Hong Kong
1962	New York	2006	Istanbul
1967	Paris		

Source: C. W. Nobes and R. H. Parker, *Comparative International Accounting*, Prentice Hall, 2006.

1

Table 2 AISG Studies.

1	Accounting and Auditing Approaches to Inventories (1968) [E2 of 1974]
2	The Independent Auditor's Reporting Standards (1969)
3	Using the Work and Report of Another Auditor (1969)
4	Accounting for Corporate Income Taxes (1971) [E13 of 1978]
5	Reporting by Diversified Companies (1972) [E15 of 1980]
6	Consolidated Financial Statements (1972) [E3 of 1974]
7	The Funds Statement (1973) [E7 of 1970]
8	Materiality in Accounting (1974)
9	Extraordinary Items, Prior Period Adjustments, and Changes in Accounting Principles [E8 of 1976]
10	Published Profit Forecasts (1974)
11	International Financial Reporting (1975)
12	Comparative Glossary of Accounting Terms in Canada, the United Kingdom, and the United States (1975)
13	Accounting for Goodwill (1975) [E22 of 1981]
14	Interim Financial Reporting (1975)
15	Going Concern Problems (1975)
16	Independence of Auditors (1976)
17	Audit Committees (1976)
18	Accounting for Pension Costs (1977) [E16 of 1980]
19	Revenue Recognition (1978) [E20 of 1981]
20	Related Party Transactions (1978) [E25 of 1983]

Source: prepared by the authors.

was set up to consider the international needs of the profession. Its report to the Tenth Congress, in Sydney in 1972, established the International Coordination Committee for the Accountancy Profession (ICCAP), the predecessor of today's International Federation of Accountants (IFAC) (which was set up at the Eleventh Congress in 1977).

In 1966, Sir Henry (later Lord) Benson was President of the Institute of Chartered Accountants in England and Wales. He had discussions with the US and Canadian institutes (the AICPA and the CICA, respectively) that led to the setting up, in 1967, of the Accountants International Study Group (AISG). By its close in 1978, the AISG had issued 20 papers (see Table 2), largely comparing the practices of the three countries. All ten of the financial reporting topics were taken up by the IASC, after a time lag of a few years, as shown in the square brackets in Table 2.[1]

In the late 1960s, the three institutes were in charge of rule-making on technical accounting issues in their respective countries, given an absence of any detailed legal requirements. It was therefore natural for them to expect to control international standard setting. However, this assumption was criticised, and change was in the air. The AICPA set up a study that led to the creation of the independent Financial Accounting Standards Board (FASB) in 1973. Over time, the FASB's structure would become the model for the IASB's, and the IASB would become the FASB's main collaborator and competitor. Also, in these years, the ICAEW and other UK-based professional accounting bodies established the Accounting Standards Committee.

The IASC was founded in 1973, following a meeting organised by Sir Henry at the Ninth Congress in Sydney, again between the Canadian, UK and US bodies. Throughout the IASC's life, it was connected, sometimes uneasily, with ICCAP and then with IFAC.

Chapters 25–7 of this volume relate to Henry Benson. The first two are his own words about the IASC, starting with an extract from his autobiography. In Chapter 27, Peter Walton conducts an imaginary interview with Benson.

As noted above, other key players in the early years of the IASC were representatives of the institutes in the USA, Australia and Canada. Chapters 28 and 29 are contributions from two of these key players. W. E. Olson (Chapter 28) was involved for the AICPA in the negotiations to set up the IASC. J. A. Hepworth (Chapter 29) was an early (Australian) chairman. Chapter 30 is by the first non-native-English-speaking chairman of the IASC, J. A. Burggraaff, a Dutchman. He reports on the IASC's state of affairs in the early 1980s.

Mason (1978), in an early academic piece concerned with the IASC, suggests that the involvement of six 'vital countries' is necessary for successful standardisation. The countries are the five mentioned above in this section, plus Japan.

Another relevant background issue to the foundation of the IASC was the negotiations for the UK to join the Common Market (now EU), concluded by the accession of Denmark, Ireland and the UK at the beginning of 1973. The UK and Irish profession were faced with the prospect of prescriptive (largely German) accounting Directives. The setting up of the IASC, an Anglo-American style of standard-setter, could be seen partly as a reaction to the EU. Olson (see Chapter 28 above) confirms this, and Hopwood (1994) discusses it.

Part 5 ends with the reproduction of three early IASC documents: the *Agreement* (of 1973) for setting up the IASC, the *Preface* of 1983 and the *Constitution* of 1992 (Chapters 31–3).

Assessments of the IASC and its standards

Part 6 comprises six papers that examine the nature and structure of the IASC and its standards.

In Chapter 34 William Violet recommends that international standards should be based on a framework of postulates. This paper's publication date preceded the publication of the IASC's conceptual framework by six years. Juan Rivera (Chapter 35) examines some of the problems facing the IASC, including the lack of enforcement, while R. S. Olusegun Wallace (Chapter 36) looks at the legitimacy of the IASC as an institution and at strategies that it could adopt in order to prosper. He notes that there was no effective competitor organisation.

Richard Goeltz, in Chapter 37, takes up a theme of Part 2 of Volume I, that is whether the importation of accounting technology is always useful. He looks specifically at the IASC's work and concludes that some aspects of standardisation are not necessary or useful.

S. E. C. Purvis, Helen Gernon and Michael A. Diamond (Chapter 38) examine a key development in the IASC's standard setting: the improvement and comparability project of the early 1990s. This led to the ten revised standards of 1993 and set the stage for the further improvement of standards that led to their recognition by IOSCO and the EU.

In Chapter 39 Sara York Kenny and Robert Larson examine the issue of lobbying of the IASC by companies, in the context of IAS 31 on joint ventures. Later, lobbying was to become a much more important issue (see Volume IV).

Compliance and harmonisation with IASs

Part 7 contains five papers concerned with the use of data to assess the effects of the IASC.

Chapters 40–42 study *de jure* uniformity or standardisation. R. D. Nair and Werner Frank (Chapter 40) look at standardisation over three periods using Price Waterhouse (PW) survey data. Since the PW data is largely about rules rather than practices, we classify this as a *de jure* study. Nair and Frank report that 'the period of the IASC's existence has coincided with a growing harmonization' (pp. 226–7). However, they are very careful about inferences of causation.

S. M. McKinnon and Paul Janell, in Chapter 41, look at three technical topics using the 1979 PW data. They saw little effect of the IASC, and suggested that it should stick to research and to persuading national legislation to adopt IASC principles.

Doupnik and Taylor (1985) updated the PW data by a survey in 1983. They found that Europe showed the lowest compliance with IASC standards, but saw some increase from 1979 to 1983. Nobes (1987) points out some problems with the use of the PW data. For example, many answers in the PW survey refer to the appropriate IAS as authority for compliance, as though most companies in a country actually followed the IAS. Perhaps, instead, PW were reporting on what they encouraged their listed clients to do in consolidated statements.

In Chapter 42 Thomas Evans and Martin Taylor examine *de facto* compliance by large companies with five IASs over six years. For example, Evans and Taylor look at the 'lower of cost and net realisable value' rule of IAS 2. They say (p. 249) that US compliance was weak because of US use of LIFO which was unacceptable in IAS 2. However, there are three problems with that. First, LIFO was not unacceptable in IAS 2 (until 2005). Second, LIFO is a way of measuring cost, so it would not contravene the rule. Third, Evans and Taylor do not mention that US companies often use replacement cost instead of net realisable value, so they break IAS 2's rule in a different way. Elsewhere, Gray (1983) and Wallace and Gernon (1991) criticise early research on international accounting as being descriptive, but another problem is that there were many errors in it, especially when authors wrote about a topic beyond their own country.

Rudolf Brunovs and Robert J. Kirsch (Chapter 43) look at the degree to which the standard-setters of various countries appear to have followed the IASC's lead on the subject of goodwill. P. Weetman *et al.* (Chapter 44) detect a reduction in harmony from 1988 to 1994 in UK practices compared to US or IAS requirements.

Note

1 Excluding interim reporting, which is not an issue for annual financial statements. That had to wait until E57 of 1997.

References

Doupnik, S. and M. E. Taylor (1985) 'An Empirical Investigation of the Observance of IASC Standards in Western Europe', *Management International Review* 25(1): 27–33.

Gray, S. J. (1983) 'International Accounting: A Review of Academic Research in the United Kingdom', *International Journal of Accounting* (Fall): 15–42.

Hopwood, A. (1994) 'Some Reflections on "The Harmonization of Accounting Within the EU"', *European Accounting Review* 3(2): 241–53.

Mason, A. K. (1978) 'Vital Countries: The National Environments', in *The Development of International Standards*, ICRA, Lancaster University, pp. 74–84.

Nobes, C. W. (1987) 'An Empirical Investigation of the Observance of IASC Standards in Western Europe: A Comment', *Management International Review* 27(4): 78–9.

Wallace, R. S. O. and H. Gernon (1991) 'Frameworks for International Comparative Accounting', *Journal of Accounting Literature* 10: 209–64.

Part 5

FOUNDATION OF THE IASC

25

ACCOUNTING STANDARDS

Sir Henry Benson

Source: Sir H. Benson, *Accounting for Life*, London: Kogan Page, 1989, pp. 102–14.

In the early years of my professional life I thought it was impossible to lay down national standards in accounting matters and I am sure that I did not give international standards a thought. It seemed to me at that time that the wide range of different conditions and circumstances which affected commercial, industrial and financial businesses made any form of uniformity out of the question. Over the years all my opinions – professional, social, religious and political – have changed or been significantly modified, and after the Second World War I began to realise that a degree of uniformity in accounting matters was not only desirable but necessary.

Two things began this change of outlook, both of which I have already described. The first was my experiences in the Royal Ordnance Factories. The second was the realisation that, if the firm was to be able to build up a national and international accounting practice, it would be quite impossible to do so without clear manuals for the guidance of partners and staff, worldwide, who were engaged on professional work. These two experiences opened my eyes; changes were beginning to take shape in other fields.

As peace-time conditions returned, professional accountancy bodies in different parts of the world began to codify the widely differing accounting treatments which were in use in their respective countries and authoritative papers began to be produced. They were called by different names – recommendations, principles, guidelines, opinions and statements. By whatever name, they were the beginnings of what we now refer to as Accounting Standards.

A great deal of time and effort was spent by dedicated men on this work. By modern standards, some of the papers now look crude, but at the time they were first issued they were up to date and a big advance in accounting thought. There was, however one serious defect. They were prepared without sufficient reference to what was happening in other countries so that authoritative publications were issued in different countries which conflicted, sometimes in minor ways, but sometimes on fundamental points of principle.

Soon after taking office as President of the Institute in June 1966 I visited Canada and the United States and had discussions with the heads of the accounting bodies there. At the annual conference of the Canadian Institute of Chartered Accountants in Regina, Saskatchewan in August 1966, a meeting took place with the President of that Institute and the President of the American Institute of Certified Public Accountants (AICPA). I suggested to them that we should set up a three-nation group to study major accounting problems and to issue an agreed statement upon each of them. We agreed quickly that such an enterprise would be worthwhile.

At the end of September 1966 I met the executive committee of the AICPA which, on that occasion, was meeting in Boston and I set out below a copy of the minute which the AICPA has allowed me to reproduce. Looking back, this minute may have some historical significance as I think it marked a turning point in international relationships in the accountancy profession.

PROPOSAL FOR INTERNATIONAL STUDY GROUP

At the invitation of President Trueblood, Sir Henry Benson of the Institute of Chartered Accountants in England and Wales appeared before the executive committee to present a proposal for the creation of a 'study group' composed of two or three representatives of the English, Canadian and American institutes to organise a programe of comparative studies of current trends in accounting thought and practice in the three countries.

In presenting his proposal Sir Henry observed that most of the three organisations pursued their separate ways with compartively little regard to, or knowledge of, accounting and auditing developments in other countries. He suggested that this was a remarkable state of affairs in view of the fact that accountants in the United States, Canada and the United Kingdom were collectively responsible each year for attesting to the fairness of financial statements involving billions of dollars.

Under the proposal the 'study group' would meet at least once a year in each of the countries in rotation and keep in touch with each other by correspondence in the intervals between meetings. The first task of the 'study group' would be to determine the subject areas for exploration and to devise a pattern for the research reports which would facilitate comparisons between the three countries.

It was suggested that the formation of such a group was a simple and effective way, but not the only way, of promoting international cooperation in accounting and it was agreed that similar groups might be organised with accounting organisations in other countries or that the original group might be expanded to include representatives from other countries in due course.

In concluding his presentation Sir Henry declared that the publications to be issued by the 'study group' might bring about a reassessment of present practices and future plans in the three countries; that they would broaden the minds of all who read them and suggest new lines of enquiry; and that they could prove helpful to the profession of accountants in other nations.

After extended discussion, the executive committee resolved to approve the proposal in principle with the understanding that the Presidents of the three organsiations would hold further conferences to develop a plan for an early implementation of the programme.

It was also the sense of the executive committee that when the proposal had received the approval of the three organisations any public announcement on the formation of the 'study group' would be coordinated between the executive staffs of the organisations.

A day or so later I had the privilege of addressing the whole council of the AICPA which happened to be meeting at that time. No formal resolution was put to the council but the proposals appeared to command its approval.

These meetings in Regina and Boston led to the formation of the Accountants International Study Group (AISG) which first met in February 1967 and began to publish papers every few months on important topics. AISG was eventually disbanded after the International Accounting Standards Committee had been launched, but during its lifetime it issued twenty authoritative papers which began to shape international thinking in the profession.

The Presidents of the three Institutes knew when the AISG was set up that it might engender some measure of discontent in other countries who were likely to feel that they should have been invited to join, or to contribute to, what would be seen as an international group, formed to speak with authority on accounting subjects. We decided deliberately to risk this criticism. It is difficult enough to get agreement on accounting subjects even within a single nation, and we felt that if this exercise was to get off the ground the maximum number of nations who should initially be involved was three, and they should start with the advantage of all speaking a common language. We all had in mind, as the minute records, that if the AISG proved to be a success other nations might be invited to join later on. There was in fact some comment by other nations who felt they had been left out unreasonably but, as far as I know, this disquiet was not deep-seated, particularly when explanations were given about the practical advantages, if not the necessity, of operating initially with a small group.

11

In the ensuing five or six years events moved faster. There were a number of scandals or failures in different parts of the world which brought criticism upon the business community and the accounting profession; the public began to demand, *inter alia*, higher and more definite accounting rules; the accumulated labour of the professional bodies in different countries since the end of the War was then beginning to bear fruit in, among many other ways, the issue of clear and precise standards; in 1969 the accountancy profession in the UK formally began the publication of Accounting Standards; international barriers were being continually lowered or removed and this was accelerated in Europe by developments within the Common Market. By the time the accounting bodies of the world met at the Tenth International Congress of Accountants in Sydney in the autumn of 1972, the mood of the accounting profession had changed. The time was right for another step forward.

The lay reader might express surprise at the slow pace at which events moved but the speed of any advance is relative. For a number of reasons major changes take a long time in the accountancy profession. Professional men by their training and upbringing are conservative in outlook; the business community has to be persuaded and convinced; any major change takes a long time to be absorbed and often involves retraining; the student body usually requires three to five years for qualification and there are administrative problems in introducing new teaching and amending examination syllabuses. My own experience is that the accountancy profession has moved surprisingly quickly both nationally and internationally.

In Sydney, therefore, another meeting of the three nations took place similar to the one in Regina six years earlier and the President of the Institute of the Chartered Accountants of Scotland was also present. On this occasion it was proposed that an international body should be set up which would write accounting standards for international use. As at the meeting in Regina, there was no difficulty in reaching agreement in principle but it was realised that there would be practical difficulties in designing a suitable organisation, in financing the enterprise and in getting the approval of the governing bodies of a number of different accountancy organisations. We agreed to meet again before the end of the year after the representatives present had had time to reflect on the proposal.

I went home from Sydney via New Zealand and America and spent all my spare time in thinking out the practical problems and sketching out some sort of organisation and plan of work. I was not alone in this; others who had been in Sydney did much the same thing so that at our next meeting early in December 1972 in London under the then President of the English Institute, there was a store of collective thought on which to draw; progress was rapid.

We had a good deal of discussion about the proposed founder members. Some of those present proposed different combinations but in the end and without much difficulty it was decided to invite the accountancy bodies of six other nations to join us – Australia, France, Germany, Japan, The Netherlands and Mexico. It would have been easy to have made the number larger but, like the original decision to limit the AISG to three, it was felt that the number of countries would have to be restricted to nine. Anything more was thought to be unworkable and anything less would not be representative from an international point of view. We also had to bear in mind that the annual cost of the enterprise would be not inconsiderable and some accounting bodies, although operating to high standards, could not be expected to find their proportion of the cost involved.

After the initial meeting of the three nations in London, a meeting took place in March 1973 at which five of the other six nations were also represented. By this time the proposals had been prepared in draft form. We decided that we would not employ solicitors to formalise the necessary documentation because if solicitors were employed in London the other nations would inevitably want lawyers in their own countries to express a view. So the representatives of the nine nations did their own redrafting of what subsequently became the Agreement and Constitution of the International Accounting Standards Committee (IASC).

The ultimate result may be open to some technical criticism but the intention of the documents was clear and they have stood the test of time. The objectives remain unaltered. The next meeting took place on 28 June 1973; this was followed by the inaugural meeting on 29 June 1973 at which the Agreement and Constitution were signed by representatives of sixteen accountancy bodies from the nine nations. The Earl of Limerick was also present representing the Department of Trade and Industry of the United Kingdom. I was appointed chairman of the IASC.

Looking back on these events it is extraordinary that the IASC was set up and in operation only some eight or nine months after the meeting in Sydney. I think the reason was a spontaneous feeling in the accountancy profession that something needed to be done quickly and that it was important to let the public see that action was being taken. I also believe that if the process had been delayed for several months every nation, not least my own, would have discovered flaws or practical difficulties in the proposals and the whole venture would have come to a stop.

When the IASC was formed it was provided that it would promulgate 'basic' standards. I, among others, was responsible for the use of this word. I am not sure precisely what others had in mind at the time, but I meant to convey the impression that the standards issued would be simple and straightforward, on topics that went to the root of published financial statements. I did not envisage highly complicated and sophisticated standards with detailed argumentation explaining all the possible alternatives – of which there are some examples in existence in different countries.

I think this view is borne out by an extract from the paper which was prepared after the meeting of the three nations in London in December 1972 and which indicates what was in mind at the time:

> Such Standards must ensure a significant improvement to the quality and comparability of corporate disclosure and yet be capable of rapid acceptance and implementation worldwide. Such Standards would need to be short, clear and uncomplicated if they were to achieve their purpose.

Indeed, the subjects which we discussed during the formative meetings at the end of 1972 and in the first half of 1973 were the very topics on which Standards or Exposure Drafts were subsequently issued by the IASC – accounting policies, inventory valuation, consolidated accounts, depreciation, the minimum information to be disclosed, and the like.

In my own country, and elsewhere abroad, the role of the IASC and the interpretation to be placed on the word 'basic' were construed by different people in different ways. Some believed that there would be great difficulty in the IASC reaching agreement on any topic, and that any standards which emerged would be unlikely to have much impact. Others saw a more positive role for the IASC but wished to see what emerged in the initial years before passing judgement. The consensus of opinion was that it was a bold experiment which was worth undertaking.

The IASC got down to work on 29 June 1973, the day it was inaugurated. It laid down a programme and timetable which, subject to some not very serious lapses, were adhered to. For the first few months everything went well. Then, as exposure drafts began to be issued it was suddenly borne in on the accountancy profession and the world that the International Standards would have teeth. More than that, under the Agreement and Constitution both founder and associate members were expected to comply with Standards.

In consequence of this realisation national prejudices were aroused; there were complaints that the subjects covered by the IASC were too advanced and were not 'basic'; the exposure drafts were said to be too detailed; the composition of the committee was criticised. It was a difficult time but the sixteen accountancy bodies which had signed the Agreement and Constitution remained steadfast, despite criticisms. The IASC reassessed its position and stuck to its guns. At the same time a growing body of opinion began to recognise that the purpose behind the IASC was important and should be supported. This was made apparent when accountancy bodies from many other nations, over and above the founder members, applied to join. Not only did they believe that it would help to keep them up to date in relation to international accounting matters but they realised that it would save the heavy cost in time and money of writing standards for their own members.

I left the chair in 1976 after three years. The detailed method of operation we adopted when I was in office was as follows. When the full Committee had decided that a particular topic was suitable for an International Standard a steering committee was appointed. Steering committees usually comprised one or more representatives from three countries but occasionally, on difficult subjects, the number of countries was increased. The countries chosen for this purpose were normally two of the nine founder countries and one country which was not.

The steering committees were serviced by the IASC secretariat who prepared a brief of all the relevant standards or pronouncements which were known to be in existence on the selected topic. In the light of this information the steering committee settled a 'point outline' which indicated the general lines on which it intended to present the Standard. This 'point outline' was debated by the full Committee at one of its three annual meetings.

In the light of this debate a preliminary draft of an Exposure Draft was submitted to a subsequent meeting of the full Committee for further comment and debate. A final Exposure Draft was then prepared which was examined with meticulous care at a further meeting of the full Committee held some months later. Normally, after appropriate alteration, this was approved for issue to the public at the latter meeting. In short, the substance of every Exposure Draft was debated by the full Committee on three separate occasions before it was authorised for issue.

The Exposure Drafts had a wide circulation; some countries sent them direct to selected people or firms; for example, about 3,000 copies were so issued in the United Kingdom and 20,000 in the United States. In other countries use was made of the professional journals. In this way every Exposure Draft was drawn to the attention of well over 100,000 people in different countries. The number of comments received in response to an Exposure Draft was relatively small. These comments were collected within the different countries and then forwarded to the secretariat of the IASC in London who reassembled the information in a way suitable for examination by the steering committee. Each comment was considered on its merits to ascertain whether it was relevant and, if so, whether a change in the Exposure Draft was warranted. In a great many cases the comments received were contradictory which did not make the steering committee's work easier.

On the basis of this study by the steering committee the exposure draft was revised and submitted to the full Committee in the form of a definite Standard. This was discussed in detail and, in the light of the decisions then made, the Standard was approved for issue. The Standards were expressed in English and it was the responsibility of each country, if English was not the mother tongue, to prepare and issue translations for local use.

One of the three full Committee meetings in each year was held outside the United Kingdom but the other two were held in London. The steering committees, on the other hand, met in different parts of the world depending on which countries were represented on them. It would be impracticable to dispense with any of these meetings and to conduct the affairs of the IASC by correspondence; it will be apparent, therefore, that the cost is considerable.

The only payments made by the IASC for work performed were to the full-time secretariat. In an age when overmanning is rampant, the IASC's record was clean. The total number of the secretariat was three and it is a tribute to their quality and industry that they were able to cope efficiently with a considerable volume of exacting work in addition to much overseas travel. The men who sat on the IASC were, and are still, leaders of the profession in their own countries. All of them had to travel many thousands of miles to sit on steering committees and to be present at the main Committee meetings. The paperwork is technical and exacting. One of the most heart-warming experiences of my professional life was the objective and unselfish work that the members devoted to the task. The cost in money was considerable but that is the least part of the cost. The cost in unpaid professional and leisure time has been enormous. I doubt whether this effort has been realised or appreciated and I am glad to place it formally on the record.

Changes and improvements in the procedures have, of course, taken place over the years but the care and attention which is given to the preparation of Exposure Drafts and Standards has in no way diminished. The Board which now controls the IASC has been widened to include representatives from thirteen countries and the number of persons who sit on each of the steering committees is larger – usually four or five. Another major improvement has been the appointment of a consultative group representing the users and preparers of financial statements. A factor which will add weight is the work of the International Federation of Accountants (IFAC) which was formed in 1977. This is the international organisation which represents the professional accounting bodies of the world. It has issued, up to the time of writing, twenty-six guidelines on auditing which provide authoritative and complementary guidance for practitioners on that subject. Accounting standards and auditing guidelines go hand in hand and in course of time should help to raise standards worldwide. Both are needed and both must be applied if the standards of the accountancy profession are to be held at the right level.

What then of the future? I believe the IASC has come through its formative years with an enhanced reputation. It is now, in 1989, an accepted part of the accountancy profession worldwide and one hundred accounting bodies in seventy-six different countries are members of it. The individual members of these accountancy bodies represent an overwhelming majority of the trained and qualified accountants in the world today. It should also be remembered that the accounting bodies who are members have between them a very large student body who will be the accountants of tomorrow.

At the time of writing twenty-eight definitive Standards have been issued and Exposure Drafts have been issued on a number of other subjects. Many of the smaller nations, who do not have adequate resources of money or personnel to prepare standards, adopt the International Standards more or less verbatim as their own national standards. The need for International Accounting Standards is becoming more widely recognised as each year goes by and the IASC is increasingly in touch with organisations, national and international, which in one way or another are concerned with the integrity of financial statements. In the Carrian trial (referred to in Chapter 12, pages 204–210) I was interested to notice that International Accounting Standards were often referred to for authoritative guidance.

I believe that the main thrust for the future should be in three ways. First, some of the present Standards reflect a compromise and proffer alternatives. I think that those Standards need to be tighter and the alternatives reduced or eliminated. The IASC is conscious of this problem and is taking steps to review the Standards already issued with this in mind. Second, I feel that whenever financial statements are issued to the public they should state whether they comply with International Accounting Standards and, if they do not, the extent to which the Standards have not been observed. Third, although progress is being made, I do not think that any accountancy body anywhere in the world has done enough to ensure that either its own national standards or International Standards are, in fact, being applied by its members in the conduct of their professional practice or in their capacity as directors of business enterprises. It is a heavy and costly operation. It needs a skilled staff to detect failures to comply, and a heavy overhead to follow this up with dispassionate investigation and, if necessary, the imposition of sanctions. This has always been my worry and I pointed out in Chapter 3 that I drew attention to the problem over twenty years ago on the day I was appointed President of the Institute.

If the accountancy, or any other, profession is to command the respect of the public which it serves and which provides it with a living, I believe that it has a duty to do more than write standards. It has a duty to take reasonable steps to see that they are in fact followed. Over and over again, when a company fails or goes into liquidation, the subsequent *post mortem* shows that a contributing factor has been the failure to observe sound accounting standards. In most countries the public is rightly indulgent to professional men, realising that they have a heavy responsibility; errors of judgement are human and are therefore pardoned, but neither the public nor governments will continue to be complacent if clear and authoritative standards are openly disregarded. Standards are written to be observed not to be ignored and the accounting profession should take the necessary steps before the public and governments demand it.

I never thought that the impact of the IASC would be revolutionary or immediate. In meetings and seminars in numerous capitals of the world

I have said that the impact would be important in the formative years and of dominating importance in the presentation of financial statements by about the year 2000. The period from the meetings in Regina and Boston to the beginning of the next century is no more than a generation – which is a short period in the lifespan of a great profession – but I am clear beyond peradventure on one issue. The accountancy profession will fall into disrepute and possibly come under government direction unless it ensures that its members comply with its own standards.

I think that this is fully appreciated in the United Kingdom. Early in 1988 the Consultative Committee of Accountancy Bodies set up a committee, under the chairmanship of Sir Ronald Dearing, to review the accounting standard setting process in the United Kingdom, including the methods of enforcement. I gave evidence to the committee in which I expressed the above views with all the conviction I could muster. The Dearing Committee reported later in 1988 and I am glad to see that it laid great emphasis on the need to ensure that in future not only the accounting profession, but also the directors of companies, observe accounting standards and that sanctions will be imposed on those who do not do so. It recommended the continued development of International Standards in the United Kingdom and the Republic of Ireland.

26

THE STORY OF INTERNATIONAL ACCOUNTING STANDARDS

A personal record

Sir Henry Benson

Source: *Accountancy* (July 1976): 34–9.

Sir Henry Benson GBE FCA writes . . . As at the end of this month I am giving up the chairmanship of the International Accounting Standards Committee, I thought it would be sensible to place on record, for the historians of the future, how the movement to establish international accounting Standards began, and to venture upon some comments about the future. I think I am the only person who has been present during all the different episodes from the early beginnings until the present time. This is essentially a personal note of reminiscence, and speculation about the future. I have never kept any records of my professional career or the different tasks on which I have been engaged. This article has therefore been written from memory, but whenever possible I have verified the facts from contemporary records.

In the early years of my professional life, I thought it was impossible to lay down national Standards in accounting matters, and I am sure that I did not give international Standards a thought. It seemed to me at that time that the wide range of different conditions and circumstances which affected commercial, industrial and financial businesses made any form of uniformity out of the question. Over the years, all my opinions – professional, social, religious and political – have changed, or been significantly modified, and after the 1939–45 war, I began to realise that a degree of uniformity in accounting matters was not only desirable, but necessary.

Two things began this change of outlook. During the war, I was seconded from the Army for a short period to reorganise the accounts of the Royal Ordnance Factories. There were between 40 and 50 of them, making weapons, ammunition and explosives. My recollection is that there were between 300,000 and 400,000 persons employed in them, and the staff in the various factories handling the accounting tasks of one sort or another, for which I was responsible, totalled about 10,000.

As a result of very rapid expansion and a shortage of skilled staff the accounting organisation and records were in chaos and the accounts months in arrears. I decided that the only course was to scrap the lot and start afresh. I therefore wrote manuals of accounting procedure which, as from named dates, I imposed upon the civilian staff in each of these factories with a military severity and discipline which would not have been tolerated except under war conditions. I returned to the Army 10 months later, by which time a simple system of accounting and stores control had been installed, which was up-to-date, and the accounting staff employed in the factories had been reduced by about 900 bodies.

After the war, when I was helping to build up my firm's national and international accounting practice, I realised that it would be quite impossible to do so without clear manuals of procedure and principles for the guidance of partners and staff world-wide who were engaged on professional work. These two experiences opened my eyes; changes were beginning to take shape in other fields.

As peace time conditions returned, professional accountancy bodies in different parts of the world began to codify the widely differing accounting treatments which were in use in their respective countries, and authoritative papers began to be produced. They were called, different names – recommendations, principles, guidelines, opinions and statements. By whatever name called, they were the beginnings of what we now refer to as accounting Standards.

A great deal of time and effort was spent by dedicated men on this work. By modern standards, some of the papers now look crude, but at the time they were first issued, they were up-to-date and a big advance in accounting thought. There was, however, one serious defect. They were often prepared without sufficient reference to what was happening in other countries, so that authoritative publications were issued in different countries which conflicted, sometimes in minor ways, but sometimes on fundamental points of principle.

It is the tradition in my Institute for the President, on his election to office, to summarise the accounting scene as he sees it, and to announce the policies which he hopes to follow or to initiate in his year of office. On my appointment as President in the summer of 1966, I had five points which seemed to me of importance the first of which was expressed as follows: 'I have had the feeling for a long time that our relations with those Institutes

(Canada and America) were very friendly, but somewhat remote, and, with the Council's approval, I shall see whether I can perhaps get them on to a rather more intimate basis.'

In pursuit of this objective, I visited Canada and the United States and had discussions with the heads of the accounting bodies there. At the annual conference of the Canadian Institute of Chartered Accountants in Regina, Saskatchewan, in August 1966, a meeting took place with the President of that Institute and the President of the American Institute of Certified Public Accountants (AICPA). I suggested to them that we should set up a three-nation group to study major accounting problems and to issue an agreed statement upon each of them. We agreed quickly that such an enterprise would be worth while.

At the end of September 1966, I met the executive committee of the AICPA which, on that occasion, was meeting in Boston, and I set out below a copy of the minute which the AICPA have kindly allowed me to reproduce. Looking back, this minute may have some historical significance, as I think it marked a turning point in international relationships in the accountancy profession.

'22. Proposal for International Study Group

'At the invitation of President Trueblood, Sir Henry Benson, of the Institute of Chartered Accountants in England and Wales, appeared before the executive committee to present a proposal for the creation of a "study group", composed of two or three representatives of the English, Canadian and American Institutes, to organise a program of comparative studies of current trends in accounting thought and practices in the three countries.

'In presenting his proposal, Sir Henry observed that most members of the three organisations pursued their separate ways with comparatively little regard to, or knowledge of, accounting and auditing developments in the other countries. He suggested that this was a remarkable state of affairs in view of the fact that accountants in the United States, Canada, and the United Kingdom were collectively responsible each year for attesting to the fairness of financial statements involving billions of dollars.

'Under the proposal, the "study group" would meet at least once a year in each of the countries in rotation, and keep in touch with each other by correspondence in the intervals between meetings. The first task of the "study group" would be to determine the subject areas for exploration, and to devise a pattern for the research reports which would facilitate comparisons between the three countries.

'It was suggested that the formation of such a group was a simple and effective way, but not the only way, of promoting inter-national co-operation in accounting, and it was agreed that similar groups might be organised with accounting organisations in other countries or that the original group might be expanded to include representatives from other countries in due course.

'In concluding his presentation, Sir Henry declared that the publications to be issued by the "study group" might bring about a reassessment of present practices and future plans in the three countries; that they would broaden the minds of all who read them and suggest new lines of inquiry; and that they could prove helpful to the professional accountants in other nations.

'After extended discussion, the executive committee resolved to approve the proposal in principle, with the understanding that the presidents of the three organisations would hold further conferences to develop a plan for an early implementation of the program.

'It was also the sense of the executive committee that when the proposal had received the approval of the three organisations, any public announcement of the formation of the "study group" would be co-ordinated between the executive staffs of the organisations.'

A day or so later I had the privilege of addressing, on the same subject, the whole Council of the AICPA, which happened to be meeting in Boston at that time. No formal resolution was put to the Council, but the proposals appeared to command its approval.

These meetings in Regina and Boston led to the formation of the Accountants International Study Group (AISG) which first met in February 1967, and began to publish papers every few months on important topics. In the last 10 years, 15 such papers have been issued, and the work of this group is still continuing.

The presidents of the three Institutes knew, when the AISG was set up, that it might engender some measure of discontent in other countries who were likely to feel that they should have been invited to join, or to contribute to, what would be seen as an international group formed to speak with authority on accounting subjects.

We decided deliberately to risk this criticism. It is difficult enough to get agreement on accounting subjects even within a single nation, and we felt that if this exercise was to get off the ground, the maximum number of nations who should initially be involved was three, and they should start with the advantage of all speaking a common language. We all had in mind, as the minute records, that if AISG proved to be a success, other nations might be invited to join later on. There was, in fact, some comment by other nations who felt that they had been left out unreasonably, but as far as I know, this disquiet was not deep-seated, particularly when explanations were given about the practical advantages, if not the necessity, of operating initially with a small group.

In the ensuing five or six years, events moved faster. There were a number of scandals or failures in different parts of the world which brought criticism upon the business community and the accounting profession; the public began to demand, *inter alia,* higher and more definite accounting Standards; the accumulated labour of the professional bodies in different countries since the end of the war was then beginning to bear fruit in, among many other ways, the issue of clear and precise accounting Standards; international barriers were being continually lowered or removed, and this was accelerated in Europe by developments within the Common Market.

By the time the accounting bodies of the world met at the 10th International Congress of Accountants in Sydney, in the autumn of 1972, the mood of the accounting profession had changed. The time was ripe for another step forward.

The lay reader might express surprise at the slow pace at which events moved, but the speed of any advance is relative. For a number of reasons, major changes take a long time in the accountancy profession. Professional men, by their training and upbringing, are conservative in outlook; the business community has to be persuaded and convinced; any major change takes a long time to be absorbed and often involves retraining; the student body usually requires about five years for qualification, and there are administrative problems in introducing new teachings and amending examination syllabuses. My own experience is that the accountancy profession has moved surprisingly quickly, both nationally and internationally. I doubt whether, relatively, we have moved any less fast than our colleagues in other comparable professions.

In Sydney, therefore, another meeting of the three nations took place similar to the one in Regina six years earlier, and the President of the Institute of Chartered Accountants of Scotland was also present. On this occasion, it was proposed that an international body should be set up which would write accounting Standards for international use.

As at the meeting in Regina, there was no difficulty in reaching agreement in principle, but it was realised that there would be practical difficulties in designing a suitable organisation, in financing the enterprise, and in getting the approval of the governing bodies of a number of different accountancy organisations. We agreed to meet again before the end of the year after the representatives present had had time to reflect on the proposal.

I went home from Sydney via New Zealand and America and spent all my spare time in thinking out the practical problems, and sketching out some sort of organisation and plan of work. I was not alone in this; others who had been present in Sydney did much the same thing, so that at our next meeting, early in December 1972 in London, under the then President of the English Institute, there was a store of collective thought on which to draw; progress was rapid.

We had a good deal of discussion about the proposed founder members. Some of those present proposed different combinations but, in the end, and without much difficulty, it was decided to invite the accountancy bodies of six other nations – Australia, France, Germany, Japan, the Netherlands and Mexico – to join us.

It would have been easy to make the number larger, but like the original decision to limit AISG to three, it was felt that the number of countries would have to be restricted to nine. Anything more was thought to be unworkable, and anything less would not be representative from an international point of view. We also had to bear in mind that the annual cost of the enterprise would be not inconsiderable, and some accounting bodies, although operating to high standards, could not be expected to find their proportion of the cost involved.

After the initial meeting of the three nations in London, a meeting took place in March 1973, at which five of the other six nations were also represented. By this time, the proposals had been prepared in draft form. We decided that we would not employ solicitors to formalise the necessary documentation because, if solicitors were employed in London, the other nations would inevitably want lawyers in their own countries to express a view. So the representatives of the nine nations did their own redrafting of what subsequently became the Agreement and Constitution of IASC.

The ultimate result may be open to some technical criticism, but the intention of the documents was clear, and they have stood the test of time. Experience in the last three years has shown that a few changes are needed to meet present conditions, but the objectives are unaltered.

The next meeting took place on 28 June 1973; this was followed by the inaugural meeting on 29 June 1973, at which the Agreement and Constitution were signed by representatives of 16 accountancy bodies from nine nations. Lord Limerick was also present, representing the Department of Trade and Industry.

Looking back on these events, it is extraordinary that the International Accounting Standards Committee was set up and in operation only some eight or nine months after the meeting in Sydney. I think the reason was a spontaneous feeling in the accounting profession that something needed to be done quickly and that it was important to let the public see that some action was being taken. I also believe that, if the process had been delayed for several months, every nation, not least my own, would have discovered flaws or practical difficulties in the proposals, and the whole venture would have come to a stop.

When IASC was formed, it was provided that it would promulgate 'basic' Standards. I, among others, was responsible for the use of this word. I am not sure precisely what others had in mind at the time, but I meant to convey the impression that the Standards issued would be simple and straightforward, on topics which went to the root of published financial statements.

I did not envisage highly complicated and sophisticated Standards, with detailed augmentation explaining all the possible alternatives – of which there are some examples in existence in different countries.

I think this view is borne out by an extract from the paper which was prepared after the meeting of the three nations in London in December 1972, which indicates what was in their minds at the time: 'Such Standards must ensure a significant improvement to the quality and comparability of corporate disclosure and yet be capable of rapid acceptance and implementation world-wide. Such Standards would need to be short, clear and uncomplicated if they were to achieve their purpose.'

Indeed, the subjects which we discussed during the formative meetings at the end of 1972 and in the first half of 1973 were the very topics on which Standards or Exposure Drafts were subsequently issued by IASC – accounting policies, inventory valuation, consolidated accounts, depreciation, the minimum information to be disclosed, and the like.

In my own country, and elsewhere abroad, the role of IASC and the interpretation to be placed on the word 'basic' were construed by different people in different ways. Some believed that there would be great difficulty in IASC reaching agreement on any topic, and that any Standards which emerged would be unlikely to have much impact. Others saw a more positive role for IASC, but wished to see what emerged in the initial years before passing judgement. The concensus of opinion was that it was a bold experiment which was worth undertaking.

IASC got down to work on 29 June 1973, the day it was inaugurated. It laid down a programme and timetable which, subject to some not very serious lapses, have been adhered to.

For the first few months everything went well – too well. Then, as Exposure Drafts began to be issued, it was suddenly borne in on the accounting profession of the world that the international Standards would have teeth. More than that, under the Agreement and Constitution, both founder and associate members were expected to comply with them.

In consequence of this realisation, national prejudices were aroused; there were complaints that the subjects covered by IASC were too advanced and were not 'basic'; the Exposure Drafts were said to be too detailed; the composition of the Committee was criticised. It was a difficult time. But the 16 accountancy bodies which had signed the Agreement and Constitution remained steadfast, despite criticisms by some of their individual members. IASC reassessed its position but stuck to its guns.

Moreover, a growing body of opinion began to realise that the purpose behind IASC was important and should be supported. This was made apparent because accountancy bodies from many other nations, over and above the founder members applied to join. Not only did they believe that it would help to keep them up-to-date in relation to international accounting matters, but they realised that it would save some of them the heavy cost in time and money of writing accounting Standards for their own members.

I do not think this record would be complete without some account of the way in which IASC conducts its business, which now follows a set routine. When the full Committee has decided that a particular topic is suitable for an international Standard, a Steering Committee is appointed. Steering Committees usually comprise one or more representatives from three countries, but occasionally, on difficult subjects, the number of countries is increased. The countries chosen for this purpose are normally two of the nine founder countries, and one country which is not.

The Steering Committees are serviced by IASC's secretariat, who prepare a brief of all the relevant Standards of pronouncements which are known to be in existence on the selected topic. In the light of this information, the Steering Committee settles a 'point outline', which indicates the general lines on which it intends to present the Standard. This 'point outline' is debated by the full Committee at one of its three annual meetings.

In the light of this debate, a preliminary draft of an Exposure Draft is submitted to a subsequent meeting of the full Committee for further comment and debate. A final Exposure Draft is then prepared, which is examined with meticulous care at a further meeting of the full Committee, held some months later; normally, after appropriate alteration, this is approved for issue to the public at the latter meeting. In short, the substance of every Exposure Draft is debated by the full Committee on three separate occasions before it is authorised for issue.

The Exposure Drafts have a wide circulation. Some countries send them direct to selected persons or firms. For example, about 3,000 copies are so issued in the United Kingdom, and 20,000 in the United States. In other countries, use is made of the professional journals. In this way, every Exposure Draft is drawn to the attention of well over 100,000 people in different countries.

The number of comments received in response to an Exposure Draft is relatively small. These comments are collated within the different countries and then forwarded to the secretariat of IASC in London, who reassemble the information in a way suitable for examination by the Steering Committee. Each comment is considered on its merits to ascertain whether it is relevant and, if so, whether a change in the Exposure Draft is warranted. In a great many cases, the comments received are contradictory, which does not make the Steering Committee's work easier.

On the basis of this study by the Steering Committee, the Exposure Draft is revised and submitted to the full Committee in the form of a definitive Standard. This is discussed in detail by the full Committee and, in the light of the decisions then made, the Standard is approved for issue. The Standards are expressed in English, and it is the responsibility of each country, if English is not the mother tongue, to prepare and issue translations for local use.

One of the three full Committee meetings in each year is held outside the United Kingdom, but the other two are held in London. The Steering Committees, on the other hand, meet in different parts of the world, depending on which countries are represented on them. It would be quite impracticable to dispense with any of these meetings and to conduct the affairs of IASC by correspondence; it will be apparent, therefore, that the cost in travel and time and expense is considerable.

The only payments made by IASC for work performed are to the full-time secretariat. In an age when overmanning is rampant, IASC's record in this respect is clean. The total number of the secretariat is three, and it is a tribute to their quality and industry that they have been able to cope efficiently with a considerable volume of exacting work in addition to much overseas travel.

On leaving the chair of IASC after the first three years of its life, I have tried to assess calmly and dispassionately where IASC stands today.

I believe that it has come through its difficult period without damage, and possibly with an enhanced reputation. It is now an accepted part of the accountancy profession world-wide, and 44 accounting bodies in 32 different countries are members of it. The individual members of these accountancy bodies number over 400,000, which must represent an overwhelming majority of the trained and qualified accountants in the world today. It should also be remembered that the accounting bodies who are members have, between them, a very large student body, who will be the accountants of tomorrow. By the end of July, it is expected that five definitive Standards and two or three Exposure Drafts on other subjects will have been issued or authorised for issue. Work on five other subjects is under way.

The International Federation of Stock Exchanges has recommended its constituent members to include in their listing requirements reference to compliance with international accounting Standards. The United Nations recently set up in New York a Centre on Transnational Corporations to consider the position of transnational companies, which has indicated an intention to embrace the work of IASC in the pursuit of its aims.

I know that the Standards so far issued or under exposure are not perfect. Sometimes they reflect a compromise, or proffer alternatives; sometimes they may not be penetrating enough. Nevertheless, they are a gallant start. Any attempt to have moved too quickly or too fast in the formative years would have been fatal and, as the years go by, the existing Standards will be tightened and strengthened. For all these reasons, I think IASC has come to stay, and that its impact will increase in the years to come.

But there is one area in which we have not gone as far or as fast as we should have done. Some of the members of IASC have not arranged compliance with the new Standards by their individual members sufficiently firmly, and sometimes not at all. My own country has been staunch in this respect. The members of the accountancy bodies in the UK have been informed that they are under an obligation to comply with international accounting Standards in the same way that they are under an obligation to comply with our own local UK Standards, and members have been told that failure to comply can lead to an appropriate enquiry. Other members of IASC, both founder and associate members, have taken similar action. But some founder and associates have not yet done so.

There are various reasons for this. Some countries take the view that they cannot require compliance locally until they are satisfied that the Standards are internationally acceptable. Some see local legislation as an obstacle to the introduction of international Standards. Some accounting bodies do not have the power of discipline over their members, and cannot therefore impose compliance with either national or international Standards. Some countries have not yet overcome stubborn local resistance from the business community. But all these impediments must be broken down, and there should be no delay in starting this process.

But the ultimate objective is more far-reaching. It is one step to write international Standards; it is another step forward for professional bodies to notify their members that they are to observe them. The ultimate goal is to make reasonable efforts to see that the members do, in fact, observe them. Although progress is being made here and in other countries, I am sure that no accountancy body anywhere in the world has yet done enough to ensure that either its own local Standards or international Standards are, in fact, being applied by its members in the conduct of their professional practice or in their capacity as directors of business enterprises.

It is a heavy and costly operation. It needs a skilled staff to detect failures to comply, and a heavy overhead to follow this up with dispassionate investigation and, if necessary, sanctions. But this must, I suggest, happen sooner or later.

If the accountancy profession is to command the respect of the public which it serves and which provides it with a living, I believe that it has a duty to do more than write accounting Standards. It has a duty to take reasonable steps to see that they are, in fact, observed. Over and over again, when a company fails or goes into liquidation, the subsequent postmortem shows that one contributing factor has been the failure to observe sound accounting Standards. In most countries the public is rightly indulgent to professional men, realising that they have a heavy responsibility; errors of judgement are human and, are therefore pardoned, but neither the public nor governments will continue to be complacent if clear and authoritative Standards are openly disregarded.

I believe that IASC will have an important influence in this new field of effort because it has been instrumental in bringing this subject out into the open. In the years to come (and, as I have pointed out, things move slowly in a profession) it will be borne in on the accounting profession of the world, that Standards are written to be observed, not to be ignored. It is important that the accounting profession should take the necessary steps before the public and governments demand it.

What then of the future? IASC has started, but it will only succeed if the Standards it issues are sound, and if it continues to enjoy in the future the same relentless dedication by its members which has characterised the past three years. The men who sit on IASC are leaders of the profession in their own countries. The majority have sat on the Committee from the beginning, and will continue to do so for some time to come. All of them have had to travel many thousands of miles to sit on Steering Committees and to be present at the main Committee meetings. The paperwork is technical and exacting.

One of the most heartwarming experiences of the 50 years of my professional life has been the objective and unselfish work that the members of the Committee have devoted to the task.

The cost in money has been considerable – between £200–300,000 – but that is the least part of the cost. The cost in unpaid professional and leisure time has been enormous. I doubt whether this effort has been realised or appreciated, and I am glad to place it formally on the record.

I have never thought that the impact of IASC will be revolutionary or immediate. In meetings and seminars in numerous capitals of the world, I have said that the impact will be important in the next 10 years, and of dominating importance in the presentation of financial statements by about the year 2000.

The period from the meetings in Regina and Boston to the next century is no more than a generation – which is a short period in the lifespan of a great profession. But let us all be clear beyond peradventure on one issue. IASC will fail unless the founder and associate bodies ensure that the Standards are complied with by their members. There is no time to lose.

27

ACCOUNTANCY—THE MOST EXCITING PROFESSION IN THE WORLD

Peter Walton

Source: *Accounting and Business* (June 1996): 12–13.

When Henry Benson officially retired in August 1983 on his 74th birthday, his professional life covered nearly 60 years of very disparate activity, and he had built a reputation in a number of different fields. As an accountant he had been the initiator of the IASC and its first chairman; he had helped develop Coopers & Lybrand from a largeish family firm to today's international giant; he had been president of the ICAEW; he had sat on numerous professional committees and helped establish, amongst other things, the Joint Disciplinary Scheme.

But to lawyers, he was the chairman of the 1976 Royal Commission on Legal Services, while to bankers he was special adviser on industrial finance to the Governor of the Bank of England. As if this were not enough, his career also takes in achieving the rank of Brigadier in the Grenadier Guards, reorganising the Royal Ordnance factories, and looking into the running of the National Trust, the Coal Board, the New Zealand shipping trade—the list is endless.

To those who know, he is a grandson of one of the original Cooper Brothers. His choice of career seems natural, but it was largely a matter of chance. Henry Benson was born in Johannesburg in 1909 and it was in 1923 when, on a visit to London, his mother decided to drop into the family firm. Benson relates: "Nobody had anything to say—it was rather a sticky meeting because everyone was rather shy, and at the end of it, in desperation, the senior partner, Stuart Cooper, said: 'Well, if you would like this lad to be articled when he has finished school, you can send him home to England, here'. And that's how I became a chartered accountant.

"When I joined the firm, which was in 1926, the total strength everywhere, all over the world, was about 150 people. The only offices we had were London, Liverpool, Brussels and New York." Today, of course, Coopers & Lybrand, at the time of the merger with Price Waterhouse, has more than 70,000 staff in 140 countries.

"While I was with Coopers it was my life, and practically everything else was subordinated to it. I do not think it was a personal ambition, but there was a definite wish to see the firm recognised as one of the best and as a leader in the profession. I think accountancy is the most exciting profession in the world."

IASC

Although the inaugural meeting of the IASC Board took place in London in June 1973, its origins go back to 1966. In the summer of that year Henry Benson became president of the ICAEW. He says: "I had had the feeling for a long time that our relations with the Institutes in Canada and America were very friendly but somewhat remote. I decided to see whether I could get them on to a rather more intimate basis." He went to the US and Canada in the autumn. "I suggested to them that we should set up a three-nation group to study major accounting problems and to issue an agreed statement upon each of them.

"I was not advocating regimentation or uniformity. I was saying no more than that a careful study of the developments in the other two countries at regular intervals would be helpful to all of us."

This initiative produced the Accountants' International Study Group (AISG). Benson became convinced that international standards were necessary. "I used not to think so, but I now speak with total conviction that they are necessary. A Japanese aircraft is approaching John F Kennedy airport in New York in fog. Should the pilot proceed by his own rules and should he attempt to converse with the ground staff in Japanese? (I deliberately introduced fog into the analogy because finding one's way through some financial statements I have seen is like groping through a fog). Business, like everything else, has to be conducted by reference to certain rules and regulations, else chaos reigns. If a multinational company is raising money on world markets there must surely be some international standards by which its operations are judged."

The AISG started work in 1967. Benson explains: "I know that, by starting with three nations, other nations were upset but I had a fixed idea that we should start in a small way and expand later. Then at the International Congress in Sydney in 1972 the next step was taken. It was decided to enlarge the scope of AISG to include other nations and to set in place something much more ambitious.

"There were the usual birth pangs: mistrust, misunderstanding and criticism. But good humour and common sense prevailed; the venture got under way and IASC came into being in June 1973."

Benson did not expect that IASC would be an instant success. "In the early years of IASC I spoke in many capitals of the world and said: 'The impact of IASC will not be revolutionary or immediate. The impact will be important in the next ten years and of dominating importance in the presentation of financial statements by about the year 2000'. At that time a great many people thought that the venture would fail and some wanted it to do so. By the work and diligence of a great many devoted persons the world over, it has met with a remarkable degree of success."

Nature of standards

Some commentators criticise international standards for being insufficiently detailed. Benson's view is that "The standard should be clear enough so as to leave no doubt as to what is intended and sufficiently precise so that users can understand what has been done in preparing the financial statements. Excessive details should be avoided as this is likely to be counter-productive. The two qualities which are essential to any accountant if he is going to succeed in the pursuit of his profession are judgement and common sense and both should be brought fully into play in writing international standards."

As regards the influence of Anglo-Saxon accounting, Benson says: "There is a natural fear in every country that, in preparing international accounting standards, the views or practices of one country will be given undue emphasis to the exclusion of those in other countries. When I was appointed as the first chairman of IASC it was made clear to me, often with a noticeable absence of tact or politeness, that other nations were determined to see that UK standards and procedures were not given special prominence. I think these fears are unfounded. In practice IASC goes to great pains to try and secure balanced standards which do not place improper emphasis in any direction."

Benson is not happy about the tendency in Europe to move towards differential reporting: the use of international standards in consolidated accounts by large companies and national rules for domestic companies. "I cannot see the sense of this and it is certainly contrary to the concepts of those of us who are members of the European Union. It is confusing and time-wasting for companies from the same country to prepare their accounts on different bases depending upon whether for the moment they do, or do not, happen to have some international connection."

And what of the future? "International Accounting Standards have been my mistress, and for the removal of doubt, my only mistress, since I first fell into her clutches in 1967. But like all mistresses, she is outwardly attractive and compliant but in fact is capricious and difficult to satisfy. By the next century I shall be viewing the scene from, I hope, a more lofty stand point. I only hope that I shall then be able to look down with a benign, if not angelic, smile of approval."

Lord Benson died in 1995. The above quotations have been taken from records of presentations made by Lord Benson and a variety of published sources, including his autobiography *Accounting for life* published by Kogan Page in 1989, and an interview with Geoffrey Holmes which appeared in *Accountancy* in May 1975. Particular thanks are due to the Hon. Peter Benson for his help in preparing this article.

28

THE ESTABLISHMENT OF INTERNATIONAL ORGANIZATIONS

W. E. Olson

Source: W. E. Olson, *The Accounting Profession – Years of Trial: 1969–1980*, New York: AICPA, 1982, pp. 223–43.

During the 1960s many American corporations expanded their operations by establishing facilities and subsidiaries in other countries. The rapid emergence of huge multinational companies made it necessary for auditors, in turn, to expand their operations worldwide.

This created an urgent need for the profession to organize internationally in order to develop uniform accounting and auditing standards and to cope with national barriers to international practice. Because the United States was in the forefront of world trade, the AICPA had to assume a leadership role. Accordingly, during the 1970s the AICPA, in cooperation with the institutes of other countries, devoted a great deal of effort toward establishing new organizations to achieve international harmonization within the profession.

The report of the working party

The international organizations that were formed in the 1970s had their genesis in a working party that was established at the Ninth International Congress of Accountants in Paris in 1967. The working party was organized to consider the international needs of the profession and to present recommendations to the Tenth International Congress of Accountants to be held in Sydney, Australia, in 1972. Serving on the working party at its first two annual meetings were representatives from France, Great Britain, the Netherlands, the United States, and Australia; representatives from India and Mexico were added to the group for the 1970 and 1971 meetings. The AICPA was represented by Clifford V. Heimbucher, a past president of the Institute, and Leonard M. Savoie, the Institute's executive vice president.

One of the principal issues discussed by the working party was whether a permanent secretariat should be established to help speed up international cooperation and the harmonization of auditing and accounting standards. The AICPA was very much in favor of this, but other members objected strongly. The English institute felt that the main emphasis should be on the development of standards within each country; eventually, the most appropriate standards would gain international acceptance. It argued that the main role of the working party and any successor body should be to encourage and assist the development of regional professional organizations.

The AICPA position reflected the fact that many American companies had expanded their operations worldwide and were struggling to cope with the variety of accounting practices in different countries. The English position, on the other hand, reflected that institute's desire to achieve a leadership role in the Union Européenne des Experts Comptables, Economiques et Financiers (UEC). The UEC was a European regional accounting group. For years the English institute had been indifferent to the UEC, but its interest had increased now that the United Kingdom was joining the European Economic Community (EEC or Common Market).

The working party presented its conclusions and recommendations in a final report to the Tenth International Congress of Accountants in October 1972. The report largely reflected the position taken by the representatives of the English institute. It recommended against a secretariat, urged the strengthening of existing regional organizations, and suggested that the international congresses concentrate on ways to harmonize auditing and accounting standards.

The report did, however, take a small step toward creating an international professional organization. It recommended that the working party be restructured and renamed the International Coordination Committee for the Accountancy Profession (ICCAP). The new body would consist of five members serving for fifteen years and an additional five members serving for five years and eligible for reappointment thereafter. The ICCAP would select the host country for international congresses, maintain liaison with all bodies participating in the congresses, and monitor and assist the progress of regional organizations. The body would recommend changes for widening or amending its work, and it would continue to review the need for an international secretariat.

The leaders of the congress did not request a vote on the report, and none was taken. Since there was no groundswell of objection from the delegates, it was presumed that the recommendations had their approval.

One delegate, Walter J. Oliphant of the AICPA, did rise to urge more aggressive action toward the international harmonization of auditing and accounting standards. Mr. Oliphant complained that the report did not go far enough toward setting up an effective international organization.

The congress, without a vote, established the new body and approved the composition that the working group had suggested. The fifteen-year members were Australia, France, the Netherlands, the United Kingdom, and the United States. The first five-year members were Canada, West Germany, India, Mexico, and the Philippines.

The delegates of the Japanese Institute of Certified Public Accountants insisted that Japan should be included as a member of the new ICCAP. Japan, after all, had become a leader in world trade, and its accounting profession was developing very rapidly. Although no action was taken at the congress, subsequently, at its first meeting, the ICCAP voted to seat the Japanese delegation. The Japanese representatives participated in the balance of the meeting, and the ICCAP became an eleven-member body.

The ICCAP would continue to function through October 1977.

The formation of the international accounting standards committee

The other important event that occurred at the Tenth International Congress of Accountants was not part of the official proceedings. Sir Henry Benson of the United Kingdom invited delegates from the Canadian and American institutes to meet with him regarding a very important proposal for setting international accounting standards.

The five institutes in England and Wales, Scotland, Ireland, Canada, and the United States had previously formed a group known as the Accountants International Study Group (AISG), which worked for several years to achieve greater uniformity in those countries' accounting standards. This body had issued nineteen publications on accounting and auditing matters over the period of its existence. It was a natural starting point for any new initiative in the field of international accounting standards.

At the meeting, Sir Henry suggested that, because of its limited membership, the AISG was not adequate to meet the urgent need for the international harmonization of accounting standards. He proposed that a new body be created to set "basic" international accounting standards. The new body, as he envisioned it, would be composed of representatives from the United Kingdom, Ireland, Australia, Canada, France, West Germany, the Netherlands, and the United States.

It later became apparent that the proposal was motivated at least partially by a desire to gain greater influence over the standards to be set by the EEC, which would become mandatory for its members, including the United Kingdom. At that time the West German institute was generally recognized as being the leading influence in the EEC deliberations of accounting, and English practitioners feared that the standards adopted by the EEC would be incompatible with their own procedures.

At the meeting President Leroy Layton and I represented the AICPA. We had several reservations about the proposal. For instance, we pressed for an explanation of what Sir Henry meant by "basic" standards, but we received no clear answer. Also, the proposed membership seemed to be designed to allow England to dominate the organization: The Common Market countries would control four of the seven votes, and two of the other three votes would go to Canada and Australia, both members of the Commonwealth. More important, we believed that any truly international standard-setting body should include representation from Asia and Latin America. Japan and Mexico were obvious candidates, and we pressed for their inclusion; Sir Henry grudgingly agreed to include Mexico but resisted any further expansion. Finally, we insisted that the proposed standard-setting body should be established as a part of the ICCAP, albeit with complete autonomy in the development of standards.

Sir Henry would not hear of placing the new body under the aegis of the ICCAP. He believed that this would guarantee failure because it would subject the standard-setting body to all the conflicting political pressures of the larger organization. The ICCAP represented more than ninety different groups, among which the degree of professional development differed widely. Sir Henry maintained that the profession in the advanced countries should agree on "basic" standards, which would then very likely be adopted by accountants in the rest of the world.

Despite these differences in opinion, everyone agreed that we should hold another meeting to develop a more detailed plan. Leroy Layton and I recognized that U.S. interests coincided with those of the United Kingdom in regard to the type of accounting standards that might be mandated by the Common Market. To avoid a potential collision between the standards of English-speaking countries and those of the Common Market, we were prepared to recommend that the AICPA support the proposal for a new body.

The AICPA Board of Directors agreed. It authorized us to seek Japan's inclusion as a member, to press for the location of the secretariat in New York City, and to continue arguing that the new body should be established as a part of the ICCAP.

The participants at the Sydney meeting assembled again in London on December 3, 1972. A major portion of the discussion was devoted to reviewing and modifying a proposed constitution, which had been prepared by Douglas S. Morpeth and Sir Henry Benson in behalf of the English institute. We reached agreement on most issues with little difficulty, but the three AICPA proposals were hotly debated. Finally, we agreed on a compromise, whereby the Japanese institute would be invited to join the new International Accounting Standards Committee (IASC), the secretariat would be permanently located in London, and the constitution would include language that acknowledged the IASC to be a part of the ICCAP but not under its control. Clarification of this ambiguous relationship was left for future consideration.

None of the parties represented at the meeting were happy with all aspects of the compromise, but we all agreed that the IASC should be established. By the end of January 1973, the institutes in Canada, the United Kingdom, and the United States had approved the tentative proposal, and a meeting was scheduled in London for March 19 to explain the plan to officials of the institutes in Australia, France, West Germany, Japan, Mexico, and the Netherlands.

The participants at this meeting strongly supported the proposed IASC, but they were skeptical about how the new body's pronouncements might be enforced. Most of the participants indicated that their institutes would not initially be able to enforce international standards that were at variance with their domestic standards. I pointed out that the AICPA was unlikely to assign the IASC pronouncements a status higher than that of the Financial Accounting Standards Board. Sir Henry, however, insisted that each institute should require its members to demand that variations from international standards be disclosed in financial statements, or to make such disclosures in their audit reports, when international financial reports were involved.

This was a fundamental issue that could not be resolved in a short time. To get around this hurdle, language was adopted whereby the member institutes would pledge

to use their best endeavors:

(i) to ensure that published accounts comply with these standards or that there is disclosure of the extent to which they do not and to persuade governments, the authorities controlling securities markets and the industrial and business community that published accounts should comply with these standards;

(ii) to ensure that the auditors satisfy themselves that the accounts comply with these standards. If the accounts do not comply with these standards the audit report should either refer to the disclosure of non-compliance in the accounts, or should state the extent to which they do not comply;

(iii) to ensure that, as soon as practicable, appropriate action is taken in respect of auditors whose audit reports do not meet the requirements of (ii) above.

On this basis the institutes represented at the meeting agreed to establish the IASC. In due course all the arrangements were made, and an agreement and a constitution were signed in London on June 29, 1973, followed by a press conference and press releases in the nine founding countries.

Joseph P. Cummings was appointed as the AICPA's first voting representative on the IASC, to be accompanied by Robert Sempier, the Institute's director of international relations. Mr. Cummings was the deputy senior partner of Peat, Marwick, Mitchell and Co. and had previously served for several years on the Accounting Principles Board.

At the suggestion of the Canadian representatives, the AICPA was asked to provide the first secretary of the IASC. Paul Rosenfield, a member of the AICPA's technical staff, agreed to serve in this capacity for a two-year period and immediately took up residence in London.

It was unanimously agreed that Sir Henry Benson should be the first chairman of the new body. He believed passionately in the need for international accounting standards, and under his leadership, which some people viewed as autocratic, the IASC made rapid progress. Sir Henry remained chairman until June 1976, when he was succeeded by Joseph P. Cummings of the United States. Mr. Rosenfield was replaced as secretary in 1975 by John Brennan, a Canadian accounting professor; thus, the terms of the chairman and secretary were staggered to avoid the disruption that would be caused by simultaneous changes in both positions.

Other changes also took place as time went on. The AICPA appointed Eugene Minahan, an officer of Atlantic Richfield Company, to serve as one of the two U.S. representatives on the IASC, reflecting the Institute's belief that its members in industry should participate in the development of accounting standards, since they were responsible for the issuance of financial statements.

A revised agreement and constitution were signed in Munich in 1977, at which time the original standard-setting committee was redesignated the International Accounting Standards Committee Board. The purpose of this change was to permit supporting bodies to become members of the IASC even though they might not be voting members of the standard-setting body.

The IASC made remarkable progress. By the end of 1980 it had published thirteen International Accounting Standards and had issued exposure drafts for eight additional standards. Many observers were pleasantly surprised that agreements were reached with a minimum of nationalistic intransigence.

Although the standards were gaining recognition by the end of the decade, there continued to be no effective means of enforcing compliance with them. Fortunately, there were few differences between the IASC standards and the domestic standards of the major developed countries. Thus, for the time being, a confrontation had been avoided.

When it became apparent that IASC had become well established there was no longer a need for the Accountants' International Study Group (AISG), which included Canada, the United States and the United Kingdom. By mutual agreement it was discontinued in 1976 after having produced a series of excellent studies of the standards differences in the participants' respective countries.

The first meeting of the ICCAP

At the same time that the IASC was being established, the new ICCAP was also getting under way. Since West Germany had been selected as the host country for the next congress in 1977, the new president of its institute, Dr. Reinhard Goerdeler, had the task of chairing the ICCAP. At his instigation the first meeting of the ICCAP was scheduled for April 26 and 27, 1973.

Prior to the meeting, the AICPA appointed Michael Chetkovich, head of Deloitte, Haskins and Sells and the chairman of the AICPA International Relations Committee, to serve as its voting representative on the ICCAP. He would be joined at the meeting by Robert Sempier, the AICPA's director of international practice, and by me.

The AICPA decided to push immediately for the establishment of an international organization with a more formal structure and greater substance. We visualized some form of an international institute to achieve an organized profession on the international level. To further this end, Mr. Chetkovich requested that the agenda for the first meeting provide for discussion of a broader role for the ICCAP. The secretary of the English institute suggested that it would help to know specifically what the AICPA had in mind, so we developed an outline of a proposed international institute and sent the outline to all ICCAP members.

When the first meeting of the ICCAP convened on April 26, Douglas E. Morpeth, representing the United Kingdom, vigorously opposed the AICPA's proposal. He urged that the role of the ICCAP should be limited to encouraging regional organizations and overseeing the international congresses every fifth year. All the other members supported the general concept of an expanded international organization, but they had varying views about the nature and timing of the changes to be made. Realistically, they recognized that progress would be difficult unless the United States and the United Kingdom could reconcile their fundamental differences.

Adding to the problem were sharp differences of views about the nature of the relationship between the ICCAP and the IASC. The United Kingdom preferred mere recognition that close cooperation was desirable. All other members felt that the IASC should be a part of the ICCAP structure, although most agreed that the IASC should be free of any interference in the setting of accounting standards.

For a time it appeared that the opposing viewpoints could not be reconciled; but, to the great credit of Chairman Goerdeler, a way was found to break the impasse. A working party was appointed to reconsider the role and structure of the ICCAP and to determine a reasonable timetable for implementing any proposed changes. Serving on the working party would be Australia, Canada, the United States, France, the Netherlands, the United Kingdom, and West Germany. In addition to taking this action, the delegates adopted the following resolution without dissent:

ICCAP endorses the endeavors that have resulted in the formation of IASC.

ICCAP formally invites IASC to be part of the world attempt to develop the accountancy profession.

ICCAP requests IASC to recognize in its charter that it is part of the ICCAP organization although it is autonomous in its issuance of exposure drafts and recommendations.

ICCAP further agrees that IASC's basic charter shall not be reviewed until the end of 1976 without the agreement of IASC and ICCAP.

A paragraph containing the substance of this resolution was subsequently included in the IASC constitution. The words *part of* remained subject to interpretation, however, since no structural ties existed between the two organizations other than sharing of the same group of sponsoring institutes.

The evolution of the international federation of accountants

Although these actions prevented a total breakdown in the discussions, a fundamental conflict between the United Kingdom and the United States remained. Their basic differences were the subject of continuing discussions during the next four years. Six more plenary meetings of the ICCAP, two meetings of the ICCAP Working Party on the Future Role and Structure of ICCAP, six meetings of a subcommittee on future organizational structure, and numerous unofficial meetings between key representatives of the United Kingdom and the United States were held between 1973 and 1977. Slowly and painstakingly, differences were reconciled, and the International Federation of Accountants (IFAC) evolved from the discussions and negotiations at these meetings.

The working party appointed at the ICCAP meeting held its first session in Paris on August 9 and 10, 1973. The group concluded that the ICCAP should adopt a formal statement of objectives and that ICCAP committees should be appointed to deal with ethics, education, regional organizations, and promotion of the ICCAP. Another committee should study the need for a formal international body with a written constitution. The preparation of background papers on each of these subjects was assigned to individual members of the working party. The United Kingdom and the United States were given joint responsibility to develop proposals regarding a constitution.

The results of these assignments were reviewed by the working party on the day preceding the next ICCAP plenary meeting in October 1973. The American and English delegates had jointly prepared a summary of the working party's conclusions in the form of a report to the ICCAP, to which the other papers could be attached. This approach won the approval of the working party, and the report was presented on the following day.

The report urged the ICCAP to appoint the committees agreed upon at the Paris meeting. It also recommended that a constitution for an international federation of accountants be developed and submitted at the next international congress in Munich in 1977. An outline for such a constitution, prepared by the American and English delegates, accompanied the report.

The ICCAP approved the recommendations without dissent and appointed the suggested committees. The new subcommittee on future organizational structure, cochaired by the delegates from the United Kingdom and the United States, included delegates from Canada, France, West Germany, and the Netherlands; this subcommittee bore the brunt of the planning and negotiations that led to the establishment of the International Federation of Accountants.

The subcommittee spent 1974 preparing and reviewing successive drafts of a constitution for the International Federation of Accountants. Robert Sempier, Douglas Morpeth, Philip Carrel (director of overseas relations for the English institute), and I drafted the original document at meetings in London and New York. The subcommittee and the ICCAP held meetings to resolve details of the proposed constitution. Everything went quite smoothly because the decision to establish a formal federation in 1977 seemed to have unanimous support.

Unfortunately, at a subcommittee meeting in New York on January 24, 1975, the apparent consensus fell apart. The Canadian representative, Gordon Cowperthwaite, expressed the belief that the constituent bodies would not agree to establish a federation unless the ICCAP had produced some solid achievements by 1977. Otherwise, there would be little enthusiasm for paying dues to a new organization. He also worried about the lack of progress being made by the other ICCAP subcommittees. If the member institutes could not complete the work assigned to them by the ICCAP, then they would have trouble performing the many chores needed to establish the new organization. With these problems in mind, Mr. Cowperthwaite prepared a paper proposing that the ICCAP engage a small staff. He suggested raising the necessary funds by seeking contributions from the large CPA firms, which had the greatest interest in international developments.

The English representative, Mr. Morpeth, responded with a swift, firm rejection of the proposal. More significantly, he also reported that the United Kingdom institutes had reconsidered the need for a federation and were no longer prepared to provide financial support for such a body.

This announcement threw the meeting into disarray. The session ended, however, with an agreement that Canada and West Germany, in consultation with the United States, would develop a more complete proposal for an ICCAP staff. The participants still hoped that somehow the United

Kingdom could be convinced to change its position since all the other members of the ICCAP solidly backed the concept of a strong federation.

The AICPA's representatives supported the proposal to engage a staff before 1977, and on February 6, 1975, I sent a letter to the heads of the large firms seeking funds for this purpose. The response was mixed. A few firms agreed to provide funds; some took a wait-and-see position, and one firm stated its opposition to a new federation. Given this response and a vigorous campaign mounted against the proposal by the large British firms, it was clear that funds for an interim ICCAP staff could not be raised from the firms.

Thus, in their definitive proposal, Messrs. Cowperthwaite and Goerdeler stated that funds for the staff would have to come from the member institutes. The proposal was mailed to the subcommittee on April 9, 1975.

The reaction of the United Kingdom was almost immediate. On April 30 Mr. Morpeth sent a long letter to the subcommittee, with copies to all the other members of the ICCAP. He repeated the British opposition to a strong, central body and urged that virtually all international harmonization efforts should be carried on through regional organizations. He did, however, support a federation with a £30,000 (approximately $60,000) annual budget and a role confined to coordination of work by other bodies and oversight of the international congresses. The letter stated emphatically that the United Kingdom institutes would not provide funds for an interim staff and argued that the lack of a defined work program for a central body and the minimal achievements of the ICCAP demonstrated that a strong federation was not needed.

The message left no room for doubt. The United Kingdom would support only a federation with little substance, and the stage was set for yet another confrontation on the fundamental issue that had been argued since the international congress in 1967.

On June 11, 1975, the subcommittee met in Amsterdam to discuss the paper that had been circulated on April 9. The discussion was acrimonious, and in the end the subcommittee agreed only to report to the ICCAP that it supported the recommendations but that the United Kingdom remained opposed.

The ICCAP met on the following day. The meeting began with a discussion of the subcommittee's report and the Morpeth letter. All the pro and con arguments were aired in a tense session. Feelings of betrayal and anger were expressed by the delegates, none of whom supported the position of the United Kingdom representatives. Since no progress was being made toward breaking the impasse, Chairman Goerdeler adjourned the discussion until the next day, when a more dispassionate atmosphere might prevail.

I decided that a private discussion with Mr. Morpeth might produce a compromise on the diametrically opposed positions of the United States and the United Kingdom. In a candid exchange over breakfast the following morning, we both conceded that our constituents distrusted each other's motives. We agreed that effective progress could not be achieved on an international level unless the United Kingdom and the United States were in agreement. Either country could block effective action simply by refusing to agree.

Mr. Morpeth explained the British perception that the United States would want to spend large sums on a federation. Many people feared that the United Kingdom would be asked to pay more dues than it could comfortably afford. He cited the large budget of the Financial Accounting Standards Board as the basis for this concern.

An additional worry seemed to be the U.K. desire to retain the situs of the IASC in London. Apparently, the United Kingdom feared that the United States might urge that the IASC be moved to New York.

With these considerations in mind, I made a very frank proposal. The secretariat of the proposed federation would be located in New York, and that of the IASC in London. The two countries would jointly provide staff for the two secretariats so that there would be mutual surveillance. The United States would agree that the ICCAP should not hire a staff before 1977 and would do its best to confine the budget of the proposed federation to only what was necessary to carry out substantive projects at the international level. In return, the United Kingdom would agree to support a stronger federation with a secretariat beginning in 1977. Mr. Morpeth agreed to these proposals.

When the ICCAP meeting resumed that morning, a more harmonious atmosphere prevailed. The members unanimously adopted motions authorizing the subcommittee on future organizational structure to prepare an interim report to all the constituent bodies represented by the ICCAP seeking approval of the establishment of an International Federation of Accountants (IFAC) and a secretariat in 1977. Included in the report would be a proposed constitution, a proposed work program for the IFAC, a proposed method of financing the IFAC, a recommendation on the location of the secretariat, a definition of the relationship between the IFAC and the IASC, a definition of the roles of regional bodies and their relationship to the IFAC, and a timetable and program for presenting the federation proposal to the congress in 1977.

When the meeting closed, the effort to create a new federation was back on track. The delegates departed with the hope that the ICCAP's primary objective finally would be achieved.

The period from July 1975 through March 1976 was devoted to preparing, reviewing, and revising drafts of an interim report. Although there were debates about many of the details, the only serious disagreements were in regard to the relationship between the IASC and the IFAC.

Defining the relationship proved particularly troublesome. Most delegates urged that the IASC be a "part of" the IFAC as an autonomous committee with authority to issue pronouncements in its own name. A few delegates insisted that both bodies should share a single secretariat at one location. The United Kingdom's delegates argued that the IASC should be a separate body with its own membership, financing, and secretariat but closely related to the IFAC.

Representatives of the ICCAP met with the chairman and other representatives of the IASC in an attempt to reach agreement on a definition of the relationship. Even though the principal sponsors of the IFAC and the IASC would be identical—the institutes from the major countries—it was believed that obtaining the agreement of the individuals serving on the IASC would avoid any bruised feelings. The IASC constitution stated that it was a "part of" the ICCAP; the strict constructionists now said that the ICCAP had no fight to assign this relationship to a new federation without the IASC's consent. Others suggested that this was nonsense because the principal sponsoring bodies were identical and were in effect dealing with themselves.

The issue was temporarily resolved when a final version of an interim report was approved in February 1976. The report included the following wording:

> ICCAP believes that its existing relationship with IASC should be carried forward to IFAC on the same general basis and recommends that IASC should continue as the body designated to have responsibility and authority to issue, in its own name, pronouncements on international accounting standards. As such, IASC would be autonomous and have its own constitution, secretariat and system of financing its activities.
>
> ICCAP recognizes that the objectives of IFAC and IASC are interdependent. The closest relationship is clearly to the advantage of both IASC and IFAC particularly since some member bodies of IASC will also be members of IFAC. Therefore, arrangements should be made to establish and maintain a continuing liaison between the two bodies.

This wording was mirrored in a revised IASC constitution, which was adopted on October 10, 1977. The description was sufficiently ambiguous to allow agreement, but in fact there continued to be little substance to the concept that the IASC was a "part of" the IFAC. The issue would arise again at a later time.

The interim, report requested the constituent bodies to respond, stating whether they would join the proposed federation and providing their reactions to the provisions of the constitution. A large number of responses were received, and the subcommittee and the ICCAP held several meetings during the months preceding the October 1977 congress. A final report and constitution were drafted, agendas were prepared, and all the necessary arrangements were made to launch the IFAC at the congress. Agreement was reached to nominate Dr. Goerdeler as president and Mr. Cowperthwaite as deputy president of the new federation. It was also agreed that the secretariat would be located in New York, that the AICPA would provide office facilities at no cost to the IFAC, and that Robert Sempier would be employed as the executive director.

The final ICCAP report was mailed to the constituent bodies in March 1977. The heads of delegations to the congress approved the report on the morning of October 7, and that afternoon a founding meeting of the IFAC constituent assembly was convened to approve and sign the constitution.

The assembly then elected four countries to serve on the council along with the eleven countries designated in the constitution. The fifteen countries that composed the initial council were Australia, Brazil, Canada, Denmark, West Germany, France, India, Japan, Mexico, the Netherlands, New Zealand, Nigeria, the Philippines, the United Kingdom (and Ireland), and the United States.

The newly formed council held its first meeting on October 8. Officers were elected, auditors were appointed, a budget was approved, standing committees were appointed, and Mr. Sempier was appointed executive director. The two elected vice presidents were Gabriel Mancera of Mexico and B. L. Kabra of India. The budget for the first year projected expenditures of $145,500.

The conclusion of the council meeting marked the culmination of five years of effort to establish a formal international organization. It had been a difficult struggle at times, but in the end there was broad support for the federation. A total of sixty-three bodies from fifty-one countries had signed the constitution.

The relationship between the IFAC and the IASC

The second meeting of the IFAC Council was held in May 1978, and on the agenda was the matter of how to implement the provision in the constitution whereby "the closest relationship should be maintained between IFAC and IASC." IASC Chairman Joseph Cummings addressed the meeting on May 3. He urged the appointment of a small joint committee to develop a plan for merger of the two bodies. He expressed the view that eventually the duplication of secretariat, funds, and membership should be resolved.

This immediately rekindled the United Kingdom suspicions that the Americans were determined to consolidate all international activities into a single secretariat located in New York. Past wounds were reopened, and the ensuing negotiations continued into 1981.

At the IASC meeting in Perth, Australia, in June 1978, IFAC President Goerdeler discussed the subject of merger with representatives of the two bodies. They agreed to hold an informal meeting in London on November 6 to explore the merger issue further.

The London meeting was attended by the president, deputy president, and executive director of the IFAC and the chairman and staff of the IASC. John Grenside, a past president of the English institute and a member of the IASC, also attended. The participants agreed that they should continue to act as a joint working group to examine the problems and benefits of merging by October 1982. It was also agreed that the AICPA representatives should be added to the working group and that the two staffs should jointly prepare a draft proposal for the next meeting.

During the next year the individuals serving on the IASC began to raise objections to a possible merger with the IFAC. They feared that such action would hinder them from bringing other interested parties into the standard-setting process. This was viewed by some as necessary to gain the recognition and support of the Economic and Social Council of the United Nations and the Organization for Economic Cooperation and Development, which were threatening to set their own accounting and financial reporting standards for multinational corporations.

The members of the joint working group expected these concerns to prove troublesome at its next meeting in June 1979. Early in the meeting, however, I proposed a series of parallel amendments to the constitutions of the two bodies that would effectively integrate them without disturbing the autonomy of the IASC in the setting of accounting standards. The proposal quickly won unanimous agreement, and the two staff heads were instructed to draft the necessary documents for presentation to the IASC and the IFAC Council. Agreement had been reached in less than two hours of discussions.

The euphoria was short-lived, however. After reviewing a joint draft, Mr. Chetkovich and I were troubled by the ambiguity created by the continuation of a separate IASC constitution. We believed that this strongly implied that the IASC was a separate body rather than a division of the IFAC. To correct this problem, we suggested an alternative approach consisting of the following documents: an agreement of integration to be signed by the members of both organizations, "Terms of Reference and Operating Procedures" to be appended to the agreement of integration, and an amended IFAC constitution. (The word *integration* had been substituted for *merger* in the discussions of the joint working group because it was believed to be less objectionable to opponents of a merger.)

The suggested alternative was adopted, and subsequent drafts were prepared in the form of a preamble, an integration agreement, and amendments to the IFAC constitution. These were circulated to members of the joint working party, modified on the basis of comments received from them, and then incorporated in a report to the IASC and the IFAC Council.

Neither body found the report acceptable. IASC members had various objections to the proposed integration, and a majority of the IFAC Council expressed dissatisfaction that the proposal did not provide for a forthright merger of the two bodies. In addition, at the urging of Washington SyCip of the Philippines, the council suggested that membership on the IASC board should be subject to rotation so that the nine founding countries would not have perpetual representation. Such a change would bring the IASC into harmony with the provisions of the IFAC constitution.

The joint working group met to consider objections that had been raised. After extensive discussions, agreement was reached in principle on the changes to be made in the proposed integration documents. A revised draft was mailed to members of the IASC board and the IFAC Council on January 7, 1980. It was hoped that by June 1980 both groups would approve the report for distribution to their respective constituent bodies.

These plans did not materialize. The Consultative Committee of Accountancy Bodies of the United Kingdom issued a letter urging delay in integration until questions about certain financing procedures and outside representation on the IASC were resolved. This position was reiterated by the United Kingdom representatives at a meeting of the IFAC Planning Committee in Bermuda on February 17, 1980. At the same meeting the Netherlands representatives expressed their opposition to the integration proposals. It came as no surprise, therefore, when the IASC board decided to defer further consideration of the proposed integration agreement pending exploration of whether outside parties could be brought into its activities.

The integration discussions resumed on May 14, 1980, at a meeting of the IFAC Council in London. IASC Chairman Hans Burggraaff reported on the action of his board and expressed the hope that a revised agreement could be reached by the spring of 1981. Other informal discussions were also held, which revealed that the United Kingdom representatives were very upset with the provision that would permit but not require the rotation of all IASC members. They believed that the principal developed countries should be guaranteed membership on the standard-setting body.

During the succeeding months Mr. Cowperthwaite, who had succeeded Mr. Goerdeler as president of the IFAC, had informal meetings with representatives of the IASC in an effort to develop a revised agreement that would gain acceptance. Despite these efforts the IASC board indicated at a meeting in November that the rotation issue was still a stumbling block. Also, the IASC had received a legal opinion on the proposed integration agreement and had been advised to recast the document in the form of mutual commitments. In the meantime the IFAC Council reconfirmed its desire to allow rotation of all IASC members. Once again it appeared that negotiations had reached an impasse.

On January 14, 1981, the joint working group met in Toronto to make yet another effort to achieve an acceptable proposal for integration. Time was running out; if action was not taken at the 1982 congress, a delay until 1987 would likely result. The group agreed to recast the relationship between the

IASC and the IFAC in the form of mutual commitments, as suggested by the IASC's legal counsel. This formally recognized that there were two separate bodies, which effectively negated any pretension that a merger would be consummated. Nevertheless, the IASC would make two concessions: Rotation of all members would be permitted after 1987, and the IFAC Council would nominate the members to serve on the IASC board. All other features of the mutual commitments would be essentially the same as those included in prior drafts of an integration agreement.

In February 1981 the IFAC Planning Committee gave its approval to the compromise. An explanation of the revised proposals was sent to the IFAC Council and the IASC board, urging their approval. At the date of this writing it appears that both bodies will approve the proposals and that the terms will be ratified at the congress in Mexico City in October 1982. If this occurs, the existence of two separate bodies will be institutionalized, but more substantive ties will be created.

It remains to be seen whether being a separate body will make the IASC more vulnerable to pressures to divorce it from any control by the accounting profession. If the American experience with the FASB is any guide, it can be expected that eventually the international accounting profession will be forced to surrender all controlling ties to the standard-setting body. It was precisely for this reason that the AICPA's representatives resisted a separate status for the IASC. The AICPA's representatives supported the participation of outside parties in standard setting but believed that the profession should retain control over the process as long as possible. We believed that a takeover by government seemed unlikely at the international level. We were more concerned that a body with separate status unnecessarily increased the chances that other interests would gain a controlling influence.

The setting of financial accounting and reporting standards internationally is perhaps less critical than on a national level since there is no effective means of enforcement across national borders. Nevertheless, uniform, standards are being adopted by the Common Market countries, and the United Nations is expected to seek actions by member nations to adopt a common set of international standards. Further evolution can be expected as the national economies become increasingly interdependent. For all these reasons, the battle over the relationship between the IFAC and the IASC was not an academic exercise.

Other international activities

Throughout the 1970s the AICPA pursued other international activities more limited in scope. These included membership in two regional organizations, the Conference of Asian and Pacific Accountants (CAPA) and the Interamerican Accountants' Association (IAA). The activities of these bodies consisted principally of holding periodic conferences devoted to technical subjects. The AICPA also invited the presidents and executive directors of various institutes to attend its annual meetings as guests of the Institute. Reciprocal invitations were also extended to representatives of the AICPA to attend similar meetings in other countries. As might be expected, the relationships with the Canadian and Mexican Institutes were especially close and cordial. In addition, the AICPA's chairman and president periodically attended various meetings in England, Scotland, Ireland, France, West Germany, the Netherlands, Australia, and New Zealand.

These visits often entailed expensive and time-consuming travel, but they helped build understanding and cohesiveness. It will be in the best interests of the AICPA and its members to continue such a policy of active involvement in professional developments around the world. All signs point toward increasing interdependence of business activities across international borders, and the profession must continue to adapt to these changing circumstances.

At the beginning of the 1980s much remains to be accomplished before the profession can become truly harmonized internationally. Technical standards, entrance requirements, rights to practice, and ethical restraints are far too disparate among the well developed countries and are too poorly developed in others. The barriers of national sovereignty guarantee that achieving uniformity will be a slow and painful process.

Nevertheless, a solid foundation for working toward this long-range goal was laid during the 1970s. It was a period of difficult negotiations and compromise. Out of the controversies emerged a keener understanding that the profession's interests will be better served by setting aside national pride. The establishment of the IFAC and the IASC were impressive accomplishments, and it behooves the profession's future generations to build on this good beginning. The profession has an opportunity to set an example by transcending nationalism for the common good.

29

INTERNATIONAL ACCOUNTING STANDARDS COMMITTEE — THE FUTURE

John A. Hepworth

Source: W. J. Brennan (ed.) *The Internationalization of the Accountancy Profession*, Toronto: CICA, 1979, pp. 49–57.

The International Accounting Standards Committee (IASC) first met in June 1973, exactly five years before I assumed office as chairman. During these first five years the committee issued 14 exposure drafts, which were followed by 10 standards, two discussion papers and the document "The Work and Purpose of the International Accounting Standards Committee." The committees are now working on a further eight topics. The IASC held its first meeting of members in Munich in October 1977, adopting a new constitution at that time.

Successful history

The committee always recognized that the achievement of its objectives would take time and, more particularly, that it was necessary to have produced standards before its performance could be assessed and accepted. The organization of the work of the IASC in developing standards is largely the result of its first chairman, Sir Henry Benson. His conviction, technical ability, dedication and drive saw to it that the work was organized, coordinated and carried out according to a schedule determined at the beginning of each project. I believe this procedure of establishing a definite timetable, as well as having the whole IASC board involved, is one of the great strengths of the organization of the committee's work.

Joe Cummings, as the second IASC chairman, carried on this task of ensuring productivity and, in addition, provided leadership in reviewing and amending the constitution.

While the committee has been fortunate in its first two leaders, another important clue to its achievements lies in its secretariat. It consists of two technically qualified staff, the secretary and the assistant secretary. This team is an integral part of the technical input, writing and editing for all the committees' work.

So far, appointments have been on a limited term basis. Various organizations have been able to release from their staff individuals with the highest technical ability for periods of between 18 and 24 months. Paul Rosenfield was seconded by the American Institute of Certified Public Accountants as the first secretary. His assistant was Richard Simmons, who was seconded by Arthur Andersen in the UK. Subsequent teams included W. John Brennan from the University of Saskatchewan in Canada as secretary, and Chris Relleen from Deloitte Haskins & Sells in London as his assistant; and Roy Nash from Arthur Young in the US as secretary and Hugh Richardson from Coopers Lybrand (UK) as his assistant. We have been extremely well served to date, and I hope that professional accountancy bodies, accounting firms, universities and companies will continue to contribute by making their staff available to serve on the secretariat.

Changes to IFAC's constitution

The changes made to the constitution — which will be the basis of IASC's organization for the next five years — were in response to observations from the board and from the total membership during the first four years of operation. The chairman and the board had recognized quite early that a review would be necessary and, accordingly, set up an Organization and Planning Committee. It is interesting to consider the reasons for and impacts of some of the changes adopted.

The original agreement specified that the IASC would formulate "basic" standards. The word "basic" caused a great deal of confusion and misunderstanding. If taken literally, the scope of the standards developed by IASC would have been very limited. For example, it was generally accepted that international standards should be set in terms suitable for universal acceptance and that they should not be too complex.

One of the changes was to delete this word "basic" so that the committee would be free to develop standards on more complex issues as well. Indeed, some of the standards now being developed fall into this category, for example, translation of foreign currencies; accounting for diversified operations and segment reporting; and disclosure in the financial statements of banks. Most will agree that current reporting practice in these topics is inconsistent and deficient, yet it is difficult to arrive at a consensus for setting an accounting standard. I believe that, more and more, IASC will see a need to give leadership in some of these areas by issuing exposure drafts or discussion papers before actually issuing a standard. The removal of the word "basic" has removed any inhibitions in this regard on the committee's work. Nevertheless, the fact that IASC standards are issued for international use requires that they should recognize that practice and law will be different in some countries and that, therefore, they cannot always be as restrictive as a national standard may be; they will probably have to start providing options to accommodate this situation. Currently, standards do identify the acceptable options and disclosure of accounting policies so that readers of financial reports do have some basis for comparability with other entities.

Another change of significance to the future of IASC is the expansion in the board membership. The term "board" is now synonymous with the term "committee" as used in the original constitution. The professional bodies from the nine countries that set up the IASC are identified as "Founder Members," and have been carried forward as members of the board. Two additional positions were created and are available to the other IASC member bodies for terms of up to five years.

The founder members had originally been selected for their commercial importance, accounting status and geographic distribution. Following the meeting in Munich in 1977, all IASC members were invited to apply to join the board; only five did so. The obligations of board membership require a considerable contribution in money, time and technical ability. The extent of these requirements caused the withdrawal of two applications and, from the remaining three, the professional accountancy bodies in Nigeria and South Africa were chosen. They are now serving three-year terms.

Adding on the extra members has been a useful amendment because it carries forward the involvement of "strategic" accounting nations, yet introduces an element of participation by all members. Since the obligations of board membership require a considerable contribution in money, time and technical ability, it is essential to have the support of the professional bodies who are able, on all counts, to participate in the board's work.

Fortunately, most of the countries who should be represented on the board are now members. And, with perhaps two exceptions — South America and Southeast Asia — the principal geographic areas are also represented on the board, virtually ensuring worldwide involvement.

The board recognizes the honest desire of members to have a greater involvement and input into the development of international standards. Therefore, it proposes to invite, when practicable, comments from all member bodies on material coming to the board for possible release as exposure drafts. IASC member bodies will have an opportunity to review and comment on proposed exposure drafts. This opportunity is similar to that exercised by board member bodies in their pre-meeting briefing of their representations. It is hoped that this arrangement will provide greater access by all IASC member bodies to the decision making process.

Financial considerations

The board's financial arrangements have been the subject of some discussion and disagreement. Basically, the arrangement is to share equally all IASC costs. Some escalation of costs above the original inflation-adjusted base is, however, shared by board members on the basis of their respective institute's size. This somewhat relieves the burden on smaller bodies.

The financial arrangements are important to the operations of a technical committee drawing its membership from all over the world. The board meets three times a year and it is essential for the continuity of its work that at least one representative from each country is present. The cost of attendance is, of course, considerably higher for the members from the more remote areas of the world. The provision therefore has been that the travelling costs of one representative for board meetings and for steering committee meetings should be shared equally; this offsets any financial inclination to be absent.

IASC's secretariat

The constitution provides that the IASC's permanent office be in London and that its rent, rates and taxes are to be borne by the UK's professional accountancy bodies. London is a good central location for the office since the majority of board members are from Europe and North America. Further, Australia, Japan, South Africa and Nigeria, although all far from London, are also quite remote from each other.

Although the original constitution placed an obligation on the UK to recruit staff for the secretariat, this has now been changed to a board responsibility. The recruitment of all members of the secretariat is critical to the board and to the committee, and all should participate in the process to ensure that the right calibre people are appointed and that the secretariat is not identified with any one country.

The other changes to the constitution made at Munich were more in the nature of procedural matters. Although desirable, they do not have a great significance in the main thrust of the objectives and work of the IASC.

IASC's current priorities

Someone looking at the future of the International Accounting Standards Committee might think that the committee will soon exhaust the range of subjects for future IASC Statements. This is not likely; not only are there numerous subjects before the committee at the present time, but the following might also be considered for addition to the IASC's current agenda:

- **General accounting topics**
  Accounting for service transactions
  Employment reports
  Financial reporting in a prospectus
  Guidelines on the presentation of financial statements
  Interim financial reporting
  Materiality in financial reporting
  Objectives in financial statements
  Published profit forecasts
  Related party transactions
  Simplified financial statements
  Value added statements

- **Specific financial statement items**
  Accounting for government grants
  Accounting for interest costs
  Accounting for marketable securities
  Earnings per share
  Reporting gains and losses from the extinguishment or restructuring of debt
  The treatment of investments in financial statements

- **Special industry problems**
  Development stage enterprises
  Extractive industries
  Governmental units
  Not-for-profit enterprises

In addition, at some stage, it will be necessary to review the standards already issued and, possibly, the board will consider a conceptual framework project on an international level.

Undoubtedly, one of the problems IASC will have is the possibility that certain of its standards may be issued before all the national accounting standards committees have tackled the same issues. The IASC will need to assess the significance of this situation for each subject and determine whether some other procedure, for example, preliminary exposure drafts or discussion drafts, is preferable to moving to the more formal exposure draft of a standard. This should not be a problem for a while yet, however.

The IASC's immediate task is to gain acceptance and observance of international accounting standards already released. A paper was presented to the Munich meeting in 1977 setting out what the member bodies undertook to do when they joined the IASC and reported on the present status of international accounting standards in various member countries. This report was based on two questionnaires sent to members in 1974 and 1976. The responses to the questionnaires did not provide a complete description of each country's position, but they made it clear that several countries still have not adopted international accounting standards.

Obviously, however, for complete credibility we must have greater acceptance and observance throughout the world. The paper presented in Munich suggested that, prior to the next International Congress of Accountants, every accounting body should:

- Publish a statement to its members indicating the status to be accorded international accounting standards in audited financial statements.
- Distribute the definitive international accounting standards to its members, appropriately translated.
- Develop an effective means to involve all interested parties in the establishment of international accounting standards via the exposure draft process.
- Establish a formal procedure for evaluating the observance of accounting standards, domestic and international.
- Prepare a report on the success being achieved in gaining the acceptance and observance of international accounting standards in its country.

It will be necessary for the IASC to regularly monitor the acceptance and observance of international standards throughout its membership. In this context, it is worth quoting the agreement to which every member subscribes in making application to join the IASC. Each member agrees to use its best endeavours:

(1) Ensure that published financial statements comply with these standards or that there is disclosure of the extent to which they do not and to persuade governments, the authorities controlling securities markets and the industrial and business community that published financial statements should comply with these standards.
(2) Ensure (1) that the auditors satisfy themselves that the financial statements comply with these standards or, if the financial statements do not comply with these standards, that the fact of non-compliance is disclosed in the financial statements, (2) that in the event of non-disclosure reference to non-compliance is made in the audit report.
(3) Ensure that, as soon as practicable, appropriate action is taken in respect of auditors whose audit reports do not meet the requirements of (2) above.

These obligations can be satisfied in different ways. For example, in some cases, an accountancy body might publish a formal statement expressing the status that IASC standards should have when members prepare or report on financial statements. Such a statement gives prominence to the existence of international accounting standards and provides an opportunity for the membership of accountancy bodies to appreciate their importance.

Some accountancy bodies have declared to their members that international accounting standards are to be accorded the same status as domestic standards. In other organizations, each international accounting standard is accompanied by an explanation of the relationship between the international standard and the national standard dealing with the same subject. This statement explaining the status of the international accounting standard is frequently published as part of the international standard.

Other accountancy bodies have issued statements declaring support for the concept of international standards and suggest that their acceptance by members of the accountancy body is desirable and should be encouraged. Some of these indicate the extent to which an international standard differs from the related domestic standard. They also often include a promise to review, or to encourage the relevant body to review, the domestic standard with the objective of eliminating any differences.

A few countries remain, however, that have published no formal statement on how IASC standards are to be treated. The problem of how to deal with these countries is now one of the major tasks facing the IASC board.

Intervention by other bodies

The recent increased interest by government agencies and other financial institutions in the setting of requirements for financial reporting in the international scene is also of significance to the future of the IASC. These moves are the logical extension of actions by these groups on the national scene. The allegation is that the accountancy profession has not performed adequately in the past and that the only satisfactory solution is to legislate or regulate the necessary control.

This development is illustrated by the October 1977 report of the Group of Experts on International Standards in Accounting and Reporting for Transnational Corporations. This report proposes standards on the publication of financial and nonfinancial information. The nonfinancial information requirements recommended go far beyond any current requirements anywhere. I feel, however, that these nonfinancial reporting requirements are an area in which accountants in general or the International Accounting Standards Committee in particular should not be involved at the present time. As for the recommendations on financial information, with the exception of reporting on segments of diversified operations, they have all been covered by IASC standards already issued. And the IASC is now, in fact, developing an exposure draft on accounting for diversified operations.

Obviously, the independence of the profession is at stake. More particularly, so far as financial reporting is concerned, the legislated regulations may be more concerned with political issues than the quality of financial reports. Thus, because of the technical and commercial experience of its members, I believe that it is the profession that is best equipped to set standards for financial reporting.

The International Accounting Standards Committee is endeavouring to liaise with all organizations expressing opinions and showing signs of wishing to become involved in the development of accounting requirements. The board has pointed out that the IASC has the independence and the objectivity to embrace all the areas contemplated by these bodies, and that the primary efforts should be directed through it rather than being complicated by a proliferation of requirements from various bodies. It would be a great pity if the IASC's work were undermined by this trend, and strenuous efforts will be necessary to avoid it.

The role of IFAC

Finally, some reference should be made to the International Federation of Accountants (IFAC) which was formed at the Munich Congress in 1977. This body replaced the International Co-Ordination Committee for the Accounting Profession, which, apart from organizing the world congresses, had the task of studying the feasibility of setting up an international federation. On its recommendation, IFAC was then formed in 1977.

The first International Accounting Standards Committee agreement in 1973 provided, in the constitution, that:

> The professional accountancy bodies which are signatories hereto, further agree that the International Accounting Standards Committee, with the objectives, functions, powers, composition, organisation and financial arrangements set out in its Constitution, shall be a part of the International Co-Ordination Committee for the Accountancy Profession established by the heads of delegations to the xth International Congress of Accountants in Sydney but shall be autonomous in the issue of Exposure drafts and Standards. The Constitution of the International Accounting Standards Committee shall not be reviewed until the end of 1976 without the agreement of the International Accounting Standards Committee and the International Co-Ordination Committee for the Accountancy Profession.

This was amended in the 1977 agreement to read:

> The professional accountancy bodies which are signatories hereto, agree that the relationship existing with the International Co-Ordination Committee for the Accountancy Profession should be carried forward to the International Federation of Accountants

on the same general basis and that the International Accounting Standards Committee should continue to be the body having responsibility and authority to issue, in its own name, pronouncements on International Accounting Standards. As such the International Accounting Standards Committee will continue to be autonomous with its own Constitution, Secretariat and system of financing its activities. The signatories recognise that the objectives of the International Accounting Standards Committee and the International Federation of Accountants are interdependent and agree that the closest relationship should be maintained between the two bodies.

The relationship between IFAC and IASC

The present arrangement does cause some confusion. It is desirable, however, to evolve to the appropriate long-term arrangement between the two bodies and it is, therefore, necessary to have a precise statement of the current relationship. It is interesting to find that, in the summary from discussion groups at the 1977 congress, there was a general consensus that the International Accounting Standards Committee should remain independent and autonomous for the time being.

At the present time, discussions are taking place between the Office Bearers of the International Accounting Standards Committee and the International Federation of Accountants, exploring what recommendations to make on the present relationship at the next meetings of members in Mexico in 1982.

In considering this relationship, there are two fundamental differences between the bodies. First, the original nine members of the IASC were selected because they each had a strong independent profession and commercial importance. I personally believe — without pre-empting the further discussions to take place — that this is essential for any committee intending to set international accounting standards. It cannot have the credibility it needs without such a background. Certainly, it would become unworkable and unacceptable if these countries were to be replaced by countries without the same status in accounting terms.

Today, as mentioned earlier, the IASC board comprises the nine original founder members, as well as two countries to be selected by the board on a rotating basis. The IFAC council comprises 15 members elected by the membership with the constraint that, for the first 10 years of IFAC's life, the council must include the 11 members specified in the constitution. The essential difference is the designed process whereby control of council is in principle held by the total membership in contrast to the permanent control of IASC that is vested in the founder members.

The second difference between the two bodies is the method of financing the operations. The IASC members share equally the cost of representatives attending meetings. The procedure involves a defined contribution to IASC and then the reimbursement of costs from IASC to the representative. IFAC representatives receive reimbursement of their costs from their accountancy body. Fees to IFAC are relatively small, but support costs by active organizations are very significant. As an Australian I have one of the heaviest time, physical effort and cost commitments when it comes to attending meetings on the other side of the world, so my own inclination is to prefer the IASC arrangement, which achieves a greater degree of equity in cost as well as reducing disincentive to participate.

As far as the future is concerned, I feel that there should be a separate, identifiable standard-setting organization to which both accountancy bodies and the commercial world attribute significant status in its own right. It must, of course, be a technically competent body, and one to which commercial and financial organizations affected by its pronouncements can make direct representations. This body should be seen as part of the world accounting profession and, therefore, part of and not in competition with or opposed to the International Federation of Accountants.

The question of financial and technical autonomy will obviously have to be discussed in depth. My view at this time is that the IASC should be responsible through its member representatives to the governing bodies of the professional organizations of the selected countries represented on its board. I do not believe that a board should be responsible to or under the authority of a separate body such as the council of IFAC.

IASC needs universal support

I believe that accounting standards are essential to the credibility of financial reports. I accept that they are not yet nearly comprehensive enough, in that too many options are exercised in areas where standards have not yet been issued. Time and voluntary technical expertise have been limiting factors in all areas of the world, but I think the development and implementation of accounting standards has been a great credit to the profession. The intention of the Accountants International Study Group set up in 1966 was to enable discussion between certain countries of these various differences. Many countries do not have accounting standards and some others simply adopt the international accounting standard as their own — a practice I would like to see universally accepted. Finally, I believe that it should be the International Accounting Standards Committee that should have the major role in harmonizing accounting standards throughout the world.

I suggest the future role of the International Accounting Standards Committee is of tremendous importance to the profession. I hope it continues to receive the support of the profession and, more particularly, that its product receives acceptance and observance throughout the world.

30

IASC DEVELOPMENTS

An update

J. A. Burggraaff

Source: *Journal of Accountancy* (September 1982): 104–10.

Businesses are no longer bound by national borders, and they affect the lives of people in other countries. Therefore, harmonization of accounting standards throughout the world is a necessity. In this adaptation of a May 11, 1982, address to the American Institute of CPAs council, J. A. Burggraaff of Binder Dijker Otte & Co., Amsterdam, the Netherlands, 1981–82 chairman of the board of the International Accounting Standards Committee, describes how IASC standards are developed and tells what is being done to promote worldwide acceptance and observance of those standards.

There have been a number of new developments related to the International Accounting Standards Committee, and this discussion attempts to bring these developments up to date as well as shed more light on the IASC's objectives and achievements.

The IASC was established in 1973 by the professional accountancy bodies in Australia, Canada, France, Germany, Japan, Mexico, the Netherlands, the United Kingdom and Ireland and the U.S. We are still grateful for the vigorous support provided by the American Institute of CPAs in getting the IASC on the road by making available an AICPA staff member, Paul Rosenfield, as our first secretary. We now have 60 professional bodies representing 47 countries as our members.

The business of the committee is conducted by a board comprising representatives of the nine founder members and, in addition, South Africa and Nigeria. We have been privileged to have in our midst the delegates from the AICPA—highly qualified individuals who share with us views and experiences gained in the U.S. during a comparatively long history of standard setting without at any time implying that what is thought best for the U.S. of necessity would be best for the world. We appreciate the AICPA's well-considered selections as an indication of goodwill toward our committee.

The objective of the IASC is twofold: to publish international accounting standards and to promote their worldwide acceptance and observance. Let me first discuss the development of standards.

The need for international standards

It is unnecessary to defend the need for standards. CPAs in the U.S. have had standards for many years; they have become one of the facts of professional life. They were born in the wake of federal regulation of the securities industry, and their purpose is to provide meaningful, reliable and comparable information to the users of financial statements.

If accounting standards are useful, and even necessary, in the national environment, the same is true on a worldwide basis. Businesses have crossed national borders; they seek capital in foreign markets; they operate facilities in foreign countries; and, in general terms, they affect through their international operations the lives and well-being of people in other countries. Those people have an interest in the foreign corporations operating in their territories. They demand information, and that information should be understandable to them. Now, although the accountancy profession is spread worldwide, accounting practices are by no means identical. There is a variety of practices even within one country; that is why the Financial Accounting Standards Board is needed. The variety of practices is substantially wider within the western world. That variety creates misunderstanding, and misunderstanding creates distrust. Therefore, from the users' perspective, international harmonization of accounting standards is essential.

The same applies when the matter is examined from the preparer's perspective. If an enterprise has to, or wants to, disseminate financial information in foreign countries, it should comply with the accounting standards prevailing in those countries. In more and more countries, standards are published on a growing number of subjects, going into increasing detail. And more and more, national standards diverge. Some countries require what others prohibit. This state of affairs is of concern to business enterprises and to the accounting profession. Clearly, life would be much easier for business and for auditors if accounting standards were in harmony worldwide.

The IASC has undertaken that harmonization. We are developing accounting standards that are meant to be truly international. That implies that we have no intention of copying the standards of any individual country, even if such country has a long and profound experience in this field. Of course, in developing a standard we carefully examine the material available in all countries with special attention to those countries in which the profession is highly developed, such as the U.S. or England or Canada. We try to discover to what extent common views exist on the direction in which accounting should move. When no clear consensus emerges we may have to try to find a compromise, leaving room for diverging views held in different countries. At times, this gives rise to criticisms that international accounting standards (IASs) are too broadly phrased and leave too many options. Obviously, in comparison with FASB statements in the U.S., several IASs are permissive indeed and do leave options. But the position of the IASC is that its first concern is to get rid of practices that are clearly misleading or that give too much latitude to management for tailoring profits to their needs. And, believe me, such practices are abundant in the world. If we wish to have an IAS at all, we have to phrase it in such a way that it gains sufficient support, that it is widely seen as workable and practical. We are not writing standards for eternity; we may come back to existing standards when the time is right. As a matter of fact, we just decided to reconsider three standards on the basis of a questionnaire sent to the member bodies.

Building an international accounting standard

Let me review how an IAS is developed. As soon as the board has selected a topic, a steering committee is formed consisting of four countries, at least one of which is a board member and at least one of which is a developing country. With the aid of the secretary, material is collected from all member countries, and a list of issues is drawn up. Those issues are presented to the board along with suggestions of the steering committee on positions to be taken. Having heard the views of the board, the steering committee prepares a provisional exposure draft which, after approval by the board, is sent to all member bodies for their comments. Having received those comments, the steering committee reworks the document into an exposure draft. The board considers this paper, amends it as the board deems appropriate and votes on its adoption as an exposure draft, with a two-thirds majority. The exposure draft is published in all member countries for comment by all interested parties, both professional and nonprofessional. These comments are considered by the steering committee, and the steering committee prepares a definitive standard for submission to the board. The board considers the paper, makes amendments when appropriate and adopts the standard by a three-quarters majority. The standard is published in all member countries, after translation if necessary.

At all stages, the board seeks the advice of a consultative group consisting of representatives of international organizations of business, labor, stock exchanges, financial executives, financial analysts and the World Bank, the Organization for Economic Cooperation and Development and the United Nations Centre on Transnational Corporations. These individuals give their advice in a personal capacity and do not commit their organizations to adopt any specific standard. However, in view of the background from which they are speaking, their advice carries considerable weight and is highly appreciated. Personally, I find the discussion with and among a group with such diverse interests a most exciting experience.

Our production since 1973 has been 17 standards, 5 exposure drafts outstanding for comment and 4 discussion papers. Four topics are under consideration. Some of our standards are rather elementary, while others address rather sophisticated issues. Accountants would not be wasting their time if they read all of them carefully.

Encouraging compliance with IASC standards

Now about our second objective—to promote worldwide acceptance and observance of IASs. This is done primarily through the member bodies. Under our constitution, they have committed themselves to use their best endeavors to persuade governments, stock exchanges and businesses that IASs should be complied with and to ensure that auditors satisfy themselves that IASs have been observed and, if not, that reference be made to departures.

The opportunities for member bodies to live up to this commitment vary from country to country. Factors of major importance are whether the professional body has the authority to set accounting standards, to discipline its own professional members or to require auditors to include in their opinions anything other than the words required by law. The opportunities may vary, but the member bodies still share a common commitment—to use their best endeavors in persuading others.

As to the effects of IASs and of the best endeavors of member bodies, we can distinguish three broad categories of countries:

1   Countries where there are no formal national accounting standards. In several of these countries, many of them less developed, the professional body adopts IASs as their own standards, lock, stock and barrel. Examples are Malaysia, Fiji, Nigeria and, quite recently, Italy. Of course, the professional body has to persuade the business community, and its own members, that IASs should be complied with—the same problem that national standard setters face in several countries.
2   Countries that have national standards but whose standards are, with minor exceptions, compatible with IASs. Examples are the U.S., England and the Netherlands.
3   Countries that have national standards but whose standards are incompatible with IASs. Examples are Germany, France and Japan.

Obviously, the profession in countries of the third category faces tremendous difficulties in achieving the adoption of IASs. In many countries the opposition is from several directions:

- Often, the commercial code gives detailed prescriptions on how financial statements should be presented. The legislator has to be persuaded that he either should incorporate IASs into the law or should couch the law in broader terms to create room for applying the IASs.
- Often, the tax law requires that financial statements presented to the public be in conformity with tax returns. In those countries the revenue service has to be persuaded that it should be satisfied with a special purpose report and shouldn't interfere with general purpose reporting to the public.
- Often, the professionals have learned to live with the commercial code and tax regulations, and the members of the business community and the national standard setters are happy with the current state of accounting practice. They have to be persuaded that their reporting should be more meaningful and directed to a true and fair view.

Now, what about the U.S.? The setting of national accounting standards is the responsibility of the FASB, an independent body in the private sector. The IASs published so far are in all material respects compatible with FASB statements, so compliance with FASB requirements implies compliance with IASs. Consequently, not much effort is required from the AICPA, apart from minor things such as persuading the Securities and Exchange Commission that compliance with IASs would be a proper requirement for foreign companies seeking a listing on a U.S. stock exchange.

In October all member bodies of the IASC will be asked as a commitment to use their best endeavors to persuade all enterprises to make positive reference to compliance with IASs in their financial statements or elsewhere in their annual reports. In Canada such an effort already has been undertaken, with promising results. Similar efforts are under way in other countries. These efforts are by no means easy. In many countries businesses aren't inclined to make that reference because of possible legal liabilities, for political reasons or because it might narrow their options. Why should the AICPA make such an arduous and prolonged effort? Let me give two reasons.

First, by becoming a founding member of the IASC, the Institute has recognized the need for worldwide harmonization of accounting practices. Such harmonization is beneficial to users, to auditors and, last but not least, to business itself. If prominent U.S. corporations make reference to IASs, which as I said are compatible with FASB statements, it will have a tremendous impact on the world. The more IASs are made visible in the U.S. and elsewhere, the more others will be encouraged to adopt them and to make reference to them as well. Clearly, IASs aren't needed to achieve meaningful reporting in the U.S. But the world needs them. And the world will get them only if the U.S. joins in the effort and sets a shining example.

The second reason is that, unless the profession makes the IASC a success, inevitably the governments will move in. It's like the story about the camel's nose entering the tent. As soon as governments take up a small part, they won't rest until they have taken the whole lot. In the U.N., the Centre on Transnational Corporations has been busy for years with reporting by multinationals. Those who attended meetings of the Working Group on Accounting Standards can relate that, to a large extent, debate was nothing but a political hassle and that expertise in accounting played a minor role. Still, that might be the profession's future. The politicians, unhampered by professional skills, will grab the subject and tell accountants how to present financial statements on the basis of worldwide standards with strong political overtones. And as soon as supranational authorities have seized the setting of accounting standards, the national governments will follow and take the standard setting way from the private sector. We have had some experience in that respect in the European communities. This might be what accountants have to look forward to, unless the private sector acts in a swift, sustained and successful effort and proves that international harmonization of accounting standards is no longer an issue because it has already been solved.

Obviously, by supporting the IASC and promoting its standards in the U.S., members of the accounting profession give the committee a lot of confidence, trusting that future standards will be sensible, workable and evenhanded. Is that confidence warranted? In answering that question, I have to point out that, in the first place, international standards are inescapable. And there is no other body in the world that has the capability, the resources and the willingness to keep the setting of those standards in the private sector. Apart from that, the IASC is a professional exercise and it will remain that way. We are prepared to share the responsibility with representatives of preparers and users, but the worldwide accountancy profession will firmly remain in control. In addition, the IASC is well aware that it would be unwise to adopt a standard that is in conflict with the views of leading professional bodies. When a clash becomes apparent, we sit down to try to find a solution. So far, we've always found a solution, and I am confident that we shall continue to do so. I am not promising that at no time will the IASC adopt a standard that goes beyond the FASB or is at variance with the FASB. That fate struck other countries on several occasions, and with the approval of their delegates. What I am promising is that the IASC will not regard lightly objections from any IASC delegate.

Our standards cannot survive without credibility in all major countries. They should be accepted by the profession as workable and evenhanded. They should be appreciated as a step forward toward reporting that is relevant, reliable, understandable and comparable. That is our aim. And that is what we shall achieve, with the support of major organizations in the accounting profession.

31

AN AGREEMENT TO ESTABLISH AN INTERNATIONAL ACCOUNTING STANDARDS COMMITTEE

London
Friday 29th June 1973

ICAEW (and others)

Source: London: ICAEW etc., 1973, 6pp.

Agreement

1 The professional accountancy bodies which are signatories hereto, hereby collectively agree:

(a) to establish and maintain an International Accounting Standards Committee, with the membership and powers set out below, whose function will be to formulate and publish in the public interest, basic standards to be observed in the presentation of audited accounts and financial statements and to promote their worldwide acceptance and observance;

(b) to support the standards promulgated by the Committee;

(c) to use their best endeavours:

(i) to ensure that published accounts comply with these standards or that there is disclosure of the extent to which they do not and to persuade governments, the authorities controlling securities markets and the industrial and business community that published accounts should comply with these standards;

(ii) to ensure that the auditors satisfy themselves that the accounts comply with these standards. If the accounts do not comply with these standards the audit report should either refer to the disclosure of non-compliance in the accounts, or should state the extent to which they do not comply;

(iii) to ensure that, as soon as practicable, appropriate action is taken in respect of auditors whose audit reports do not meet the requirements of (ii) above;

(d) to seek to secure similar general acceptance and observance of these standards internationally.

2 The professional accountancy bodies which are signatories hereto, further agree that the International Accounting Standards Committee, with the objectives, functions, powers, composition, organisation and financial arrangements set out in its Constitution, shall be a part of the International Co-ordination Committee for the Accountancy Profession established by the Heads of Delegations to the Xth International Congress of Accountants in Sydney but shall be autonomous in the issue of exposure drafts and standards. The Constitution of the International Accounting Standards Committee shall not be reviewed until the end of 1976 without the agreement of the International Accounting Standards Committee and the International Co-ordination Committee for the Accountancy Profession.

Constitution

Membership

1 (a) The membership of the International Accounting Standards Committee will consist of not more than 2 members per country (and for the purposes of this Constitution the United Kingdom and the Republic of Ireland shall be treated as though they were one country), nominated by the accountancy bodies thereof which are signatories to this Constitution. The members may be accompanied at meetings of the Committee by a staff observer.

(b) An accountancy body of a country not represented on the Committee under (a) above may, on request, become an Associate Member provided that the Committee is satisfied that it is prepared to subscribe to the objectives set out in the Agreement; is representative of the profession in that country; has standards and resources which would enable it to contribute towards the work of the Committee; and is willing, on the invitation of the Committee, to nominate members to carry out particular assignments or to join working parties or groups constituted to undertake tasks allotted by the Committee. Associate Members would not be entitled to attend meetings of the Committee nor to vote but may attend the meetings of the Committee by invitation.

(c) The members of the Committee and the persons nominated by Associate Members shall not regard themselves as representing sectional interests but shall be guided by the need to act in the public interest and the general interest of the accountancy profession as a whole.

Officers

2 The Committee shall be presided over by a Chairman elected by a simple majority for two years by the members of the Committee from amongst their numbers and shall not be eligible for re-election.

Voting

3 Each country represented on the Committee shall have one vote which may be taken by a show of hands or by postal ballot. Except where otherwise provided, the decisions of the Committee shall be taken on a simple majority.

Powers

4 (a) The Committee shall have power, subject to a vote of two-thirds in favour, to issue proposals (including amendments to existing statements) in its own name in the form of exposure drafts for comment. Exposure drafts shall be addressed to professional accountancy bodies entitled to participate in International Congresses. They may also be addressed to such governments, securities markets, regulatory and other agencies as the Committee may determine.

   (b) After a suitable period has been allowed for comment, the Committee shall review such proposals and approve, amend or abandon them as it may consider fit. No standard shall be issued for publication unless it is approved, on a vote, by at least three-quarters of the total voting rights. Every standard so approved shall be published by the participating professional accounting bodies, which are signatories hereto, and in the countries to which Associate Members belong. The standards will also be addressed to other professional accountancy bodies entitled to participate in International Congresses. They may also be addressed to such governments, securities markets, regulatory and other agencies as the Committee may determine.

   (c) Dissentient opinions will not be included in any exposure drafts or standards promulgated by the Committee. Exposure drafts will however include the arguments for and against the adoption of a particular standard.

Operating procedures

5 (a) The Committee shall determine its operating procedures so long as they are not inconsistent with the terms of this Constitution.

   (b) The definitive text of any exposure draft or standard shall be that published in the English language. The Committee shall give authority to the individual participating bodies to prepare translations of exposure drafts and standards. The responsibility for and cost of translating, publishing and distributing copies in any country shall be borne by the professional bodies of the country concerned.

Financial arrangements

6 (a) An annual budget for the ensuing calendar year will be prepared by the Committee and submitted in August each year to the Councils of the accountancy bodies which are signatories hereto.

(b) Each country shall contribute on 1st January each year a sum equal to one-ninth of the annual budget for that year.

(c) The following expenses will be a charge against the revenues of the Committee:

(i)   costs of staff employed in, and the operating costs of, the permanent office of the Committee *excluding* the rent, rates and any taxes of the permanent office which shall be borne by the professional body or bodies of the country where the permanent office is located;

(ii)   the travelling, hotel and incidental expenses of one member of each of the countries represented on the Committee;

(iii)   the travelling, hotel and incidental expenses of the permanent staff who are required to attend meetings of the Committee.

(d) Any surplus of revenue over expenditure in any one year shall be retained by the Committee and carried forward to the following year.

(e) The travelling, hotel and incidental expenses of the second member of the Committee and of the staff observer from each of the countries represented shall be borne by the professional body(ies) of the country concerned. The same arrangement will apply to persons nominated by Associate Members to working parties constituted by the Committee or to carry out specific assignments on behalf of the Committee.

Meetings

7 Meetings of the Committee shall be held at such times and in such places as the members of the Committee may mutually agree.

Permanent office

8 The location of the permanent office of the Committee shall be London.

Secretariat

9 The accountancy bodies in the United Kingdom and the Republic of Ireland will be responsible, subject to the approval of the Committee, for recruiting staff for the permanent office in London.

signed for and on behalf of
The Institute of Chartered Accountants in Australia
Australian Society of Accountants
E. H. BURGESS

signed for and on behalf of
The Canadian Institute of Chartered Accountants
P. HOWARD LYONS

signed for and on behalf of
Ordre des Experts Comptables et des Comptables Agréés
ROGER CAUMEIL

signed for and on behalf of
Institut der Wirtschaftsprüfer in Deutschland eV
Wirtschaftsprüferkammer
DR. KRAFFT FRHR. VON DER TANN

signed for and on behalf of
The Japanese Institute of Certified Public Accountants
SHOZO TATSUMI

signed for and on behalf of
Instituto Mexicano de Contadores Públicos, A.C.
J. FREYSSINIER

signed for and on behalf of
Nederlands Instituut van Registeraccountants
J. W. SCHOONDERBEEK

signed for and on behalf of
The Institute of Chartered Accountants in England and Wales
The Institute of Chartered Accountants of Scotland
The Institute of Chartered Accountants in Ireland
The Association of Certified Accountants
The Institute of Cost and Management Accountants
The Institute of Municipal Treasurers and Accountants
HENRY BENSON

signed for and on behalf of
American Institute of Certified Public Accountants
WALLACE E. OLSON

32

PREFACE TO STATEMENTS OF INTERNATIONAL ACCOUNTING STANDARDS

IASC

Source: London: IASC, 1983, 5pp.

This Preface is issued to set out the objectives and operating procedures of the International Accounting Standards Committee (IASC) and to explain the scope and authority of the Statements of International Accounting Standards. The Preface was approved in November 1982 for publication in January 1983 and supersedes the Preface published in January 1975 (amended March 1978). The approved text of this Preface is that published by the International Accounting Standards Committee in the English language.

1.   The International Accounting Standards Committee (IASC) came into existence on 29 June 1973 as a result of an agreement by accountancy bodies in Australia, Canada, France, Germany, Japan, Mexico, the Netherlands, the United Kingdom and Ireland, and the United States of America. A revised Agreement and Constitution were signed in November 1982. The business of IASC is conducted by a Board comprising representatives of up to thirteen countries and up to four organisations having an interest in financial reporting.

The objectives

2.   The objectives of IASC as set out in its Constitution are:

'(a)   to formulate and publish in the public interest accounting standards to be observed in the presentation of financial statements and to promote their worldwide acceptance and observance, and

(b) to work generally for the improvement and harmonisation of regulations, accounting standards and procedures relating to the presentation of financial statements.'

3. The relationship between IASC and the International Federation of Accountants (IFAC) is confirmed by the Mutual Commitments into which they have entered. The membership of IASC (which is the same as that of IFAC) acknowledges in the revised Agreement that IASC has full and complete autonomy in the setting and issue of International Accounting Standards.

4. The members agree to support the objectives of IASC by undertaking the following obligations:

'to support the work of IASC by publishing in their respective countries every International Accounting Standard approved for issue by the Board of IASC and by using their best endeavours:

(i)   to ensure that published financial statements comply with International Accounting Standards in all material respects and disclose the fact of such compliance;
(ii)   to persuade governments and standard-setting bodies that published financial statements should comply with International Accounting Standards in all material respects;
(iii) to persuade authorities controlling securities markets and the industrial and business community that published financial statements should comply with International Accounting Standards in all material respects and disclose the fact of such compliance;
(iv) to ensure that the auditors satisfy themselves that the financial statements comply with International Accounting Standards in all material respects;
(v)   to foster acceptance and observance of International Accounting Standards internationally.'

Published financial statements

5. The term 'financial statements' used in paragraphs 2 and 4 covers balance sheets, income statements or profit and loss accounts, statements of changes in financial position, notes and other statements and explanatory material which are identified as being part of the financial statements. Usually, financial statements are made available or published once each year and are the subject of a report by an auditor. International Accounting Standards apply to such financial statements of any commercial, industrial, or business enterprise.

6. The management of such an enterprise may prepare financial statements for its own use in a number of different ways best suited for internal management purposes. When financial statements are issued to other persons, such as shareholders, creditors, employees, and the public at large, they should conform to International Accounting Standards.

7. The responsibility for the preparation of financial statements and for adequate disclosure is that of the management of the enterprise. The auditor's responsibility is to form his opinion and to report on the financial statements.

Accounting standards

8. Within each country, local regulations govern, to a greater or lesser degree, the issue of financial statements. Such local regulations include accounting standards which are promulgated by the regulatory bodies and/or the professional accountancy bodies in the countries concerned.

9. Prior to the formation of IASC there were frequently differences of form and content between the published accounting standards of most countries. IASC takes cognisance of exposure drafts, or of accounting standards already issued on each subject, and in the light of such knowledge produces an International Accounting Standard for worldwide acceptance. One of the objects of IASC is to harmonise as far as possible the diverse accounting standards and accounting policies of different countries.

10. In carrying out this task of adaptation of existing standards, and in formulating International Accounting Standards on new subjects, IASC concentrates on essentials. It therefore endeavours not to make the International Accounting Standards so complex that they cannot be applied effectively on a worldwide basis. International Accounting Standards issued by IASC are constantly reviewed to take into account the current position and the need for updating.

11. International Accounting Standards promulgated by IASC do not override the local regulations, referred to in paragraph 8 above, governing the issue of financial statements in a particular country. The obligations undertaken by the members of IASC, as explained in this Preface, provide that where International Accounting Standards are complied with in all material respects, this fact should be disclosed. Where local regulations require deviation from International Accounting Standards, the local members of IASC endeavour to persuade the relevant authorities of the benefits of harmonisation with International Accounting Standards.

The scope of the Standards

12. Any limitation of the applicability of specific International Accounting Standards is made clear in the statements of those standards. International Accounting Standards are not intended to apply to immaterial items. An International Accounting Standard applies from a date specified in the standard and unless indicated to the contrary is not retroactive.

Working procedure – exposure drafts and standards

13. The agreed working procedure is to select certain subjects for detailed study by Steering Committees. As a result of this work an exposure draft is prepared on a particular subject for consideration by the Board. If approved by at least two-thirds of the Board, the exposure draft is addressed to accountancy bodies and to governments, securities markets, regulatory and other agencies and other interested parties. Adequate time is allowed for consideration and comment on each exposure draft.

14. Since the formation of the Consultative Group in 1981, their views are taken into account at each major decision-making stage.

15. The comments and suggestions received as a result of this exposure are then examined by the Board and the exposure draft is revised as necessary. Provided that the revised draft is approved by at least three-quarters of the Board, it is issued as an International Accounting Standard and becomes operative from a date stated in the standard.

16. At some stage in the above process, the IASC Board may decide that, in order to promote discussion of a topic, or to allow adequate time for points of view to be put forward, a discussion paper should be issued. A discussion paper requires approval by a simple majority of the Board.

Voting

17. For the purpose of voting referred to in paragraphs 13 to 16 above, each country and each organisation represented on the Board has one vote.

Language

18. The approved text of any exposure draft or standard is that published by IASC in the English language. Members are responsible, under the authority of the Board, for preparing translations of exposure drafts and standards so that, where appropriate, such translations may be issued in the languages of their own countries. These translations indicate the name

of the accountancy body that prepared the translation and that it is a translation of the approved text.

The authority attaching to the Standards

19.   Standing alone, neither the IASC nor the accountancy profession has the power to enforce international agreement or to require compliance with International Accounting Standards. The success of IASC's efforts is dependent upon the recognition and support for its work from many different interested groups acting within the limits of their own jurisdiction. In most countries of the world, the accounting profession has a prestige and standing which is of great significance in these efforts.

Conclusion

20.   The members of IASC believe that the adoption in their countries of International Accounting Standards together with disclosure of compliance will over the years have a significant impact. The quality of financial statements will be improved and there will be an increasing degree of comparability. The credibility and consequently the usefulness of financial statements will be enhanced throughout the world.

33

IASC CONSTITUTION

(Approved by the Members of IASC on 11th October 1992)

IASC

Source: London: IASC, 1992, 5pp.

Definitions

The following terms are used in this Constitution with the meanings specified:

Members of IASC shall be the Members defined in clause 3.

Board Members shall be the countries and organisations defined in clause 4. Board Members need not be Members of IASC.

Board Representatives shall be the individuals appointed to represent the Board Members in accordance with clause 6.

Country shall include two or more countries that may be appointed jointly as a Board Member.

Name and objectives

1. The name of the organisation shall be the International Accounting Standards Committee (IASC).
2. The objectives of IASC are:
   (a) to formulate and publish in the public interest accounting standards to be observed in the presentation of financial statements and to promote their worldwide acceptance and observance; and
   (b) to work generally for the improvement and harmonisation of regulations, accounting standards and procedures, relating to the presentation of financial statements.

Membership

3. The Members of the International Accounting Standards Committee shall consist of all professional accountancy bodies that are members of the International Federation of Accountants (IFAC).

The Board

4. The business of IASC shall be conducted by a Board consisting of:
   (a) up to thirteen countries as nominated and appointed by the Council of IFAC that shall be represented by Members of JASC, and
   (b) up to four organisations having an interest in financial reporting co-opted under clause 12(a).
5. (a) The term of appointment of a Board Member selected under clause 4(a) shall be no more than five years. A retiring Board Member shall be eligible for re-appointment.
   (b) The term of appointment of a Board Member co-opted under clause 4(b) shall be determined by the Board at the time of appointment.
6. The Board Members may nominate not more than two Board Representatives from their country or organisation to serve on the Board. The Board Representatives from each country or organisation may be accompanied at meetings of the Board by a Technical Adviser.
7. The Board Representatives and the persons nominated to carry out particular assignments or to join steering committees/working parties/groups shall not regard themselves as representing sectional interests but shall be guided by the need to act in the public interest.
8. The President of IFAC, or his designate, accompanied by not more than one technical adviser, shall be entitled to attend meetings of the Board of IASC, be entitled to the privilege of the floor, but shall not be entitled to vote.
9. The Board shall prepare a report on its work each year and send it to the Members of IASC, the Council of IFAC, and other interested individuals and organisations.

Chairman

10. The Board shall be presided over by a Chairman elected for a term of two-and-a-half years by the Board Representatives from among their number. The Chairman shall not be eligible for re-election. The Board Member providing the Chairman shall be entitled to a further Board Representative.

Voting at Board meetings

11. Each Board Member shall have one vote which may be taken by a show of hands or by written ballot. Except where otherwise provided either in this Constitution or in the operating procedures, decisions shall be taken on a simple majority of the Board.

Responsibilities and powers

12. The Board shall have the power to:
    (a) invite up to four organisations having an interest in financial reporting to be co-opted on to the Board;
    (b) remove from membership of the Board any Board Member whose financial contribution determined under clause! 14(d) is more than one year in arrears or which fails to be represented at two successive Board meetings;
    (c) publish documents relating to international accounting issues for discussion and comment provided a majority of the Board votes in favour of publication;
    (d) issue documents in the form of exposure drafts for comment (including amendments to existing Standards) in the name of the International Accounting Standards Committee provided at least two-thirds of the Board votes in favour of publication;
    (e) issue International Accounting Standards provided that at least three-quarters of the Board votes in favour of publication;
    (f) establish operating procedures so long as they are not inconsistent with the provisions of this Constitution;
    (g) enter into discussions, negotiations or associations with outside bodies and generally promote the worldwide improvement and harmonisation of accounting standards;
    (h) seek and obtain funds from Members of IASC and non-members which are interested in supporting the objectives of IASC provided that such funding is organised in such a way that it does not impair the independence, or the appearance of independence, of IASC.

Issue of discussion documents, exposure drafts and International Accounting Standards

13. (a) Discussion documents and exposure drafts shall be distributed by the Board to all Members of IASC. A suitable period shall be allowed for respondents to submit comments.
    (b) Dissentient opinions will not be included in any exposure drafts or International Accounting Standards promulgated by the Board.

(c) Exposure drafts and International Accounting Standards may be distributed to such governments, standard-setting bodies, stock exchanges, regulatory and other agencies and individuals as the Board may determine.

(d) The approved text of any exposure draft or International Accounting Standard shall be that published by IASC in the English language. The Board may give authority to the Members of IASC and others to prepare translations of the approved text and to publish the approved text of exposure drafts and International Accounting Standards.

Financial arrangements

14. (a) An annual budget for the ensuing calendar year shall be prepared by the Board each year and sent to the Board Members and to the Council of IFAC.

(b) The Board shall determine the aggregate amount of the net budgeted expenditure which should be borne by the Board Members and by IFAC.

(c) IFAC shall contribute 5% of the aggregate amount determined under (b) in January and 5% in July of each year. The remainder of the aggregate amount determined under (b) shall be borne by the Board Members, except that the Council of IFAC may decide to reimburse wholly or in part the share charged to one or more Board Members.

(d) The Board Members shall contribute on 1st January and 1st July each year a sum in such proportions, as shall be decided by a three-quarters vote of the Board. Unless otherwise agreed, Board Members shall contribute equally to the annual budget. Board Members which are represented on the Board for part only of a calendar year shall contribute a pro rata' proportion calculated by reference to the period of their representation on the Board in that year.

(e) The Committee shall reimburse the travelling, hotel and incidental expenses of attendance at Board meetings by one Board Representative from each Board Member. In addition, the Committee shall reimburse the Chairman for expenses incurred in attending Board meetings and otherwise on behalf of IASC.

(f) The Board shall determine in its operating procedures what other expenses shall be a charge against the income of the Committee.

(g) The Board shall annually prepare financial statements and submit them for audit and send copies thereof to the Members of IASC and to the Council of IFAC.

Board meetings

15. Meetings of the Board shall be held at such times and in such places as the Board Members may mutually agree.

Meetings of the Members of IASC

16. A meeting of the Members of IASC shall be held in conjunction with each General Assembly of IFAC.
17. Each Member of IASC shall have one vote. The method of voting shall be determined by the meeting and shall be either by a show of hands or by ballot. A Member of IASC may give a proxy to another Member of IASC to vote on its behalf subject to the Chairman receiving notice from the Member of IASC giving the proxy prior to the meeting.

Administrative office

18. The location of the administrative office of the Committee shall be determined by the Board.

Amendments to constitution

19. Amendments to this Constitution shall be discussed with the Council of IFAC and shall require a three-quarters majority of the Board and approval by the Members of IASC as expressed by a simple majority of those voting.

> This revised Constitution was approved by the Members of IASC at a meeting in Washington D.C., United States of America on 11th October 1992.

Part 6

ASSESSMENTS OF THE IASC AND ITS STANDARDS

34

THE DEVELOPMENT OF INTERNATIONAL ACCOUNTING STANDARDS

An anthropological perspective

William J. Violet

Source: *International Journal of Accounting* (Spring 1983): 1–12.

Introduction

In the past few decades, the international business community has become increasingly aware of the importance of accounting in reporting financial data.[1] Multinational transactions have precipitated the evolution of truly international corporations. Demands of owners, creditors, and many other users of financial reports have encouraged the development of International Accounting Standards (IAS). The official body established for promulgating IAS has been the International Accounting Standards Committee (IASC). The necessity for IAS results from the needs of users for financial data that are relevant, meaningful, understandable, comparable, verifiable, timely, neutral, and adequate for making economic decisions.[2] IAS form the "standardized" basis for comparing and contrasting financial activities of multinationals at the international level.

The preceding summary merely suggests the ambitious efforts by the IASC to instill some accounting uniformity into the reporting of the complex business transactions of multinational concerns.[3] Standards promulgated by the IASC have come under criticism, however, from some of the countries which earlier vociferously advocated their esetablishment.[4] The author suggests that the success of the IASC has been limited by cultural variables and attempts to delineate several cultural determinants which influence the promulgation and acceptance of international accounting theories and standards. Hopefully, some of the cultural constraints limiting the establishment and development of both IAS and the IASC in their current context will be clarified.

In the past, several accounting authors have considered determinants of international accounting standards from political, economic, and social contexts.[5] This paper considers international accounting from a systems concept of culture in the hope that an anthropological viewpoint will stimulate further cultural research toward the establishment of a truly international accounting system and will enable accountants of various countries to visualize their particular accounting systems from the perspective of a cultural relativist.

Cultural determinants

Herbert Feigl, in his introductory lecture on the philosophy of science, categorized the sciences with a simple analogy. All disciplines, hence the knowledge of man, are comparable to a glass of ice water. Philosophy is the glass, anthropology the water on which all the ice cubes of knowledge float and into which they melt. Each ice cube represents a particular science such as physics, chemistry, biology, history, and logic. From this example, anthropology is clearly an important "fluid" in the flow of knowledge between peoples.

Anthropology may be defined simply as the study of mankind and his relationships to the universe.

> Depending on the methods and goals of the anthropologists, anthropology may be a biological science, a social science — or humanity. Because man is a part of nature, anthropology is a natural science with two major subdivisions: physical anthropology (or human biology) and cultural anthropology.[6]

Anthropology studies mankind in its entirety; it is a synergistic analysis of man's being and his relationships to the external world.

Since no discipline is independent of philosophy and anthropology, the author will be concerned with the role of anthropological thought as it relates to the establishment and enforcement of international accounting standards and examines accounting as a social function, that is, a product of its culture.

Sociocultural theories of anthropology attempt to explain social phenomena. Social phenomena occur between individuals and the institutions created by their society. These institutions may be intangible but are symbolized or represented by various types of tangible matter. For example, the religion of a society incorporates the philosophical beliefs and very often the legal statutes of the society. Physical representations consist of printed matter, symbols, and other tangible forms of animal and plant life.

Social phenomena are products of a given culture. Culture may still be described by the classical definition — it is learned behavior.[7] Culture and the social institutions of a culture must be learned in contrast to instinctive reactions to environmental factors. While instinctive reactions are determined through genetic codes, culture is an

> . . . integrated system of learned behavior patterns that are characteristic of the members of a society and that are not the result of biological inheritance. . . . Culture is therefore acquired behavior. But it is as much a part of the natural universe as the stars in the heavens, for it is a natural product of man's activities, and man is part of nature.[8]

Culture is a product of mankind, invented to cope with the natural environment as well as social phenomena. Mankind has, in turn, become a product of that culture. Culture and mankind are in a constant state of evolution, creating and refining one another.[9] Mankind's basic needs — described by Maslow as food, shelter, sex, social relationships, and self-actualization — have driven mankind to formulate a culture to satisfy them.[10] Maslow's list of needs may be expanded, however, to include needs beyond the basic ones.

Claude Levi-Strauss was an early pioneer in French structuralism which searched for basic or universal structures underlying cultural behavioral patterns.[11] The search for accounting postulates by Moonitz[12] would be characteristic of employing structuralism as defined by Levi-Strauss. Levi-Strauss employed structuralism to search for relationships between social institutions and social behavior. He expanded Maslow's classification of basic social needs to include a need for order.[13] For this, consider the importance of accounting, not accounting as currently practiced, but rudimentary accounting for order, that is, classification, control, and safeguarding of assets. In a primitive hunting society, for example, hunters will need to classify, control, and safeguard their resources to ensure their continuance and that of their society. Since their essentials may include spears, each hunter may be responsible for producing and ensuring availability of an appropriate number of weapons. The hunters are responsible for controlling and safeguarding their spears. In effect, the rudiments of accounting for resources exist in even the most basic societies. As such, the accounting for scarce resources is a function utilized by most individuals. In this instance, accounting is informal and relies on an individual's memory and oral communication. A need for order, as advocated by Levi-Strauss, fosters a need for accounting for resources.

Anthropologists have long since noticed a great diversity of cultures and cultural developments in various civilizations. A culture grows and develops in response to environmental stimuli. An imperative selection exists for each culture. Ruth Benedict explains imperative selection as follows:

Our only scientific course is to consider our own culture, so far as we are able, as one example among innumerable others of the variant configuration of human culture.

The cultural pattern of any civilization makes use of certain segments of the great arc of potential human purposes and motivations . . . any culture makes use of certain selected material techniques or cultural traits. The great arc along which all the possible human behaviors are distributed is far too immense and too full of contradictions for any culture to utilize even any considerable portion of it. Selection is the first requirement. Without selection no culture could even achieve intelligibility, and the intentions it selects and makes its own are a much more important matter than the particular detail of technology or the marriage formality that it also selects in similar fashion.[14]

Culture is selected, then, through a process of determining what needs and wants are to he satisfied and, also, what needs have priority and how mankind interacts with the environment and other people. The diversity of cultural development proceeds from a foundation of satisfying wants and needs. To satisfy these insatiable wants, mankind and society evolve a culture which defines and establishes an economic system to allocate scarce resources efficiently for the satisfaction of human wants. Culture is the system which encompasses and determines the evolution of social institutions, social phenomena and mankind itself. In turn, these elements formulate culture. A constant evolutionary state exists. On a broader scale, it can be argued that cultures evolve from hunting to agriculture to industrialization. Cultural evolution involves the development of a culture through the acceptance of customs. Customs entail employing tangible or intangible elements by a society in a particular manner.

Various customs are employed throughout a culture. When observing and analyzing a culture, the ethnographer must be familiar with the concept of synergy as it relates to a cultural system. Each element of a culture cannot be understood by itself. Culture is more than the sum of each of the elements attributed to it. The definition of synergy is applicable: "The whole is greater than the sum of its parts." Customs and their interrelationships form a culture which is in a constant stage of evolution as external and internal influences alter its functioning. Customs are selected by a culture through reference to basic assumptions.

The selection of the customs that go to make up a culture is never wholly random and haphazard. Selection is made with reference to a set of deeplying assumptions, or postulates, about the nature of the external world and the nature of man himself. These assumptions as to the nature of existence are called existential postulates . . . about whether things or acts are good and to be sought after or bad and to be rejected. These are called normative postulates or values. . . .

Both existential and normative postulates are the reference points which color a people's view of things, giving them their orientation toward the world around them and toward one another.[15]

Culture enables mankind to interpret the environment and explain the immediate, surrounding social phenomena. Mankind has developed and assimilated customs to cope with social phenomena.

Postulates of a culture determine a systematic choice by a society for explaining and rationalizing social phenomena. Based on these postulates, customs are created and adopted. Customs develop into or exist as social institutions. Further, social institutions envelop various customs which enable a culture to adapt to a causal environment within the parameters and constraints of the postulates it has established.

As a social institution, an accounting system must reflect the postulates of its culture. By examining and studying the normative and existential postulates of a culture, society's accounting system and its use in communicating financial data to various users may be defined and understood. It is essential to understand a given culture's postulates before an analysis or judgment concerning a particular system can be formulated. An accounting system represents its postulates and as a language reflects those postulates.

Accounting as a language

Language is the most pervasive of the cultural variables. A language facilitates flexibility of thought and at the same time restricts thought development. Each language is as unique as its cultural setting which creates it. In turn, a language contributes to its culture's evolution.

Accounting, as a communication process, is a symbolic language which researchers have recently analyzed.[16]

What is language?

Language is the foundation for establishing culture and, like culture, it is learned behavior.[17] Languages are created, developed, and evolved within the framework of cultural postulates established by a particular society. Therefore, language reflects the postulates established by the society which employs it. Cultural postulates define the boundaries within which a language operates. Culture, through language, enables mankind to interpret the environment and explain the social phenomena occurring around it within the context of its postulates. Obviously, then, postulates directly determine language evolution. A diversity of languages represents a broad spectrum of postulates and cultures. In fact, "without language, culture ... would be wholly impossible."[18]

As a subpart of a culture, language is influenced continually by all other elements or subparts of its culture. Language can only be understood from within the framework where it operates and is maintained. Our perceptions of reality and phenomena are established through language. The importance of language in shaping perceptions and personality was introduced in the Sapir-Whorf Hypothesis: "language and our thought grooves are inextricably interwoven, are, in a sense, one and the same."[19] Language and accounting, as a symbolic written system, are determinants of behavior, personality, and thought process. Edward Sapir comments:

> Human beings do not live in the objective world alone, nor alone in the world of social activity as ordinarily understood, but are very much at the mercy of the particular language which has become the medium of expression for their society. It is quite an illusion to imagine that one adjust to reality essentially without the use of language and that language is merely an incidental means of solving specific problems of communication or reflection. The fact of the matter is that the "real" world is to a large extent unconsciously built up on the language habits of the group. No two languages are ever sufficiently similar to be considered as representing the same social reality. The worlds in which different societies live are distinct worlds, not merely the same world with different labels attached.[20]

The impact of language on our culture and its importance in formulating perceptions and interpretations of causal events is great.

Specifically, Belkaoui in his sociolinguistic research examines accounting as a language:

> Accounting can be viewed as a language, which embodies both lexical and grammatical characteristics (Belkaoui [1978]). Within the linguistic relativity school, the role of language is emphasized as a mediator and shaper of the environment; this would imply that accounting language may predispose "users" to a given mode of perception and behavior. This explanation is congruent with the "Sapir-Whorf Hypothesis". . . .

> . . . accounting may be defined as a set of lexical or symbolic representations, such as debit, credit, etc., assigned a meaning through translation rules known as accounting terminologies and used as parameters for a set of grammatical or manipulative rules known as accounting techniques.[21]

His definition classifies accounting as a language. Interacting with other cultural phenomena, accounting shapes and is shaped by its culture, postulates, and native language.

Defining and employing accounting as a language enables accountants to obtain a new perspective for understanding the role of accounting in society. Accountants refer to accounting as the language of business. It is a product and a symbolic expression of the existing culture. Though largely symbolic, accounting possesses the necessary attributes of a language. It is a language between the entities and individuals of a culture. Linguistically, accounting may appear to lack the classical oral elements of a specific language. It is a specialized symbolic communication. Because accounting is integrated into a cultural system, its growth and evolution within a society are strongly influenced by a particular society's language.

Earlier, cultural postulates were defined as normative and existential. Normative postulates are developed by a society to evaluate human behavior and goals, that is, values and direction. Existential postulates determine a people's view on how causal relationships are interpreted. A culture's language is created according to its cultural postulates and subsequently reflects those postulates. Further, these postulates contribute to the evolution of the language which defines them. In turn, individual behavior perceptions and responses arise from language constraints. Accounting as a symbolic language is formulated and evolved on the cultural postulates of a society. The postulates of a particular culture are the postulates of its accounting language.

Evidence demonstrating the individuality of accounting languages and their particular normative-existential postulate structures can be derived from Frederick Choi's recent cross-cultural comparison of a Japanese firm and a U.S. firm.[22] The financial statements of the Japanese firm were translated through generally accepted accounting principles to facilitate comparability of the firms. Mr. Choi's results are most interesting:

> In our preceding analysis, translating the primary financial statements of a Japanese company to secondary reports consistent with U.S. accounting norms proved potentially misleading. . . . secondary financial statements, as presently construed, fail to recognize that a foreign reader's investment risks and rewards are highly dependent on the socioeconomic environment of the reporting company's country of domicile.[23]

The individuality of the two diverse accounting languages, U.S. and Japanese, inhibits comparability. The accounting languages of the two firms are different. These languages were created within the postulate framework found in their respective countries. Comparability is inhibited because the underlying cultural postulates are different. "Something is lost in the translation," so to speak.

IAS and cultural relativism

Accounting is a social institution established by most cultures to report and explain certain social phenomena occurring in economic transactions. As a social institution, accounting has integrated certain cultural customs and elements within the constraints of cultural postulates. Accounting cannot be isolated and analyzed as an independent component of a culture. It is, like mankind and other social institutions, a product of culture and contributes to the evolution of the culture which employs it. Since accounting is culturally determined, other cultural customs, beliefs, and institutions influence it.

Consider the accounting system employed in the United States. Early accounting practices and concepts were assimilated and adopted through acculturation from the British.[24] The British practices were a product of British culture. Since American culture has significantly paralleled British culture, the acculturation process was adaptive rather than revolutionary, and early British accounting practices were adapted to the American culture.

As domestic business expanded beyond the national borders, American culture was and is being presented to neighboring countries. American business transactions are, in effect, an ambassador to the American way of life. The U.S. accounting system reflects the country's culture. Being pragmatically developed and applied to various social phenomena, American accounting has been developed to cope with specific American business problems. With the rapid increase in international business operations, several accounting organizations have attempted to adapt this domestic system to the international environment. Considering cultural theory, one may question this attempt. Consider the adaption of generally accepted accounting principles to the translation of foreign currencies. Certain foreign currencies may be translated, but in reality the originating country may not even be able to substantiate the value of its currency because of internal or external circumstances.

Does the American accounting system provide a rational system of accounting for other nations? This system has been highly praised for its efficiency and reliability in portraying financial data for economic decisions. In a highly industrialized and technological society, generally accepted accounting principles may be sufficient to resolve most issues concerning the practical and the conceptual. Accounting as a cultural product has evolved in the United States to resolve certain business-related issues. The complexity of this accounting system has grown in response to the complexity of the technology, the sociopolitical system, and financial transactions.

Cultures parallel to the American industrialized techno-structure exist throughout the world in Britain, Canada, West Germany, Japan, and, to a lesser extent, several other countries. If cultural differences concerning political structures, beliefs, traditions, philosophies, and social phenomena are mentioned, however, an infinite variety of cultural variables could be illustrated. Each unique culture produces a unique accounting structure shaped by a multitude of cultural constraints and variables. Visualize an accounting structure for two societies which are both industrialized but diametrically opposed philosophically. The systems may be parallel industrially, yet conventions and cultural variables may contribute to substantial differences of accounting procedures. One nation's culture may well have been determined largely by geographical and physical barriers.

One can expect accounting principles to vary depending on cultural variances. Can an accounting system of one culture be compared or contrasted with an accounting system of another culture? Comparisons are essential for practicability and perspective, but arbitrary contrasts offer little relevance. Since accounting is the product of a culture, similarities and differences will be present between cultures. Contrasting two cultural products becomes very subjective. Ethnocentrism is highly probable. Cross-cultural comparisons suffer from variables beyond the observer's control. Cultural impressions cannot be totally alienated from an observer formulating observations and conclusions. Franz Boas was extremely critical of cross-cultural comparisons and the evolutionary theories comparing cultural similarities.[25]

Even though cross-cultural comparisons have been facilitated through the gathering of statistical data,[26] cultural comparisons must be viewed with skepticism. Many cultural variables can be compared with respect to the concept of synergy. In this regard, the theory of cultural relativism is explained by Hoebel:

> The concept of cultural relativity states that standards of rightness and wrongness (values) and of usage and effectiveness (customs) are relative to the given culture of which they are a part. In its most extreme form, it holds that every custom is valid in terms of its own cultural setting. In practical terms, it means that anthropologists learn to suspend judgment, to strive to understand what goes on from the point of view of the people being studied, that is, to achieve empathy, for the sake of humanistic perception and scientific accuracy. . . . [He] who lacks this trait — who cannot put aside all chauvinist ethnocentrism, that is, the habit of uncritically judging other peoples' behavior according to the standards set in his own culture — can never become a . . . cultural anthropologist.[27]

Cultural relativity does not refute cultural comparison but qualifies the comparisons which can be made. In the areas of economics and finance, even comparisons of different industries are subject to qualifications. Often comparisons between companies of different industries are extremely limited. An individual company's financial data are relative to other companies operating in the same or in essentially a similar industrial setting.

Therefore, comparisons made between two companies of different industries are often irrelevant. Adding the dimension of internationalism further complicates defining an individual company's industry.[28] Cultural variables further dissipate a definable industry.

Cultural products, like the cultures which produce them, can be compared, but only if certain assumptions and qualifications are made by the researcher. All too often, accounting systems of various countries are compared without reference to the unique cultures or cultural variables which produce them. Such cross-cultural comparisons are limited in relevance.[29] Ethnographic field work for considering an accounting system may yield a better result. In this view, the concept of cultural relativism becomes a determining variable. Judgments concerning a particular country's accounting concepts and practices should be made in light of its cultural system and environment.[30] It is because of the infinite diversity of cultural systems that a diversity of accounting methods may continue to exist in the world. A country which does not recognize a parent-subsidiary relationship cannot be expected to condone consolidation practices. At an Arthur Young Professors' Roundtable, Mr. Sy Cip introduced the concept of cultural relativism:

> Accounting principles, standards, and practices are usually a direct product of the circumstances and influences of their environment and are most meaningful if viewed against such factors. Accordingly, accounting methods and applications originating in one country have probably the greatest utility in that country or in one with a similar environment. They could be quite inappropriate or may work undue hardships in countries of dissimilar environments.
>
> In the development of international accounting standards it is therefore essential that the diverse and differing environments where such standards are intended to be applied are first understood and appreciated. Failure to consider environmental differences or circumstances will likely deter the acceptance of any established international standards.[31]

The evolution of an accounting system is a complex process, and comparisons between such systems should be qualified. Comparisons between economies and technologies must also be qualified. An accounting system, in some stage of development, exists in all societies. As technology develops and complexities of economic transactions arise, an accounting system must evolve to interpret and report economic transactions to its society. Eventually, multinationals develop in some societies requiring an accounting system which reports to various cultures under the constraints of legalistic statutes and ownership. An accounting system is a culture's response for supplying owners and society with essential financial data for making economic decisions. Cultural determinants may limit the growth of this system. To critique or compare accounting systems is difficult because a particular accounting methodology may be the best accounting practice employable in a particular culture. The concept of cultural relativism inhibits value judgments. If a given culture or society is satisfied with the accounting information generated by its system, a criticism may not be relevant. An inference may be drawn that a particular accounting system may be "the best possible system" for a society because it reflects that society's cultural variables and technology.

IAS will someday be established and enforced for the majority of nations. Their acceptance and enforcement must be done by individual nations on a voluntary basis. Understanding cultural variances will lend credibility to these standards and hasten their establishment, not by a few industrialized nations, but by the world accounting community.

The ethnographic studies performed by cultural anthropologists, if considered, will assist in the establishment of IAS. At least an ethnographic perspective will provide an awareness of cultural differences. Such an awareness will contribute to an overall flexibility in establishing and enforcing IAS within the cultural parameters characteristic of every society.

Notes

1 Norlin G. Rueschhoff, *International Accounting and Financial Reporting* (New York, London: Praeger Publishers, 1976), p. 3.
2 American Institute of Certified Public Accountants, *Professional Standards*, vol. 3 (New York: Commerce Clearing House, 1981), pp. 7225–27.
3 Joseph Cummings, "The International Accounting Standards Committee: Current and Future Developments," *International Journal of Accounting* (Fall 1975): 31–37.
4 For a more complete discussion, see Gerhard Mueller, *International Accounting* (New York: Macmillan, 1967), pp. 1–26.
5 For in-depth discussion, see Mueller, *International Accounting*, pp. 205–37; and Rueschhoff, *International Accounting and Financial Reporting*, pp. 108–12.
6 E. Adamson Hoebel, *Anthropology: The Study of Man*, 4th ed. (New York: McGraw-Hill, 1972), p. 18.
7 For an in-depth introduction to culture, see Hoebel, *Anthropology*, pp. 21–54, 541–59. A more technical analysis beyond the introductory level is discussed by Bronislaw Malinowski's functional theory of culture, *A Scientific Theory of Culture and Other Essays,* 8th printing (Chapel Hill: University of North Carolina, 1977).
8 Hoebel, *Anthropology*, p. 22.
9 Ibid., pp. 21–53.
10 Ernest Hilgard, Richard Atkinson, and Rita Atkinson, *Introduction to Psychology*, 6th ed. (New York: Harcourt Brace, Jovanovich, 1975), pp. 334–35.
11 For a further detailed discussion on French structuralism, see James A. Boon, *From Symbolism to Structuralism* (New York: Harper & Row, 1972).
12 Maurice Moonitz, "Why Do We Need 'Postulates' and 'Principles'?" *The Journal of Accountancy* (December 1963): 42–46.

13 For a complete discussion of structuralism and the relationship of classification as a universality, see Claude Levi-Strauss, *Structural Anthropology* (New York: Basic Books, 1963).

14 Ruth Benedict, *Patterns of Culture*, preface by Margaret Mead (Boston: Houghton Mifflin, 1934), p. 237.

15 Hoebel, *Anthropology*, p. 26.

16 Current linguistical analysis of accounting has been carried out by A. Belkaoui, "The Interprofessional Linguistic Communication of Accounting Concepts: An Experiment in Sociolinguistics," *Journal of Accounting Research* (Autumn 1980): 362–73; E. Flamholtz and E. Cook, "Cognitive Meaning and Its Role in Accounting Change: A Field Study," *Accounting Organizations and Society* (October 1978): 115–40; and R. Libby, "Bankers' and Auditors' Perceptions of the Message Communicated by the Audit Report," *Journal of Accounting Research* (Spring 1979): 99–122.

17 Hoebel, *Anthropology*, pp. 610–11.

18 Ibid., p. 594.

19 Edward Sapir, *Language* (New York: Harcourt, 1921), p. 232.

20 David G. Mandelbaum, ed., *Selected Writings of Edward Sapir* (Berkeley: University of California press, 1949), p. 162.

21 Belkaoui, "Linguistic Communication of Accounting Concepts," pp. 362–63.

22 For a complete discussion of this cross-cultural comparison and its resulting implications, see Choi, "Primary-Secondary Reporting: A Cross-Cultural Analysis," *International Journal of Accounting* (Fall 1980): 83–104.

23 Ibid., pp. 96–97.

24 William Kanaga, "International Accounting: The Challenge and the Changes," *Journal of Accountancy* (November 1980): 55–56.

25 For an in-depth discussion of Franz Boas and his interpretation of cultural relativism, see *Social Evolution* (Cleveland: Meridan, 1963).

26 A coded data retrieval system created by George Murdock and implemented by John Whiting and Irvin Child was employed for hypothesis testing in contrast to Boasian anthropology. See John Whiting and Irvin Child, *Child Training and Personality: A Cross-Cultural Study* (New Haven: Yale University Press, 1953).

27 Hoebel, *Anthropology*, pp. 27–28.

28 See Choi, "Primary-Secondary Reporting: A Cross-Cultural Analysis."

29 Ibid.

30 See the American Accounting Association, *A Statement of Basic Accounting Theory* (Evanston, Ill.: AAA, 1966), for a discussion on considering environmental information as a financial data.

31 Sy Cip, "Establishing and Applying Standards in Diverse Economic and Social Environments," *International World Accounting Challenges and Opportunities*, ed. John Burton (New York: Arthur Young, 1981), pp. 85–96.

35

THE INTERNATIONALIZATION OF ACCOUNTING STANDARDS

Past problems and current prospects

Juan M. Rivera

Source: *International Journal of Accounting* 24(4) (1989): 320–41.

Abstract

The search for international accounting standards continues. Several groups are contributing to the process. The most prominent is the International Accounting Standards Committee which has issued nearly 30 international accounting principles. Despite these results, concerns as to the validity and worth of the harmonization process remain. A lack of a structured theoretical accounting framework underlying the specific standards, a multiplicity of permitted reporting and reporting alternatives introduced in the issued standards, a tendency to address only those issues developed or related to advanced economic evironments, and a lack of enforceability have all been mentioned. Problems of acceptance and enforcement of these international standards remain. To be accepted, the international accounting standards must recognise the existence of domestic requirements and needs of individual nations to assure that international standards are representative and responsive to all the countries and not simply to the larger members of the standard setting group.

The topic of international accounting standards is thought to have received the most attention in recent international accounting literature, with approximately half of the papers written addressing this issue.[1] Moreover, interest in the subject is not circumscribed to only a few institutions. Most (Ref.2, p.10) identified a variety of organizations involved in the international accounting standard-setting process. They include intergovernmental groups such as the United Nations (UN), the European Economic Community (EEC), and the Organization for Economic Co-operation and Development (OECD); professional accounting bodies, such as the International Accounting Standards Committee (IASC), and the Union of European Accountants (UEC); and regional accounting associations, such as the Arab Society of Certified Accountants (ASCA) and the Confederation of Asian and Pacific Accountants (CAPA).[3] Among these groups, the most prominent and prolific in setting standards has been the IASC, which has issued 29 international accounting principles and a comprehensive accounting framework for financial statements since its formation in 1973.[5]

Attempts to harmonize accounting standards at the international level began in 1966 when accountants from the United States, Canada, and the United Kingdom formed the Accountants International Study Group (AISG). Subsequently, a group of nine countries, including the member countries of the AISG, constituted the IASC, the multinational accounting organization that now includes 98 professional accounting associations from 74 countries. Also important in this process of international accounting standardization has been the International Federation of Accountants (IFAC), an organization that developed parallel to the IASC and currently has the same membership. Distinct from its twin institution, the IFAC has focused exclusively on the issuance of international guidelines which deal with auditing, ethics, and accounting educational requirements.

Notwithstanding the amount of interest in this area of international accounting standardization, doubts about the validity and worth of this harmonization process remain. Even though the number of accounting standards issued by the IASC is substantial (29 official pronouncements), their recognition and general acceptance is still an unrealized goal (see, for instance, Ref.7). The IASC's attempts at accounting harmonization have been unsuccessful because of the following observable conditions:

(1) lack of a structured theoretical accounting framework underlying the issuance of specific standards,[8]
(2) a multiplicity of permitted reporting and recording options introduced in the current standards,
(3) a tendency to address only those issues developed in or related to advanced economic environments where sophisticated markets and information prevail, and
(4) lack of enforceability of those international standards at the local and international levels.

Because of all these conditions, the persistent variety of inherent accounting practices in different geographical settings remains.[10] These conditions have divided academicians and practitioners alike between those who support harmonization at the international level and those who consider it a futile exercise.

Support for standardization

There is a general consensus that a world-wide standardization of accounting principles could benefit users of financial information which originates in different geographical locations (see, for instance, Ref.12). Mason[13] identified 10 types of beneficiaries from international standardization. Increasing the comparability of financial reports of companies from different countries is another reason to support standardization.[2, 14] In general, the interests of the investor as a user of financial information must be met.[15] The recent expansion of international capital markets and the availability of instantaneous global communications have placed on accounting the onus to provide useful and comparable information across international borders.

The demand for the international standardization of accounting principles stemmed from a need for information by the capital markets in developed countries and in accounting problems arising from a corporation's foreign operations.[16] Even with the proliferation of accounting statements by the IASC, many still perceive the absence of international accounting standards to be a fundamental problem. Studies by Scott[17] and Scott and Troberg[18] found that a group of accounting experts from different countries placed the lack of international accounting standards as sixth in a list of 88 problems in international accounting.

Standardization of accounting principles internationally is more of a harmonizing than a uniformity process. Nobes and Parker[19] considered harmonization as a process of making diverse accounting principles from different countries more compatible. The issue is also related to principles of accounting for private enterprises, exclusive of those for governmental entities in a centrally planned economy.

Arguments against harmonization

Even though the general trend in the literature supports harmonization some significant arguments have been advanced against that process. Both practical and theoretical considerations are mentioned as reasons for discouraging the standardization of accounting principles internationally (see, for instance, Ref.20, pp.100–108). The main argument is that socioeconomic and cultural differences between countries that cause the objectives of those countries' accounting systems actually or potentially to be different (Ref.21, pp.23–28; Ref.22), will always exist.[23] Thus the harmonization of accounting standards in different countries would tend to fail.

Choi and Mueller[21] identified numerous environmental variables that affect accounting development. For example, the degree of sophistication of a country's capital market affects business information requirements. Few of the less-developed countries have a structured capital market. The specific ownership structure of business enterprises constitutes another variable. In some countries, ownership is widely spread among investors who are normally absent from managing the business. In other countries, ownership and management fall to the same individuals. The need for disclosure and the emphasis on agency theory, so common in the more developed countries, are not a concern in many developing nations.

At the national level, unresolved questions remain on the objectives of accounting, and on the standards themselves, if any have been issued. A strong argument against the standardization of international accounting principles proposes that the conditions in developing countries differ from those in the developed nations. Because the process of standard setting has been predominantly controlled by the developed countries, the less-developed nations complain of not having enough participation in the process.[24]

The question remaining is whether a need for international accounting standards really exists, especially because lack of compliance with the international accounting rules has not impeded the development of international financial markets and foreign operations. Even before the IASC was formed, Most[27] found that when comparing financial statements of U.S. and European companies, a skilled analyst could find the information useful. Using financial statements of five leading chemical companies from five different countries to prepare a ratio analysis, he observed that European financial reports were comparable to those published in the United States. In the same vein, Choi and Bavishi[28] examined 1000 financial statements from public corporations with headquarters in 24 countries. A major finding of their comparison of the set of foreign companies with those based in the United States was that the fundamental differences in accounting standards among the countries sampled were not as extensive as expected. Also, using a sample of 26 foreign companies registered with the Securities and Exchange Commission (SEC), Meek[29] detected that responses in U.S. share prices were similar when the earnings announcements occurred, whether those earnings were measured with foreign or U.S. generally accepted accounting principles (GAAP).

Harmonization of international accounting principles by intergovernmental organizations

Both the UN and the OECD have studied the activities of transnational corporations (TNCs). The UN has shown concern with the divergent accounting and reporting practices TNCs follow and with the lack of comparability in the information they disclose. The Group of Experts on International Standards of Accounting and Reporting, an *ad hoc* unit appointed by the UN Centre on Transnational Corporations, seeks the harmonization of accounting practices and disclosures to meet user needs, particularly the needs of users in the developing countries. The Group of Experts has issued a few objectives upon which accounting standards could be built (Ref.11, pp.4–5). However, most of the work of the Centre on Transnational Corporations on the subject of accounting standards has consisted of a description of the development of accounting practices and standards in different countries.[11, 30, 31] Even though the intention of the UN and its Group of Accounting Experts is to formulate lists of minimum requirements of corporate financial information and disclosure, they have opted to reserve that task for private professional groups.

An important intergovernmental body involved in the establishment of international accounting standards is the European Economic Commission. This regional group attempts to harmonize accounting practices in the 12 member countries of the EEC through its Fourth and Seventh Directives. On a supranational level, this is the only organization at present capable of enforcing its accounting norms. According to the EEC parliamentary agreements, its member nations must enact the appropriate laws to implement the accounting methods and standards contained in the Commission's Directives.[32] With the upcoming elimination of trade barriers among the 12 members of the EEC in 1992, a surge in the harmonization of accounting policies and practices in that region is expected to develop. Whether those EEC directives would be compatible with the IASC pronouncements or with accounting standards in non-EEC countries is still uncertain.

The record of the IASC: many pronouncements and few endorsements

The IASC has been successful in publishing 28 pronouncements and in attracting new member countries since its inception in 1973. Unfortunately, the IASC's standards are not enforceable and have not yet received "generally accepted" status world-wide.

The model under which the IASC operates is strongly influenced by the accounting practice of developed countries, particularly the United States. Hall[34] observed that the IASC was created under the tutelage of a few dominant countries, especially the United States, the United Kingdom and, to a lesser extent, West Germany and The Netherlands. There was the patronizing assumption that the standards from these developed countries could be adapted to other countries, particularly those in the Third World. Attempts to transplant elaborate principles to environments where different conditions prevail make the accounting standards process questionable and often inefficient. Thus, recent subjects addressed by the IASC's principles, such as those dealing with pension accounting and leases, are superfluous for countries where capital-lease transactions are not practiced.[35] Even the IASC has been self-critical when stating that in the past, it "tended to follow

101

the developments in standard-setting that have taken place in countries where the regulatory environment and the accounting profession are well developed" (Ref.26, p.16)

Evidence of a strong dependent relationship between the IASC's standards and the accounting principles (GAAP) issued in the United States is provided by the comparative analysis presented in the Appendix. It should be noted that only two of the 28 international standards advanced by the IASC – IAS 20: Accounting for Government Grants, and IAS 29: Financial Accounting in Hyperinflationary Economies – had not been preceded by a U.S. accounting pronouncement which dealt with the same subject matter and arrived in general at the same acceptable methods and procedures. The fact that the AICPA has found very few and only minor differences between the IASC's standards and U.S. GAAP[25] corroborates the perceived relationship between those two sets of accounting principles.[36]

Additionally, the harmonization of international accounting standards that the IASC has tried to achieve has been limited because flexibility is ingrained in its outstanding pronouncements. In a search for the intrinsic uniformity of international accounting standards, Rueschhoff[37] found that flexibility is permitted in the international standards, just as flexibility is present in the U.S. GAAP in a number of cases. Most[2] found that in eight of the 24 international standards issued up to 1984, i.e., in one-third of the standards, alternative solutions were permitted. Similarly, Choi and Bavishi[28] found that eight of the initial 16 standards issued by the IASC permit alternative accounting treatments, and hence allow flexibility.

The IASC has recognized the impediments to improved harmonization caused by the free choices of accounting treatment permitted for similar transaction or events in its current international standards. The flexibility introduced in those standards was probably an attempt to accommodate the variety of treatments that existed in reporting standards already adopted by developed countries.[38] In an effort to ameliorate the problem of the observance of international accounting standards in the future and thus aim for wider comparability of financial statements, the IASC has proposed amendments to 13 of its existing standards.[6] The changes would eliminate choices of treatments and/or prescribe preferred solutions whenever options cannot be dismissed. Reporting companies which opt for an allowed alternative would need to disclose information reconciling the effect of the alternative selected against the one considered as preferred.

The problem of enforcement of IASC standards

The degree to which IASC standards are observed world-wide is generally discouraging. In a few countries, such as Cyprus, Malawi, Malaysia, and Zimbabwe, where the accounting profession is relatively young, the international accounting standards (IAS) generally have been incorporated into the official local accounting principles (Ref.26, pp.9–12). For other countries, such as Fiji, India, Kenya, and Singapore, the principles issued by the IASC serve as a basis for the formulation of local accounting rules (Ref.26, pp.12–14). Still only in exceptional cases do particular firms make reference to compliance with IAS in the financial statements. Likewise, reference to IAS in the auditors' reports of published financial statements of these countries is missing. It is evident that professional accountants must abide by existing accounting standards at the local level, and that the power or persuasion to incorporate the use of and reference to IAS has not materialized into disclosure of their observance.

Because of the large number of options permitted in the published IAS, the actual level of agreement with IAS is conceivably substantially higher than the level of disclosure of that compliance. In an effort to test the use and application of its international standards, in 1987 the IASC conducted a survey among its member bodies from 70 countries (see Ref.26). Results of this survey showed that in most of the responding countries, the national requirements or accounting practice conformed with 23 of the 25 IAS then outstanding (Ref.26, p.3). The two exceptions corresponded to IAS 14 and IAS 15, which deal with segmental information and with information to reflect the effect of changing prices, respectively.

A close scrutiny of the IASC's survey results provides additional evidence that its standards have accommodated accounting principles in effect in a few of the developed countries. The responses received from the United Kingdom, Canada, the United States, France, Belgium, and Japan indicated the highest level of conformity between the standards developed there and those promulgated by the IASC[39] (Ref.26, pp.21–69). This would imply that, at least on issues such as those covered by IAS, a good level of accounting harmonization has been achieved in those countries. Therefore, the development of standards to mirror those where agreement already exists would be a redundant task. Nonetheless, the apparent high level of conformity may be the result more of the flexibility allowed by the IASC's standards than of the actual correspondence of accounting rules and practices among those countries surveyed.

Whatever power of enforcement the IASC could have possessed, it has diminished substantially through time. When the IASC was founded, its members agreed to use their best endeavors and persuasive influence to ensure compliance with the standards. Each professional accounting association within the IASC was to ensure that the external auditors would satisfy themselves of the standards' observance and would disclose cases of noncompliance. Appropriate action was to be taken against any auditor who did not follow these recommendations. Later, revised wording of the agreement among members acknowledged that the IASC's pronouncements would not override the standards followed by individual countries. In the most recent version of the agreement, dated October 1982, the members' obligation is to use "their best endeavors to ensure that financial statements comply with the IAS in all material respects and disclose the fact of such compliance" and "to ensure that auditors satisfy themselves that the financial statements comply with those standards in all material respects" (Ref.25, Appendix). However, the earlier requirement that auditors should disclose the extent of noncompliance and refer to it in the audit report is no longer present. Actual observance of the IASC's standards is very difficult to document in practice because very few companies make reference to them in their financial reports. For instance, although the International Stock Exchange of the United Kingdom and the Republic of Ireland permits foreign companies to file financial statements that comply with IAS rather than with the British ones, disclosure of that fact is still very rare (Ref.25, p.77). The exception to the norm is Canada, where efforts undertaken by the organized accounting profession have led to a widespread practice of listed companies disclosing their observance of IAS.[40]

To assess the extent of references to IAS in published financial statements, a search for these disclosures was performed, using financial reports compiled by the National Automated Accounting Research System (NAARS). The sample included approximately 22 600 documents filed during the years 1983–1988. The sample comprised entities that were listed companies traded in the major U.S. stock exchanges or in the over-the-counter market. The results of this analysis, as reported in Table 1, reveal that disclosures of compliance with IAS are extremely limited. Although this type of disclosure is increasing, on average only 14 financial statements have alluded to IAS every year.[41] In general, the references reported in footnotes have outnumbered those included in the management report by a margin of two to one. As for the country of origin of the disclosing companies, 17 of those 26 reporting firms were incorporated in Canada. Only four U.S. companies referred to IAS during the 6-year period examined. With the exception of one Italian company, no mention to IAS was found in the auditor's report of the corporate financial statements reviewed.

Criticism of the IASC's standard-setting process

A basic criticism of the IASC is that it has not paid sufficient attention to the objectives of financial accounting and reporting in an international context. The IASC's focus has been more on legitimizing certain practices already tried in influential, developed economies. Initially, the IASC (Ref.42, para.6–10) recognized the following three fundamental assumptions in accounting: (1) going concern; (2) consistency; and (3) accrual process, together with the following three governing "considerations" in the preparation of financial information: (1) prudence; (2) substance over form; and (3) materiality.[43] However, the viability of assumptions such as these has not been tested under different economic environments. Assessment of the applicability of

Table 1 References to IAS in Published Financial Reports.

Name of company or institution	Country	Years covered and type of disclosure												Total cases	
		1983		1984		1985		1986		1987		1988			
		F	M	F	M	F	M	F	M	F	M	F	M	F	M
1. Alcan Aluminum, Ltd.	Canada		x		x		x		x		x		x		6
2. AICPA	U.S.A.	x		x		x		x						4	
3. Bell Canada (BCE)	Canada	x		x		x		x		x		x		6	
4. Bow Valley Industries, Ltd.	Canada	x					x		x		x		x	1	4
5. CPC Intl. Corp.	U.S.A.										x		x		2
6. Campeau Corporation	Canada							x		x				2	
7. Dominion Textile Inc.	Canada							x	x	x	x	x	x	3	3
8. Echo Bay Mines, Ltd.	Canada			x		x		x		x				4	
9. Elscint, Ltd.	Israel					x								1	
10. Exxon Corporation	U.S.A.						x	x		x		x		3	1
11. FMC Corporation	U.S.A.								x		x		x		3
12. Gandalf Technologies	Canada											x		1	
13. General Electric Co.	U.S.A.				x		x		x		x		x		5
14. Hudson Bay Mines, Ltd.	Canada				x		x								2
15. Imperial Oil, Ltd.	Canada	x		x		x		x		x				5	

Table 1 (cont'd)

Name of company or institution	Country	Years covered and type of disclosure 1983		1984		1985		1986		1987		1988		Total cases	
		F	M	F	M	F	M	F	M	F	M	F	M	F	M
16. Interhome Energy, Inc.	Canada											x		1	
17. IFAC^a	U.S.A.											x		3	
18. Interprovincial Pipe Line, Ltd.	Canada	x		x		x		x						5	
19. McIntyre Mines, Ltd.	Canada	x		x										2	
20. Montedison, SPA^a	Italy									x				1	
21. Northern Telecom, Ltd.	Canada	x		x		x		x		x		x		6	
22. Page Petroleum, Ltd.	Canada	x		x		x		x						4	
23. Texaco Canada, Inc.	Canada			x		x								2	
24. Transcanada Pipeline, Ltd.	Canada	x	x	x	x		x	x	x	x	x		x	4	6
25. Union Gas, Ltd.	Canada									x	x			1	1
26. Velcro Industries, Ltd.	Neth. Antilles							x		x				2	
Cases per type/year		9	2	11	4	9	5	12	6	13	9	7	7	61	33
Total companies/year		10		14		14		16		19		13			

^aCase reported included a reference to IAS compliance in the auditor's report.

F = Footnote in financial statements.

M = Included in the text of the management report.

Source: Annual files from the National Automated Accounting Research System (NAARS) for the years 1983–1988, comprising ca. 22 600 financial reports.

standards on materiality, prudence, cost–benefit, and relevance under varying conditions of inflation, unemployment, exchange controls, absence or inefficiencies of capital markets, and similar factors has not yet occurred.

The internationalization of accounting principles has suffered from a lack of synchronization between the issuance of standards at the national level in difference countries and the formulation of standards by the IASC. Based on the type of subjects covered, it seems that the IASC follows those undertaken by the Financial Accounting Standards Board (FASB), as can be inferred from the analysis of corresponding standards presented in the Appendix. In itself, the IASC's process for formulation of accounting principles is very similar to that followed by the FASB, its U.S. counterpart. Thus, for each standard, an exposure draft invites comments from interested parties. Further, an international standard in its definite form requires the approval of at least two-thirds of the members of the steering committee before its final release to the membership for implementation.[44]

The first standards from the IASC were basic and simple, and largely non-controversial. Later they became more complex, with attempts to deal with problematic subjects in vogue in the leading accounting countries. Some researchers stated that the IASC is generally reluctant to issue a standard that conflicts with U.S. or U.K. principles (Ref.45, p.31). This implies that the task of standard setting cannot remain politically neutral. Both the IASC and the U.S. FASB have been categorized as political bodies whose standards are those appropriate for industrial countries with a large private sector and a well-developed capital market.[46, 47] Most of the IAS issued probably have been made deliberately flexible so as not to upset any of the leading accounting countries. This produces more confusion in a profession already overburdened with an overload of standards and multiple accommodating options that hinder comparison and harmonization.

Shortcomings of past research

Smith and Shalchi[48] have signalled a lack of rigorous methodology and analysis in international accounting research. Many of the international accounting papers are descriptive and show an excessive concern with one aspect of the problem, namely, the harmonization of accounting principles. The research undertaken in this area is generally not supported by theory or paradigms but depends rather on subjective opinions. The studies have been of the fact-finding, data-collection type, and the results have not been sufficient to conclude with confidence whether recommendations or statements made by the researchers constitute the "best" alternative. It is still not possible to determine whether current harmonization attempts such as those of the IASC, lead to better investment decisions or whether a uniform accounting system, such as that of France, facilitates national economic planning and true harmonization.

Much of the literature on international accounting has concentrated on describing the methods used in a particular country or comparing them with those used elsewhere. Another popular topic, the classification of countries into groups according to their accounting practices or economic features, provides logical comparisons but has not produced normative research (Refs.22;49;50, pp.15–19). Even the more scientific approaches of discriminant and factor analyses for classification of countries have been criticized for using a secondary, inefficient empirical base.[51] In any event, the classification of accounting practices using sophisticated techniques has accentuated the reasons for international differences in accounting and has challenged the rationale for harmonization.[52]

Toward a research agenda for the future

No apparent agreement exists on the objectives of the international standards-setting process, and serious research on this subject has good potential. Worldwide, at least 20 national standard-setting organizations or boards exist, with very little interaction and synchronization among them.[53] The area of standards harmonization demands better answers on its validity and future direction. A cost–benefit assessment of the international standards process could produce interesting research results. Also, although some research of the descriptive-comparative type[54] has been conducted, the subset of international auditing standards and practices holds promising research potential.

The level of financial reporting reached in a particular environment depends on two main forces, namely, the needs of the users and the interest of corporations in supplying the information that is demanded. At the international level, the information needs of users in different environments is yet to be defined, thus opening an area for potentially interesting research. The information needs of users as distinct from shareholders and lenders, and the impact of these needs on the nature of accounting standards constitute another area for research.

The process of harmonization could operate at lower levels of aggregation, apart from the attempts at global standardization that have been proven far from successful. As a practical solution, the classification of countries could be used to create standard-setting organizations for those regions of the world identified as homogeneous. This process could function with direct participation of the countries involved. At some point, some basic, but, it is hoped, useful, standards could be formulated at higher levels of national aggregates. Gray et al.[1] advanced this idea of segmenting the area where international standards of accounting should be applied. They discussed the use of standards by only multinational corporations as a desirable alternative to the IASC's approach.[55] To date, the IASC's standards have been destined for application to all companies without distinguishing those that are uninational from those multinational firms – an essential distinction. Research endeavors which deal with these alternatives could produce interesting findings.

In the area of international accounting, new approaches should be introduced, borrowing from other disciplines such as statistics or behavioral sciences, as has already happened in other fields of accounting research. Attention should be turned also to issues of management accounting, particularly because in many countries the same individuals own and manage businesses. In Third World countries disclosure of accounting information for outsiders, on which the traditional accounting model has been based, is not common because there are essentially no capital markets.[56]

For empirical research, opportunities are plentiful in international accounting. So far, for instance, no research has asked U.S. investors who have passive investments in foreign companies what type of information would be useful for their decisions. The same kind of questions can be asked of foreign investors in U.S. companies. Determining a risk–return paradigm for such decision-makers is a subject worth investigation. Comparing their decision models with a standard used by a U.S. domestic investor could give support for more or less financial reporting uniformity on a world-wide or regional basis.

If a need for harmonization in international accounting practices were perceived, and assuming that harmonization efforts by the different organizations are not successful, other options could be identified through direct investigation. If the need for re-expression or adjustments of financial data to fit the particular needs of some decision-makers is essential, empirical analysis would help to determine whether it is worth producing. Perhaps the services of financial analysts or public accounting firms, either foreign- or U.S.-based, are already filling the gap.

If the harmonization of international accounting practices and standards is proven to be theoretically unsustainable, consideration of the need for and availability of other types of business information is in order. The traditional accounting information model should then be set aside and instead other indices should be built on market, management, or risk considerations more susceptible to measurement and international comparisons.

The areas for research mentioned here must be addressed through rigorous research techniques, if for no other reason than to provide evidence to critics of international accounting that this area has achieved the mature status it deserves.

Summary

More than a decade of efforts by an array of organizations in the development of international accounting standards has not produced the world-wide harmonization of accounting and reporting practices that was intended. As proven many times, the financial reporting process must attend to domestic requirements of information, which derive from the specific economic, legal, and cultural circumstances encountered in each geographical location. Often the standard-setting apparatus within specific countries lacks sufficient consensus and support from the professional groups involved in standards implementation. This is understandably so because the process is commonly characterized as a political one, with the interested parties vying for a particular course of action concomitant with their interest. Normally, the local accounting professional associations are in charge of issuing accounting principles "generally acceptable" among their membership.

The most prominent of the accounting standard-setting bodies at the international level, the IASC, follows the structural pattern of the local accounting organizations. Composed of the professional accounting associations from 74 countries, it suffers from the same defects that have plagued the determination of accounting principles at the local level. In its attempts to be politically acceptable, the IASC has followed the practice of endorsing accounting principles applied in the leading accounting countries, mainly the United States. Flexibility has also been permitted in the accounting pronouncements to accommodate divergent practices in different nations or not to upset accounting as practiced in the leading influential economies. This approach produces a result that can hardly claim to advance "harmonization". Recent attempts by the IASC[6] to reduce the free choices allowed in the current international standards could provoke further reluctance of companies to comply. The distinction of preferred and allowed methods introduced in the proposed amendments[6] would burden those companies that choose the allowed options. In these cases, the reporting company would have to reconcile its financial reported data not only against the national accounting requirements, but also against those prescribed in the "preferred" method.

It is time to question through serious research the value of the harmonization of international accounting standards. Measuring the real benefits and costs of harmonization could provide clues to support or challenge the existence of institutions such as the IASC. Even though these organizations have issued general standards, they have failed to ensure observance and disclosures even among their member countries. Part of the reason might be that the peculiar economic and cultural characteristics of each country defy any attempt for a global harmonization of accounting principles. Essentially, it is not theoretically acceptable to envision a set of accounting standards without previously defining a fundamental core of accounting theory with basic postulates. The IASC has only recently amended this mistake through the issuance of a theoretical accounting framework.[9] Whether this is the basic accounting theory acceptable on a world-wide basis remains questionable. Assuming that these basic postulates are proven operational in different geographical settings, the review and implementation of international accounting standards might have better chances of success.

Finally, perhaps a more realistic option is to seek regional harmonization. This could develop from the classification of countries into homogeneous economic or cultural regions where common accounting standards have a better chance of being observed. Perhaps institutions such as the IASC should be only guiding mechanisms or clearing houses of the accounting principles, measurement, and disclosures as applied in different parts of the world.

Acknowledgements

Financial support for this study from Peat, Marwick and Main is acknowledged and appreciated.

Appendix. Accounting standards issued by IASC

IAS	Subject area and content	Issue date	U.S. GAAP	Subject area and content	Issue date
1	Disclosure of Accounting Policies. Three fundamental assumptions and three criteria given for selection and application of accounting policies. Disclosure of all policies required.	January 1975	APB Opinion 22	Disclosure of Accounting Policies. Requires disclosure of accounting policies selected among permitted alternatives.	April 1972
2	Valuation and Presentation of Inventories in the Context of the Historical Cost System. Inventories to be valued at lower of cost or net realizable value. Several methods permitted to report cost, including LIFO base stock and standard costing.	October 1975	ARB 43 (Chapter 4)	Inventory Pricing. Inventory Valuation at cost or lower-of-cost-of-market. Cost methods are FIFO, Average or FIFO.	June 1953
3	Consolidated Financial Statements. Defines relationship between investor and investee and degree of control for application of consolidation or equity methods. Cost method applied when no significant influence exercised by investor.	June 1976	ARB 51, and APB Opinion 18	Consolidation of Foreign Operations; and The Equity Method of Accounting for Investments in Common Stock. Provide criteria to apply consolidation, cost or equity methods to report investments in other entities.	August 1959 and March 1971 respectively
4	Depreciation Accounting. Discusses concept of depreciation and type of assets subject to depreciation accounting. Disclosures required include methods of depreciation, and useful lives of assets or depreciation rates used.	October 1976	ARB 43 (Chapter 9c) and APB Opinion 12	Depreciation Concepts, Methods and Disclosures.	June 1953 and December 1967 respectively

No.	Standard and Description	Date	Comparable Standard and Description	Date
5	Information to be Disclosed in Financial Statements. Identifies the balance sheet, income statement, notes and other statements and explanatory material as part of the financial statements. Lists specific items and groups of accounts for presentation in the statements.	October 1976	ARB 43 (Chapters 2 to 9) Discusses the main elements comprising a set of comparative financial statements and the applicable methods to recognize, report and classify them.	June 1953
7	Statement of Changes in Financial Position. Considers the statement of changes in financial position as integral part of financial statements. Funds provided from or used in the operation should be disclosed separately. Funds broadly defined to be cash, cash and cash equivalents, or working capital.	October 1977	APB Opinion 19 Reporting Changes in Financial Position. Concept of Funds to mean working capital or cash. Funds from or used for operations to be disclosed separately from other sources and uses.	March 1971
8	Unusual and Prior Period Items and Changes in Accounting Principles. Gains/losses from unusual transactions or events should be separately disclosed within the income statement. Prior period adjustments reported either in retained earnings or in current income. Effect of changes in accounting estimates can be accounted in the current or in both current and future periods.	February 1978	APB Opinion 9 and SFAS 16 Treatment of Extraordinary Items and Prior Period Adjustments. Accounting treatment and disclosures for prior period adjustments, changes in accounting principles, and effects of changes in accounting estimates.	March 1971 and June 1977 respectively
9	Accounting for Research and Development Activities. Lists typical items included in research and development costs. These costs are charged as expenses in the period when they are incurred. Development costs may be deferred to future periods if certain criteria for ensuring future benefits are satisfied.	July 1978	SFAS 2 Accounting For Research and Development Costs. Defines activities that constitute research and development and the cost elements associated with them. All research and development costs should be charged to expenses when incurred.	October 1974

113

Appendix *(cont'd)*

IAS	Subject area and content	Issue date	U.S. GAAP	Issue date	Subject area and content
10	Contingencies and Events Occurring After the Balance Sheet Date. Dictates accrual of contingency losses if contingent future event is probable, and if a reasonable estimate of the loss can be made. Contingency gains are not to be accrued. After balance sheet events require adjustment of the balance sheet if related to conditions	October 1978	SFAS 5	July 1975	Accounting for Contingencies. Establishes criteria to help define if a loss contingency exists and if actual and/or disclosure in the financial statements should proceed.
11	Accounting for Construction Contracts. Permits the recognition of income through a percentage of completion or a completed contract method, establishing the conditions under which one or the other method applies.	March 1979	ARB 45	October 1955	Long-Term Construction-Type Contracts. Income from construction contracts recognized under a percentage of completion or a completed contract approach, depending on the conditions of the contractual operation.
12	Accounting for Taxes on Income. Prescribes tax expense which should be recorded according to tax effect accounting, using the deferral or the liability method. Effect of timing differences to be included in deferred assets or liabilities, unless no reversal is foreseeable in at least 3 years ahead.	July 1979	APB Opinion 11	December 1967	Accounting for Income Taxes. Income tax expense calculated on reportable pre-tax accounting income. Resulting timing differences are included in deferred taxes receivable or payable. Includes accounting for loss carry-back and carry-forward.
13	Presentation of Current Assets and Current Liabilities. Decision to present the classification of current/non-current assets and liabilities in the financial statements is left to the enterprise. Typical items to include among the current assets/liabilities group are listed.	November 1979	ARB 43 (Chapter 3)	June 1953	Current Assets and Current Liabilities. Criteria to define the current/non-current attributes of an asset or liability. Corresponding disclosures.

14	December 1976 — SFAS 14	Financial Reporting for Segments of a Business Enterprise. Requires disaggregated information by line-of-business or geographical units for segments of a firm representing 10% or more of the company's consolidated sales, profits, or assets. The existence of major customers, representing 10% or more of total sales, should also be reported.	August 1981	Reporting Financial Information by Segment. Disclosure of material line-of-business and geographical segments for firms whose securities are publicly traded. For each reportable industry or geographical segment, sales, profit, assets and inter-company pricing should be disclosed. Materiality of a segment to trigger its disclosure is set at 10% of consolidated total sales, profits, or assets.
15	September 1979 — SFAS 33[a]	Financial Reporting and Changing Prices. Applies to public enterprises of a given material size as defined in the standard. Supplementary information to reflect effect of changing prices on selected items, plus the current cost of inventories, property plant and equipment.	November 1981	Information Reflecting the Effects of Changing Prices. Superseded IAS 6. Applies to businesses whose levels of revenues, assets, profits or employment are significant in their environment. Information adjusted for price changes can be prepared though price indices or current cost methods. Disclosures are in the form of supplementary data, unless the firm routinely presents that information in the primary financial statements.
16	December 1985 — FASB Concept 6	Elements of Financial Statements. Replaced FASB concepts statement No. 3, thus extending the theoretical concepts supporting valuation and reporting of the items in the financial statements.	March 1982	Accounting for Property, Plant and Equipment. Carrying value of an asset in property, plant and equipment is historical cost or revaluation amount. General guidelines for acquisition of assets through asset exchanges are established. Revaluation of assets is permitted, provided the difference between revalued amount and cost is directly reported in shareholders' equity.

115

Appendix (cont'd)

IAS	Subject area and content	Issue date	U.S. GAAP	Subject area and content	Issue date
17	Accounting for Leases. Provides general guidelines for the accounting and disclosure of operating and finance leases for both the lessee and the lessor. Finance leases are classified into sale-type or strict financing ones. Sale and lease-back option is also covered.	September 1982	SFAS 13	Accounting for Leases. Leases classified into operating and capital types, according to criteria that focus on the substance of the transaction. Capital leases can be sales- and financing-types. Disclosures for the lessee and the lessor are discussed. Accounting treatment for sale–leasebacks is included.	November 1976
18	Revenue Recognition. Establishes criteria to recognize revenue from sales or service transactions. Recognition of service revenue is permitted under the completed contract or percentage of completion methods.	December 1982	ARB 43 (Chapter 1A and 8)	Recognition of revenue and gains as part of realization and matching concepts.	June 1953
19	Accounting for Retirement Benefits in the Financial Statement of Employers. Definitions of current and past service costs, vested benefits, funding, actuarial methods, accrued and projected benefits, etc., are introduced. Gives guidelines for the accounting and reporting of a defined benefit plan in the financial statements of the employer.	January 1983	SFAS 36	Disclosure of Pension Information. Requires revised disclosures of defined benefit pension plans in the financial statements of the employer. The disclosures include the present value of the accumulated plan benefits, and the funded assets for the pension plan obligations.	May 1980
20	Accounting for Government Grants and Disclosure of Government Assistance. Government grants are to be included in the income statement. Recognition is during the period(s) when the corresponding costs intended to be compensated with the grant are incurred.	April 1983		No corresponding standard is available.	

116

No.	Title / Description	Date	Standard	Date	Title / Description
21	Accounting for the Effects of Changes in Foreign Exchange Rates. Provides guidelines to account and report transactions involving foreign operations. Exchange differences from intercompany monetary items are to be reflected in shareholders' interests. Exchange rate differences from long-term monetary items can be deferred, or recognized in current income.	July 1983	SFAS 52	December 1981	Foreign Currency Translation. Superseded SFAS No. 8. Introduces the concept of "Functional Currency" to translate foreign operations to a reporting currency, using current exchange rates. Translation adjustments are accrued in a separate component of consolidated shareholders' equity. Special treatment is applied to translating foreign operations from a subsidiary operating in highly inflationary environments.
22	Accounting for Business Combinations. The general treatment for a business combination is to account it under the purchase method. If combination is deemed a uniting of interests, the pooling of interests method may be applied. Differences between the cost of acquisition and fair values of the assets acquired can be recognized in income or adjusted to shareholders' equity. Positive goodwill arising in the acquisition should be recognized as a deferred asset.	November 1983	APB Opinion 16	August 1970	Business Combinations. Considers the purchase method and the pooling of interest method as acceptable approaches to account for business combinations. The combination must meet specified criteria to be treated as a pooling of interest case. For acquisitions considered purchases, if cost of acquisition exceeds the fair value of net assets bought an amortizable goodwill is recorded.
23	Capitalization of Borrowing Costs. Borrowing costs should be capitalized as part of the cost of an asset up to the point in time when the asset is ready for its intended use or sale.	March 1984	SFAS 34	October 1979	Capitalization of Interest Cost. Standards for capitalizing the interest cost as part of the acquisition cost of an asset. Interest is for the period required to complete the asset. Interest cannot be capitalized for inventories that are routinely manufactured.

117

Appendix (*cont'd*)

IAS	Subject area and content	Issue date	U.S. GAAP	Subject area and content	Issue date
24	Related Party Disclosures. After identifying who constitutes related parties, full disclosure is called for transactions involving the reporting enterprise and the related party.	July 1984	SFAS 5	Related Party Disclosures. Establishes the required content for disclosures of material related party transactions. Excludes compensation arrangements, expense allowance and similar items from the obligation to disclose.	March 1982
25	Accounting for Investments. Valuation and disclosure rules are stated for both short-term and long-term investments in securities. Accounting is for investments in securities different from those reportable under consolidation or equity methods. Long-term investments in tangible assets are also covered.	April 1986	SFAS 12	Accounting for Certain Marketable Securities. Provides standards for accounting and reporting investments in marketable equity securities, including the resulting gain or loss from their valuation and disposal.	December 1975
26	Accounting and Reporting by Retirement Benefit Plans. Addresses the disclosures needed in reports by defined retirement benefit plans. The report should disclose net assets available for benefits, present value of the promised retirement benefits, and the resulting excess or deficit between those two items.	January 1987	SFAS 35	Accounting and Reporting by Defined Benefit Pension Plans. Establishes guidelines for supplying information relevant to the status of the plan. Disclosures must include net assets available in the plan, present value of accumulated benefits, and changes affecting the actuarial computations of the accumulated plan benefits.	March 1980

	IAS	Date	US Standard	US Description	Date
27	Consolidated Financial Statements and Accounting for Investments in Subsidiaries. Relates to the preparation and reporting of consolidated financial statements for parent and subsidiaries. Control needed to proceed with consolidation is presumed if the investor owns more than 50% of the voting shares of the investee.	April 1989	SFAS 94	Consolidation of All Majority-Owned Subsidiaries. Requires consolidation of all majority-owned subsidiaries on substantially all cases, except where control is likely to be temporary or when special circumstances preclude control by the majority owner.	
28	Accounting for Investments in Associates. Modifies IAS 3 in relation to investments in associated companies under the equity method. It is assumed than an investor holding 20% or more of the voting stock of the investee has "significant influence" over the investee's policies and decisions to require reporting under the equity method.	April 1989	APB Opinion 18	The Equity Method of Accounting for Investments in Common Stock. Provides guidelines in using the equity method for investments where the investor, not having majority control, exercises significant influence on the investee. Significant influence is presumed if investor holds 20% or more of the investee's voting stock.	March 1979
29	Financial Reporting in Hyperinflationary Economies. Requires enterprises reporting in the currency of a hyperinflationary economy to restate the primary financial statement to account for changes in the domestic price levels. Gains or losses resulting from the adjusted net monetary position should be included in net income.	April 1989		No corresponding standard is available (for a related item, see IAS 15 and the corresponding footnote to SFAS 33).	

119

References

1. S. J. Gray, J. C. Shaw and L. B. McSweeney. "Accounting Standards and Multinational Corporations," in F. D. S. Choi and G. G. Mueller (eds.), *Frontiers in International Accounting, An Anthology* (Ann Arbor, MI: UMI Research Press, 1985), 136–156.

2. K. S. Most. *International Conflict of Accounting Standards, A research Report* (Vancouver: The Canadian Certified General Accountants' Research Foundation, 1984).

3. A similar list and discussion of the actors involved in this process was presented by Belkhaoui (Ref.4, pp. 57–84).

4. A. Belkhaoui. *International Accounting. Issues and Solutions* (Westport, CT: Quorum Books, 1985). 57–84.

5. The Appendix presents a list of the accounting standards issued by the IASC, with a brief description of their content and a cross-correspondence to U.S. accounting principles which address similar subject matters. In addition to the standards issued, there are currently three IASC Exposure Drafts (E) outstanding, namely, E32: Comparability of Financial Statements;[6] E33: Accounting for Taxes on Income; and E34: Disclosures in the Financial Statements of Banks and similar Financial Institutions.

6. IASC. E32 Exposure Draft. *Comparability of Financial Statements* (New York: AICPA, Product G00392, 1989).

7. D. T. Hayes. "The International Accounting Standards Committee: Recent Development and Current Problems," *International Journal of Accounting* (Fall 1980), 1–10.

8. The recent accounting framework prepared by the IASC[9] is expected to provide the basis needed to develop international accounting standards in the future.

9. IASC. *Framework for the Preparation and Presentation of Financial Statements* (London: IASC, 1989).

10. A survey conducted by the UN (Ref.11, pp. 21–64) on 42 of its affiliated members exemplified the diversity of accounting principles followed by the countries surveyed.

11. UN. *International Accounting and Reporting Issues: 1984 Review* (New York: United Nations, 1985).

12. CCA (The Canadian Chartered Accountant). "The Need for International Standards in Accounting," in K. B. Berg, G. G. Mueller and L. M. Walker (eds.). *Readings in International Accounting* (Boston: Houghton Mifflin, 1969), 189–191.

13. A. K. Mason. *International Financial Reporting Standards: Problems and Prospects* (Lancaster, U.K. University of Lancaster, 1977).

14. J. C. Burton (ed.). *The International World of Accounting, Challenges and Opportunities, 1980 Proceedings of the Arthur Young Professors' Roundtable* (Reston, VA: Arthur Young, 1981).

15. S. J. Gray. "The Impact of International Accounting Differences from a Security-Analysis Perspective: Some European Evidence," *Journal of Accounting Research* (Spring 1980), 64–76.

16. B. R. Doyle and S. D. Spencer. "International Accounting Standards. Why They Merit Support?" *Management Accounting* (October 1986), 28–29.

17. G. M. Scott. "Topical Priorities in Multinational Accounting," in F. D. S. Choi (ed.), *Multinational Accounting. A Research Framework for the Eighties* (Ann Arbor, MI: UMI Research Press, 1981), 5–19.

18. G. M. Scott and P. Troberg. *Eighty-eight International Accounting Problems in Rank Order of Importance – A DELPHI Evaluation* (Sarasota, FL: American Accounting Association, 1980).

19. C. W. Nobes and R. H. Parker. *Comparative International Accounting* (Oxford: Philip Allan, 1981).

20. J. M. Samuels and A. G. Piper. *International Accounting: A Survey* (New York: St. Martin Press, 1985).

21. F. D. S. Choi and G. G. Mueller. *An Introduction to Multinational Accounting* (Englewood Cliffs, NJ: Prentice-Hall, 1978).

22. W. G. Frank. "An Empirical Analysis of International Accounting Principles," *Journal of Accounting Research* (Autumn 1979), 593–605.

23. The variety of social, economic, and legal circumstances as causal factors for differences in financial statements across countries has been acknowledged by the IASC (Ref.9, Preface).

24. Although the operating structure of the IASC calls for a policy preferably to include a minimum of three developing countries in its 13-member Board (see IASC Objectives and Procedures in Ref.25, p.11 053) only one developing country (Jordan) is currently included. In addition, only the U.S. standard-setting type of institution (The Financial Accounting Standards Board) is a representative in the IASC's 10-member Consultative Group (Ref.26, Appendix 2).

25. AICPA (American Institute of Certified Public Accountants). International Accounting and Auditing Standards (New York: AICPA, 1988).

26. IASC.; *Survey of the Use and Application of International Accounting Standards* (London: IASC, 1988).

27. K. S. Most. "How Bad are European Accounts?" in K. B. Berg, G. G. Mueller and L. M. Walker (eds.) *Readings in International Accounting* (Boston: Houghton Mifflin, 1969), 208–222.

28. F. D. S. Choi and V. B. Bavishi. "Financial Accounting Standards: A Multinational Synthesis and Policy Framework," *International Journal of Accounting* (Fall 1982), 159–183.

29. G. K. Meek. "U.S. Securities Market Responses to Alternate Earnings Disclosures of Non-U.S. Multinational Corporations," *The Accounting Review* (April 1983), 394–402.

30. UN (United Nations Centre on Transnational Corporations). Towards International Standardization of Corporate Accounting and Reporting (New York: United Nations, 1982).

31. UN. *International Accounting and Reporting Issues: 1985 Review* (New York: United Nations, 1985).

32. Rueschhoff[33] analyzed similarities and differences between the IASC's and the EEC's pronouncements as well as between the IFAC's and the UEC's statements and guidelines.

33. N. G. Rueschhoff. "European Accounting and Auditing Standards: A Comparative Study with International Standards and Guidelines," in V. K. Zimmerman (ed.), *The Recent Accounting and Economic developments in*

Western Europe (Champaign, IL: University of Illinois, Center for International Education and Research in Accounting, 1985), 91–114.

34. W. Hall, "Establishing Standards for International Financial Reporting," in J. J. Davis (ed.), *1977 Accounting Research Convocation on the Subject of Patterns of Change* (Tuscaloosa: University of Alabama Press, 1977), 95–106.
35. As another example, in many countries – particularly those in Latin America – the severance payment to an employee upon dismissal or retirement is a totally different construct from pension benefits as thought of in the United States.
36. The trend is apparently continuing, because two of the three IASC's exposure drafts outstanding and one under study – on financial instruments – have also been in the agenda of the FASB.
37. N. G. Rueschhoff. "The Intrinsic Uniformity of International Accounting Standards," in K. S. Most (ed.), *Advances in International Accounting*, Vol. 1 (Greenwich, CT: JAI Press, 1987), 23–38.
38. As an example, IAS 9 on Accounting for Research and Development allows development costs to be either expensed (as required in U.S. GAAP) or deferred if certain conditions are met (as dictated in the U.K. standards).
39. For the countries listed, conformity in all material respects was reported for 17 or more of the 25 standards issued. On the other hand, the West German and Swiss accounting requirement did not conform to those advanced by the IASC in 18 and 15, respectively, of the 25 standards checked.
40. The recent IASC (Ref.27) survey states that in 1987, from a sample of 129 companies listed in the Toronto Stock Exchange, 102 disclosed such compliance.
41. In most cases, referral to IAS consisted in stating that the financial statements have been prepared according to the generally accepted accounting principles of the particular country, and that such principles were in conformity, in all material respects, with IAS.
42. IASC (International Accounting Standards Committee). International Accounting Standard. IAS 1. Disclosure of Accounting Policies (London: IASC, 1975).
43. The assumption of consistency is absent in the new framework developed by the IASC. The "considerations" have been broadened and renamed "qualitative characteristics of accounting information" (see Ref.9).
44. Details of this process are described in the IASC's Objectives and Procedures (Ref.24, pp. 11 051–11 057)
45. H. Benson, "Establishing Standards Through a Voluntary Professional Process Across National Boundaries," in J. C. Burton (ed.). *The International World of Accounting, Challenges and Opportunities, 1980 Proceedings of the Arthur Young Professors' Roundtable* (Reston, VA: Arthur Young, 1981), 27–48.
46. J. M. Samuels and J. C. Oliga. "Accounting Standards in Developing Countries," *International Journal of Accounting* (Fall 1982), 69–88.
47. R. G. May and G. Sundem. "Research for Accounting Policy: An Overview," *Accounting Review* (October 1976), 747–763.
48. C. H. Smith and H. Shalchi. "Multinational Accounting: Some Methodological Considerations," in F. D. S. Choi (ed.), *Multinational Accounting: A Research Framework for the Eighties* (Ann Arbor, MI: UMI Research Press, 1981), 21–37.
49. R. C. Da Costa, J. C. Burgeois and W. M. Lawson. "A Classification of International Financial Accounting Practices." *International Journal of Accounting* (Spring 1978), 73–85.

50. G. G. Mueller, H. Gernon and G. Meek. *Accounting: An International Perspective* (Homewood, IL: Irwin, 1987).
51. C. W. Nobes. "An Empirical Analysis of International Accounting Principles: A Comment," *Journal of Accounting Research* (Spring 1981), 268–270.
52. C. W. Nobes. *International Classification of Financial Reporting* (London: Croom Helm, 1984).
53. L. A. Daley and G. G. Mueller. "Accounting in the Arena of World Politics: Crosscurrents of International Standard-setting Activities," in F. D. S. Choi and G. G. Mueller (eds.), *Frontiers of International Accounting, An Anthology* (Ann Arbor, MI: UMI Research Press, 1985), 157–170.
54. B. E. Needles, Jr. *Comparative International Auditing Standards* (Sarasota, FL: American Accounting Association, 1985).
55. The proposal that harmonization should apply only to companies with international dimension has also been suggested by Nobes (Ref.52, p. 96).
56. Although academicians and practitioners have discussed topics of managerial accounting, these have been approached from the standpoint of the multinational corporation's interest only.[57]
57. V. K. Zimmerman (ed.). *Managerial Accounting: An Analysis of Current International Applications* (Champaign, IL: University of Illinois Center for International Education and Research in Accounting, 1984).

36

SURVIVAL STRATEGIES OF A GLOBAL ORGANIZATION

The case of the International Accounting Standards Committee

R. S. Olusegun Wallace

Source: *Accounting Horizons* 4(2) (1990): 1–22.

This paper is based on the premise that the IASC is a legitimate organization because it continues to be acceptable to its constituencies, in spite of the challenges posed to its credibility by the inevitable crises that surround the pursuit of its goals. In fact, legitimacy implies acceptability in the face of uncertainty; and that, in turn, as Johnson and Solomons[1] argue, implies organizational durability. Whether they focus on the IASC's explicit objectives or its standards, current explanations treat the IASC too superficially and posit a relationship between it and its social environment that seems inflexible. Given the IASC's survival, this paper abandons the assumption that the worst will happen and that unintended consequences will invariably be negative. It separates out the IASC from its standards or actual activity so as to explain why and how it continues to survive.

The paper is in three parts. The first part introduces the topic in the context of a contingency theory which provides the stimulus for the study of the survival strategies of the IASC. The second part presents the survival strategies concerned with the management of technical core resources and the procedural process. The third part explains how the IASC manages its external environment.

Introduction

Researchers studying the IASC have emphasized its standards and treated these standards as choices made by a single actor, and have likened them to those of an individual human being. The authors state propositions about the explicit goals of the IASC which are then presumed to be the only principles for evolving accounting standards. An alternative approach is to focus upon the IASC itself rather than upon its standards, in order to utilize its peculiar characteristics to examine the rationality of its goals, options and consequences. This will enable a researcher to consider either (a) the propensities or institutional traits of the IASC, (b) the values shared by its membership or (c) the special principles of action such as a change in its goals or a narrowing of its alternatives or consequences. This focus could concentrate on the IASC's strategic objectives including its own perpetuation rather than its explicit goals. Yet another approach is the political; the recognition of the existence of several actors within the IASC's central mechanism. The last two approaches could help to explain how the IASC has adapted to, created or shaped its own environment. As Solomons[2] has pointed out:

> International accounting standards [IASs] are not exclusively the concern of any one organization, for governments have not been willing to leave this matter entirely to private initiative. The IASC is unquestionably the voice of the private sector in this field, but it does not have the field to itself. The OECD, made up of highly developed countries, has prepared a Code of Conduct for Multinational Enterprises, which includes, among other things, prescriptions for financial disclosure by multinationals. At the urging of the developing nations, the United Nations has formed an Intergovernmental Group on International Accounting Standards and Reporting.

This quotation emphasizes the market for the supply of global accounting standards in which the IASC is a dominant (not the sole) supplier. To understand such a dominant role, one needs to consider the factors which affect the structure and effectiveness of the IASC. Such an understanding can be informed by a contingency theory of the existence (and survival) of the IASC.

Contingency theory

Previous studies of the IASC have conceptualized the contingency approach very restrictively. Choi and Mueller[3] use varying cross-national differences in environmental characteristics of countries to argue that the IASC cannot be a sustainable entity.[4] Aitken and Islam[5] disagree with this contention. They argue that the transactions and events which accountants seek to measure, value and report are similar across countries and that the IASC's task is to harmonize the different measurement, valuation and reporting practices.

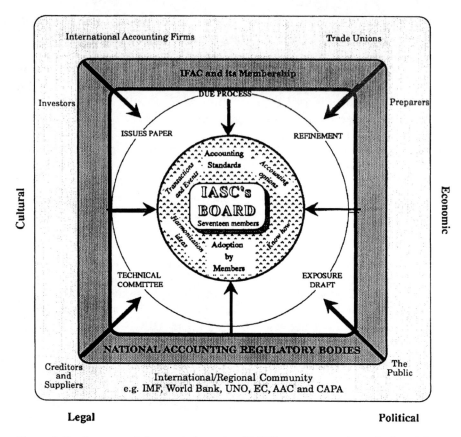

Figure 1 Environmental factors influencing IASC's patterns and survival social.

Similarity of business transactions and events occurring in different countries and different environmental factors are two of the many variables capable of informing an understanding of the IASC's activities and survival. An enlarged perspective on contingency theory, with the inclusion of contextual, environmental and socio-cultural variables can provide a comprehensive understanding of the determinants of the organizational patterns and effectiveness of IASC. An integrative model [Figure 1] provides a means of conceptualizing these variables by visualizing three successive environments: the IASC's internal environment (the core); its tasks and constituencies (the inner boundary) and the varying international environment (the outer boundary). This model stresses the "patterns of relationships" rather than causal linkages. It is from these patterns that one can perceive the intentions of the IASC and its membership.

The internal environment is shown in the center with the Secretary-General and Chairman to the Board determining, in consultation with the Organization and Planning Committee [OPC], the patterns and survival strategies of the IASC. Also determining the scope of operations of the IASC is the size of its staff and budget. Shown on either side to represent what keeps the IASC in existence are business transactions and events, and accounting policy options. Accounting standards are developed, after due process, to resolve measurement, valuation and reporting problems arising from business transactions and events. The standards are the result of choices from among many accounting and disclosure options. Guiding all these operations is the primary goal of the IASC [harmonization] and the know-how of the Board's members.

Surrounding all these activities are the various groups of coalition. The members of International Federation of Accountants [IFAC] who are also members of the IASC are shown at the top. The national accounting standards setting bodies which determine the international recognition of the IASC are shown below. The various external constituencies including investors, preparers, creditors/suppliers and other external parties are shown to form a ring around the entire core, in effect influencing or being influenced by every part of it. Finally, all these groups of interested parties are influenced by different (national) and sometimes common (international) social, cultural, legal, political and economic factors.

This contingency model equates social behavior with political and rational behavior. It posits the existence of a core structure within the IASC composed of some member-bodies (nominated to its Board) with regular, routine and easy access to the IASC's core activities. Member-bodies excluded from the core are denied the ready access and some strive to join the core to gain such privileges. The core is dominated by developed countries while the excluded group is populated by developing countries. However, the core is a conglomeration of independent bodies that promote and defend their own interests.

But many member-bodies share a sufficient level of individual needs (e.g., harmonization of accounting practices) and grievances (e.g., increasing power of transnational enterprises [TNEs]) to produce a common purpose. Their support of the IASC can be seen as a product of environmental forces, internal and external to the IASC. Internal forces include leadership qualities, level of available resources, and the small size and level of professional competence of the IASC's establishment. External forces include the level of the IASC's recognition, extent of external sympathizers [third party constituencies] and the professional capability, capacity and influence of each non-core member-body. The interplay of these various factors can be said to determine the development and behavior of the IASC.

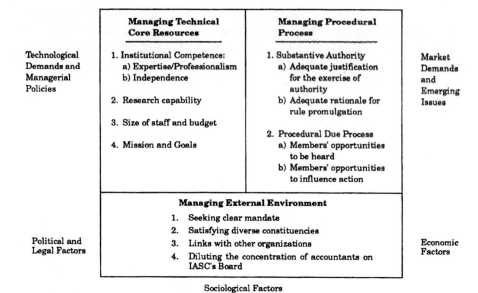

Figure 2 IASC's survival strategies.

Survival strategies: managing core activities

It may be argued that the survival of IASC is a non-issue because the IASC has been functioning since 1973. Institutional survival is an elusive concept which needs to be bounded for a meaningful discourse. Survival, in the context of this paper, connotes the methods by which the IASC sustains itself, adapts to change and the demands of its internal and external environment. The requirements for IASC's survival are examined along the following lines: (a) the resources at its disposal; (b) the diversification of its tasks; (c) the goals it pursues and how such goals are sustained and renewed; (d) the legitimacy of its tasks and procedures and (e) the management of its external environment. Each of these requirements is discussed below and summarized in Figure 2, as the management of (a) technical core resources, (b) procedural process and (c) external environment.

Gradualism and discretion are the hallmarks of the IASC's survival in a potentially hostile environment. Abrupt pursuit of harmonization would attract resistance and place the IASC in jeopardy. But if it acts gradually and quietly, positive steps can be taken, while letting its constituencies build up their support, to help the process of harmonization along. This evolutionary process can be perceived in the way the IASC seeks the support of its member-bodies. It started off in 1973 by emphasizing and strengthening the independence of individual member-bodies. In the 1980s, it sought to strike a sensitive balance between its collective actions and the desires of individual members. This balancing act is now giving way to the need to strengthen the organs of collective responsibility; to let the IASC emerge as a rational actor, different from its individual members.

Technical core resources

The core activities of the IASC can be categorized for analytic convenience into two: the management of technical core resources like the organization of the IASC's office, staffing; and the management of the procedural process. The IASC operates on a meager budget[6] compared to any national regulatory body in the developed world. It has no more than three professionally qualified accountants (including the Secretary-General) on its staff at any time. Ninety percent of the IASC's annual budget is financed, on an equal basis, by its Board members and the rest by IFAC on behalf of its entire membership. No funding comes from its constituencies. As McCarthy and Zald[7] state, "the growth or maintenance of organizations whose formal goals are aimed at helping one population but who *depend* on a different population for funding is ultimately more *dependent* on the latter than the former." This suggests that the IASC is more likely to conform to the wishes of the funding population [its Board members] than the wishes of the beneficiary population [TNEs, stock exchanges, national accounting regulatory bodies of the Third World]. Thus it can be argued that the IASC cannot be said to represent the views of the constituencies it is supposed to serve.

An underlying assumption of the small budget and administrative machinery is that the IASC can draw on the knowledge, perspectives, experience and resources of its many member-bodies especially those of its Board members. The raw materials for forging solutions to global accounting problems are neither concentrated in a single country nor a global accounting profession, but rather are widely dispersed among the various countries' accounting professions and other global non-accounting professional bodies. For any given accounting problem there is a variety of classes of expertise. Every affected party is an expert on some aspect of the problem and its solution. But members do not and cannot contribute equally to the resolution of IASC's problems. For example, the extent of participation in IASC's technical committees, and "procedural due process" depends on the extent of standard-setting experience of a member country.[8] There are three different ways of classifying countries on the basis of capability to set standards:[9]

1. those that originate standards with little or no references to other countries. These are countries with developed standard-setting procedures [i.e., the standard setters]; for example, Australia, Canada, the UK, the Netherlands, and the US. The first three countries, however, make reference to the US and to each other.

2. those that take standards prepared in other countries or by other agencies outside their own countries, without ensuring that such standards are suitable for their environment because they lack the capability and capacity, that is, they do not possess the technical expertise, cannot afford the costs, are afraid of being exposed to *ex ante* complaints or do not want to be held responsible for the scandals which may arise from such disclosure rules *ex post*. Examples are Cyprus, Malawi, Pakistan, Trinidad, and Zimbabwe.
3. those that blend standards from outside sources into their internally generated standards; for example, Egypt, France, Fiji, Germany, India, Japan, Kenya, Nigeria and Singapore.

Many countries in category 1 have accounting professional bodies or regulators that are keenly interested in exporting their internally generated accounting standards to other countries. Although every country is free to "set" its own standards, only a few can originate their standards from scratch. This requires knowledge of available options, exposure to situations requiring accounting regulation (such as an active stock exchange) and adequate resources. While it might be argued that there is usually no need to travel through a well-trodden path in search of a similar solution to a similar problem, it is important to realize that such a journey may be worthwhile if the solution is to be relevant to its environment.

Essentially, if a country has greater resource endowments and capabilities, relatively superior experience in accounting practice and standard-setting process, a litigious citizenry (as in the U.S.), a knowledgeable and free financial press and many companies with foreign subsidiaries and branches, it is more likely that such a country would have more to offer to (than receive from) any institution concerned with international harmonization of financial disclosure practices. This may explain why some members are more capable than others of serving the IASC and why the IASC seeks to utilize the capabilities of these members. Table 1 provides information on the level of participation of member countries in the IASC's technical committees since its establishment.[10]

There are two methods for assessing the extent of the IASC's utilization of individual member's capabilities. The first is to measure the difference between the scope and contents of IASs and the average scope and contents of member countries' standards to reflect how effectively the IASC has benefitted from its members' capabilities in arriving at its output.[11] The second is to measure whether the IASC's output exceeds that of its best member country.[12] Both methods would focus on the synergistic effects of the interaction of the members of IASC. Synergy would exist if the IASC's capabilities surpass those of its members. This is likely to arise when members effectively exchange, constructively criticize and build upon each other's ideas.

Table 1 Participation in All 46 IASC's Technical Steering Committees 1973–1989+.

Countries	Number of Committees		
Board Members	Active	Concluded	Total
Australia (1973)	2	8	10
Canada (1973)	3	10	13
Denmark (1988)	1	2	3
France (1973)	3	9	12
Germany (1973)	1	10	11
Italy (1983)	2	2	4
Japan (1973)	3	8	11
Jordan (1988)	1	–	1
Korea (1988)	–	–	–
Netherlands (1973)	4	9	13
South Africa (1978)	2	4	6
United Kingdom (1973)	5	10	15
USA (1973)	5	10	15
ICCFAA (1986)	1	1	2
Former Board Members			
Mexico (1973–87)	1	8	9
Nigeria (1978–87)	–	3	3
Taiwan (1984–87)	–	1	1
Non-Board Members			
Austria	–	1	1
Belgium	–	1	1
Brazil	1	2	3
Egypt	–	1	1
Greece	1	–	1
Hong Kong*	–	1	1
India	1	1	2
Indonesia	–	1	1
Israel	1	2	3
Lebanon	–	1	1
Malaysia	–	1	1
New Zealand	2	2	4
Norway	–	2	2
Pakistan	–	2	2
Philippines	1	1	2
Singapore*	–	1	1
Spain	–	1	1
Sri Lanka	–	1	1
Sweden	1	2	3
Venezuela*	–	1	1
Yugoslavia	–	1	1
Zimbabwe	–	1	1
Former Non-Board Member			
Argentina**	–	1	1

Table 1 (cont'd)

Non-Board members which have never participated in a Steering Committee

Bahamas	Ghana	Paraquay
Bahrain	Iceland	Portugal
Bangladesh	Iraq	Swaziland
Barbados	Jamaica	Switzerland*
Bolivia	Kenya	Syria
Botswana	Kuwait	Tanzania
Chile	Lesotho	Thailand
Colombia	Liberia	Trinidad & Tobago
Cyprus	Libya	
Dominican Rep	Luxembourg	Tunisia
Ecuador	Malawi	Turkey
Fiji	Malta	Uruguay
Finland*	Morocco	Zambia
	Panama*	

Participation by Board Members in Active Technical Steering Committees

Australia (2)	Fin. Instruments
	Joint Ventures
Canada (3)	Joint Ventures++
	Fin. Instruments
	Improvements
Denmark (1)	Cash Flows
France (3)	Comparability of F.S.
	Review of IAS 12++
	Fin. Instruments
Germany (1)	Banks' F.S.
Italy (2)	Fin. Instruments
	Intangibles
Japan (3)	Banks' F.S.
	Comparability of F. S.
	Fin. Instruments
Jordan (1)	Improvements
Netherlands (4)	Review of IAS 15++
	Comparability of F.S.
	Fin. Instruments
	Improvements
South Africa (2)	Comparability of F.S.
	Cash Flows++
UK (5)	Banks' F.S.++
	Review of IAS 15
	Fin. Instruments
	Intangibles++
	Improvements
USA (5)	Banks' F.S.
	Comparability of F.S.++
	Fin. Instruments++
	Joint Ventures
	Improvements++
ICCFAA (1)	Review of IAS 15

Notes:
+ The author is grateful to David Cairns, Current Secretary-General of the IASC, for supplying this information, on request. This information is current to the end of October 1989 and excludes membership of the Task Force on the needs of developing countries.
++ Chairman of Technical Steering Committee.
* These non-Board members have, in the past, declined an invitation by the IASC to participate in a particular proposed technical Steering Committee.
** This non-Board member has served on an IASC technical Steering Committee but is no longer a member of IASC and IFAC.
( ) Date since joining the Board of IASC or period on the Board.

Degree of professionalization

The Board of the IASC is a professional polity in the sense of achieving coordination essentially by calling upon the professional skills and experience of members acquired through education, training and exposure in their respective countries.[13] Most of the representatives of its members enter with professional qualifications and experience in accounting and/or auditing. Many have had experience as members of national accounting regulatory boards. Many have served as Presidents or Council members of their country's accountancy profession or as heads of the nominating organization. The high professional profile of each person nominated to the Board of the IASC by each member-body springs from the need of each Board member-body to ensure that its candidate goes to represent and secure for it the best terms (output) from the IASC. The concentration of expertise on the Board probably accounts for the high quality of the IASs and the emphasis of those standards on transactions and events that are not peculiar to a particular industry or region; thus ignoring issues of particular relevance to developing countries.

Diversification strategy

The IASC seems to prefer topics of a general nature to industry-specific and region-specific topics. This is probably because the IASC is a mirror of what prevails in many member countries, where industry regulation is less preferred to regulation of transactions and events of a general nature. To embark upon industry-specific regulation is to limit the scope of the IASC's market.[14] Such a regulation will create a bilateral monopoly, where there will be one user group of the IASC's standards—the relevant industry. Also if the IASC regulates all aspects of corporate reporting for such an industry, the industry has only one place where it can buy such regulation. But by adopting the general transactions/events regulation strategy the IASC seeks not only to expand its market, but also to produce parcels of standards which can be distributed across many separated markets and countries. In short, general transactions/events regulation is an improved product. It increases the scope of the IASC's activities immensely, increases the number of affected interest groups and reduces the IASC's dependence on any one industry or group of countries. This diversification strategy provides one explanation of the IASC's global influence.

Under industry- or sector-specific regulation, the IASC would serve fewer groups—the specific industry/sector and its customer class.[15] Since the marginal benefits to the customer class are probably very small, that group will most probably not bother to seek regulation.[16] Therefore, the standards would exist to serve only one industry or one sector. Under general transactions/events regulation, the market for IASs is expanded in two ways. First, the IASC provides service to more than one industry/sector. Second, the standards are likely to be perceived as having a larger impact on many users because they deal with topics from which many different issues and interpretations tend to emerge. Rutherford's[17] specification of the wide variety of the different ways the IASC's standard is used confirms the preceding argument:

> [IASC standards] are used as a vehicle for harmonization within the developed Anglo-American oriented world; as a means by which sophisticated enterprises in one country can communicate with sophisticated investors in other countries; as a source of standards for indigenous enterprises in Third World countries; as a means of regulating the activities of multinationals within the Third World; as a uniform body of standards to be used by companies quoted on several national stock exchanges.

There are innumerable difficulties in balancing these tasks. As McDougall[18] has suggested:

> What is, perhaps, not so obvious is that there are, and must be differences between "what is good for General Motors" [a transnational enterprise] on the one hand and what is good for any nation-state (not excluding the USA) as regards the relations within its own territory between that nation-state and General Motors, between that nation-state and its own companies, and between those national companies and the local subsidiary of General Motors. Problems such as those relating to group accounts, associated and subsidiary companies, transfer pricing, translation of foreign currencies, inflation accounting and costing policies in the extractive industries are among the many where highly skilled accountants can produce very different proposed solutions, all backed by strong arguments that are likely to appeal to those whose interests it is their duty to serve.

> It follows that the profession must not allow itself to be dominated—nationally and internationally—by thinking dictated by consideration only of what is good for, say, transnational companies. There must be an opportunity for the interest of all types of businesses to be represented both on the national and international level.

The preceding discussion suggests a multiplicity of underlying rationales. The internationality of an accounting problem, transboundary transactions (including related-party transactions and debt swaps), the perceived seriousness of an accounting problem in the light of the inadequacy of most or even all national solutions (e.g., financial instruments and off balance sheet transactions), the greater efficiency of collective solutions and the objective of eliminating distortions of the global market for capital—all may help to explain the identification and development of candidates for harmonization and/or the substantive solutions adopted. The interests of Third World countries require, in some cases, particular attention like IAS 29 on financial reporting for hyper-inflationary economies. It is, of course, not easy to identify a single rationale even for an accounting standard.

A genuinely global system of standard-setting contains serious internal strains. If it is to be a system, there must be a measure of coherence between the purposes being pursued by its different member-bodies. If it is to be global, there must be a measure of independence accorded the different members, so that standard-setting in each member-country may respond appropriately to the particular constellations of interests confronting corporate reporting. The IASC's system has evolved a set of arrangements and procedures which may alleviate these internal strains in its quest for harmonization. Before these are discussed, it is necessary to determine what the IASC means by harmonization.

The mission and goals of the IASC

The implicit primary goal of the IASC is harmonization but its official goal (or mission) is "to formulate and publish, in the public interest, accounting standards to be used in the presentation of financial statements." Harmonization can, however, be attained by means other than the development of IASs.

Types of harmonization

The definition of harmonization provided by Nobes[19] as "a process of increasing the compatibility of accounting practices by setting bounds to their degree of variation," suggests that there are other ways of achieving harmonization. For example, each national stock exchange can issue certificates to its domestic registrants whose financial statements have met its standardized review protocols. If such certification is recognized by other national stock exchanges, harmonization is enhanced by the elimination or reduction of repetitive review procedures. Another process of harmonization may be to allow countries to set accounting and disclosure standards in the first instance, subject to centralized review under general criteria, as in the European Communities [EC] model. Yet another is the institutional mechanism operated by the defunct Accountants International Study Group [1966–1977]. This Group founded by Canada, the UK and the US undertook research into the differences in the accounting practices of the three countries and made recommendations on how to harmonize the different practices.

In the context of the approach adopted by the IASC, harmonization is not a matter of either-or propositions but a matter of degree. In an objective appreciation of its inability to force its standards on member-countries, the IASC acknowledges, in its Constitution, that its standards are not intended to supersede local standards. It expects, however, that its member-bodies will use their best endeavors in their respective countries to procure the acceptance of its standards. The problem with this expectation is that member-bodies are not, in many cases, the bodies responsible for regulating accounting principles and practices in their countries. The degree of harmonization which the IASC can pursue and attain depends, therefore, upon the ability of each member-body to use its "best endeavors" to ensure that IASs are adopted within its own country. A full knowledge of the different degrees, will help our understanding of the one which represents the IASC's goals.

Total harmonization would occur when all countries[20] adopt and enforce the same accounting and disclosure standards. This would strengthen the concept of collective responsibility. While there are overwhelming disincentives to total harmonization [variation in preferences, differences in geographical, economic, political, social and cultural conditions; resentment of centralized directions and opposition from reporting TNEs], there are other degrees of harmonization which can mediate the competing claims of total harmonization and national autonomy. These are minimum, partial, optional and alternative harmonization.

Minimum harmonization would occur when member countries adopt standards which are at least as stringent[21] as those recommended by the IASC. But it would not allow member countries to adopt less stringent standards. The minimum "floor" limits member countries' use of weaker accounting standards as incentives for attracting companies to locate in their territories, but allows countries to give effect to more stringent standards. This approach can, however, increase the reporting costs of companies seeking to enter these countries from a country with minimum standards; thus increasing the height of barriers to entry.

Partial harmonization would allow a country to impose stricter or laxer standards on domestic enterprises[22] but forbids imposition of stricter standards on foreign companies. This is what the IASC's current comparability exercise is seeking to achieve: a situation where corporate reports presented on the basis of its own standards will be acceptable to securities regulating organizations in other countries. This may give foreign companies unfair advantage or disadvantage over domestic companies.

Optional harmonization would allow a country to adopt standards different from the global standards but requires the country to allow domestic or foreign companies operating in that country to elect which of the standards to comply with. This is similar to partial harmonization but there are two important differences. First, a country must specifically "opt out" of the global standards. Second, when Country X adopts less stringent standards, foreign companies located in Country X need only comply with its standards rather than the global standards, undercutting the competitive advantage that domestic companies would otherwise enjoy.

Alternative harmonization is the current option of the IASC which allows two or more alternative accounting and/or disclosure methods from which a member country may elect. The IASC may identify a clear preference for one set of methods as in its current proposal to limit allowable options. In such cases, selection of alternatives will ordinarily be allowed only under narrowly defined criteria and this may be subject to later reviews.

The preceding discussion on the resources and mission of the IASC does not explain the potential weaknesses of the IASC's standard-setting process, its vulnerability to political manipulation, its lack of constitutional and legalistic legitimacy and its potential conflict with the culture of many countries. How can (or does) the IASC protect itself against political interference (or manipulation) and ward off attacks on its regulatory process on constitutional and other grounds? This is a question of institutional legitimacy.

Institutional legitimacy

Three conditions for assessing legitimacy (acceptability or defensibility) of a regulatory machinery were presented by Johnson and Solomons.[23] The three conditions for the defense of institutional legitimacy they suggested as collectively sufficient to ward off attacks on the standard-setting process are:

1. The organization must possess a level of authority sufficient to carry out its intended regulatory function given the environment in which it must operate. Possession of "sufficient authority" comes about as a result of proper delegation and institutional competency.[24]
2. The decision-making process of the organization must be impartial and objective and each exercise of authority must bear a direct and substantial relationship to the organizational remit. This condition, referred to as "substantive due process" requires that the organization acts as a fiduciary in arbitrating disputes that may arise between the various interested parties, not as agent of any one party or group.[25]
3. The organization must provide an adequate and an impartial opportunity for interested parties to provide input into the standard-setting process. This "procedural due process" requires that interested parties are kept informed of matters considered by the organization and be given an adequate opportunity to have their views and evidence heard.[26]

In short, institutional legitimacy [IL] is a function of sufficient authority [SA], substantive due process [SDP] and procedural due process [PDP]. An organization's survival is potentially threatened if it lacks any of the characteristics of the elements of IL.

Sufficient authority

SA can be attained when there is a clear mandate and institutional competence. It has been argued that the IASC possesses institutional competence. However, the IASC has no clear mandate, that is, it lacks *de jure* IL. No country has delegated to it the power to prepare its accounting standards. Neither the United Nations which has a broad though vague remit for global order, the OECD concerned with economic cooperation and development among industrialized nations nor the EC has asked it to regulate accounting at the global level on its behalf. Although the IASC does not act directly as agent for any group, the present situation whereby some countries have a permanent seat[27] on its Board creates an apparent over-representation of the interests of developed countries. While it might be argued that the exposure draft procedure and the consultative committee process offer some opportunities for many member countries and non-accounting groups to participate in its substantive due process, it is not apparent that the views and evidence of the majority [the developing countries] are being heard and considered.

Substantive due process

SDP legitimacy exists if the IASC can justify its authority and provide adequate rationale for its standards. It has been suggested that there are multiple rationales for its standards. The lack of adequate justification tends to invite political interference. Solomons[28] has suggested three kinds of defenses against political interference to national accounting regulation: educational, conceptual and structural. One would agree with Solomons that much of the political heat generated by so many accounting arguments could be avoided if the limited significance of many accounting numbers were better understood. Much of the argument arises from the need to enhance the "bottom line" in corporate reports. Educational defense involves the use of persuasive devices to remove the "bottom line" mentality. On conceptual defense, Solomons emphasized that an explicit theoretical foundation, that is, the provision of a conceptual framework [and the IASC has recently issued its own framework] is an indispensable defense against political interference, but as Peasnell[29] argued, this is not the case with the Accounting Standards Committee in the U.K. whose regulatory process is characterized by bargaining. The conceptual framework might be more of a hindrance than a help, since flexibility is the more important in a predominantly bargaining environment; but flexibility seems to be what a conceptual framework is intended to eliminate.

Structural defense is the installation of institutional machineries to ensure that constituencies perceive the legitimacy of the standard-setting process. Solomons does not give a clear statement of how to determine the acceptability of a regulatory process. The two illustrations provided in his paper are only inferential. One is the validity of the process which, in the U.K. context, requires that an accounting standard developed by the Accounting Standards Committee [ASC] needs the approval of each member-body of the Consultative Committee of Accounting Bodies [CCAB] to be operative. The other concerns the independence of the Board members of the ASC who as part-time members are not likely to be perceived as neutral by the very fact of their affiliation to bodies which may be interested in the output of the ASC. These two points apply to the IASC as well. In the first place, there is the expectation that member-bodies of the IASC would use their best endeavors to ensure that the standards issued by the IASC would become acceptable in member countries. A recent survey by the IASC[30] provides overwhelming evidence that only in a few developing countries have such endeavors resulted in a total incorporation of the provisions of IASs into national accounting rules, though many other countries have used the IASs as a basis for their own national standards. If member-bodies have little or no clout in the standard-setting process of their countries, they are not likely to succeed in ensuring the conformity of their national standards with IASs. In respect of the independence of Board members, many of them have affinity with the big international auditing firms or TNEs—two major groups likely to be affected by the output of the IASC. In this case, there is the potential for the IASC to be captured by those it seeks to regulate.

Procedural due process

A legitimate PDP must provide interested parties with sufficient opportunities to be heard and to influence outcome. The presumed endeavor of the IASC, its Board and its entire membership is to arrive at a consensus based on the preferences of the various participants. That is why information about the topic and contents of a future standard is widely circulated among members of the Board, other member-bodies and an international consultative group of interested institutions. In the process a topic takes, on the average, two to three years to become a standard. It is also possible for the Board, at any time during this period, to stop the progress of an evolving standard and to decide to issue a discussion paper on the topic instead.

In resolving differences on any topic, attention is paid to criteria which would ensure the acceptability of a standard. The unwritten but operational procedure is to ensure that the document which finally evolves is satisfactorily received by all target groups—this involves an *ex ante* estimation of the preferences elicited from its membership, various national accounting standard setting bodies and the other target groups such as TNEs and national stock exchanges. To achieve this, there are three possible options which provide alternative ways of understanding the actions or reactions of member-countries to IASs.

The first is the flexibility option. This seeks to capture all present and potential regulators of corporate reporting practices across the world. It aims at the maximization of the number of feasible or acceptable methods (or techniques) for each and every issue covered by a standard. It is because this option recognizes rather than harmonizes differences in accounting practices that the IASC is seeking to reduce the number of options in its current IASs.

The second is the maximum likelihood option. In contrast to the flexibility option, this seeks to identify those methods and techniques with which all countries from which Board members are drawn agree, in the belief that the Board membership is truly representative of the member countries. This belief assumes "vicarious representation" which is the satisfaction or dissatisfaction felt by one member as the direct consequence of the representation of another. Concern about the welfare of others can motivate individuals just as self-interest does. This option suggests as a decision criterion the probability that a choice from among competing methods of recognizing, measuring or disclosing a transaction or event will be optimal when there is uncertainty with regard to preferences associated with the different alternatives by member countries. The task of the IASC will then be to focus on the methods which are acceptable to all its members—a sort of convergent standard or what is described as the lowest common denominator approach.[31] This means that the IASC seeks a middle path between more detailed and less detailed standards. It draws heavily on the work of other national standard setting bodies (especially the U.S., the U.K., Canada, Australia and the Netherlands). It does not carry out much, if any, original work, and it is therefore, not surprising that its standards represent some sort of compromise. This reduces IASs to the level of "second-rate" standards in countries with greater "topic" coverage but it has also enabled the IAS to become a sort of minimum benchmark which some other countries seek to attain. This probably suggests that most member-bodies see the attainment of minimum harmonization as the goal of the IASC.

The third option, which derives from the previous one (though different from it), is the versatility option by which the IASC would prefer to see itself as an organization independent of and distinguishable from its member-bodies. The aim of the IASC would be to ensure that its standards would attain an acceptable level of adoption across the world. The strategy for generating this acceptability would be:

1. to ensure that any group most likely to determine its continued survival as an organization is not "offended" [the 'vital countries hypothesis' of Mason[32]]; or
2. to seek to develop standards which will be acceptable to the majority rather than all the membership.

This strategy is based on the assumption that the IASC is a risk-averse satisficer[33] that aims to minimize the likelihood of not attaining its chosen objectives, one of which is the adoption of its standards by all possible target groups. In this endeavor, the IASC makes it a point of duty to go round all member countries to persuade national accounting regulatory bodies to adopt or recognize its standards. The versatility option is more useful than the others in explaining (i) the strategies of the IASC for survival in an international arena where there are heterogeneous preferences about the IASC's agenda of regulatory items, information needs and the targets which should be regulated and (ii) the adoption of IASs by developing countries instead of the development of accounting and disclosure standards suited to their needs.

Without SA, the drive toward harmonization, to which the IASC has contributed so much, may ultimately be futile. Without SDP legitimacy based on the superiority of solutions to measurement and disclosure problems, the effects of continuing harmonization of corporate disclosure may be the increasing repression of the IASC. These deficiencies of the IASC are presently being overcome by a deliberate management of its external environment, to convert potentially hostile external parties to friendly and supportive allies.

Managing the external environment

The UN link

The United Nations' interest in the standardization of the contents of corporate reports started in the early 1970s, when it created the United Nations Commission for Transnational Corporations [UNCTNC] which discovered in its attempt to assess the impact of TNEs on international business and developing countries that there was a lack of usable financial and non-financial information on TNEs. The different styles of corporate reporting made it difficult to compare TNEs. This led to the creation of a 14-man Group of Experts on International Standards of Accounting and Reporting [GEISAR] in 1974. The experts were chosen from different regional groupings on the basis of professional and academic experience with accounting practices in their regions. The group reported in 1977 and recommended, among other things, the compilation of a list of minimal disclosure items which should be found in TNE's corporate annual report and accounts. The desire to elaborate on the broad and vague recommendations of GEISAR led to the creation in 1979 of an "Ad Hoc Intergovernmental Working Group of Experts on International Standardization of Accounting and Reporting" [Group of Experts]. This 34-member group of experts is made up of government representatives many of whom do not possess the technological competence of the members of GEISAR. Their discussion became more politicized and polarized and fundamental issues in accounting were viewed more from the perspective of economic and regional consequences than from professional validity. This made it impossible for the group of experts to pursue the task of compiling a list of minimum disclosure items with a singular focus. But their deliberations revealed deficiencies in current "general purpose" corporate reporting and led to the conclusion that each country should not discriminate between foreign and domestic companies in its corporate disclosure regulation [one step toward partial or optional harmonization]. The effort of the group of experts towards the development of global accounting standards waned because (i) the UN has no technical competence in the development of accounting standards, (ii) members of the group of experts from the developed world saw this as a duplication (if not dissipation) of the effort of the IASC, (iii) the IASC was granted an observer status at the group's meeting, thus recognizing it as the global standard-setting body and (iv) the group's discussions and deliberations tend to be overwhelmed by political rather than technical considerations. The group decided in 1984 that it should not become involved in standard-setting but should serve instead as a forum for discussion of member needs. The group now sees its role as that of compiling, comparing and reporting regulatory practices in different countries. This shift in emphasis is probably a reflection of the growing influence of the IASC, the difficulty of obtaining a mandate from the Security Council to take on the role, and the concerted efforts of developed countries to discourage the group from pursuing that course.[34] The IASC in concert with others has succeeded in out-maneuvering the UN's attempt to set corporate reporting standards for the TNEs.

Link with regional bodies

The major strategy of the IASC's relationship with regional groups is to keep its secretariat and Board membership informed of regional activities, to attend major regional conferences with potential impact on accounting harmonization and present papers on the IASC and its activities at such conferences. In addition, the Board members of IASC in Europe have continued to play a significant role in weakening the potential threat[35] to the survival of IASC because of the effect of the apparent incongruence between the objectives of the EC intent on harmonizing accounting regulation by the use of alternative harmonization and those of the IASC on those countries which are members of the two institutions.

Link with IFAC

Although IFAC was founded in 1977, four years after the IASC, an agreement of the nature of an absorption [described as "mutual commitments"] was entered into between IFAC and the IASC. This "mutual commitment" came into effect in January 1983. It allows the rationalization of the membership of the two bodies. This meant that professional bodies no longer need to be members of both bodies but only need to be fee-paying members of IFAC to enjoy the benefits of the IASC's membership. The agreement allowed the IASC to retain full autonomy in setting corporate reporting standards and IFAC to endorse automatically all such standards. For the loss of direct subscription from its membership the IASC was to be (and is) given 10 percent of its annual budget by IFAC which also agreed to defray the costs incurred by non-Board member-bodies for participating in steering committees. In return for these contributions, IFAC appoints 13 member-bodies to the 17-member Board of the IASC from July 1986 and has an observer status at the Board meeting of the IASC. The remaining four members of the IASC's Board are co-opted from non-accounting user and interest groups that are not members of IFAC.[36]

The mutual commitment between IFAC and the IASC probably ensures the capture of the IASC by the accounting profession which founded it but prevents it from adopting the current practice of broadening the membership of accounting standard-setting bodies across the world. National accounting regulatory bodies are no longer the exclusive monopoly of the accounting profession.[37] Many now have non-accountants on their boards and are controlled by bodies which seek to protect the interests of the predominant users of corporate annual reports. In the interest of international harmonization of corporate reporting and the legitimacy of the IASC, it is appropriate that both IFAC and the IASC reconsider the propriety of their mutual commitments. Membership of the IASC should belong to standard-setting organizations [not accounting professional bodies] from each country. This is because the "best endeavor pledge" of professional accounting bodies that are not responsible for standard setting in their countries is ineffectual. The IASC should be made up of such organizations as the Council for Annual Reporting in the Netherlands, the Financial Accounting Standards Board in the U.S. and the Australian Accounting Standards Review Board. There is also a need for IFAC to (a) relinquish its hold on the IASC and (b) sponsor the formation of a Global Financial Reporting Foundation to superintend over the affairs of the IASC (that is, to take over the functions now performed by IFAC) and to seek to resource it adequately. The Foundation may comprise IOSCO, IFAC, ICCFAA, the International Financial Executive Institutes, the UNCTNC and the World Bank among others.

Link with Board member countries

The most important and pervasive aspect of the IASC's influence is its practice of rotating the venue of its Board meeting from one Board member country to another. Another is the special alliance which the IASC cultivates with its Board members. This relationship is embedded in the understanding which has evolved over time that the IASC's staff are to deal with such professional bodies through their representatives on its Board and vice versa. This special relationship has two disadvantages. First, there is the danger of the IASC being captured by its professional member-bodies for their domestic purposes. Second, such relationships limit the IASC's access to other agencies that might be more suitable for negotiating certain aspects of its agenda. A good example is the time it took the IASC to evolve a working relationship with the FASB in the U.S. and the little or no relationship between the IASC and other regulatory bodies in countries where the member-bodies do not control accounting regulation.

Link with Non-Board member-countries

The link with non-Board member-countries includes (a) the use of IASs by member-countries; rather than duplicate the IASC's effort, some members rely on the IASC's standards for input into their standard setting process or adopt them with or without amendments as their own standards; (b) the request for nominations to the technical committees on issues in which the IASC believes a member-country can contribute. The most critical issue concerning the adoption of IASs is their relevance to developing countries.[38] For example, a comparative study of the perceptions of users and accountants in Nigeria on the one hand and those of the Board members of the IASC on the other revealed that the IASC does not perceive the same set of measurement and disclosure items as important as do users and accountants in Nigeria.[39] Another critical link is the desire to develop standard setting procedures in member-countries with no experience in this area. The Chairman and Secretary-General of the IASC make regular visits to member-countries to discuss their problems and to advise them on how to use IASs or on how to embark on the development of corporate disclosure standards.

Link with user groups

Initially the IASC was less interested in the views of dominant users of its standards, relying principally on the pledge of its members to use their best endeavors to ensure that IASs are adopted in their respective countries. This may be the most appropriate strategy to start with but it did not seem to work, and the legitimacy of the IASC, as a body composed of professional accountants, to set corporate financial reporting standards at the global level was regularly questioned. At a low level, prior to 1982, and more so thereafter, the IASC opened up a "continuing dialogue" with regulatory bodies and international organizations [such as the potential users of corporate reports prepared on the basis of its standards] as an essential part of its program. It is the increasing intensity of this "continuing dialogue" with the international user community that is a distinguishing feature of the IASC's management of its environment. Although only a few members of the user community recognize what the IASC is, the IASC makes sure that that part of the user community most active in influencing corporate reporting activities of TNEs and government-owned enterprises operating in and from different countries know what it is doing and what it can do for them. These awareness activities are pursued in two ways.

The first is the introduction, in October 1981, of user consultation into the standard-setting process. A consultative group comprising international bodies representing valuers, bankers, financial executives, lawyers, chambers of commerce, trade unions, securities commissions, the World Bank, the International Finance Corporation, and the FASB in the U.S. was formed. The European Commission has recently been invited to join this group. The goal is for the group to include representatives of preparers and users of financial statements and standard-setting bodies. The group meets regularly with the IASC Board to discuss matters of principles and policy arising from the IASC's work and the practical and conceptual issues that affect the acceptability of IASs. The OECD and UNCTNC attend as observers.

The second approach is to co-opt some representatives of international preparers and users to its Board. One such co-option was the admission of the International Coordinating Committee of Financial Analysts Association to the Board in June 1985. Another is the moral suasion of national member-bodies to ensure that their nominations to the Board include both preparers and auditors.

Link with stock exchanges and securities organizations

Apart from the best endeavors of its members, the IASC has sought to make the adoption of its standards visible by advocating the desirability of TNEs to disclose conformity with or identify deviations from IASs. The most important ally in the propagation of IASs is Canada. In that country, the President and Chief Executive of the Toronto Stock Exchange invites, on an annual basis, enterprises listed on the Exchange to disclose the fact of conformity with IASs. Similarly, the Chairman of the Canadian Accounting Standards Committee urges all major accounting firms to encourage their audit clients to comply with IASs and disclose the fact of such compliance in their financial statements. These efforts have resulted in increased disclosure in the annual reports of Canadian listed enterprises. The IASC reported that in 1980, 49 out of a sample of 140 of the large Canadian enterprises listed on the Toronto Stock Exchange made a compliance disclosure. By 1987, 102 out of a sample of 129 such enterprises disclosed compliance with IASs.[40] This overwhelming support is limited to Canada but the IASC will probably not relent in its efforts to increase the support of other national Stock Exchanges.

In February 1985, the US SEC published a consultative document calling for comments on two approaches for the harmonization of disclosure practices in prospectuses and facilitation of transnational securities offerings by enterprises in Canada, the UK and the US.[41] The document suggested two harmonization approaches: (a) *reciprocal*—by which the offering document used by an issuer in its own country would be accepted for offerings in each of the other countries and (b) *common prospectus*—to which all three countries would agree on disclosure standards for an offering document which would be used in more than one country. Although there were 70 responses[42] (50 of which favored the reciprocal approach and 21 [including the IASC's] the common prospectus approach), the US SEC has not decided on how to proceed. This is probably due to the desire to extend the arrangement to other countries, especially Japan. This desire has led to the transformation of the Interamerican Conference of Securities Agencies and Similar Organizations from a regional group to a global body now named the International Organization of Securities Commissions and Similar Organizations [IOSCO]. This new organization has 49 regular members from 45 countries and one affiliate member [the International Finance Corporation]. IOSCO's objectives include (a) to establish standards and an effective surveillance of international securities transactions and (b) to provide mutual assistance to ensure the integrity of the markets by a rigorous application of the standards and by effective enforcement against offenses. IOSCO has set up six working parties to review and propose solutions to regulatory problems related to international securities transactions. One working party would work with the IASC with a view to identifying accounting standards which securities regulators might be ready to accept in the case of multinational offerings. It is more likely that a global grouping of national organizations with jurisdiction over corporate disclosure regulation in their respective countries would want to take over the control of a global body formulating corporate reporting standards.

In 1987, IOSCO accepted an invitation to join the IASC consultative group. IOSCO's membership has meant that it could influence the work of the IASC especially if it believes that IASs could form the basis of the common standards of accounting in prospectuses which it desires to evolve. While IOSCO does not agree that the present portfolio of IASs is adequate for this purpose, it has agreed to take part in IASC's projects concerned with the (a) reduction of options in IASs and (b) improvement of extant IASs to a level which would be acceptable to IOSCO.

At its recent meeting in November 1988, IOSCO issued the following statement which confirms its desire to support the harmonization efforts of the IASC:

> The Technical Committee of IOSCO supports the initiatives by the IASC to revise and expand international accounting standards.

A primary impediment to international offerings of securities is that different countries have different accounting standards. Mutually acceptable international accounting standards are a critical goal because they will reduce the unnecessary regulatory burdens resulting from current disparities between the various national accounting standards, while protecting investors through adequate disclosure in financial statements.[43]

Future directions

Recently [November 1988], the Board of IASC considered and approved that the IASC should focus its attention, during the five years to 1993, on the demands for:

a. truly international standards of accounting and disclosure that can be used by international capital markets and the international business community;
b. the comparability of national and international standards; and
c. accounting standards that developing (and other) countries can use as the basis for national standards and assistance with the implementation of such standards.

If the IASC continues with the "co-option" policy of inviting non-accounting international bodies to join its Board as well as emphasizing its consultation strategies, it will soon become a multilateral professional organization with a potential for responding to emerging international business transactions and events based on its expertise and neutrality. Such a potential would arise from the fact that it would be in a position to draw from a global pool of diversified competences in the interest of international harmonization of accounting practices. This will probably increase its influence as a dominant actor in international regulation of business. As the world of "big" business becomes more and more integrated through the coordination of the world's major stock exchanges and the continuation of cross-national merger arrangements of businesses and auditing firms, the need for corporate reporting standards at the global level will become more pronounced and the legitimacy of a private-sector body affiliated to an international accounting organization [IFAC] will be intensely questioned. At present, enterprises seeking finance for growth from other countries and those seeking to be quoted on foreign stock exchanges have to bear the costs of preparing different sets of corporate reports to satisfy the regulatory bodies in the different countries in which they operate. Such increasing costs make it more compelling that these enterprises welcome any international efforts to narrow and rationalize the many corporate reporting differences into a set of identifiable rules. But that set of rules must not be too permissive. If the IASs cannot be prescriptive [i.e., identify a particular option as the only preferred option], they can at least be proscriptive [i.e., disallow one or more options by reducing the domain and range of options allowable in its standards]. The IASC has decided to adopt the latter.

The IASC has recently issued Exposure Draft No. 32 on "Comparability of Financial Statements." The aim of this draft is "to eliminate most of the choices of accounting treatment currently permitted under IASs," so that like transactions and events can be accounted for in the same way, wherever in the world they are being reported.

The IASC indicated that it will be guided by the undernoted preferability criteria in its attempt to proscribe accounting practices:

a. current worldwide practice and trends in national accounting standards, law and generally accepted accounting principles [especially if they all point to one or two specific options];
b. conformity with its Framework for the Preparation and Presentation of Financial Statements which is its own conceptual basis of accounting;
c. the views of regulators and their representative organizations, such as IOSCO; and
d. consistency within an IAS and with other IASs.

There are many reasons for this obvious change of direction in the IASC's operational strategy. The first is the increasing presence of many non-accounting organizations in the IASC's core deliberations—many of these organizations desire accounting standards documents to have internal consistency and integrity. Of particular relevance is the indication of many securities regulators [including the SEC in the U.S.] that they are willing to consider the possibility of allowing foreign TNEs quoted on their stock exchanges to file corporate annual reports and accounts prepared on the basis of IASs if the IASC will reduce many of the options in its current stock of IASs. The second reason is the increasing convergence of the different corporate reporting rules of the member countries of the EC. Their demands for the inclusion of country-specific accounting options in IASs is probably not as intense as it was before the 4th Directive of the EC was implemented by member countries. The third is the need to enhance the comparability of accounting statements prepared by enterprises located in different parts of the world.

There are, however, potential problems for the IASC. The Dearing Committee (set up to review the accounting standard-setting process in the UK) suggests that the attempt of the IASC to reduce the number of options in its standards may pose some difficulties for the U.K. Accounting Standards Committee, especially if the IASC comes down against some options favored in the U.K.[44] This is probably true of many countries with developed accounting standard-setting procedure. Another problem is the possibility that some Third World countries currently conforming with the IASs may discontinue the practice because the options they prefer are no longer permitted and the permitted options are evolved on the assumptions that there is an efficient stock market and that the accounting competence of all countries is comparable to that in the developed world. For example, it is proposed to eliminate the completed contract method as an option for the recognition of revenue and net income on construction contracts. Many construction contracts in developing countries are undertaken by joint ventures between Third World investors and/or governments and TNEs/governments of developed countries. If profits are only allowed to accrue without recognition of the uncompleted portion of a contract, an abandoned contract would create a burden on local investors especially if foreign partners have remitted their share of recognized profits and have left the resolution of post-completion problems to local partners. In some cases, the post-completion costs may overwhelm the profits which had accrued to local partners.

The point was made earlier that Third World countries require more assistance if they are expected to move along with the international community. In pursuit of this goal, the IASC can play the role of a catalyst by introducing programs which will help to train people of the Third World in setting their own standards. The IASC can also develop a system of providing exports on secondment to accounting standard-setting bodies of the Third World. This would require more funds than is available to the IASC at present. But given the will, and its international prestige, the IASC can collaborate with international development organizations to raise such funds. The IASC can also undertake research studies of the state of accounting in specific countries and sectors and on specific accounting problems. This will provide immense assistance to the international community and will also identify many issues worthy of inclusion in the agenda of the IASC.

There are still important accounting topics and corporate disclosure issues which require further harmonization and collective solutions at the global level. One such issue is accounting for financial instruments. Many new financial instruments (including the swapping of Third World debts) which are being created across national borders by financial institutions do not come under any extant national corporate disclosure regulation and are hardly reported in corporate reports of the affected parties. An attempt is presently being made to evolve a global solution. The IASC and the Canadian Institute of Chartered Accountants have formed a joint working party to study the problems and to develop an exposure draft in this area for adoption by the two bodies. There are other disclosure problems—like the treatment of taxation in corporate reports, cash flow statements, interim financial reporting and the computation and reporting of earnings per share—where divergent national measures justify the intervention of the IASC in the interest of international harmonization of corporate financial reporting. There is also the need to enhance the level of participation of the Third

World. The present situation whereby these countries adopt the standards developed by the IASC and some standard setting bodies from the developed world regardless of the relevance of these standards to their environments will not do.

Conclusion

The IASC is probably here to stay. Its inadequacies and survival strategies have been examined. Despite its lack of *de jure* institutional legitimacy, the IASC has managed to generate a global constituency of broad public support. Its survival is being sustained by (a) the increasing internationalization of business and finance which make global harmonization of accounting and disclosure practices desirable, (b) the composite nature of its standards and its preoccupation with topics of a general nature, (c) its evolutionary strategy and (d) the absence of a rival organization with keen and prolonged interest in the development and marketing of global accounting standards.

If the IASC did not exist, there would be a need for an organization to harmonize differing national accounting and disclosure standards. The appearance of IOSCO in 1985 with a desire to harmonize differing national rules for securities offerings increases the need for an international organization to harmonize differing national and international corporate disclosure rules and poses a threat to IASC's survival. But IOSCO seems to have left this task to the IASC. So the critical question is not whether one needs an IASC but whether we have the appropriate IASC. One suggestion concerns the potential benefit to the Board of the IASC of a restructuring of its membership and the injection of non-accounting international bodies interested in corporate reporting as regulators, users, preparers and advisers. Another suggestion is the improvement in the manpower and funding of the IASC. International harmonization of corporate disclosure practices seeks to serve more than the accounting profession. Such pursuits should be endowed with much more financial and technical staff than is presently available. Yet another suggestion concerns the probable improvement in the acceptance and relevance of IASs if the IASC seeks to evolve a tiered standardization process which can differentiate between big and small TNEs found in developed countries, and smaller TNEs emerging from developing and newly industrialized countries on the one hand, and big and small domestic enterprises on the other. It seems inappropriate to apply a single IAS uniformly to all reporting enterprises of different sizes, especially when it is obvious that the benefits of that application far outweigh the costs for only a few of them. An IAS that is worthwhile in terms of benefit/cost analysis for a TNE may be less worthwhile for a domestic enterprise in a developing country.

As enterprises, investors and lenders continue to ignore national boundaries and cultures they would continue to support those efforts which seek to encourage the increasing internationalization of business and finance. It is on such a support that the survival and future prospects of the IASC depend. The comparability project is probably a turning point in the history of the IASC. It is more likely that the IASC will spend less time on the development of new standards but more on the review of existing standards and the removal of options which are mutually unacceptable in the international arena. The IASC may increase its interest in the promotion and liaison work in order to increase further the use of IASs. Following from its ongoing project on the search for the needs of financial reporting in developing and newly industrialized countries, the IASC could begin to provide help to developing countries in the creation of a standard-setting process and the interpretation of IASs.

Acknowledgements

The author acknowledges the helpful comments on earlier drafts of this paper from Professor R. H. Parker and Dr. Terry E. Cooke of the University of Exeter, Professor C. W. Nobes of the University of Reading, Professor Helen Gernon of the University of Oregon and David Cairns, Secretary-General of the IASC. The author served as Technical Adviser to the Nigerian members on the IASC's Board from 1983 to 1988. The personal views expressed in this paper are neither those of the Nigerian delegation nor of the IASC.

Notes

1 Steven B. Johnson and David Solomons, "Institutional Legitimacy and the FASB," *Journal of Accounting and Public Policy* (Vol. 3, No. 3, Fall 1984), p. 167.
2 David Solomons, *Making Accounting Policy: The Quest for Credibility in Financial Reporting* (New York, Oxford University Press, 1986), pp. 59–60.
3 F. D. S. Choi and G. G. Mueller, *International Accounting* (Englewood Cliffs, New Jersey: Prentice-Hall Inc., 1984).
4 Other scholars have doubted the continued survival of the IASC. These include D. De Bruyne, "Global Standards: A Tower of Babel?", *Financial Executive* (February 1980) and C. W. Nobes, "Is the IASC Worthwhile?", *International Accounting Bulletin* (February 1986), p. 14.
5 M. J. Aitken and M. A. Islam, "Dispelling Arguments Against International Accounting Standards," *The International Journal of Accounting Education and Research* (Vol. 19, No. 2, Spring 1984), pp. 35–46.
6 Its annual revenue and capital expenditure has risen from £100,000 in 1973 to £400,000 in the 1989 budget. Its earnings from sales of standards and other publications are insignificant.
7 J. D. McCarthy and M. N. Zald, *The Trend of Social Movements in America: Professionalization and Resource Mobilization* (Morristown, NJ: General Learning Corporation, 1973), p. 18, emphasis added.
8 A member country is one in which a member body of the IASC is located.
9 Examples of countries suggested are taken from the LASC's *Survey of the Use and Application of International Accounting Standards, 1988* (London: IASC).

10 There have been 46 technical steering committees between June 1973 and October 1989. These are made up of (a) nine ongoing (active) committees, three of which have issued Exposure Drafts 32, 33 and 34; (b) completed committees resulting in 29 IASs [two of which have been withdrawn—IASs 3 and 6]; (c) one on the completed conceptual framework; (d) one led to the issue of a discussion paper on accounting for banks; (e) three committees reviewed IASs 1, 3 and 6 and (f) three committees on assets, liabilities and objectives of financial statements dissolved when the committee on the conceptual framework was constituted.

11 This method assumes that all members have developed the standards under investigation before the IASC issued its own which is not always the case. For three examples of IAS topics not covered by any extant accounting standards in the U.S. see C. W. Nobes "A Note on the Compliance by U.S. Corporations with IASC Standards," *British Accounting Review* (Vol. 22, No. 1, March 1990), pp. 41–49.

12 This is based on the belief that two or more heads are better than one. However, compared to the U.S., which can, intuitively, be described as the "best" member of the IASC in the context of the number and quality of extant accounting standards developed by each member country, the IASC's standards are poorer "cousins."

13 For more on the concept of professional bureaucracy, see H. Mintzberg, *The Structuring of Organizations* (Englewood Cliffs: Prentice-Hall, 1979).

14 It can be argued that the evolutionary (rather than revolutionary) profile of the IASC compels the pursuit of transactions/events of general nature and that industry regulation may follow after key underlying issues have been dealt with as in the U.S. and the U.K.

15 The customer class includes national accounting regulators for the specific industry/sector, preparers, users and auditors of corporate annual reports in the specific industry/sector not all of which actively seek regulation.

16 IASC's detour into regulation of financial reporting in the banking industry may be due to the fact that it perceives the marginal benefits to its constituencies to be high.

17 Brian Rutherford, "A Pat on the Back but Time for a Change," *Accountancy* (July 1987), p. 18.

18 E. H. V. McDougall, "Regional Accountancy Bodies," in *The Internationalization of the Accountancy Profession*, J. W. Brennan (ed.) (Toronto: The Canadian Institute of Chartered Accountants, 1979), p. 18. For a similar argument with an explicit diagrammatic illustration see C. Nobes, "Harmonization of Financial Reporting," in C. W. Nobes and R. H. Parker (eds.), *Comparative International Accounting* (Oxford: Philip Allan, 1985), pp. 341–42.

19 C. Nobes, "Harmonization . . . ," op. cit., p. 331.

20 A country represents a national accounting regulatory body. It may be a professional accounting body that is a member of the IASC, a government agency, a body made up of a mixture of accounting profession, government agency and other interested users and preparers of accounts. It may also stand for generally accepted accounting practices in a country with no identifiable regulatory agency.

21 Stringency, in the context of accounting standards, refers to a demand for more rather than less disclosure and to a decision to prescribe or proscribe specific measurement and/or disclosure (i.e., presentation) methods rather than to permit all available options.

22 This raises the problem of which entities should come within global harmonization rules—should it be TNEs, local companies with no multinational interests, public or private limited companies, government-owned enterprises, joint

ventures between two or more enterprises/governments from different countries? The IASC believes that its standards apply to all. The earlier quotation from Brian Rutherford ("A Pat on the Back . . ." op. cit.), a former Assistant Secretary of the IASC, attests to this belief.

23 Johnson and Solomons, op. cit., pp. 172–79.

24 Ibid., p. 172.

25 Ibid., p. 173.

26 Ibid., p. 174.

27 As will become clear in the discussion of the link between the IASC and IFAC, no member now has a permanent seat. In practice, however, some probably will have, because of their expertise and long-standing experience in the standard-setting process. Since membership of the IASC implies neither activity nor much in the way of financial support, the members with little or no expertise and finance to contribute could not have been expected to have a serious voice in the policy formulation of the IASC.

28 D. Solomons, "The Political Implications of Accounting and Accounting Standard Setting," *Accounting and Business Research* (Vol. 13, No. 50, Spring 1983), p. 115.

29 K. V. Peasnell, "The Function of a Conceptual Framework for Corporate Financial Reporting," *Accounting and Business Research* (Vol. 12, No. 48, Autumn 1982), pp. 243–56. Recently, more interests have been shown by some members of the Accounting Standards Committee in the U.K. David Solomons addressed to the Accounting Standards Committee a report, *Guidelines for Financial Reporting* (1989), prepared for the Research Board of the Institute of Chartered Accountants in England and Wales. The Institute of Chartered Accountants, Scotland also produced a document on *Making Corporate Reports Valuable* (1988). More importantly, the Accounting Standards Committee in the U.K. announced that it proposes to use the IASC's *Framework for the Preparation and Presentation of Financial Statements* (1989) as a benchmark against which its future proposals will be measured.

30 IASC's Survey . . . op. cit.

31 This term was used to describe the IASC's approach by R. D. Fitzgerald in "International Harmonization of Accounting and Reporting," *The International Journal of Accounting Education and Research* (Vol. 17, No. 1, Fall 1981), pp. 22–32. Fitzgerald's meaning of the term must be distinguished from its meaning here. In the context used here, it refers to a set of standards or practices applicable in all countries—a sort of convergent standard. In the context of Fitzgerald's meaning, an IAS is a set of composite standards from different countries. What prevailed when Fitzgerald wrote was an IAS that allowed each country to more or less have its own way.

32 A. K. Mason, *The Development of International Financial Reporting Standards*, ICRA Occasional Paper No. 17 (International Centre for Research in Accounting, University of Lancaster, U.K., 1978), p. 40.

33 See Herbert Simon, "A Behavioural Model of Rational Choice," *Quarterly Journal of Economics*, (Vol. 69, No. 1, 1955), pp. 99–114.

34 This is probably because the developed countries, particularly the U.S., were concerned that their influence would not be as extensive at the UN compared with the IASC.

35 For a full discussion of such a threat see, D. McComb "International Accounting Standards and the EEC Harmonization Program: A Conflict of Disparate Objectives," *The International Journal of Accounting Education and Research* (Vol. 17, No. 2, Spring 1982), pp. 35–48.

36 Only one of these seats has been filled by the International Coordinating Committee of Financial Analysts' Associations [ICCFAA]. It has recently been suggested that one of the seats be offered to the International Organization of Securities Commissions.

37 In countries like France, Germany, Japan, etc., accounting regulatory bodies never were in the hands of the accounting profession.

38 For arguments on the irrelevance of the IASC's standards to developing countries see, R. J. Briston, "The Evolution of Accounting in Developing Countries," *The International Journal of Accounting Education and Research* (Vol. 14, No. 1, Fall 1978), pp. 105–20 and J. M. Samuels and J. C. Oliga, "Accounting Standards in Developing Countries," *The International Journal of Accounting Education and Research* (Vol. 18, No. 1, Fall 1982), pp. 69–88.

39 R. S. O. Wallace, "Intranational and International Consensus on the Importance of Disclosure Items in Financial Reports: A Nigerian Case Study," *British Accounting Review* (Vol. 20, No. 2, December 1988), pp. 223–65.

40 IASC's Survey . . . op. cit., pp. 70–71.

41 See Securities Act Release No. 6568 (February 28, 1985) or *Federal Register*, Vol. 50, No. 45, March 7, 1985.

42 See Clarence Sampson, "Facilitation of Multinational Securities Offerings," in *Research in Accounting Regulation*, edited by Gary J. Previts, Volume 2 (Connecticut, JAI Press Inc., 1988), p. 216.

43 See *IASC News*, The Newsletter of the IASC, Vol. 18, No. 1, January, 1989, pp. 2–3.

44 Accounting Standards Committee (UK), *The Making of Accounting Standards*, Report of the Review Committee under the Chairmanship of Sir Ron Dearing CB (London: The Institute of Chartered Accountants in England and Wales, 1988), p. 5.

37

INTERNATIONAL ACCOUNTING HARMONIZATION

The impossible (and unnecessary?) dream

Richard Karl Goeltz

Source: *Accounting Horizons* 5(1) (1991): 85–8.

If financial measurement standards are to be made more meaningful, one of the first issues to be confronted is the need for harmonization across national boundaries. While it may appear obvious that such a step is desirable, I believe that there are serious questions as to whether much money or effort should be expended to achieve a unified set of accounting principles across borders.

To be sure, a common denominator would be beneficial. To argue by analogy, most historians would agree that the nearly universal use of the English language and a single currency contributed greatly to the economic development of the United States. One language and one monetary unit reduce costs and friction, leading to greater economic efficiency. These benefits are still believed to be valid as is evidenced by the European Community's objective of ultimately creating one currency for that region.

It might seem that an equally strong case can be made for the harmonization of accounting standards. Clearly, advantages would be obtained from this step. Adjustments, often arbitrary and perhaps based on faulty assumptions, would no longer be needed in order to place the financial reports of companies in different domiciles on the same basis. Accuracy would be enhanced and effort saved. Investors, security analysts, academicians and other users would take comfort in a Global GAAP. Some have even asserted that international accounting standards are requisite for the development of a global securities market. I would not only challenge that contention, but go further. Full harmonization of international accounting standards is probably neither practical nor truly valuable.

Consider first the matter of practicality. The record of domestic stand-ard setting bodies in the United States where they have been well funded and supported by government regulators does not offer much hope that the infinitely more difficult task of gaining international agreement can be achieved in any reasonable time period.

An examination of the limited progress of the FASB in recent years leads quickly to the conclusion that consistent worldwide accounting standards are virtually certain to remain an elusive goal. In the last three years, for example, the FASB has promulgated only one completely new standard — FAS 105. It requires the disclosure of information about financial instruments. All the other standards during this period merely have modified in some way previous pronouncements. To illustrate, FAS 101 provides that when a regulated company becomes deregulated, regulatory accounting is no longer appropriate. This standard is certainly not contentious, nor does it seem to push forward the frontiers of accounting theory.

The recent decision to require a super majority at the FASB rather than a simple one seems likely to result in even more plodding, piecemeal efforts. I fear that this will lead to the Board addressing arcane but simple issues, while more important one will be avoided or deferred. As an example, there is speculation that the FASB may postpone yet again the implementation of FAS 96 to field test its position on the recognition of deferred tax assets. If an adopted standard cannot be implemented in three years, how long might we expect it to take for a standard covering an important but difficult and politically contentious topic such as accounting for inventories to reach fruition?

My purpose is not to attack the FASB. Rather, I cite the lack of signi-ficant output in recent years to support my contention that harmonization of international accounting principles is unlikely to come about. Too many different national groups have vested interests in maintaining their own standards and practices which have developed from widely different perspectives and histories. There is not a single, powerful champion of the proposal for harmonization. There is no authoritative body with the ability to mandate the adoption of Global GAAP. The situation is not analog-ous to that of the single currency unit (ECU) in the European Community. Even Canada and the United States, linked by many common business and accounting traditions and now by a common market as well, have been unable to agree on an entire corpus of sound accounting principles and financial statement presentation. We have been coming closer, but the melding is not complete.

An issue as potentially important as harmonization of international accounting standards should not be dismissed solely because numerous impediments to its adoption exist. If the value of the objective were sub-stantial enough, a means would be found to achieve it. But it is not clear whether significant benefits would be derived in fact. A well developed global capital market exists already. It has evolved without uniform accounting standards.

Deregulation, the elimination of capital controls, improved communications, dis-intermediation and greater sophistication on the part of issuers and their advisors have expanded the sources of funds available to corporations. Absent a massive shock such as a worldwide depression, I am confident that the global capital market will continue to expand both in size and scope. Funds can flow to areas and activities which promise the highest returns or reduce risks with diversification.

Statistics from the IMF illustrate the robustness of the global capital market. Equities are more likely than debt instruments to be adversely affected by different accounting principles and therefore provide the more rigorous test. Equity securities sold to investors outside the issuer's home country jumped from $300 million in 1984 to $15 billion in 1989, a fifty-fold increase. Equity linked bonds placed internationally increased from $11 billion to $88 billion in the same period. While straight bonds grew less proportionately during these years, in absolute terms their growth was even greater, from $110 billion to $250 billion. It is not hyperbole to describe the recent growth of the international capital market as explosive, and it took place despite the absence of Global GAAP.

Focusing exclusively on new international equity and debt instruments does not, however, provide a comprehensive understanding of the extent of global integration of capital markets. The increasing importance of swap transactions must be recognized as well. Interest rate and currency swaps were virtually nonexistent ten years ago, while today their total value probably exceeds $2 trillion. These derivative products are a substitute in many ways for the direct issuance of a debt security in a foreign market. A corporation can use swaps effectively to borrow fixed rate sterling or floating rate Swiss francs without ever leaving North America. Any discussion of the global capital market must recognize the economic substance of swaps. The lack of accounting harmonization has not hampered the growth of the swap market.

If issuers of securities have been well accommodated by international capital markets, it is reasonable to hypothesize that investors have also been cared for. This proposition is supported by empirical evidence. Transactions in domestic stocks involving non-residents have grown rapidly in the past decade. Such transactions now account for roughly 12 percent of the total world stock exchange trading value. One out of every nine equity trades involves a non-resident. It is worth noting in this connection that foreigners have been particularly enthusiastic investors on the Tokyo Stock Exchange, notwithstanding prodigious price/earnings multiples, numerous insider trading scandals and inscrutable Japanese accounting principles.

In addition to the increase in international transactions, there has been an equivalent increase in the cross border holding of investment assets.

The percentage of pension plan assets held in foreign securities has risen steadily for every major industrial country. In the U.K. at the present time, 20 percent of private pension funds are dedicated to overseas investments. Even U.S. pension fund investors have broadened their view. From almost zero in 1980, over 5 percent of U.S. pension fund assets is not committed overseas.

There has also been a blossoming of closed-end country investment funds. As recently as five years ago these virtually did not exist in the United States. In the period from 1985 to the present, 41 closed-end country funds were launched in the U.S. raising a total of almost $5 billion for foreign investment.

These data suggest that investors as well as issuers seem able to make investment decisions without the convenience of international accounting standards. There seems no reason to expect that our integrated global capital markets are likely to shrink in the future as a result of this lack. Indeed, it seems much more plausible to expect these markets to continue to grow.

One related development which may help to expand international capital markets is the recent adoption of Rule 144A by the SEC. This rule provides an exemption from SEC registration and reporting requirements in connection with sales of securities to large institutional investors. This should result in a broader, deeper, more liquid market in the United States for instruments of foreign companies, since they will be able to issue debt and equity in the U.S. without complying with SEC registration requirements which include U.S. GAAP financial statements. Investors will, of course, demand financial information but the issuer's accounts prepared on the basis of its home country standards are likely to suffice. To the extent more data are necessary, the determination will be made by the market, not by accounting standard setters or regulators. This rule is still in its embryonic stage, and its effects cannot be forecast with confidence, but my assessment is that both foreign issuers and U.S. institutional investors are likely to embrace the opportunity enthusiastically. The fact that this is a step away from accounting standardization is not likely to weigh heavily in their thinking.

I have argued that Global GAAP is unlikely to be achieved due to the institutional impediments in the standard setting process, and because there is no demonstrated need in order to fuel the growth of robust international capital markets. My final argument is that evidence also seems to suggest that rational investors are able to pierce the accounting veil and focus on real economic results. This ability to use accounting and other data to predict future cash flows which are the ultimate source of investment value seems to rest on the effective use of data rather than its uniformity. Academic researchers in the U.S. have generally concluded that the market does not respond to changes in earnings caused by cosmetic changes in accounting policies. Accounting alternatives which have been tested for market impact include FIFO/LIFO, flow through vs. deferral of investment tax credits, full cost vs. successful efforts methods for oil exploration, and the effect of volatility in net income resulting from various foreign currency translation methodologies. The conclusions from this research suggest that the market does not simply accept reported earnings. Security analysts, portfolio managers and investors examine footnotes and other textual disclosures for differences in accounting when comparing the performance of and prospects for companies. The evidence for the U.S. stock market is that all publicly available information is included in market price; in other words, the market is information efficient.

While the evidence developed to date refers largely to the U.S. stock market, and I cannot conclude from it that fully efficient markets exist outside the U.S., I do believe that analysts around the world are able to adjust published financial statements sufficiently to determine the relative attractiveness of an investment vehicle, at least to the point where the crucial investment decision making variables are not based on accounting differences. Investors are rational and will expend the necessary time and money to analyze investment opportunities correctly.

38

THE IASC AND ITS COMPARABILITY PROJECT

Prerequisites for success

S. E. C. Purvis, Helen Gernon and Michael A. Diamond

Source: *Accounting Horizons* (June 1991): 25–44.

Introduction

As the volume of international financial operations and cross-border investments continues to surge, the need for a common language of business in
financial statements is increasing in urgency. It has long been argued that
different national accounting standards militate against the efficiency of
international capital markets and may even impair the ability of corporations to compete effectively for capital in those markets. Barthes observed
that the:

> business community is tired of differences in accounting. These
> differences lead to increased costs for those companies that operate
> and raise capital abroad and to an unlevel playing field for those
> international companies that are competing with one another for
> business opportunities.[1]

In the last three decades, standard-setters[2] and regulators[3] in different
countries have grappled with the problems posed by different national standards. Several international institutions have risen to the challenge presented
by the development of international accounting standards. These include
the United Nations (UN), the European Community (EC), the Organisation for Economic Cooperation and Development (OECD), all governmental
or quasi-governmental institutions, and the International Accounting
Standards Committee (IASC), the only private standard-setter in the international arena. Two years ago, the IASC released Exposure Draft 32 (ED32),
"Comparability of Financial Statements," proposing an improved set of

international standards.[4] ED32 represents the culmination of a two-year project which had been encouraged by the International Organisation of Securities Commissions (IOSCO), and stakes the IASC's claim to be the preeminent provider of international financial accounting and reporting standards.

The purpose of this article is to assess the likely compliance with ED32 and to debate the prerequisites for the success of the IASC's proposal for international accounting comparability. The next section analyzes national compliance with existing IAS, and identifies several factors which may hinder this comparability attempt. The third section briefly reviews ED32 and discusses the likely compliance of five major countries with ED32. In the fourth section, possible responses from different groups of countries to the IASC's move are considered. In the fifth section, prerequisites for success of the Comparability Project are reviewed. In the sixth section, the desirability of harmonization is debated. Finally, it is concluded that the IASC needs the cooperation and endorsement of standard-setters and regulators in the major markets in order to realize the aims of the Comparability Project.

Review of compliance with existing IAS

In 1988, the IASC published a major survey[5] of compliance with international accounting standards (IAS) in force at that time. Member institutions were asked to indicate the extent to which national standards or practices conformed with the 25 IAS.[6] Responses received from 54 member countries were reported in tabular form, but were not subjected to examination by the IASC. This study analyzes the IASC data from several different perspectives, including compliance by standard and by country.

Compliance by standard

Table 1 shows the current level of compliance with existing IAS on a standard by standard basis. The numbered columns record the presence or absence of substantial conformity, as defined in the table.

The categories employed by the IASC in its questionnaire may be distinguished into conforming versus non-conforming responses (columns 1–4 and 5–6 respectively). In order to evaluate the degree of compliance with the 25 existing standards, two conformity indices were constructed. In each percentage-based index, the numerator represents the sum of all *conforming* responses (in columns 1–4). There are two possible choices for the denominator: (A) the sum of conforming and nonconforming responses (in columns 1–6), or (B) 54, the number of countries surveyed.[7] The difference between the two denominators is column 7, which represents the number of countries omitting a response, or otherwise indicating that a particular standard was not applicable. The two indices are highly correlated (Spearman's

Table 1 Conformity with existing standards: analysis by standard.

Standard	Response Category							Conformity Index A	Conformity Index B
	1	*2*	*3*	*4*	*5*	*6*	*7*		
IAS 1	7	7	25	9	3	2	1	90.6%	88.9%
IAS 2	7	4	30	7	5	1		88.9%	88.9%
IAS 3	7	4	21	13	4	4	1	84.9%	83.3%
IAS 4	7	7	29	10	1			98.2%	98.2%
IAS 5	7	6	28	11	2			96.3%	96.3%
IAS 7	7	4	24	15	1	3		92.6%	92.6%
IAS 8	7	3	30	8	4	2		88.9%	88.9%
IAS 9	7	4	18	12	7	2	4	82.0%	75.9%
IAS 10	7	6	28	11	1	1		96.3%	96.3%
IAS 11	7	6	21	15	2	2	1	92.5%	90.7%
IAS 12	7	3	16	8	9	6	5	69.4%	63.0%
IAS 13	7	5	26	13	2	1		94.4%	94.4%
IAS 14	7	2	6	10	7	19	3	49.0%	49.3%
IAS 15	4	5	11	5	22		7	42.6%	37.0%
IAS 16	7	3	26	14	2		2	96.2%	92.6%
IAS 17	7	3	15	10	6	11	2	67.3%	64.8%
IAS 18	7	4	18	18	2	1	4	94.0%	87.0%
IAS 19	6	4	13	9	3	11	8	69.6%	59.3%
IAS 20	6	1	17	14	4	7	5	77.6%	70.4%
IAS 21	7	6	17	11	6	4	3	80.4%	75.9%
IAS 22	6	2	15	14	5	8	4	74.0%	68.5%
IAS 23	7	4	15	17	2	5	4	86.0%	79.6%
IAS 24	4	1	15	12	2	14	6	66.7%	59.3%
IAS 25	4	3	16	14	5	4	8	80.4%	68.5%
IAS 26	4	3	6	9	3	15	14	55.0%	40.7%
Total	160	95	480	295	93	145	82	80.5%	76.3%

Notes: The response categories are defined as follows:
  1. "IAS adopted as national standard"
  2. "IAS used as the basis for a national requirement"
  3. National requirements conform "in all material respects with IAS"
  4. National practice "generally conforms with IAS"
  5. National requirements do "not conform with IAS"
  6. "National practice does not generally conform with IAS"
  7. Not applicable[1]
2. The values represent the number of countries (out of 54) that selected each response category.

[1]Some countries were not assigned a response in the IASC survey results. Recent correspondence with the IASC indicates that these should be coded "Not applicable," and therefore they have been assigned to category 7.

correlation coefficient, rho = .849), and strongly statistically significant (p = .0001). Note that the number of countries in column 7 increases directly with the recency of the standard. Indeed, Spearman's correlation (rho) of the standard number (as a proxy for issue date) with column 7 is .746, a very high degree of association, which explains more than half of the observed variance (r^2 = .558).

Some of the missing responses surely reflect a lack of compliance with the standards rather than the standards' lack of relevance to the country. It is difficult to imagine that a country could argue that IAS1 "Disclosure of Accounting Policies" is 'not applicable'! Consequently, Index B is used in subsequent analyses because it more accurately reflects *active* compliance.

Conformity by standard

An examination of Table 1 shows a high level of conformity with the first group of standards issued, but much lower levels for standards issued more recently. Both conformity indices show a strong negative correlation with the date on which each standard came into effect (Index A, rho = −.534, p = .006; and Index B, rho = −.640, p = −.0006). There are (at least) two explanations for this negative relationship. First, the early standards tended to address more fundamental issues at a high level of generality, which enabled many countries to conform with a minimum of effort. As noted by Stronge,[8] "compliance with International Accounting Standards means little because of the range of permitted alternative treatments." Second, the passage of time has perhaps permitted other countries with initially non-conforming standards or practices to adopt new approaches that are in line with IAS.

To test this suggestion, cluster analysis of the country responses by standard was performed. Clustering techniques essentially sort observations (raw data) into groups (or clusters) based on the degree of similarity that an observation bears to existing members of a cluster. The results suggest that the IASC has issued three types of standards: (1) standards issued early in the IASC's life and with which conformity was easily achieved; (2) standards issued more recently, perhaps requiring additional procedures for some countries to achieve conformity; and (3) some standards which have not been adopted by the majority of the IASC's member countries. The first group contains 12 standards (IAS1–5, IAS7–8, IAS10–11, IAS13, IAS16 and IAS18), which have been in effect for an average of 11.0 years and have achieved an average conformity of 92 percent. The second group contains 10 standards (IAS9, IAS12, IAS17, and IAS19–25), which have been in effect for an average of 5.7 years. Only 69 percent of the member countries have demonstrated some form of conformity with these standards. The third group contains only three standards (IAS14–15 and IAS26), achieving conformity in only 41 percent of the member countries. IAS14 (segment disclosure) and IAS15 (price-level changes), which became effective in 1983, are apparently unwelcomed by the international accounting community. IAS26 (retirement benefits) came into effect in 1988, the year in which the data was collected.

Conformity by country

Conformity Index B was calculated for each of the 54 countries resonding to the IASC survey. The score represents the percentage of the 25 IAS with which each country complied (i.e. the country response to the questionnaire was one of columns 1–4). While the mean conformity score was 76.3 percent, there was substantial inter-country variation. Fifteen countries have scores of 90 percent or more and five have scores lower than 50 percent, meaning that they comply with fewer than half of the existing IAS.

There are, of course, many reasons why a country has or has not adopted an accounting treatment which conforms with IAS. One contributing factor is the strength of the national accounting institutions, which affects the way in which standards are developed (see Table 2). Countries with weak or newly established accounting professions may lack a formalized system for developing, issuing and enforcing accounting and reporting standards. These countries were identified from IASC questionnaire categories 4 and 6, conforming and non-conforming national *practices*. For example, Trinidad and Tobago and Bahrain have no national requirements at all in the areas covered by the 25 IAS in the survey. Other countries, such as India and Hong Kong, have national practices, but no standards, in 11 and 13 areas respectively. Altogether, a total of 18 countries have not codified or otherwise standardized the majority of their accounting treatments (abbreviated as "unstandardized," see Table 2 column 1). On average, this group has issued standards corresponding to 5.5 of the 25 IAS.

The other 36 countries have a formalized system for promulgating and enforcing the majority of their accounting treatments, either via national laws, via the accounting profession, or a combination of both. This group may be further subdivided into two groups, one of which includes 11 countries which rely upon the IASC for the development of standards (abbreviated as "dependent," see Table 2 column 2) and a group of 25 countries which have a strong tradition of accounting or powerful accounting institutions and typically issue standards independently of the IASC (abbreviated as "independent," see Table 2 column 3).

In developing countries, the tendency is for local accounting institutions to adopt or adapt IAS for their own standards (IASC questionnaire categories 1 and 2 respectively). Illustrative of the dependent category are Botswana and Cyprus (both 100 percent), which have adopted the IAS as their own. Other countries, such as Jamaica and Singapore, use the IAS as a basis for developing their own standards. It is interesting to note that all the

Table 2 Development of accounting standards.

Practice not yet standardized		Dependent on IASC		Independent of IASC	
Country	*%*	*Country*	*%*	*Country*	*%*
Abu Dhabi	96	Botswana	100	Belgium	84
Bahrain	100	Cyprus	100	Brazil	92
Dubai	100	Fiji	44	Canada	84
Greece	80	Jamaica	76	Finland	100
Kuwait	88	Malawi	88	France	76
Lesotho	72	Malaysia	72	Germany	96
Malta	100	Oman	96	Ireland	84
Saudi Arabia	96	Pakistan	92	Japan	88
Switzerland	96	Singapore	96	Mexico	76
Trinidad and Tobago	100	Sri Lanka	44	Netherlands	88
		Zimbabwe	92	Spain	84
				Sweden	88
				United Kingdom	84
				United States	100
Ghana	64			Australia	64
Hong Kong	52			Austria	68
India	44			Denmark	60
Kenya	52			Iceland	60
Morocco	56			Indonesia	72
Nigeria	52			Italy	64
South Africa	36			New Zealand	64
Taiwan	60			Norway	60
				Swaziland	52
				Tanzania	60
				Yugoslavia	68
Total 18	Av. 74.7	Total 11	Av. 81.8	Total 25	Av. 76.6

Note: The figures indicate the percentage of the 25 standards which were developed in that mode for each country. Only the predominant mode is reported.

countries in column 2 of Table 2 are (or have been) members of the British Commonwealth. On average, these countries have adopted or followed 20.5 of the 25 IAS.

The independent category comprises countries which have national accounting requirements that were not developed from IAS (i.e., IASC questionnaire categories 3 and 5). On average, these 25 countries developed requirements corresponding to the IAS for 18.6 standards out of 25. The leading examples in this category are the United States (100 percent) and Germany (96 percent) (see Table 2, column 3). The authority underlying national accounting treatments in these countries typically predated the creation of IASC. For example, in the U.S.A., the Securities Acts of 1933 and 1934, the Committee on Accounting Procedure and the Accounting Principles Board paved the way for the Financial Accounting Standards

Board (FASB), which came into being in 1973. In Germany, the Commercial Code is the major source of accounting regulation. Both countries have created national guidelines or issued standards on topics well before the IASC pronounced on these issues.

In order to test the similarity of the three country grouping (IASC-dependent, independent, and unstandardized with respect to accounting treatments), the 54 country responses (level and type of conformity with the 25 existing IAS) were further analyzed by group. The intergroup correlations suggest that they are capturing significantly different behavior. The conformity indices of those countries which may be classified as independent of the IASC show a strong negative correlation (rho = $-.597$, p $\leq$ .001) when compared to the conformity indices of the dependent group. The indices of the unstandardized group show similar negative correlations when compared to the independent group (rho = $-.409$, p $\leq$ .002) and with the dependent group (rho = $-.488$, p < .001). Each group is distinctly different from the others, as is shown by the negative correlations, all highly significant, statistically. In particular, the strong negative Spearman correlation (rho = $-.597$) between the dependent and independent groups evidences the wide gulf that the IASC must bridge if the Comparability Project is to be realized.

The development of accounting standards in each country (Table 2) is associated with the level of conformity with existing IAS standards (Table 1). The mean Conformity Index for the "dependent" category is 89.1 percent, with a standard deviation of 12.7 percent. By way of contrast, the mean Conformity Index for the "independent" group is substantially lower, 74.2 percent, and has a larger standard deviation, 20.3 percent, and the mean for the "unstandardized" group is 71.3 percent, with a standard deviation of 19.5 percent. The dependency scores from Table 2 were correlated with the Conformity Index B scores from Table 1 for each country, using Spearman's rho. The IASC-dependent group scores were positively associated with the Conformity Index score (rho = .382), at a high level of statistical significance (p = .001). In other words, the statistical analysis suggests that the greater the degree of dependence on the IASC, the greater the country's score on the Conformity Index. Also, as expected, the "unstandardized" group scores were negatively associated with the Conformity Index (rho = $-.227$) but at a marginal level of statistical significance (p = .107).

The weak and negative correlation (rho = $-.170$) of the "independent" group with Conformity Index B reflects the bipolar distribution of countries on this dimension. Several countries with well-established accounting professions have issued standards or passed laws at variance with existing IAS, while others with their own standard-setting function have produced standards that are largely comparable with IAS. Typical of the latter are Canada, France, the United Kingdom and the United States, with Conformity Index scores ranging from 84 percent to 96 percent. Remarkably, the former includes some of the founding members of the IASC, with comparatively low scores on Conformity Index B, notably Germany (28 percent) and Mexico (48 percent).

An examination of the individual country responses to the IASC survey shows that, as a group, the IASC founders demonstrate an average compliance that is fractionally worse than non-founders (75.7 percent and 76.4 percent respectively). The IASC survey respondents included 10 of the EC's 12 members. (Luxembourg and Portugal were omitted). These countries, all in the "independent" category (except for Greece, which was "unstandardized"), obtained a mean score of 71.6 percent on Index B, which is consistent with Doupnik and Taylor's[9] observation of lower levels of conformity with IAS within the EC. These findings pinpoint a major obstacle to the IASC's comparability quest. The cooperation of the major "independent" standard-setting groups must be obtained in order to progress.

Country patterns of conformity

Choi[10] observed a correlation between financial disclosure and the development and efficiency of capital markets. More recently, Pratt and Behr[11] suggested that, in the case of the United States and Switzerland, differences in the standard-setting process and the types of standards promulgated may be explained in terms of differences in the "size, complexity, and diversity of capital transactions, the wide distribution of ownership and the opportunistic nature of the market participants". These contentions were examined in the context of the IASC survey data.

The country responses were subjected to two cluster analysis procedures available on SAS to ascertain whether discernible patterns of conformity existed. These two clustering techniques differ in two important ways: (1) the method used to structure initial clusters, and (2) the method of calculating similarity. When the SAS[12] CLUSTER procedure was used with the average link metric of similarity, the 54 countries were allocated to five clusters. The results are shown in Table 3. The first cluster includes all the countries that have not yet standardized their accounting practice, which may explain the low average Index B score of 66.4 percent for this cluster. Cluster 3 comprises countries which are highly dependent on the IASC and, in general, have high scores on Conformity Index B, with an average of 89.1 percent. Cluster 2 contains the countries which set standards independently of the IASC, and which have a lower level of conformity, 72.9 percent, largely attributable to the non-conforming standards of Finland, Germany and Mexico. Countries which had medium scores on the Unstandardized Index (ranging from 36 percent to 64 percent) were in cluster 4, and those with similar scores on the Independence Index (ranging from 52 percent to 72 percent) were grouped in cluster 5. As the results of the second cluster procedure were very similar,[13] there is evidence that these clusters represent different groupings on a meaningful dimension.

Table 3 Cluster analysis of responses to standards.

Cluster 1: Unstandardized				Cluster 4: Unstandardized			
	B	U	r^2		B	U	r^2
Abu Dhabi	80	96	.99	Ghana	84	64	.92
Bahrain	80	100	.99	Hong Kong	80	52	.98
Dubai	68	100	.99	India	56	44	.94
Greece	24	80	.78	Kenya	52	52	.84
Kuwait	72	88	.98	Morocco	96	56	.96
Lesotho	68	72	.91	Nigeria	100	52	.85
Malta	68	100	.99	South Africa	76	36	.82
Saudi Arabia	68	96	.99	Taiwan	76	60	.95
Switzerland	36	96	.91				
Trinidad and Tobago	100	100	.95				
Mean	66.4	92.8	.95	Mean	77.5	52.0	.91

Cluster 2: Independent				Cluster 5: Independent			
	B	I	r^2		B	I	r^2
Belgium	76	84	.99	Australia	92	64	.97
Brazil	76	92	.99	Austria	80	68	.95
Canada	96	84	.96	Denmark	80	60	.99
Finland	12	100	.61	Iceland	76	60	.98
France	84	76	.96	Indonesia	100	72	.93
Germany	28	96	.78	Italy	68	64	.94
Ireland	88	84	.98	New Zealand	80	64	.97
Japan	68	88	.99	Norway	72	60	.98
Mexico	48	76	.95	Swaziland	72	52	.99
Netherlands	84	88	.96	Tanzania	60	60	.93
Spain	96	84	.96	Yugoslavia	56	68	.93
Sweden	84	88	.99				
United Kingdom	88	84	.98				
United States	92	100	.98				
Mean	72.9	87.4	.94	Mean	76.0	62.9	.95

Cluster 3: IASC-Dependent		
	B	D	r^2
Botswana	100	100	.96
Cyprus	100	100	.96
Fiji	60	44	.77
Jamaica	88	76	.97
Malawi	88	88	.98
Malaysia	100	72	.97
Oman	96	96	.97
Pakistan	92	92	.98
Singapore	96	96	.95
Sri Lanka	68	44	.80
Zimbabwe	92	92	.98
Mean	89.1	81.8	.94

Notes:
1. The B column denotes the country's percentage compliance with IAS, as captured by Conformity Index B.
2. The columns headed I (Independent), D (Dependent) and U (Unstandardized) indicate each country's dominant mode of developing standards (see Table 2).
3. The r^2 column measures each country's degree of association with its own cluster.

The clusters confirm the deep difference in country attitudes to the IASC, the IAS and standard-setting that was highlighted by Table 2. The importance of the country differences in standard-setting is compounded by the presence of major stock exchanges (refer to Table 5). The latter are usually supervised by regulatory bodies that are independent of the accounting profession, and which may stipulate accounting treatments and specify disclosures as a condition of listing. Cluster 3 (IASC-dependent) and cluster 1 (unstandardized) each contain only one major stock exchange country (Singapore and Switzerland respectively). Eight of the world's major stock markets are located in countries appearing in cluster 2, which exhibits high IASC-independence. Three major markets operate in countries in cluster 5, which represents medium to high levels of IASC-independence. (The remaining exchange is in Luxembourg, which was not included in the IASC survey.) These findings are consistent with Choi (1973) and Pratt and Behr (1987), who noted the association between accounting disclosure and the development of capital markets.

If the IASC is to make real progress with its comparability initiative, the preceding analysis of conformity with IAS suggests that the IASC must win the support not only of the standard-setters but also of the regulators in the countries hosting the world's major stock exchanges. At the very minimum, ED32 requires the active endorsement of the United States, Japan, and the United Kingdom, which are the three largest markets and together have 50.8 percent of the total listings on major exchanges.

Country conformity with ED32

The existing accounting requirements of five major countries were reviewed for confortuity with ED32. Canada, France, Japan, the United Kingdom and the United States were chosen for three reasons: (1) they were founder members of the IASC; (2) they are economically significant; and (3) they each host major stock exchanges, which together accounted for 91.1 percent of the annual turnover on major exchanges in 1986. Table 4 indicates the potential areas of conflict if ED32 in its present form were to be issued as a standard.

Revised IAS11 eliminates the completed contract method of accounting for construction contracts, whereas the five countries currently permit this treatment. Likely to be of greater economic significance are the changes that would ensue from the adoption of revised IAS22, which requires that positive goodwill be amortized over 5 and certainly no more than 20 years. Canada follows the American practice of a 40 year amortization period. The preferred (at the time of writing) British treatment, the immediate write-off of goodwill, would also be unacceptable.

The number of "No discussion" entries in the table is quite compelling. Some reflect an absence of a standard on a particular topic while there may be an understood practice which is not documented in country GAAP.

Table 4 Current country compliance with revised IAS.

Standard	Canada	France	Japan	UK	USA
IAS 2 Inventory	FIFO-Preferred LIFO-Allowed	Preferred	Possibly NIC	Preferred	FIFO-Preferred LIFO-Allowed
IAS 8 Prior Period Adjustments	Preferred	Statement disclosure may be acceptable. Footnote disclosure may not be in compliance.	Statement disclosure may be acceptable. Footnote disclosure may not be in compliance.	Preferred	Preferred
IAS 9 R & D	Preferred	Preferred	Preferred	Preferred	Preferred
IAS 11 Contracts	Capitalization-Allowed Percentage-Required Completion-NIC	Capitalization-Allowed Percentage-Required Completion-NIC	Capitalization-Allowed Percentage-Required Completion-NIC	Percentage-Required Completion-NIC	Percentage-Required Completion-NIC
IAS 16 p. 36 Fixed assets	Cost-Preferred Valuation-Allowed	Preferred	Preferred	Cost-Preferred Valuation-Allowed	Preferred
IAS 17 p. 47 Leases	ND ND	NIC ND	N/A ND	ND Required	ND Required
IAS 18 Revenue recognition	ND	ND	ND	ND	ND
IAS 19 p. 45a Retirement Benefits	Accrued-Preferred Projected-Allowed	NIC	NIC	NIC	Preferred
p. 5	Required	ND	ND	NIC	Required
p. 45c	Required	NIC	NIC	NIC	Required

IAS 21 p. 28–30 Foreign Currency	Required	NIC	Required	Required	Required
p. 31	ND	ND	ND	ND	ND
p. 32c	Required Closing-NIC	Average-Required	NIC	Required	Required
p. 33	ND	Possibly NIC	ND	Required	Required
p. 34	ND Gains-NIC	Losses-Preferred	ND	ND	ND
IAS 22 Business combinations					
p. 36–38	Required Pooling-NIC	Purchase-Required	Required	Required Pooling-Possibly NIC	Purchase-Required
Positive goodwill p. 40–42	Asset-Required Life 40-NIC	Required	Required	NIC	Asset-Required Life 40-NIC
Negative goodwill	Preferred	NIC	ND	NIC	Required
Minority interests p. 45	ND	ND	ND	ND	ND
IAS 23 Capital. interest	Preferred Asset-Allowed	Expense-Preferred Asset-Allowed	Expense-Preferred Asset-Allowed	Expense-Preferred Asset-Allowed	Expense-Preferred
IAS 25 Long term investments					
p. 47	Preferred	ND	Preferred	Preferred	Preferred
Individual	Preferred	ND	Preferred	Preferred	NIC
p. 45	ND	ND	ND	NIC	ND
p. 46	Possibly NIC	ND	ND	ND	NIC
p. 48, 49	ND	ND	ND	ND	Required
p. 50	ND	ND	ND	ND	ND

*NIC = Not in compliance
N/A = Not applicable
ND = Not discussed in standards

However, a number have arisen because ED32 is breaking new ground, particularly in the areas of foreign currency and long-term investments. The IASC has also undertaken a major project on financial instruments, which were therefore excluded from the Comparability Project.

Canada and the United Kingdom would continue to exhibit a high degree of conformity with revised IAS, as each has only four areas of conflict. The United States has five, Japan six and France nine potential departures from revised IAS. There will doubtless be opposition from countries whose accounting treatments are to be eliminated by ED32. While many countries are in compliance with either required, preferred, or allowed treatments, there are a number of instances where prevailing domestic practice would not conform. Even in those countries whose standards are in complete agreement with existing IAS, major adjustments may have to be made by companies that had selected any of the 23 treatments now prohibited, and minor adjustments would be necessary to provide a reconciliation from any allowed alternative selected to the benchmark provided by the preferred treatment. If each country chooses to ignore IAS in the area of non-compliance, little progress will be made in the quest for comparability. Perhaps the only practical way is for each country to "suffer" to some extent in the interest of achieving standards that are more comparable internationally.

The IASC comparability project: what next?

Significant accounting policies in individual countries are likely to be at variance with revised IAS as prescribed by ED32. This raises the question of how national policy-setters and regulators will react to the Comparability Project. The responses from these groups will largely determine the future for comparable international standards. The spectrum of responses ranges from adoption of the revised IAS, through lobbying to change the less attractive features of the proposed standards, to maintaining the status quo. Potential responses to the Comparability Project, from the most optimistic to the most pessimistic, include:

(A) IASC standards as amended by Exposure Draft 32 are adopted or incorporated in national standards by both national policy-setters and regulators.

(B) Regulators and/or national policy-setters *require* reconciliation to the IASC required or preferred standards in the primary financial statements.

(C) Regulators and/or national policy-setters encourage adoption of or reconciliation to the IASC's benchmark in supplementary financial statements or notes to the primary financial statements.

(D) There is no international movement toward adoption of the new IASC standards.

This section debates the potential responses from two groups of countries: (1) those that are dependent on the IASC for setting standards; and (2) those that set standards independently of the IASC. The third group, countries that have not yet fully standardized their accounting treatments, may move closer to the IASC or may follow the leading independent countries in their economic sphere influence.

IASC-dependent countries

ED32 eliminates some 23 presently acceptable accounting policies. Immediate adoption of the revisions could have adverse economic consequences for companies required to comply with the revised standards. The stock market reaction to the new presentation (or new information) is unpredictable. However, if compliance with revised IAS alters accounting income, there may be an impact on tax flows. The dependent group, which in the past required primary financial statements prepared in accordance with international generally accepted accounting principles (I-GAAP), may be reluctant to endorse full adoption of ED32. Instead, they may encourage, rather than require, conformity with IAS, at least in the near-term, to permit companies to phase in the new standards. The creation of a transitional period also allows the accounting profession and the corporate CFOs time to debate the tax impact of these changes with national revenue authorities. Alternatively, these countries may require the preparation of secondary financial statements in accordance with I-GAAP. This approach is without tax consequences and may promote greater domestic comparability than presently obtains. However, companies are then burdened with the additional reporting requirements. A hybrid alternative would give companies the option of preparing either primary or secondary financial statements in accordance with revised IAS. This may be a viable option in the short-run for countries like Singapore that have adopted IAS in the past.

IASC-independent countries

As noted earlier, these countries have strong accounting institutions and, as hosts to most of the world's major stock-markets, have well-developed regulatory functions. The response of the standard-setters and regulators in these countries is critical for the Comparability Project. If IASC standards, as revised, are adopted by many countries as their national standards, international comparability in practice would be greatly enhanced. This is especially true if countries with large capital markets adopt these standards. However, for IASC standards permitting a preferred and/or alternative treatment, domestic comparability may be somewhat inhibited, despite the reconciliation that is required for the allowed alternative in countries that currently permit only one accounting treatment. National standard-setters, if unwilling to relax their standards in such cases, may adopt the IASC's proposals piecemeal.

If IASC standards are widely adopted, it would be appropriate for the current composition of the IASC to change. National standard-setting groups, such as the FASB, and other groups currently recognized on a consultative basis, such as the UN, the OECD, or the EC, might be invited to become full members of the IASC. There arises an interesting question of the relationship between the IASC and the national standard-setting groups. If the IASC emerges as a forum for consultation, a cooperative relationship may develop. On the other hand, if the IASC becomes the primary originator of new financial accounting and reporting standards, the role of the national standard-setting groups may diminish. Daley and Mueller have argued that national standard-setters might find that they were "relegated" to "lobbying for the interests of their local constituencies at the international level."[14] The current behavior of European Community members lends support to this view. The resolution of this issue may hinge on the locus of enforcement powers.

In theory, existing IAS apply to all public and private companies in the member countries. However, as there is no enforcement mechanism, current conformity varies greatly within this group (see cluster 2, Table 3). In our opinion, it is highly unlikely that this situation will improve with ED32. If these countries support ED32 at all, they may choose to restrict required conformity to a subset of firms in their jurisdiction. For example, in declining order of size of domain, IAS conformity may be required of (1) only listed domestic public companies; or (2) listed public companies whose securities are registered on foreign exchanges; or (3) foreign companies seeking a listing on a domestic exchange. The first case has obvious implications for national standards. The second and third cases create the possibility of dual standards if countries were to accept I-GAAP in lieu of domestic GAAP for foreign registrants. Alternatively, countries may require that foreign financial statements be supplemented by a reconciliation to I-GAAP.

A. IASC standards adopted as the national standards

It could be argued that all listed public companies should use international standards. No company is purely domestic if individuals or institutions from other countries can purchase its shares. The needs of a German, Japanese, or Australian investor for adequate and accurate information, coupled with investor protection, when purchasing shares of a U.S. company on the New York Stock Exchange, should be given as much consideration as the needs of a domestic investor.

It is possible that IASC standards could be adopted as the national standards in those countries which have in the past partially or fully adopted IASC pronouncements. However, the likelihood that both national standard-setters and regulators would adopt or revise national standards to conform with IASC standards is remote in countries with strong national policy-setting groups. For example, consider the posture of the EC regulators. The Fourth Directive permits a variety of accounting treatments, whereas ED32 permits at most a choice of two. In the Brussels Conference, the Commission concluded:

> The time is not ripe for future accounting directives ... for the foreseeable future, there will be no reduction of options and no extension of the directives to cover subject areas not previously addressed.[15]

More than a decade ago, the International Federation of Stock Exchanges "recommended to its member exchanges situated in IASC countries to require as part of the listing requirements reference to the adherence to international standards of accounting."[16] No country has yet undertaken this step. Canada, a prominent exception in this regard, currently encourages companies to follow IAS, and to disclose that fact in their annual report (Turner, 1983).[17] For example, GE Canada's 1988 annual report indicated in the Summary of Significant Accounting Policies: "These principles also conform in all material respects with International Accounting Standards on a historical cost basis." Some 100 Canadian companies, barely 9 percent of the listed companies, make such disclosures.[18] Even fewer companies in other countries disclose conformity with IAS. A rare exception is the French company Lafarge Coppée (see its English language annual report for 1988).

B. Regulators require use of or reconciliation to IASC standards (in effect dual standards are promulgated)

Here, the regulators would require compliance with IASC standards only by foreign filers. For example, the SEC may require Mexican or Thai companies to use IASC standards if they wish to list on U.S. exchanges.

If a country does restrict the range of companies required to conform with IAS, two tiers of financial reporting are erected. Dual standards on a single exchange pose the question of preferential treatment for international filers vis-a-vis domestic filers. (Foreign international filers on the London Stock Exchange have been permitted to file statements prepared in accordance with I-GAAP for some years.) This problem is particularly salient in countries where domestic standards may be reconsidered more complete or more rigorous than comparable IASC standards. The dual standards issue also creates a problem for international filers in the preparation of their domestic statements. This happens to a certain extent today, and some believe that it clouds rather than clears the comparability issue, and raises

175

questions about the "fair presentation" of any given set of financial statements.

From a preparer's point of view, this approach might result in extra costs to prepare and disseminate dual sets of financial statements, designed for the domestic and international marketplaces. Whether this cost is great enough to offset the benefits of being able to file on various exchanges that recognize IAS is an empirical question. At the OECD forum in 1985, representatives of Shell International and Du Pont spoke in favor of international harmonization. In their view, it "would save costs, help understanding of accounting numbers of overseas subsidiaries, open up capital markets, etc."[19] There is little concrete evidence for these beliefs. However, Eiteman and Stonehill suggest that the "recent trend for European and Japanese firms to request bond ratings by Moody's and Standard and Poor's (supports) the idea that executives may believe further disclosure may reduce the cost of debt."[20] However, it is expected that using one set of financial statements to access several exchanges at the very least would provide considerable cost savings.

This scenario raises problems of attestation. Are the revised IASC standards set forth in such a complete and detailed manner that two different preparers would arrive at the same treatment? If not, it may be difficult for auditors to issue an opinion that states the financial statements "fairly present" or present "a true and fair view."[21] Further, would the regulators accept unaudited I-GAAP financial statements? Would domestic auditors extend the domestic opinion to the international financial statements, or would a separate opinion be required?

C. Regulators encourage the use of or reconciliation to IASC standards

Countries which are in the independent group and display low levels of conformity with current IAS, such as Germany and Mexico, are likely to do nothing, or at the most, encourage some form of reconciliation. Members of the unstandardized group may do likewise. Optimistically, some of these may encourage the preparation of secondary financial statements, as may high conformity members of the independent group. A lower cost, and less useful alternative, would be the preparation of a statement reconciling the reported income number to the one which would have resulted if revised IAS has been applied.

A reconciliation requirement for all filers would place a burden on preparers in countries with significant differences between domestic and I-GAAP. For example, Table 2 shows that eight of the 54 countries in the IASC survey currently do not comply with IAS3 (consolidations), 27 are not in compliance with IAS15 (inflation accounting), and 18 countries do not comply with IAS26 (post-retirement benefits). Clearly, the costs of preparing a reconciliation in these countries would be significant. The legal ramifications of reporting under two standards must also be resolved. A reconciliation requirement, whether imposed on domestic or on international filers, also raises the attestation issues discussed earlier. Thus, standard-setting groups might be pressured by preparers and international audit firms to adopt at least some IASC standards in order to reduce financial statement preparation time and expense. Alternatively, the IASC might face continual pressure to permit more options, which would defeat the purpose of the Comparability Project.

The (British) Accounting Standards Committee, chaired by Mr. Renshall, has already opposed ED32's reconciliation requirement on two grounds. There was concern that the IASC would seek:

> to override the requirements of national securities exchanges. There was a danger that there would be two reconciliation statements, one from the relevant securities exchange and one from the IASC and that would not be particularly useful (quoted by Spink).[22]

Doubtless, there will be support for the ASC's position from other policy-makers. The disclosure of two sets of income and shareholders' equity amounts might prove confusing to users of the financial statements, thrusting the issue of dual standards into prominence. Whether the benefits of this reconciliation process outweigh the problems related to dual standards is an unsettled issue. However, even with the extra preparation time required for a reconciliation, international filers would most certainly benefit if IOSCO members accept a single reconciliation to I-GAAP income for access to their exchanges.

The comparability project: prerequisites for success

It would seem that there are three major obstacles which must be overcome in order for the Comparability Project to be successful. First, the members countries must be willing to cooperate with the IASC, rather than fight to promote their national interests. Second, regional efforts at harmonization must be restrained or otherwise subordinated to the IASC's endeavours. Third, the IASC must vigorously pursue its aims, and must be sufficiently funded to enable it to achieve them. These points are developed further below.

The level of cooperation among IASC members appears to be the most critical concern. If, for example, each IASC member vehemently opposes the parts of the ED32 having the greatest effect on its national standards, the IASC may be unable to go forward with the project. Alternatively, the project may be so diluted as a result of lobbying that it garners little support from bodies such as IOSCO. Such a scenario would weaken the position of the IASC and reduce its influence over the development of international standards. Some fear that the "do nothing" alternative might lead to the de facto international adoption of American standards.[19, 23] Simmonds considered that:

> there are only two credible pretenders to the crown of international standards setter—US GAAP and the IASC. The case in support of US GAAP is that it is already in a commanding lead over other national alternatives. . . . its standards show the natural signs of domestic influence—including unavoidable fiscal implications that are not applicable elsewhere. . . . I question whether US standards could adequately reflect the needs of groups operating in non-US international environment.[24]

Following Simmonds' reasoning, there may be a corps of countries that prefer the IASC to the alternative.

There are two different, but perhaps overlapping, approaches to harmonization, the first focusing on accounting practices and the second on disclosure.[25] The IASC Comparability Project has addressed measurement issues, and has not broadened the disclosure requirements. The SEC Policy Statement[26] suggests that the ultimate goal should be the development of an integrated international disclosure system and would like to see more detail in IAS standards and greater coverage of topics. IOSCO has hinted that international accounting standards might eventually be used in prospectuses of MNE offerings, provided several problems can be overcome: the elimination of most accounting choices, and increased detailed guidance contained in each statement and increased breadth of coverage of the standards as a whole. The SEC has made similar statements. FASB's current chairman indicated in a presentation to the IASC that:

> FASB would support an objective that seeks to create superior international standards that would gradually supplant national standards as the superior standards become universally accepted.[27]

As to the question of restraining regional efforts at harmonization, Choi argued that "harmonization efforts within clusters may be a more fruitful and feasible development strategy that attempts to harmonize accounting standards on a worldwide basis.[28] Others have warned that the present efforts[29] of the EC to harmonize accounting standards within that community "pose a serious obstacle to development of worldwide standards."[30] Similar observations have been made by McComb[31] and Choi and Mueller.[32] Damant commented, "it is bad enough having so many different national standards. The last thing which is needed is a complication of international harmonization by the establishment of regional standards."[33]

Despite the comments expressed earlier, members of the EC Commission in Brussels, such as Van Hulle,[34] see their efforts as consistent with international harmonization. Clearly, the IASC and the EC must work together to develop international standards. The current president of the Federation of European Accountants (FEE) also espoused this view.[35] Mr. Carey of the Accounting Standards Committee (ASC) said, "the UK prefession's view is very clear. We believe harmonization should be through international standards and the IASC".[36] These views apparently prevailed, for the Commission Conference on accounting standards, held in Brussels in January 1990, recognized the IASC as "the appropriate forum for world-wide work in this field, and it was decided that the community would strengthen its input to IASC."[15]

Sir Henry Benson, a former IASC chairman, noted the key prerequisites of harmonization: focused leadership; reconciliation to a single set of international standards; compliance with international standards to be a requirement for stock exchange listing; national standard-setters to be on the IASC standard-setting board; greater industry involvement in standard-setting; and national accounting bodies to use disciplinary action to enforce IAS.[37] During the last decade, the IASC has worked diligently on Benson's program for harmonization, perhaps spurred by the fear that the accounting profession might lose control of setting international standards,[38] and is now poised to meet several of Benson's prerequisites if the major funding problems of the IASC can be overcome: funding structure and level of financial support.

Currently, the IASC's budget is funded by IFAC, which, in turn collects membership fees from the member institutions. The IASC's effectiveness as a supplier of international accounting standards would doubtless be enhanced by restructuring the funding procedures to include direct contributions and increasing the membership fees. Without significant increases in the budget, there is little hope that the IASC can meet the challenge of providing detailed and complete international standards, without excessive reliance upon its previous pillars of support, the United Kingdom and the United States.

Is harmonization desirable?

Many professionals have questioned whether harmonization is feasible or even desirable.[39] They acknowledge that individual and institutional investors are not deterred by country boundaries in the selection of investment portfolios. Total transactions in US corporate securities for foreigners in 1988 totaled US$452.7 billion. Total transactions in U.S. securities (including treasury and government securities) amounted to US$3,579.3 billion, an increase of US$263.9 billion over 1987. U.S. investors purchased or sold a total of US$594.5 billion worth of foreign stocks and bonds in

1988.[40] Foreign direct investments into the United States increased by US$58.4 billion in 1988.[41] Similarly, institutions in search of capital are addressing the global marketplace. For example, funds raised in international capital markets totalled US$225 billion in 1986, but amounted to US$347 billion in 1989.[42] Many companies have already obtained listings on stock exchanges outside their own country.

Table 5 summarizes the relative size of the stock markets in 14 countries and their annual turnover and activity levels. While the United Kingdom has the most listings, the United States is the largest market in terms of size and turnover. However, the Tokyo Stock Exchange is a very strong second on both dimensions.

The table also indicates the percentage of listings that are "foreign." The huge variation in the foreign percentage is readily discerned, with the smaller exchanges heavily dependent on foreign registrants. (For example, 61.5 percent of Singapore's and 59.2 percent of the Netherlands' listings are foreign.) However, the percentage of foreign listings on the world's busiest exchanges is still rather small (NYSE and AMEX combined, 4.6 percent; Tokyo, 3.4 percent). This lends support to the argument advanced by the Technical Committee of IOSCO that a "primary impediment to international offerings of securities is that different countries have different accounting standards."[43]

As the table confirms, there is a significant volume of foreign registrations. However, the countries with stringent listing requirements (for example, the U.S.A. and Japan) are capturing little of this market (4.6 percent and 3.4 percent respectively of their total listings are foreign). By way of contrast, foreign registration in Singapore comprise 61.5 percent of the total. This table is significant evidence that companies seek to avoid rigorous accounting and disclosure requirements. (Saudagaran[44] has recently confirmed this finding).

The economic consequences of this maneuvering are profound. First, the paternalistic notion, so dear to the regulators, of investor protection is completely undermined where investors can (and do) purchase securities in jurisdictions with relatively fewer requirements. Second, the financial services industry (from stockbrokers to analysts and beyond) is separated from market transactions that take place in Belgium or Luxembourg, for example, rather than at home, with significant loss of revenue to that sector. Third, it has been suggested that the costs of raising debt and equity in different markets is affected by the perceived rigor of the accounting policies and disclosure requirements. Fourth, there is anecdotal evidence from analysts, and others, suggesting that funds are misallocated (see Damant in Gernon, Purvis & Diamond[45]) because economic differences between investment vehicles in different jurisdictions are obscured by different financial accounting treatments and disclosure practices. Trade negotiators representing the United States, in response to initiatives from FEE, have recently acknowledged that the use of I-GAAP "would facilitate expansion of trade

Table 5 Major stock exchanges in 1986.

	Total Listings	Foreign Percentage	Market Size US$B	Av. size per listing US$M	Annual Turnover US$B	Activity
Australia	1,193	2.6	78	65.4	27.0	34.6
Belgium	331	42.3	36	108.8	7.0	19.4
Canada	1,085	4.7	166	153.0	57.0	34.3
Denmark	281	2.5	*	NC	1.9	NC
France	1,100	20.5	150	136.4	56.0	37.3
Germany	673	26.9	246	365.5	136.0	55.3
Italy	184	0.0	141	766.3	45.0	31.9
Japan	1,551	3.4	1,746	1,125.7	954.0	54.6
Luxembourg	421	39.9	*	NC	*	NC
Netherlands	409	59.2	73	178.5	30.0	41.1
Singapore	317	61.5	33	104.1	5.0	15.2
Switzerland	339	57.2	132	389.4	*	NC
United Kingdom	2,613	19.6	440	168.4	133.0	30.2
United States	2,373a	4.6	2,203	928.4	1,374.0b	62.4
Total	12,870		5,444		2,825.9	
Mean	919.29	24.63	388.86	299.32	201.85	29.74
Std. dev.	759.65	22.43	662.25	345.14	403.01	19.90

Notes:
US$B = US$ billions
US$M = US$ millions
* = Not given in data source
NC = Not calculable
a = New York and American Stock Exchanges combined
b = NYSE only
Activity is defined as Turnover/Market size and may be viewed as a measure of market breadth.
Market size and turnover data is taken from Exhibits 10.8 and 10.9 in Eiteman and Stonehill, 1989.[20] Total listings are taken from, and the foreign percentages are derived from data presented in the report of the Staff of the U.S. Securities and Exchange Commission to the Senate Committee on Banking, Housing and Urban Affairs and the House Committee on Energy and Commerce on the Internationalization of the Securities Market, July 29, 1987, p. II–66.

in services by removing barriers caused by different national accounting requirements." Accordingly, they "have proposed that the General Agreement on Trade and Services (GATS) agreement should recognize the importance of International Accounting Standards."[46] In view of these factors, we share IOSCO's view that increased comparability is an important objective, and that the IASC is the best vehicle to realize this goal.

Conclusion

Moulin,[47] amongst others, identified prerequisites for improved IAS: sufficient detail to guide interpretation; increased scope to cover key areas, including earnings per share, discontinued operations, and accounting for specialized industries; additional disclosure requirements; and standards developed with the needs of users in mind. It seems clear that ED32 does not meet all of these preconditions, yet that does not mean that the IASC's venture is a failure. The Comparability Project has narrowed the range of choices, a major criticism in the past, and has provided a forum for debate of comparability issues. The IASC offers an institutional means of addressing (and implementing) subsequent steps in the quest for comparability.

If global comparability of accounting standards is ever to be achieved, significant effort will have to be expended to alter the direction of accounting evolution, to emphasize international, rather than national, interests. It is important to recognize that whatever scenarios evolve, progress toward international comparability of accounting standards is likely to be slow and will not proceed in the same direction nor at the same pace in the various IASC-member countries. Changing domestic standards is a slow process; the economic, legal and professional differences among countries provide additional complexity in the international arena.

The pace of a planned evolution to comparable international accounting standards will be affected by several important factors: the responses of the national standard-setters and regulators to the Comparability Project and the extent to which the intent of the Steering Committee survives the exposure draft phase; the reaction of IOSCO and national regulators to the final version, and the extent of their subsequent support for the IASC's international standards; and the way in which future IASC standards are developed. It is essential that they be drafted with a breadth of coverage and sufficient detail to provide implementation guidance, thus promoting the comparability envisioned by the IASC and to ally the concerns of certain regulatory bodies. Even standards that require one treatment or have a preferred and allowed alternative with a reconciliation will not result in comparability if they do not provide adequate implementation guidance. The IASC Board has accepted this criticism. In its updated five year plan, the Board has pledged to revise existing IAS "to ensure that they are sufficiently detailed and complete and contain adequate disclosure requirements to meet the needs of capital markets and the international business community."[48]

To realize the intent of the Comparability Project will require a long-term sustained effort on the part of the IASC, which will need to increase its staff. Member countries must provide greater support, not merely in terms of financial contributions, but also in active promotion of IAS. As Kanaga observed, "if the IASC fails in its mission, the UN or regional governmental bodies will step in as the clamor grows to improve transnational reporting," (cited in Burton).[37] Finally, the IASC must win the commitment of standard-setters and regulators in at least three major markets—the United Kingdom, the United States and Japan—for comparability to proceed.

Notes

1 Georges Barthes, "Meeting the Expectations of Global Capital Markets." *IASC News*, Vol. 18, No. 3 (July, 1989): 1–2.

2 *Standard-setters* are institutions or groups responsible for setting national accounting and reporting standards. These groups may be in the private sector, e.g., the Financial Accounting Standards Board (FASB) and the current Accounting Standards Committees in Canada and the United Kingdom. In some countries, these national standard-setters may be government agencies, related to government agencies, or even the government itself. For example, in Japan, the Business Accounting Deliberations Council, affiliated with the Ministry of Finance, is involved in setting accounting standards, whereas in Germany, accounting standards are set by Parliament through the Ministry of Justice. In the Netherlands, Parliament has primary responsibility (again through the Ministry of Justice), but there is also an independent, private sector Council for Annual Reporting.

3 *Regulators* are groups or institutions with statutory authority to regulate stock exchanges, and, which, in so doing, may prescribe accounting standards and disclosure requirements. These groups also have enforcement to insure compliance. In many countries, the regulatory function is separated from the standard-setting function. For example, in the U.S., the Securities and Exchange Commission (SEC), while having statutory authority to set standards, has generally looked to the private sector (presently, the FASB) for the development of accounting standards. The SEC, however, has mandated disclosure requirements which apply to listed companies through regulations S-X and S-K. In other countries, the regulating body may be the same as the standard-setting body. The Swedish Accounting Standards Board is such an example.

4 International Accounting Standards Committee (a). "Comparability of Financial Statements: Proposed amendments to International Accounting Standards 2, 5, 8, 9, 11, 16, 17, 18, 19, 21, 22, 23, and 25." *Exposure Draft 32* (London: IASC, 1989).

International Accounting Standards Committee (b). "Towards the International Harmonisation of Financial Statements: An Invitation to Comment on an Exposure Draft on the Comparability of Financial Statements." (London: IASC, 1989).

5 International Accounting Standards Committee. *Survey of the Use and Application of International Accounting Standards.* (London: IASC, July 1988).

6 A complete list of international accounting standards, titles, and release dates may be found in the inside back cover of ED32.

7 It is recognized that this coding scheme is rather generous in that it weights each category of conformity equally. It could be argued that category 4 should be assigned a lower weight that categories 1–3. Similarly, one could argue that a national standard conflicting with IAS should receive greater weight than a non-conforming national practice. Different weights were used in a sensitivity analysis (not reported here). While the absolute scores changed according to the weights used, the relative rankings of each standard in the table were not significantly affected.

8 Chris Stronge, "Financial Reporting: Disturbing Lack of a Common Language." *Accountant*, (July 1988): 22–23.

9 S. Doupnik and M. E. Taylor, "An Empirical Investigation of the Observance of IASC Standards in Western Europe." *Management International Review*, Vol. 25, No. 1 (1985): 27–33.

10 Frederick D. S. Choi, "Financial Disclosure and Entry to the European Capital Market." *Journal of Accounting Research*, Vol. 11, No. 2 (Autumn 1973): 159–175.

11 Jamie Pratt and Giorgio Behr, "Environmental Factors, Transaction Costs, and External Reporting: A Cross-National Comparison." *International Journal of Accounting, Education and Research*, Vol. 22, No. 2 (Spring 1987): 1–24.

12 SAS Institute. "SAS Users' Guide", Version 6, (Cary, NC: SAS Institute Inc., 1989).

13 Because cluster analysis can yield unstable results, the data was subjected to a very different cluster procedure, VARCLUS, also available on SAS. Varclus, which utilizes an oblique principal component methodology, generated four clusters. Three clusters formed under this procedure were indentical to the first three clusters shown in Table 3, with the sole exception of Yugoslavia, which was placed in Cluster 2. The fourth cluster combined Clusters 4 and 5 (again with the exception of Yugoslavia). The cluster summary for this procedure is shown below:

Oblique Principal Component Cluster Analysis

Cluster	Members	Cluster Variation	Variation Explained	Proportion Explained	Second Eigenvalue
1	10	10.00	9.49	0.940	0.415
2	15	15.00	14.06	0.937	0.798
3	11	11.00	10.30	0.936	0.579
4	18	18.00	16.88	0.937	0.649

Total variation explained = 50.72 Proportion = 0.939

14 Lane A. Daley and Gerhard G. Mueller, "Accounting in the Arena of World Politics." *Journal of Accountancy*, Vol. 153, No. 2 (February 1982): 40–46, 48, 50.

15 Federation des Experts Comptables Europeens (FEE). "The Future of Harmonisation of Accounting Standards within the European Communities." Memorandum on Commission Conference 17/18 January, 1990, dated January 19, 1990.

16 Seymour M. Bohrer, "Harmonization of Accounting." Pp. 198–205 in *Accounting for Multinational Enterprises*. Edited by Dhia D. AlHashim and James W. Robertson (Indianapolis: Bobbs-Merrill Inc., 1978).

17 John N. Turner, "International Harmonization: A Professional Goal." *Journal of Accountancy*, Vol. 155, No. 1 (January 1983): 58–64, 66.

18 John Kirkpatrick, "The Case for Visible Conformity." *Accountancy*, Vol. 99, No. 1121 (January 1987): 17–18.

19 Rolf Rundfelt, "Views From Abroad: Europe." *Journal of Accounting, Auditing & Finance*, Vol. 9, No. 1 (Fall 1985): 85–88.

20 David K. Eiteman and Arthur I. Stonehill, *Multinational Business Finance* (5th ed.). (Reading, Mass: Addison-Wesley, 1989).

21 The recent issue of Statement on Auditing Standards No. 51, "Reporting on Financial Statements Prepared for Use in Other Countries," by the (US) Auditing Standards Board has heightened the U.S. auditing profession's awareness of the difficulties.

22 Hazel Spink, "ASC Refuses to Yield on World Standards." (Newspaper, 1989).

23 Paul Rutteman, "Demands of a Different Environment." *Accountancy*, (October 1987): 17–18.

24 Andy Simmonds, "Bridging the European Gap." *Accountancy*, (August 1989): 29.

25 Philip M. Reckers and D. J. Stagliano, "International Accounting Standards: Progress and Prospects." *Survey of Business*, Vol. 16, No. 4 (Spring 1981): 28–31.

26 Securities and Exchange Commission (SEC). "Regulation of International Securities Markets." Policy Statement (November 1988).

27 Dennis R. Beresford, "Internationalization of Accounting Standards: The Role of the Financial Accounting Standards Board." *Financial Accounting Standards Board Status Report*, Series 065, No. 195 (June 1988): 3–6.

28 Frederick D. S. Choi, "A Cluster Approach to Accounting Harmonization." *Management Accounting*, Vol. LXIII, No. 2 (August 1981): 17–31.

29 For a more detailed discussion of the progress of harmonization within the European Community, see the following articles by Van Hulle: Karel Van Hulle, (a). "The EC Experience of Harmonisation—Part I." *Accountancy*, (September 1989): 76–77. (b). "The EC Experience of Harmonisation—Part II." *Accountancy*, (October 1989): 96–99.

30 Richard D. Fitzgerald, "International Harmonization of Accounting and Reporting." *International Journal of Accounting, Education and Research*, Vol. 17, No. 1 (Fall 1981): 21–32.

31 Desmond McComb, "International Accounting Standards and the EEC Harmonization Program: A Conflict of Disparate Objectives." *International Journal of Accounting, Education and Research*, Vol. 17, No. 2 (Spring 1982): 35–48.

32 Frederick D. S. Choi and Gerhard G. Mueller, *International Accounting*. (2nd ed.) (Englewood Cliffs: Prentice-Hall Inc., 1984).

33 David Damant, "Accounting Standards: Europe and the World." *European Accounting Focus*, (May 1989): 14–15.

34 Karel Van Hulle, "Harmonisation of Accounting Standards Throughout the EC." *European Accounting Focus*, (Spring 1989): 11–13.

35 IASC. "FEE address to the IASC, April 1989." *IASC News*, Vol. 18, No. 2 (June 1989).

36 Carey, quoted in *Accountancy Age*, (August 31, 1989).

37 J. C. Burton (ed.), *The International World of Accounting. Challenges and Opportunities*. (Reston, VA: Council of Arthur Young Professors, 1981).

38 J. A. Burggraaff, "IASC developments: an Update." *Journal of Accountancy*, Vol. 154 (September 1982): 104, 106–110.

39 Richard Karl Goeltz, "International Accounting Harmonization: The Impossible and (Unnecessary?) Dream." *Accounting Horizons*, Vol. 5, No. 1 (March 1991): 85–88.

40 U.S. Bureau of the Census. "Statistical Abstract of the United States, 110th Edition." (Washington, DC: 1990): Tables 840 and 841.

41 Federal Reserve Bulletin. "Monetary Policy Report to the Congress." (August 1989): A55.
42 Organisation for Economic Cooperation and Development (OECD). "Financial Statistics." (December 1990).
43 Quoted in *IASC News*, Vol. 18, No. 1 (January 1989): 2.
44 Shahrokh M. Saudagaran, "An Empirical Study of Selected Factors Influencing the Decision to List on Foreign Stock Exchanges." *Journal of International Business Studies*, Vol. 19, No. 1 (Spring 1988): 101–127.
45 Helen Gernon, S. E. C. Purvis and Michael A. Diamond. "An Analysis of the Implications of the IASC's Comparability Project." *Topical Issues Study No. 3* Los Angeles: SEC and Financial Reporting Institute, School of Accounting, University of Southern California, 1990).
46 IASC. "Board Supports Commitment to International Accounting Standards." *IASC News*, Vol. 19, No. 4 (December 1990): 1.
47 Donald J. Moulin, "Practical Means of Promoting Common Accounting and Auditing Standards." Paper presented at the 13th Annual Conference of IOSCO, Melbourne, 1988.
48 IASC. "IASC's Five Year Plan—Update." *IASC News*, Vol. 19, No. 4 (December 1990): 3.

39

LOBBYING BEHAVIOUR AND THE DEVELOPMENT OF INTERNATIONAL ACCOUNTING STANDARDS

The case of the IASC's joint venture project

Sara York Kenny and Robert K. Larson

Source: *European Accounting Review* 3 (1993): 531–54.

Abstract

This paper studies the role of lobbying in an international (i.e., harmonization) accounting standards setting and examines the IASC's process of promulgating International Accounting Standard (IAS) 31, 'Financial Reporting of Interests in Joint Ventures'. Our study begins with an examination of the Exposure Draft (ED 35, 'Financial Reporting of Interests in Joint Ventures') preceding IAS 31 and analyses the lobbying efforts observed during the promulgation process. Consistent with prior literature, the paper analyses lobbyists and their lobbying positions. During the time frame of the study (1989 and 1990), the IASC changed its due process, which affords us the opportunity also to analyse the IASC's strategic approach to public input. Accordingly, this study incorporates aspects of institutional theory as it relates to strategic choice by organizations.

The comment letters received by the IASC regarding ED 35 were analysed using a form of content analysis. The analyses generally support the hypothesized relationships; namely, lobbying firms tend to be very large, and they lobby against any change in the *status quo*; professional and trade organizations lobby on behalf of their constituents and tend to support the majority positions held by those constituents; and the regulatory body (IASC) seeks acceptance from its constituency by adapting its position to that which is more palatable to the lobbyists. The interaction between respondents and the IASC is consistent with an institutional theory explanation of organizational change and adaptation to environment pressures.

Few individual firms lobbied the IASC. Rather, the bulk of the respondents to ED 35 were professional associations and organizations. The result contrasts markedly with both our expectations and prior research involving lobbying of the FASB. The dearth of corporate respondents to ED 35 implies that multinational corporations do not yet see the IASC as a serious regulatory organization. Further, few legal, governmental or regulatory organizations required compliance with IASs during 1989 and 1990, when IAS 31 was being deliberated, but many organizations and countries were considering such regulation (Guy, 1992; Denman, 1991). As of early 1993, both the London and Hong Kong Stock Exchanges began allowing foreign issuers to provide only reconciliations from home country GAAP to IASs (Cairns, 1992). Additionally, the International Organization of Securities Commissions (IOSCO) has been increasingly supportive of the IASC's harmonization efforts (Chandler, 1992; Wyatt, 1992; Wallace 1990). Coupled with the IASC's efforts to achieve institutional legitimacy (Wallace, 1990), the lack of corporate respondents might be rather disturbing except for one factor: the Exposure Draft (ED) analysed in this study represents one of the first standards promulgated under the IASC's new due process, and it may be that multinational corporations (MNCs) simply have not yet focused on the IASC. If this is the case, a steady increase in both the number and the intensity of respondents to future IASC exposure drafts would be expected.

This study raises several questions for future study. As the IASC embarks on its future goals towards internationalization and harmonization of accounting standards, these questions of legitimization, acceptance, flexibility and economic consequences will grow in importance.

A substantial amount of academic literature addresses the role of lobbying in the accounting standards-setting process. These studies primarily focus on lobbyists and lobbying positions directed towards the Financial Accounting Standards Board (FASB) or the Governmental Accounting Standards Board (GASB) in the United States (Watts and Zimmerman, 1978; Kelly, 1983; Deakin, 1989; Roberts and Kurtenbach, 1990; Tandy and Wilburn, 1992). Of increasing importance, however, is the development and harmonization of international accounting standards, i.e., financial reporting standards and practices which apply in a wide range of countries and economies. Although there is some descriptive and theoretical research comparing lobbying behaviour in the US to that in the UK (Benston, 1980; Sutton, 1984), little research addresses the question of lobbying efforts directed towards the International Accounting Standards Committee (IASC), the major international accounting standards-setting organization (Coopers & Lybrand, 1991; Wallace, 1990; Grinyer and Russell, 1992).[1]

Since its inception in 1973 until 1989, the IASC invited commentary from selected interested parties regarding proposed international accounting issues, but carried out its deliberations in relative private, with little, if any, unsolicited public input. Written commentary submitted to the IASC was not released to the public. In 1989, the IASC changed the policy and began soliciting a wider range of public input. Comment letters received by the IASC began being released, upon request, to the general public. In other words, the IASC changed from a relatively introverted strategy of standards setting to a more public strategy, which is similar to that followed by the FASB.

This paper provides the first study dealing with the role of lobbying in an international (i.e., harmonization) accounting standards setting and examines the IASC's process of promulgating International Accounting Standard (IAS) 31, 'Financial Reporting of Interests in Joint Ventures'. Our study begins with an examination of the Exposure Draft (ED 35, 'Financial Reporting of Interests in Joint Ventures') preceding IAS 31 and analyses the lobbying efforts observed during the promulgation process. Consistent with prior literature, our paper analyses lobbyists and their lobbying positions. The observed change in the due process affords us the opportunity also to analyse the IASC's strategic approach to public input. Accordingly, this study incorporates aspects of institutional theory as it relates to strategic choice by organizations.

The comment letters received by the IASC regarding ED 35 were analysed using a form of content analysis. The analyses generally support the hypothesized relationships; namely, lobbying firms tend to be very large, and they lobby against any change in the *status quo*; professional and trade organizations lobby on behalf of their constituents and tend to support the majority positions held by those constituents; and the regulatory body (IASC) seeks acceptance from its constituency by adapting its position to that which is more palatable to the lobbyists.

Few individual firms lobbied the IASC. Rather, the bulk of the respondents to ED 35 were professional associations and organizations. The result contrasts markedly with both our expectations and prior research involving lobbying of the FASB. The dearth of corporate respondents to ED 35 implies that multinational corporations do not yet see the IASC as a serious regulatory organization. In light of the IASC's efforts to achieve institutional legitimacy (Wallace, 1990), the lack of corporate respondents might be rather disturbing except for one factor: the Exposure Draft (ED) analysed in this study represents one of the first standards promulgated under the IASC's new due process, and it may be that multinational corporations (MNCs) simply have not yet 'tuned in' to the IASC. If this is the case, a steady increase in both the number and the intensity of respondents to future IASC exposure drafts would be expected.

While few legal, governmental or regulatory organizations required compliance with IASs during 1989 and 1990, when IAS 31 was being deliberated, many organizations and countries were considering such regulation (Guy, 1992; Denman, 1991). As of early 1993, both the London and Hong Kong Stock Exchanges began allowing foreign issuers to provide only reconciliations from home country GAAP to IASs (Cairns, 1992). Additionally, the International Organization of Securities Commissions (IOSCO) has been increasingly supportive of the IASC's harmonization efforts (Chandler, 1992; Wyatt, 1992; Wallace, 1990). Support from IOSCO is considered to be very important to the IASC because IOSCO represents securities commissions throughout the world, and harmonization is considered to be most possible through efforts of the international capital and securities markets (Guy, 1992; Radebaugh and Gray, 1993; Wyatt, 1992). The relationship between accounting and capital flows is well documented (Radebaugh and Gray, 1993). Therefore, as Fogarty (1992: 348) suggests, studying the organizations which determine acceptable accounting techniques should be 'a special priority'.

The remainder of the paper is organized as follows. Background information about the IASC's due process and the evolution of ED 35 into IAS 31 are presented in the first section. Prior economic consequences literature is reviewed and applied to the IASC case in the second section. Institutional theory is discussed and applicable hypothesized relationships are introduced in the third section. The fourth section contains research design and data collection discussions. The results are analysed in the next section and the final section presents the conclusions and implications of the study.

Background

From its formation in 1973 until 1989, the IASC promulgated IASs with input from a select group of interested parties. Besides the IASC Board members the IASC invited commentary from IASC members, professional associations, government agencies, public accounting firms and corporations. Eventually part of this process was formalized into an official IASC Consultative Group. Table 1 lists the board members and Table 2 lists the members of the consultative group during the focus of this study's time frame. Most of the IASC's deliberations were conducted essentially in private, and comment letters were not released to the public.

Beginning with ED 32, issued in 1989, the IASC began a new due process which more closely mirrors that of the FASB, including public input and a form of public hearings, ED 32, 'Comparability of Financial Statements', generated over 125 comment letters, including forty-seven from various multinational enterprises; most of the comment letters concerning ED 32 were released to the public. However, ED 32 did not result in an IAS; rather, ED 32 was split into several separate exposure drafts. At the time of

Table 1 Members of IASC Board (1989).

Representatives of the accountancy profession from:

Australia*
Canada*
Denmark
France
Germany
Italy
Japan
Jordan
Korea
Netherlands
South Africa
United Kingdom
United States*

and representations of up to four other organizations with an interest
in financial reporting (then only one):

International Co-ordinating Committee of Financial Analysts' Associations

* Participated on Joint Venture Technical Steering Committee.
Source: ISAC (1989).

Table 2 Members of IASC Consultative Group (1989).

Federation Internationale des Bourses de Valeurs (FIBV)
Financial Accounting Standards Board (FASB)
International Association of Financial Executives Institutes (IAFEI)
International Banking Associations
International Bar Association (IBA)
International Chamber of Commerce (ICC)
International Confederation of Free Trade Unions (ICFTU) and World
Confederation of Labour
International Finance Corporation (IFC)
International Organization of Securities Commissions (IOSCO)
The World Bank
Organization for Economic Co-operation and Development (OECD)*
United Nations Centre on Transnational Corporations (UNCTC)*
* Denotes observer status.

Source: IASC (1989).

this study, the comment letters on the separate exposure drafts had not been
released to the public. ED 33, 'Accounting for Income Taxes', was released
in 1989 and generated considerable commentary as well. As of early 1993,
the IASC has not resolved the issue of accounting for income taxes (IASC
1993). Thus, neither ED 32 or ED 33 followed smoothly the IASC's new
due process and, thus, could not be used in this study.

Two EDs, 34 and 35, followed the IASC's new due process from inception to promulgation of an IAS. ED 34, 'Disclosures in the Financial Statements of Banks and Similar Financial Institutions', generated thirty-three comment letters which were released to the public and culminated in IAS 30. ED 35, 'Financial Reporting of Interests in Joint Ventures', generated fifty comment letters and culminated in IAS 31. Since the issue addressed in ED 34 applied only to financial institutions, we hypothesized that ED 34 might not generate much public input from industrial multinationals. ED 35, however, dealt with a salient issue of MNCs, accounting for joint ventures, and we expected considerable public input from multinationals. Accordingly, we chose to study the deliberation process of ED 35 (IAS 31) in this research project. We were interested in the entire deliberation process, so we analysed both lobbying behaviour (comment letters from constituents) and the IASC's reactions and behaviour.

The IASC issued ED 35, 'Financial Reporting of Interests in Joint Ventures', in December 1989. Comment letters were due to the IASC by May 1990. The IASC received fifty comment letters on ED 35 from fifty-two organizations, trade/professional associations and individuals from eighteen different countries.[2] The final standard, IAS 31, 'Financial Reporting of Interests in Joint Ventures', was issued in November 1990.

ED 35 defines the nature of joint operations and prescribes various accounting treatments for several types of joint venture operations. ED 35 defines joint ventures broadly, including not only jointly controlled entities, but also jointly controlled operations and jointly controlled assets. The general tone of the ED stresses the relative importance of the economic substance of relationships within the joint ventures over the legal form of those relationships. Also, the lack of unilateral control by any one venturer and consensus in all major decision making is key to the joint venture relationship in ED 35. Thus, venturers would include in their own financial statements their ownership/responsibility of jointly controlled assets, liabilities, revenues and expenses. Further, ED 35 suggests proportional consolidation for jointly controlled entities. Gains and losses on capital contributions are then to be limited to that portion attributable to the interests of the other venturers/partners. ED 35 also encourages substantial disclosures regarding the nature and scope of joint venture operations.

Although IAS 31 retains much of the flavour of the ED, the IASC did recant its insistence on proportional consolidation for jointly controlled entities by allowing the equity method as an acceptable accounting alternative. In addition, the IASC deleted some of the disclosure requirements in ED 35 and more carefully defined 'unilateral control' and consensus in decision making to encompass a wider range of joint venture arrangements.

Literature review

Prior literature regarding lobbying activities directed towards accounting standards-setting organizations follows two basic paths: (1) as a subset of accounting choice research, lobbying has been studied from management's perspective, and (2) the relevant influence of various parties on standards setters has been analysed. Both of these paths of research follow an economic consequences model, assuming self-interest motivations on the part of the lobbyists. To date, the literature has not tied together these two lines of research in an international accounting lobbying context. Rather, the extant literature has tended to study behaviour of standards-setting organizations (primarily the FASB) as separate from that of the lobbyists. Our research introduces an institutional theory framework which affords us the opportunity to study the relationship of the standards-setting organization (in this case, the IASC) to its constituents from a strategy standpoint.[3]

Much of the prior literature views lobbying accounting standards setters as a subset of accounting choice research (Francis, 1987; Deakin, 1989; Kelly, 1985). In this context, the purpose of the research has been to identify economic incentives associated with management's choices, with respect to either accounting methods or lobbying activities (Francis, 1987). From this line of research, several hypotheses have evolved and have been well supported:

1. Lobbying firms tend to be very large because lobbying is costly, and only the very large firm can receive enough benefit to justify the cost. Additionally, the very large firms are the only ones which can hope to influence standards setter. Finally, lobbying is a means of mitigating political costs (such as tax or antitrust) borne by the very large firms.
2. Debt position (leverage) is a factor significantly influencing a firm's decision to lobby because of the impacts of accounting upon lending agreements (debt covenants) and perceived risk in the marketplace for debt financing.
3. In general, firms will lobby for accounting treatments which broaden their abilities to manage reported income.
4. If management's compensation is based upon reported income, management will prefer accounting methods which maximize its income.

The accounting choice research in lobbying behaviour assumes that lobbying will significantly influence the standards setters' activities, and that lobbyists will get what they want in the process. This line of research implicitly assumes that management feels financial reporting techniques have economic consequences and that changes in accounting standards can significantly impact on firm valuation. Further, as Tandy and Wilburn (1992) note, disagreement with a proposed standard seems to induce response.

In terms of the question addressed in this study, accounting for joint ventures, the economic consequences literature should lead us to hypothesize that large MNCs involved heavily or contemplating involvement in joint venture projects should be interested in the ED. Further, since the ED supported a method which differed from that which the MNC was presently using (as in the case of proportional consolidation), the economic consequences literature would predict voluminous and negative commentary on the part of MNCs.

Another area of lobbying research studied the relative influence of various lobbying organizations. Initially, the research studied the contention that public accounting firms have undue influence on standards-setting organizations (US Senate, 1976; Hating, 1979; Hussein and Ketz, 1980; Brown, 1981; Newman, 1981). Although the research has evolved into more general studies of the relative influence of various types of organizations on standards-setting bodies (Puro, 1985; Taylor, 1987; Tandy and Wilburn, 1992), the question of public accounting influence on the IASC has been noted (IASC, 1992). While the general consensus of this line of research is that public accounting firms do not exhibit undue influence on standards-setting organizations (at least, not on the FASB), at least two observations about the lobbying behaviour of public accounting firms have been supported in the literature:

1. Accounting firms will lobby to express their views.
2. Large multinational accounting firms are more likely to lobby than are small and medium-sized firms.

In summary, the prior literature seems to tell us who will lobby and why, and the prior literature implicitly assumes the standards-setting organization will be influenced by lobbying activities. However, the strategy of the standards-setting organization to deal with and/or encourage participation has not been addressed in the economic consequences literature. In the next section, we discuss this dimension as guided by institutional theory.

Institutional theoretical framework

Institutional theory places organizations within a social setting and explicitly recognizes the influences and interactions of the external social environment on the internal activities of the organization (Selznick, 1957; Scott, 1987). A key element of institutional theory is that an organization strives to be legitimized by becoming or remaining acceptable within the social environment (Dowling and Pfeffer, 1975; Oliver, 1990; Meyer and Scott, 1983; Meyer and Rowen, 1977). In this context, organizations such as the IASC must remain acceptable to their constituencies to survive. Therefore, organizations will continuously monitor the needs and influences of their constituencies and will adjust accordingly to meet those needs.

In the case of the IASC, we observe an organization which solicits direct commentary about its products (accounting standards) from its constituents. An institutional theory framework would assume that the IASC plans to use the commentary in its deliberations. Lobbying in the form of commentary on exposure drafts should be an effective way for constituencies to make known their wishes and influence the outcome of the regulation, e.g. accounting standard. Consistent with the predictions of economic consequences theories in this instance, institutional theories would predict that constituents will respond to the IASC's requests for commentary.

Institutional theory predicts that an organization will be responsive to its environment and will change itself to adapt to (real and/or perceived) shifts in its environment (Scott, 1987). Institutional theorists emphasize that environmental forces make organizations adopt forms which best meet imposed needs, thereby encouraging continuous interaction between an organization and its environment (Thompson, 1976). Although changes in organizational form and strategy may be induced by a variety of factors and may be explained under a variety of rhetorics in the institutional theory literature, organizational change, while difficult, is virtually a foregone conclusion (Zucker, 1977, 1983, 1988; Fogarty, 1992; Scott, 1987).

The IASC's 1989 policy shift triggered our interest in the organization and the process by which it established international accounting standards. The policy shift seemed consistent with an institutional theory explanation of mimetic institutional influence (DiMaggio and Powell, 1983).[4] Mimetic institutional influence suggests that organizations will try to model themselves after other organizations which they perceive as successful or legitimized because to do so enhances their own legitimacy and reduces their exposure to environmental uncertainty. Since the FASB and the IASC were formed in the same year (1973), and the FASB has been more fully legitimized, the mimetic institutional influence explanation might predict that the rational strategy for the IASC to take was to imitate the FASB's format.[5]

International stock exchanges, professional accounting organizations and multinational corporations (MNCs) are the IASC's targeted constituency. Based upon this relationship, MNCs and organizations representing MNCs should be highly inclined to respond to IASC exposure drafts. Institutional theory would also predict that the IASC will try to accommodate the strongest wishes of its constituency when doing so enhances the organization's acceptability without seriously impairing its integrity. This 'give and take' process will usually result in at least some flexibility in the accounting standards in order to accommodate as many of its constituents as possible.[6]

As Fogarty (1992) points out, the notion of resource dependency also enriches the institutional theory perspective. Resource dependency concepts focus on the firm's competition for external sources of funding (Tolbert, 1985; Oliver, 1990). The successful competition for scarce resources enhances the organization's legitimization and increases its likelihood of survival

(Dowling and Pfeffer, 1975; DiMaggio, 1988; Oliver, 1990). In the case of the IASC, resources consist primarily of contributions and, to a lesser extent, rhetorical support. In this regard, the IASC may be in competition with the FASB and other standards-setting organizations for contributions. As we studied the IASC, we observed increasing levels of support from various international organizations, including the International Federation of Stock Exchanges (FIBV), the International Bar Association and the IOSCO.[7] Coupled with the IASC's deliberate attempts to invite a wider range of participants into the standards-setting process, we hypothesize an adaptation and resource-seeking strategy designed to further legitimize the IASC. The change in due process policy may simply be a survival strategy, as Wallace (1990) suggests, but even that explanation is generally consistent within an institutional theory framework.

Consistent with the accounting choice research and economic consequences theory, we agree that very large firms will respond to IASC's exposure drafts because (1) the cost of response is relatively high, (2) very large (multinational) firms are significantly affected by IASC standards and (3) only very large (multinational) firms can hope to have the clout to influence the behaviour of standards-setting organizations. The accounting choice/economic consequences theory hypothesizes that debt position, income manipulation and management compensation plans are factors in the decision to lobby. These three factors are only relevant if the proposed standards affect them. While ED 35 cannot be used to test the income manipulation and management compensation issues because it does not increase or decrease income, the debt position is relevant since proportional consolidation may result in a different balance sheet.

In summary, a large number of MNCs are expected to respond because the issue, joint venture accounting, affects most MNCs. Further, we expected MNCs to oppose any method which required a change from their current practice, such as would be the case with proportional consolidation. Finally, we expected responses from IASC member bodies, the large international accounting firms and other interest parties, especially those who oppose at least part of ED 35.

Research design

Table 3 lists the respondents to ED 35. Respondents were categorized by size, type of organization, country of origin, multinational operations and activity in joint ventures. This data was gathered from a variety of sources, including Disclosure, ABI Inform and NAARS.

The responses were analysed using content analysis and categorized based upon their general support of the standard and/or the IASC's joint venture project as well as their comments on various parts of ED 35. Consistent with Holsti (1969), responses were analysed both for commentary and tone

Table 3 Respondents to IASC Exposure Draft 35 on Joint Ventures.

Member bodies of the IASC:

CIC	Accounting Standards Steering Committee of the Canadian Institute of Chartered Accountants
CGA	Certified General Accountants' Association of Canada
CYP	Institute of Certified Public Accountants of Cyprus
FRN	Compagnie Nationale des Commissaires aux Comptes and Orde des Experts Comptables et des Comptables Agrees (France)
GER	Institut der Wirtschaftsprufer (Federal Republic of Germany)
JPN	Japanese Institute of Certified Public Accountants
NZ	New Zealand Society of Accountants
NRW	Norwegian Institute of State Authorized Public Accountants, Norwegian Accounting Standards Board, and Oslo Stock Exchange
SNG	Institute of Certified Public Accountants of Singapore
SA	South African Institute of Chartered Accountants
SWD	Foreningen Auktoriserade Revisorer FAR (Sweden)
SWZ	Schweizereische Kammer der Bucher-Steuer-und Treuhendexperten (Switzerland)
AIC	American Institute of Certified Public Accountants
NAA	National Association of Accountants (now IMA)
ZMB	Institute of Chartered Accountants of Zimbabwe

Regional and other accounting bodies:

FEE	Federation des Experts Comptables Européens
NJ	New Jersey Society of Certified Public Accountants

Standard-setting bodies:

NTH	Raad Voor De Jaarverslaggeving – Council for Annual Reporting (The Netherlands)
UK	Accounting Standards Committee of the United Kingdom and Ireland
GSB	The staff of the Governmental Accounting Standards Board

Stock exchanges:

JSE	Johannesburg Stock Exchange

Other organizations:

SEC	Securities and Exchange Commission
FEI	Financial Executive Institute
SJP	Security Analysts Association of Japan

Corporations – industry and commerce:

BHP	Broken Hill Proprietary (Australia)
RDS	Royal Dutch Shell (Netherlands & UK)
ABL	Abbott Laboratories
ELI	Eli Lilly and Company
ITT	ITT Corporation
MRC	Merck & Co., Inc.
SAL	Salomon Inc
SHL	Shell Oil Company
TEX	Texaco Inc

Table 3 (cont'd)

Representative organizations – industry and commerce:
100   The Hundred Group (UK)

Banks and banking associations:
CIT   Citicorp – Citibank N.A.
BAA   British Bankers' Association

Accounting firms:
AA   Arthur Andersen & Co (International)
HI   Hodgson Impey (UK)
PW   Price Waterhouse (USA)

Individual, but member of accounting firm:
CLC   M. P. Carscallen, Coopers & Lybrand (Canada)

Those who responded, but desired that their responses remain confidential:
Bahamas Institute of Chartered Accountants
Association for Investment Management and Research (USA)
CIGNA Corporation
E. I. Du Pont de Nemours & Company
General Electric Company
Texas Instruments
AT&T
Coopers & Lybrand (USA)
Plus two other unknown respondents

---

of commentary. In general, however, respondents' letters were quite straightforward and often almost terse, so the concerns often present in content analysis may be somewhat lessened in this study.

The demographic data about the respondents was combined with the results of the content analysis in order to perform several tests analysing the existence of any patterns between responses and respondents.

Finally, the comments and suggestions of the respondents were compared to the requirements in the final standard to see what influence, if any, the respondents had on the IASC. This last step was designed to test the IASC's adaptability and desire to be acceptable to its constituency, as well as to be a weak test of the significance of influence of any one group on the IASC.

Results

Characteristics of respondents

The bulk of the fifty comment letters to ED 35 came from professional organizations and standards-setting bodies. Four public accounting firms and one partner of a large international accounting firm also submitted responses. Of the fifty responses, only fifteen responses were from industrial or financial institutions, contrary to expectations. Of the fifty responses, however, only forty were made public.[8]

The fifteen corporations that did respond were, as predicted, extremely large MNCs. Thirteen of the fifteen businesses responding were US-based multinational corporations, representing several industries, including the oil and gas, financial services and pharmaceutical sectors. The two non-US firms were gigantic mining and oil and gas firms (Royal Dutch Shell and BHP). Each of the US responding corporations was consistently listed in the Fortune 500 in the past decade. The 1988, 1989 and 1990 annual reports for the MNC respondents were reviewed and, interestingly, only six of the thirteen US corporate respondents mentioned international joint venture activities in their annual reports.[9]

Further, NAARS search indicated that the corporate respondents were not particularly representative of those firms which engage heavily in joint ventures. One hundred and nine companies reported significant international joint venture activity in either their 1989 or 1990 annual reports. The companies represented several industries, including oil and gas, automotive, manufacturing and pharmaceutical industries. Several of the joint venture discussions in the annual reports were lengthy and discussed activities in virtually all sectors of the world. We wondered why these firms had not responded to the IASC's exposure draft regarding joint venture accounting. We thought at first that perhaps these firms simply did not lobby standards-setting organizations at all, but a quick review of FASB respondents found the contrary. More often than not these firms did officially comment on FASB exposure drafts.

So, while this study finds some evidence that only very large firms lobby, it does not fully support the economic consequences theory literature. The paucity of responses from seemingly affected firms casts doubt on the perceived economic consequences of the IASC's standards. An alternative explanation may be that many of these firms do not perceive themselves to be affected by IASC standards and, thus, are not part of its constituency. The ramifications of this alternative explanation are discussed more fully later in the paper.

Content analysis of comment letters

Respondents' comment letters were analysed to determine the major areas of comment or concern. The content analysis indicated that the respondents were concerned with three major issues: (1) general need for a joint venture standard, (2) proportionate consolidation and (3) disclosure requirements. On each of these points, respondents were fairly clear and consistent; that is, respondents either supported the issue or they did not, and there was very little evidence of indecision or 'degrees' of support. Accordingly, responses were coded nominally.

Analysis of respondents' positions

Tables 4 and 5 present the results of the content analysis.[10] In general, the comment letters expressed support for the process of internationalization and harmonization of accounting standards, even though many comments had specific disagreements with certain aspects of this particular proposed standard.

The first column in Table 4 presents the 'overall support' category. 'Overall support' is based on respondents' general comments regarding ED 35 and/or their comments regarding the mission of the IASC in the area of joint venture accounting. Sixteen respondents expressed support for ED 35. While less than the majority of respondents, we interpret these responses as evidence to suggest that at least a portion of the IASC's constituency seems to be legitimizing the IASC by acceptance and support. Although twenty-one respondents expressed strong concerns about the appropriateness of ED 35, these respondents seemed to focus primarily on proportionate consolidation issues, as opposed to the overall intent of harmonization of joint venture accounting and the IASC.

The second column of Table 4 presents the issue of proportionate consolidation for jointly controlled entities. The area of proportional consolidation generated the most responses of all separable issues in ED 35. Two diametrically opposed groups formed. The larger group of twenty-four respondents opposed proportional consolidation and is dominated by most of the US, UK and German professional organizations and industrials which responded.

The other group of thirteen respondents supported proportional consolidation and represents a diverse group, including one US public accounting firm (Price Waterhouse), two US pharmaceutical corporations (Merck and Abbott Labs), the British Bankers Association and the professional accounting organizations for France, South Africa, Japan, Sweden and Switzerland. Interestingly, while both Canadian professional accountancy organizations are in this group and support proportionate consolidation, a representative of Coopers & Lybrand (Canada) opposed proportionate consolidation. However, since no Canadian corporations responded, it is not possible to assess which position is representative of Canadian industrials.

The link between the respondents in each opposing group is not well explained by either of the theoretical frameworks used in this study. The evidence appears to support most strongly the view that firms and organizations lobby to maintain the status quo. Inasmuch as the equity method is presently acceptable in the US, the UK and Germany, the domination of the group opposing proportionate consolidation by representatives from these countries appears consistent.

Next, comparisons were made of the first two columns in Table 4, based on general support and proportionate consolidation. Interestingly,

Table 4 Respondents' positions listed and grouped based upon overall support, proportionate consolidation and disclosure requirements.

Respondent		Overall support (S=support, N=neutral or no comment, O=oppose)	Proportionate consolidation (S=support, N=neutral or no comment, O=oppose)	Disclosure requirements (S=support, N=neutral or no comment, O=oppose)
CLC	Can Coopers & L	O	O	N
HI	UK Hodgson Imp	O	O	N
CIT	US Citicorp	O	O	N
ITT	US ITT	O	O	N
RDS	Royal Dutch Sh	O	O	N
TEX	US Texaco	O	O	N
FEE	Fed Eurp Accts	O	O	N
GER	Germany	O	O	N
GSB	US GASB	O	O	N
NAA	US NAA (IMA)	O	O	N
NZ	New Zealand	O	O	N
SEC	US SEC	O	O	N
SAL	US Salomon	O	O	S
100	UK Hundred Grp	O	O	O
ELI	US Eli Lilly	O	O	O
SHL	Shell Oil	O	O	O
FEI	Finl Exec Inst	O	O	O
NTH	Netherlands	O	O	O
UK	UK ASC	O	O	O
AA	Arthur Andersn	S	O	N
BHP	Aust Broken HI	S	O	N
NRW	Norway	S	O	N
SJP	Jp Security Anl	S	O	N
CYP	Cyprus	N	N	N
SNG	Singapore	N	N	N
ZMB	Zimbabwe	N	N	N
ABL	US Abbott Labs	S	S	O
BAA	UK Bankers	S	S	O
FRN	France	S	S	O
PW	Price Waterhse	S	S	S
SA	South Africa	S	S	S
MRC	US Merck	S	S	N
CGA	Can CGA	S	S	N
JSE	JohannesburgSE	S	S	N
NJ	US New Jersey	S	S	N
JPN	Japan	S	S	N
SWD	Sweden	S	S	N
SWZ	Switzerland	S	S	N
CIC	Can CICA	O	S	O

Table 5 Summary of respondents' positions on three main issues.

	Overall support	Proportionate consolidation	Disclosure requirements
Support	16	13	3
Neutral/no comment	3	3	27
Oppose	21	24	10

respondents who oppose proportionate consolidation also seem to dismiss ED 35 in general. Even though the relationship is interesting, it tends to cloud the application of institutional and legitimacy theories to this scenario. From the tenor of the responses, it was not determined if the respondents generally support the IASC's efforts and simply oppose proportionate consolidation, or if they dismissed both. To try and understand this relationship, the respondents to ED 34 were briefly analysed. Seventeen of the ED 35 respondents also responded to ED 34, although none of the dual respondents were corporations. Thus, if response can be at all interpreted as either support, legitimization or acknowledgement of importance, then legitimization is being given to the IASC only by the professional accounting organizations. At this time corporations may not feel a need to respond to each ED from the IASC, either because the IASC is not important, the accounting issue is not important or because corporations are willing to allow professional organizations to handle it.

The third column in Table 4 lists whether respondents support the disclosure requirements. Only ten of the respondents to ED 35 opposed or suggested an alteration in the proposed disclosure requirements. While that number does not, on the surface, seem important, it is because twenty-seven of the respondents made no comment on the disclosure requirements.

Next, all three issues were examined together: general support, proportionate consolidation and support of disclosure requirements. The first group of thirteen respondents oppose both ED 35 in general and proportionate consolidation specifically. They are silent with respect to additional disclosures, which might mean that by dismissing the overall content of the ED, they have also effectively dismissed the disclosure requirements. While this cluster is dominated by US respondents, it is by no means representative of all US respondents, either corporations, regulatory bodies or professional organizations.

Other respondents, when grouped by their common position, were fairly diverse and did not appear to have a common link, at least as explained by the theoretical frameworks. The BHP, AA, NRW and SJP group of respondents, however, while tiny, is quite interesting. This group is made up of respondents who expressed general support for ED 35, opposed proportionate consolidation and were silent with respect to additional disclosures.

This might be the type of response one would expect to see to support the legitimizing theories; that is, the constituencies support the institution in principle, but oppose some of its edicts. This is precisely the type of response a 'legitimate' organization would generate, much like that observed with respect to the FASB.

That this group is so tiny may be interpreted in the context of institutional theory. One might argue that, since the IASC has a new due process, the need for public legitimization by respondents is not understood by the IASC's constituents. Further, the 'constituency' may not yet realize that it is the constituency. This interpretation would imply that, once constituents understand this need, future EDs should generate more responses and interest by both professional organizations and corporations. Of course, any increase in the level and/or intensity of response might also indicate an increasing economic consequences perspective.

Analysis of positions by group membership

We further analysed the groups formed by the issues 'overall support', 'proportional consolidation' and 'disclosure', to see if certain types of organizations held similar views. The respondents were grouped by country (grouping US and UK together and comparing them to other countries), and industry (including categories for corporate, public accounting and professional organizations). These analyses are presented in Table 6.

Grouping by industry/organization was uniformly insignificant. No issue identified divided respondents based on their type of organization. Grouping by country, however, was significant in the 'overall support' and 'proportional consolidation' issues. With a mean response of −.43, the US/UK group is significantly different (and generally non-supportive of ED 35) from the other countries responding. This difference is significant at a .035 level 38 with degrees of freedom. In other words, in general, US or UK respondents were less likely to support ED 35 than respondents from other countries. Further, the US/UK group tended generally to oppose proportional consolidation, with a mean response of −.52; and was significantly

Table 6 Analysis of responses by country of origin: difference of means tests.

	N	Overall support	Proportional consolidation	Disclosure requirements
US/UK	21	−.4286	−.5238	−.2381
Other countries	19	.2105	.0000	−.1053
t-value		2.19**	1.82*	.76

* significant at .076 confidence level (two-tailed test).
** significant at .035 confidence level (two-tailed test).

203

different from respondents from other countries on this issue, with a confidence level of .076. We find this result odd in light of recent criticisms directed towards the IASC which claim that the IASC is dominated by US and UK influences. Though this criticism appears somewhat validated later by the IASC's response to objections from the US and UK.

The US/UK versus everyone else split led us to review the comment letters again. The data lend supports to the economic consequences view that respondents are unwilling to change from the status quo. In the case of ED 35, proportional consolidation represented a change from the status quo, which appeared to be unacceptable to US and UK respondents. Proportional consolidation, while having no differential impact on net income than the equity method, changes the picture of the balance sheet. The relationships on the balance sheet should be similar under both methods, but the increase in both assets and liabilities may be undesirable to companies used to using the equity method, especially those with debt covenant restrictions.

Analysis of the IASC's response

The final analysis compared the requirements of the ED with the IAS, given the nature and intensity of respondents' comments. Of major importance was that the IASC modified the ED to allow the equity method for accounting for jointly controlled entities. The IASC also modified the descriptions and requirements for disclosures in accordance with respondents' comments. This action is consistent with institutional theory. Seeking legitimization and survival, the IASC must remain acceptable to its constituency. If the IASC is to achieve its goal of harmonization, it must accomplish these objectives (Wallace, 1990). One strategy to accomplish these goals is to maintain a posture of flexibility and receptivity to public input (Wallace, 1990).[11] This does, however, also reinforce criticism of the IASC as being dominated by UK and US interests (Hove, 1990).

One important note is that the IASC, in order to pass a new IAS, must get three-fourths of the vote of the IASC board members (IASC, 1989). Thus the IAS must be acceptable to the vast majority of the Board. Of the letters from respondents from countries represented on the IASC Board, a majority opposed proportional consolidation (see Table 7). Therefore,

Table 7 Analysis of respondents from IASC board member countries

	All support	Most support	Split	Most oppose	All oppose
Position on proportionate consolidation	France South Africa	Canada	Japan	United Kingdom United States	Australia Germany Netherlands

assuming that Board members at least consider the desires of those in their own country as well as seek general legitimacy, some compromise was required in order to achieve the required number of votes to approve a joint venture IAS.

A final issue considered was the relationship of the funding of the IASC to its decision, i.e. the resource dependency issue. Historically, the primary sources of funding for the IASC were the International Federation of Accountants (IFAC) and the IASC board members themselves. More recently, funds have also been contributed by the six largest international accounting firms, as well as by other accounting firms and corporations, including BHP (Australia) and ITT (IASC, 1991). Of those known for both taking positions on ED 35 and contributing to the IASC, both corporations (BHP and ITT) were opposed to proportional consolidation, while the accounting firms were split on the issue. While contributions may be made in order to increase an organization's influence on the IASC, insufficient information is currently available in order to reach any real conclusion on this matter.

Conclusion

This study examined the IASC's process of promulgating IAS 31, 'Financial Reporting of Interests in Joint Ventures', the lobbying efforts observed during the process and the interaction between the IASC and its constituents. The interaction between respondents and the IASC is consistent with an institutional theory explanation of organizational change and adaptation to environment pressures. The results were also consistent with an economic consequences model in that only very large firms lobby and they lobby against virtually any change in the *status quo*. Further, the respondents did tend to cluster around a few salient issues. However, their behaviour and the small number of corporate respondents did not strongly support an economic consequences explanation.

Also interesting from both an economic consequences viewpoint and an institutional legitimacy standpoint is the fact that US companies heavily involved in international joint ventures did not respond to the IASC. Given the recent attention paid to harmonization of financial reporting standards in both the academic and popular press and the attention the issue is receiving from international stock exchanges, more responses from MNCs were expected. However, further study of both the data and MNCs active in international joint venture activity led us to conclude that the IASC probably was not perceived as a salient regulatory body by most of those companies. In addition, we studied one of IASC's 'new due process' standards, which may not have attracted much attention from these corporations since the IASC's new standards-setting process was such a recent event.

The study, like most lobbying studies, is subject to several limitations. For example, the decision to lobby is inherently a respondent specific choice, and, thus, any study of lobbyists represents a choice-based sample. In this context, that bias is acceptable since we were primarily interested in those who did lobby as opposed to those who did not. However, future research in this area may choose to concentrate on those organizations involved in joint venture activities who did not lobby, especially given evidence to suggest that this population is large.

Another criticism of lobbying studies is that each study tends to treat lobbying as a single-issue, single-period decision, when it actually may be a multiple-issue, multiple-period decision. Inasmuch as ED 35 represents only one of the first two standards to have endured the entire process under the IASC's new rules, we have no way currently of assessing the impact (if any) of this criticism. As the IASC continues under its new due process, future research may involve longitudinal studies of the process of lobbying over time by particular firms and/or organizations. Another area for future research may focus on multiple entity lobbying, i.e., a study of firms who lobby a variety of accounting standards-setting bodies.

Additionally, we chose to study an ED which eventually became an IAS. From an institutional theory standpoint, a study of those EDs which did not become IASs may also be relevant. Our focus in this paper was the more complete due process, but future research may include studies of 'unsuccessful' EDs.

The conclusions of this study suggest a basis for future research examining MNC reaction to forthcoming IASC exposure drafts. The IASC is publicizing its activities more fully and has recently gained the support of IOSCO and the interest of the SEC. Harmonization continues to be a popular idea, both in the EC and the Pacific Rim. Even the AICPA (American Institute of Certified Public Accountants) and the IMA (Institute of Management Accountants) are now regularly announcing new IASC EDs in their publications. Accordingly, we expect to see an increase in both the number and intensity of responses to future IASC exposure drafts. The current study provides a base from which to launch those future studies.

This study also motivates future research dealing with the IASC's move towards more restrictive accounting standards (as evidenced by the many recently released EDs). As these EDs, most of which are components of ED 32, move through the due process, the interaction between the IASC and its constituencies may be compared to the actions predicted by institutional theories and economic consequences theories.

While this study raises interesting questions for future study, it also contributes to the current literature in at least two important areas. First, this study represents some of the first empirical work examining lobbying accounting standards setting bodies in an international context. Second, this study addresses the applicability of two theoretical frameworks, each developed in a US context, to an international context.

Notes

We gratefully acknowledge the helpful comments from our colleagues at the University of Utah, Jerry Searfoss of Deloitte and Touche, Anne Loft (the editor) and an anonymous reviewer. We thank the Center for International Business Education and Research at the University of Utah for its support of this project. Any remaining errors are our own.

The data used in this study were purchased from a variety of sources, all of which are available to the public. Included in the data sources are: the IASC, *NAARS, Disclosure* and *ABI Inform.*

1 Wallace (1990) discusses the issue of lobbying the IASC, but his focus is the IASC's reactions to lobbying as opposed to the motivations and/or behaviours of the lobbyists. While Grinyer and Russell (1992) discuss whether the IASC affects the UK standard setting process, their focus is lobbying efforts towards the UK's Accounting Standard Committee.
2 In one instance three Norwegian organizations jointly penned responses to ED 35, thus providing fifty letters in total from fifty-two organizations.
3 Fogarty (1992) suggests studying the FASB from an institutional theory standpoint.
4 For a discussion of mimetic institutional influence as applied to the FASB, see Fogarty (1992).
5 For a discussion of the legitimization of the FASB, see Johnson and Solomons (1984).
6 Though with the increased involvement of IOSCO in the activities of the IASC, the push for narrower standards may eventually outweigh the push for flexible standards.
7 For a more detailed discussion of this point, see FIBV (1991) and IOSCO (1991).
8 In the transition to the 'new due process', the IASC allowed respondents confidentiality if they so chose. Five corporate respondents elected that option.
9 Respondents mentioning joint venture activity in the Form 10-K include AT&T, General Electric, ITT, Merck, Shell and Texaco.
10 Cluster analysis was also performed with the data and provided similar results.
11 Again, it will be interesting to see if the IASC continues to allow flexible IASs in the future, given that IOSCO, a new major constituent, is strongly lobbying for narrower IASs.

References

Benston, G. J. (1980) 'The Establishment and Enforcement of Accounting Standards: Methods, Benefits and Costs', *Accounting and Business Research*, Winter: 51–60.

Brown, P. R. (1981) 'A Descriptive Analysis of Select Input Bases of the Financial Accounting Standards Board', *Journal of Accounting Research*, 19: 232–46.

Cairns, D. (1989) 'IASC's Blueprint for the Future', *Accountancy*, 104 (1156): 80–2.

Cairns, D. (1992) 'FIBV/Toronto Stock Exchange Workshop: Should Listed Companies Conform with IAS?', *IASC Insight*, July: 7–8.

Campbell, A. (1990) *Lobbying Intensity and Corporate Management's Opinion: The Marketable Securities Case, 1975*, working paper, University of Colorado at Boulder.

Chandler, R. A. (1992) 'The International Harmonization of Accounting: In Search of Influence', *International Journal of Accounting*, 27: 222–33.

Choi, F. D. S. and Mueller, G. G. (1992) *International Accounting*, 2nd edition. Englewood Cliffs, NJ: Prentice-Hall.

Coopers & Lybrand (International) (1991) *1991 International Accounting Summaries: A Guide for Interpretation and Comparison*. New York: Wiley.

Deakin, E. B. (1989) 'Rational Economic Behavior and Lobbying on Accounting Issues: Evidence from the Oil and Gas Industry', *The Accounting Review*, January: 137–51.

Denman, J. H. (1991) *The Comparative Analysis of Financial Statements by Use of International Accounting Standards*, paper presented at the Third Asian-Pacific Conference on Accounting Issues, Honolulu, 18 October.

DiMaggio, P. (1988) 'Interest and Agency in International Theory,' in *Institutional Patterns and Organizations*, Zucler, L. (ed.) Cambridge, MA: Ballinger Press: 3–21.

DiMaggio, P. and Powell, W. (1983) 'The Iron Cage Revisited: Institutional Isomorphism and Collective Rationality in Organizational Fields', *American Sociological Review*, 48: 147–60.

Dowling, J. and Pfeffer, J. (1975) 'Organizational Legitimacy: Social Values and Organizational Behaviour' *Pacific Sociological Review* 18(1): 122–36.

Francis, J. R. (1987) 'Lobbying Against Proposed Accounting Standards: The Case of Employers Pension Accounting', *Journal of Accounting and Public Policy*, 6: 35–57.

Federation Internationale Des Bourses De Valeurs (FIBV) (1991) *Annual Report 1990*. Paris: FIBV.

Fogarty, T J. (1992) 'Financial Accounting Standard Setting as an Institutionalized Action Field: Constraints, Opportunities and Dilemmas', *Journal of Accounting and Public Policy*, 11: 331–55.

Grinyer, J. R. and Russell, A. (1992) 'National Impediments to International Harmonization: Evidence of Lobbying in the UK', *Journal of International Accounting Auditing and Taxation*, 1(1): 13–31.

Guy, P. (1992) 'Regulatory Harmonization to Achieve Effective International Competition', in Edwards, F. R. and Patrick, H. T. (eds) *Regulating International Financial Markets: Issues and Policies*. Boston: Kluwer Academic.

Haring, J. R. (1979) 'Accounting Rules and "The Accounting Establishment" ', *Journal of Business*, 52(4): 507–19.

Holsti, O. E. (1969) *Content Analysis for the Social Sciences and Humanities*. Addison-Wesley.

Hove, M. R. (1990) 'The Anglo-American Influence on International Accounting Standards: The Case of the Disclosure Standards of the International Accounting Standards Committee', in R. S. O. Wallace (ed.) *Research in Third World Accounting*, Vol. 1. London: JAI Press, pp. 55–66.

Hussein, M. E. and Ketz, J. E. (1980) 'Ruling Elites of the FASB: A Study of the Big Eight', *Journal of Accounting, Auditing and Finance*, 3(4): 354–67.

Hussein, M. E. and Ketz, J. E. (1991) 'Accounting Standards-Setting in the U.S.: An Analysis of Power and Social Exchange', *Journal of Accounting and Public Policy*, 10: 59–81.

International Accounting Standards Committee (1988) *Survey of the Use and Application of International Accounting Standards 1988*. London: IASC.

International Accounting Standards Committee (1989) *International Accounting Standards 1990*. London: IASC.

International Accounting Standards Committee (1990) 'Financial Reporting of Interests in Joint Ventures: From E35 to IAS 31', *IASC News*, 19: 7–11.

International Accounting Standards Committee (1991) 'IASC Funding: New Contributions From Business Community', *IASC Insight*, October: 2.

International Accounting Standards Committee (1992a) *International Accounting Standards 1993*. London: IASC.

International Accounting Standards Committee (1992b) 'Involving the Business Community', *IASC Insight*, March: 1.

International Organization of Securities Commissions (IOSCO) (1991) *Annual Report 1991*. Montreal: IOSCO.

Jensen, M. C. and Meekling, W. H. (1976) 'Theory of the Firm: Managerial Behavior, Agency Costs and Ownership Structure', *Journal of Financial Economics*, October: 305–60.

Johnson, S. B. and Solomons, D. (1984) 'Institutional Legitimacy and the FASB', *Journal of Accounting and Public Policy* 3(2): 165–83.

Kelly, L. (1982) 'Corporate Lobbying and Changes in Financing or Operating Activities in Reaction to FAS No. 8', *Journal of Accounting and Public Policy*, 1(2): 153–73.

Kelly, L. (1983) 'The Development of a Positive Theory of Corporate Management's Role in External Financial Reporting', *Journal of Accounting Literature*, 2: 111–50.

Kelly, L. (1985) 'Corporate Management Lobbying on FAS No. 8: Some Further Evidence', *Journal of Accounting Research*, 23: 619–33.

Meyer, J. W. and Rowan, B. (1977) 'Institutionalized Organizations: Formal Structure as Myth and Ceremony', in Meyer, J. W. and Scott, W. R. (eds) *Organizational Environments*. Beverly Hills, CA: Sage, pp. 45–67.

Meyer, J. W. and Scott, W. R. (1983) *Organizational Environments*. Beverly Hills, CA: Sage.

Newman, D. P. (1981) 'An Investigation of the Distribution of Power in the APB and FASB', *Journal of Accounting Research*, 19: 247–62.

Oliver, C. (1990) 'Determinants of Interorganizational Relationship: Integration and Future Developments', *Academy of Management Review*, 15(2): 241–65.

Puro, M. (1985) 'Do Large Accounting Firms Collude in the Standards-Setting Process?', *Journal of Accounting, Auditing, and Finance*, 8(3): 165–77.

Radebaugh, L. and Gray, S. (1993) *International Accounting and Multinational Enterprises*, 2nd edition. New York: Wiley.

Roberts, R. W. and Kurtenbach, J. M. (1990) 'An Analysis of Lobbying Activities before the Governmental Accounting Standards Board', working paper, University of Missouri-Columbia.

Scott, W. R. (1987) 'The Adolescence of Institutional Theory', *Administrative Science Quarterly*, 32: 493–511.

Selznick, P. (1957) *Leadership in Administration*. New York: Harper & Row.

Sutton, T. (1984) 'Lobbying of Accounting Standard-Setting Bodies in the U.K. and the U.S.A.: A Downsian Analysis', *Accounting, Organizations; and Society*, 9(1): 81–95.

Tandy, P. R. and Wilburn, N. L. (1992) 'Constituent Participation in Standard-Setting: The FASB's First 100 Statements', *Accounting Horizons*, 6: 47–58.

Taylor, S. L. (1987) 'International Accounting Standards: An Alternative Rationale', *Abacus*, (23)2: 157–71.

Thompson, J. D. (1976) *Organizations and Beyond: Selected Essays of James D. Thompson*, ed. W. A. Rushing and M. N. Zald. Lexington, Mass.: Lexington Books, D. C. Heath.

Tolbert, E (1985) 'Institutional Environments and Resource Dependence: Sources of Administrative Structure in Higher Education', *Administrative Science Quarterly*, 30(1): 1–13.

US Senate (1976) 'Subcommittee on Reports, Accounting and Management of the Senate Committee on Government Operations, 94th Congress, 2nd Session', *The Accounting Establishment.. A Staff Study (Metcalf Report)*. Washington, DC: Government Printing Office.

Wallace, R. S. O. (1990) 'Survival Strategies of a Global Organization: The Case of the International Accounting Standards Committee', *Accounting Horizons*, 4: 1–22.

Watts, R. L. and Zimmerman, J. L. (1978) 'Towards a Positive Theory of the Determination of Accounting Standards', *The Accounting Review*, 53: 112–34.

Watts, R. L. and Zimmerman, J. L. (1986) *Positive Accounting Theory*. Englewood Cliffs, NJ: Prentice-Hall.

Wyatt, A. R. (1991) 'International Accounting Standards and Organizations: Quo Vadis?' in Choi, F. D. S. (ed.) *Handbook of International Accounting*. New York: Wiley.

Wyatt, A. R. (1992) 'An Era of Harmonization', *Journal of International Financial Management & Accounting*, 4(1): 63–80.

Zucker, L. (1977) 'The Role of Institutions in Cultural Persistence', *American Sociological Review*, 42(5): 726–43.

Zucker, L. (1983) 'Organizations as Institutions', in Bacharach, S. (ed.) *Advances in Organizational Theory and Research*. New York: JAI Press, pp. 1–43.

Zucker, L. (1988) 'Where Do Institutional Patterns Come From?', in Zucker, L. (ed.) *Institutional Patterns and Organizations*. Cambridge, Mass.: Ballinger, pp. 23–49.

Part 7

COMPLIANCE AND HARMONISATION WITH IASs

40

THE HARMONIZATION OF INTERNATIONAL ACCOUNTING STANDARDS, 1973–1979

R. D. Nair and Werner G. Frank

Source: *International Journal of Accounting* (Fall 1981): 61–77.

In the decade of the 1970s, serious attempts were made to harmonize international accounting practices. This effort was deemed important because the growth of international trade and of multinational corporations necessitated the comparison of accounting data across national boundaries. Differences which existed in accounting practices constituted a barrier to international communication of valid financial data.

An assessment of these efforts at harmonization now needs to be made. Sufficient time has elapsed, a large number of accounting issues have been addressed in this effort, and enough empirical data are now available for such an assessment to be neither premature nor impractical. This assessment is particularly necessary because the barriers to harmonization are considerable. Economic, social, and political environments of nations differ, and these influences may lead to corresponding differences in accounting practices. Frank, and Nair and Frank found that underlying environmental variables were closely associated with groupings of countries based on their accounting practices.[1] Nair and Frank state the implications of such a finding are that "reaching the goal of harmonization may be difficult because, given the . . . association, countries may be reluctant to make a change in accounting practices so long as the underlying environmental variables are significantly different."[2] It is of interest to see whether attempts at harmonization have succeeded despite such hurdles. In spite of these obstacles, the growing interdependence of countries and the growing commonality of worldwide economic conditions might have provided an added impetus to the trend toward harmonization.

213

The authors find in this study that the attempts at harmonization of accounting practices have met considerable success. The study isolates those practices on which progress has been made; relates those practices to the pronouncements of the major international standards-setting organization, the International Accounting Standards Committee (IASC); and examines which countries have made changes regarding those accounting practices. The authors also find that practices adopted in the United States seem to have had a considerable influence on the direction taken in the international accounting standard-setting process.

The first section of this study describes the institutional efforts directed toward harmonization. The second section describes the data sources used in this study, the accounting practices which were studied, and the countries which were examined. The third section details the methods of analysis which were used and the results of those analyses. The next section presents the analysis of national involvement in harmonization, and the final section presents the conclusions of this study.

Efforts at harmonization

Several institutions have addressed the problem of differences in accounting standards between nations and the need to eliminate all unnecessary differences and to understand better those differences which are justified. A discussion of such efforts can be found in Cummings and Chetkovich[3] and Berton.[4] The most important of these institutions is undoubtedly the IASC, established in 1973 by the accounting bodies of nine countries: Australia, Canada, France, Germany, Japan, Mexico, the Netherlands, the United Kingdom and Ireland (jointly), and the United States. At present, IASC's board consists of a representative from each of the founding countries and two representatives selected for members admitted after 1973. Members of the IASC have as their goal to ensure (1) that conformity exists between accounting standards in their own countries and those of the IASC, (2) that independent auditors examine financial statements for compliance with these standards, and (3) that noncompliance is either disclosed in the statements, or is referred to in the audit report. A discussion of the working procedures of IASC can be found in a publication from Deloitte Haskins & Sells.[5]

The authors have restricted their study to the first ten Statements of International Accounting Standards. These ten standards, listed in exhibit 1, were issued during the period for which the authors have survey data on the prevalent accounting practices in a wide range of countries, 1975 to 1978.[6]

An examination of these standards shows that many of them are quite similar to the authoritative pronouncements on those topics in the United States, although differences of varying degrees do exist. For example, with respect to valuation of inventories in the context of historical cost, IASC

Exhibit 1. IASC Statements of International Accounting Standards Issued Prior to January 1, 1979.

(Date of issuance in parentheses)

No. 1 — Disclosure of Accounting Policies (January 1975)

No. 2 — Valuation and Presentation of Inventories in the Context of the Historical Cost System (October 1975)

No. 3 — Consolidated Financial Statements (June 1976)

No. 4 — Depreciation Accounting (October 1976)

No. 5 — Information to Be Disclosed in Financial Statements (October 1976)

No. 6 — Accounting Responses to Changing Prices (June 1977)

No. 7 — Statement of Changes in Financial Position (October 1977)

No. 8 — Unusual and Prior Period Items and Changes in Accounting Policies (February 1978)

No. 9 — Accounting for Research and Development Activities (July 1978)

No. 10 — Contingencies and Events Occurring after the Balance Sheet Date (October 1978)

Statement No. 2, "Valuation and Presentation of Inventories," states that valuation should be at the lower of historical cost and net realizable value. The first-in, first-out or weighted-average methods are preferred, although the last-in, first-out or base-stock methods are also permitted. The treatment of unusual and prior period items by IASC is similar to the treatment outlined by the Accounting Principles Board (APB) in *Opinion No. 9*, "Reporting the Results of Operations," rather than the more stringent requirements of *Opinion No. 30*, "Reporting the Results of Operations," and *Statement of Financial Accounting Standards No. 16*, "Prior Period Adjustments," of the Financial Accounting Standards Board (FASB).

On the other hand, IASC required in June 1977, in *Statement No. 6*, "Accounting Responses to Changing Prices," that if no procedures had been adopted to show the impact of changing prices, whether of general or specific prices or both, that fact should be disclosed. In *Statement No. 9*, "Accounting for Research and Development Activities," IASC also permits deferral, and subsequent amortization, of research and development costs if certain criteria are satisfied, contrary to FASB *Statement of Financial Accounting Standards No. 2*, "Accounting for Research and Development Costs."

In sum, of the ten pronouncements, only the two dealing with changing prices and research and development can be regarded as being substantially in conflict with the U.S. posture on those topics at the time the standards were issued by the IASC. This is not surprising considering that five countries — Canada, Germany, Japan, Mexico, and the Netherlands — of the original nine members of IASC from 1973 were identified by Frank to be members of the "U.S. model."[7] In other words, these other countries followed accounting practices very similar to those in the United States. The authors would, therefore, expect the U.S. influences to prevail on IASC.

Data sources

The data for the analyses were drawn from three Price Waterhouse surveys of accounting principles and reporting practices in different countries, the first of which was published in 1973, the second in 1975, and the third in 1980.[8] These surveys constitute an important data source for a longitudinal study of change such as this one, especially since the time span of the three surveys corresponds with the existence of IASC.

The Price Waterhouse survey data were compiled from information provided by their various offices around the world. Uniform procedures were used worldwide in collecting and compiling the data. Strenuous efforts were made to ensure accuracy of the data. The firm also made a conscious effort not to bias the responses in favor of the accounting practices of its own clients or its own views on the desirability of a given practice. However, in countries where a lack of publicly available information prevents an assessment of the degree of conformity of a given practice, the response represents the best judgment of the Price Waterhouse people in those countries. Similarly, judgment was used when a diversity of practice existed in a country. Moreover, the format of the survey responses makes it impossible to detect local variations in practice which may be of importance.

All responses were based on requirements applied to financial statements prepared for the shareholders of profit-oriented firms which issue their statements to the general public. The responses were also based on any other document which a firm is required by law to produce as part of its annual report to shareholders. It should be noted that the firms whose practices are surveyed may not themselves be comparable across countries. For example, many of the firms in one country may be involved in extracting natural resources, agriculture, or in the retailing industry while in another, manufacturing firms may constitute the major sector. However, the firms from a given country whose practices are surveyed are likely to be comparable over time. These shortcomings of the data should be kept in mind when evaluating the results. These limitations could not be corrected by the authors, who nevertheless feel that the value of the data, especially for a longitudinal study such as this, far outweighs their defects.

Although the procedures for collecting the data have been consistent over time, the number of countries in the survey, the type and number of questions asked, and the nature of the possible responses have changed. The methods for correcting for these changes are discussed next.

The 1979 survey included sixty-four countries whereas the 1975 and 1973 surveys included forty-six and thirty-eight countries, respectively. The current study concentrated on the thirty-seven countries which were common to all three surveys because these were the countries for which comparisons at the three points in time could be made. These countries are listed in exhibit 2.

Exhibit 2. Countries Common to 1973, 1975, and 1979 Price Waterhouse Surveys.

Argentina	Ireland	Philippines
Australia	Italy	Singapore
Bahamas	Jamaica	South Africa
Belgium	Japan	Spain
Bolivia	Kenya	Sweden
Brazil	Mexico	Switzerland
Canada	Netherlands	Trinidad and Tobago
Chile	New Zealand	United Kingdom
Colombia	Pakistan	United States
Fiji	Panama	Uruguay
France	Paraguay	Venezuela
Germany	Peru	Zimbabwe
India		

The number of accounting practices surveyed also changed; there were 233 practices in the 1973 survey, 264 in 1975, and 267 in 1979. In addition, not all the practices surveyed in a given year were included in subsequent surveys. Finally, the form in which some questions were asked also changed from one survey to the next. To ensure a consistent and comparable data set, the authors identified 131 practices which had been included in all three surveys.[9] In terms of general categories, these 131 practices could be classified as follows:

Broad concepts	7 practices or concepts
Accounting policies	2
Fixed assets and depreciation	25
Inventories	16
Investments	6
Receivables and liabilities	11
Long-term liabilities	3
Shareholders' equity	14
Other balance-sheet items	6
Income statement	18
Consolidations	16
Foreign currency	6
Directors' activities	1
	131 practices or concepts

This selection procedure had the effect of ignoring changes with respect to certain accounting practices which were surveyed in 1979 but not in 1973 or 1975. Such issues were not as noteworthy during the early part of the decade but received greater attention in the latter part. Examples of such issues are accounting for price changes, and for segments of a business.

A bias is therefore created in the sense that the study does not deal with a random sample of practices on which the authors were able to collect data in these thirty-seven countries in the three different years. Instead, these practices were the survivors in the sense that they were considered important in all three years. Because of this, practices on which harmonization took place toward the end of the period may have been excluded; alternatively, a disproportionately large number of those practices on which harmonization had already taken place may have been included. However, the fact that these practices were included in all three surveys indicates that they are not trivial issues.

The format of the responses also changed over time. The categories into which a country's position on a practice was classified were different in each of the three surveys. These categories are listed here.

In 1973	*In 1975*	*In 1979*
1. Required	1. Required	1. Required
2. Majority	2. Majority	2. Majority
3. About half	3. About half	3. Predominant practice
4. Minority	4. Minority	4. Minority practice
5. No application	5. Not found in practice	5. Rarely or not found
6. Not permitted	6. Not permitted	6. Not accepted
	7. No application	7. Not permitted
		8. No application

Before the analyses could proceed, these categories had to be made consistent over time. This was accomplished by collapsing certain categories in each survey to yield the following five broader categories:

1. Required (including Insisted upon from 1979);
2. Predominant practice (including Majority and About half from both 1973 and 1975);
3. Minority practice;
4. No application (including Not found in practice from 1975 and Rarely or not found from 1979); and
5. Not permitted (including Not accepted from 1979).

The analyses, presented in the next section, deal with these five new categories.

Analysis and results

To harmonize accounting standards is to bring them into agreement. Thus, with respect to the data base of this study, the authors accepted that harmonization on a given practice has taken place if all countries are in the same category with respect to that practice. Complete harmonization would require that all countries were in one or the other *extreme* category, Required or Not permitted. Even if all countries fell into one of the two intermediate categories, Predominant or Minority practice, this would indicate that true uniformity has not yet been achieved since some diversity of practice does exist within the individual countries. Clustering of all countries in the remaining category, No application, would indicate that the practice is not important with respect to these thirty-seven countries. Thus, for the purposes of this study, the authors concentrated on the extent to which the thirty-seven countries were to be found in either the Required or Not permitted categories.

An analysis was therefore conducted on each of the 131 accounting practices to determine how the thirty-seven countries were classified in each of the three years that the survey was conducted. For example, for the practice Depreciation methods are disclosed, the following distribution appeared:

Category/ Years	Required	Predominant practice	Minority practice	No application	Not permitted	Total
1973	9	7	15	6	0	37
1975	16	8	9	3	1	37
1979	28	2	5	2	0	37

This indicates that whereas only nine of the thirty-seven countries required disclosure of depreciation methods in 1973, twenty-eight of the same thirty-seven required such disclosure in 1979.

There was no accounting practice among the 131 for which all thirty-seven countries were in either the Required or Not permitted categories, that is, there was no practice on which complete harmonization had been achieved. Accordingly, a less stringent operational definition of harmonization was adopted. The authors looked for those practices on which more than half of the thirty-seven countries (nineteen or more countries) were to be found in either the Required or Not permitted categories by 1979. We identified 49 such practices, or approximately 37 percent, from the original 131. For 39 of these practices, the majority of countries were in the Required category while for the other 10, the majority were in the Not permitted category.

Even though more than half the countries were in agreement on these forty-nine practices, this harmony cannot be ascribed to the activities of the IASC without further analysis. For example, the countries may have been in agreement long before IASC came into existence. Therefore, the next step of the analysis was an attempt to determine the number of accounting practices of these forty-nine for which significant changes in distribution had taken place during the period 1973 to 1979.

To determine whether the shifts during the period were statistically significant, Friedman's Analysis of Variance[10] was utilized. The Friedman test can be used to examine the rankings on a criterion for the same group of cases (that is, countries) under two or more different conditions (such as might exist at different points in time). This technique was appropriate for the purposes here since the three surveys were not independent but instead constituted repeated measures on the same sample of thirty-seven countries. For this statistical test to be used, the data had to be recast in a different form. For example, assume the extent of usage on a given practice in two countries for the three years were as follows:

Country/Year	1973	1975	1979
Country A	Minority practice (coded as 3)	No application (coded as 4)	Not permitted (coded as 5)
Country B	Predominant practice (coded as 2)	Predominant practice (coded as 2)	Required practice (coded as 1)

Then this data for each country (row) could be transformed into ranks as follows:

Country/Year	1973	1975	1979
Country A	1	2	3
Country B	2.5	2.5	1

These rankings can then be analyzed by Friedman's Analysis of Variance to determine whether the overall change in ranks during the time period is statistically significant. The null hypothesis in such a test is that there is no difference in ranks over time. The test statistic follows a Chi-square distribution, and for the purposes of this study, a significance level of 5 percent was selected.

The results indicate that of these forty-nine practices (those for which the presence of harmony of practice between countries had been detected), twenty-nine had significant changes in ranks between the three surveys.[11] Investigating further, it was found that for twenty-five of these twenty-nine practices, the significant shift occurred between the 1975 and 1979 surveys. (IASC Statement No. 1 was issued in January 1975, and thus it is not surprising that most of the significant changes should be observed after that date.) The twenty-nine practices are listed in exhibit 3. All of these practices except numbers 7, 21, 25, and 29 had significant shifts between 1975 and 1979. For nine of the practices, the majority of countries were in the Not permitted category rather than the Required category. These nine were numbers 13, 15, 16, 17, 21, 22, 23, 26, and 27.

In comparing the general topic areas covered by these twenty-nine practices with those covered by the IASC in their first ten pronouncements, it is of interest to note that all pronouncements except those dealing with

Exhibit 3. Accounting Concepts and Practices Which Had Significant Movement
to Harmonization — Sample of Thirty-seven Countries, 1973–1979.

Accounting concept or practice (Description below title)	Applicable IASC standard	Direction of movement
1. Going Concern Concept Financial statements are drawn up on the premise that the business will continue in operation indefinitely.	Standard No. 1	Required
2. Consistency Concept Accounting principles and methods are applied on the same basis from period to period.	Standard No. 1	Required
3. Accrual Concept Revenues and costs are recorded in the financial statements of the period in which they are earned or incurred, and not as money is received or paid.	Standard No. 1	Required
4. Realization Concept Revenue is recognized when its realization is reasonably assured.	—	Required
5. Matching Concept Cost of sales and expenses are appropriately matched against sales and revenue.	—	Required
6. Historical Cost Convention Departures from the historical cost convention are disclosed.	—	Required
7. Accounting Policies When accounting principles or methods have not been applied on the same basis from period to period in the determination of results of operations or financial position, the effect of the change is disclosed.	Standard No. 1	Required
8. Fixed Assets When fixed assets are stated, in historical cost statements, at an amount in excess of cost, the basis of revaluation is disclosed.	—	Required
9. Fixed Assets When fixed assets are stated, in historical cost statements, at an amount in excess of cost, depreciation based on the revaluation is charged to income.	—	Required
10. Depreciation Depreciation methods are disclosed.	Standard No. 4	Required
11. Inventories The basis on which inventories are stated is disclosed.	Standard No. 2	Required
12. Inventories A breakdown of inventory by types, such as finished goods, work-in-progress, and materials is disclosed.	Standard No. 2	Required

Exhibit 3 (cont'd)

Accounting concept or practice (Description below title)	Applicable IASC standard	Direction of movement
13. Inventories Market value ("market") of inventories is interpreted to mean net realizable value defined as estimated selling price less reasonably predictable costs of completion and disposal and normal profit margin.	Standard No. 2*	Not Permitted
14. Inventories Inventories are stated at cost or market, whichever is lower.	Standard No. 2*	Not Permitted
15. Inventories Inventories are stated at cost although this may exceed market.	Standard No. 2*	Not Permitted
16. Inventories In historical cost statements, inventories are stated at market although this may exceed cost.	Standard No. 2*	Not Permitted
17. Inventories Own manufactured goods are stated at estimated net realizable value when sale is assured.	Standard No. 2*	Not Permitted
18. Inventories The method of determining the cost of inventories (LIFO, FIFO, average, etc.) is disclosed.	Standard No. 2	Required
19. Investments When the carrying amount of an investment is permanently impaired, a provision is made for impairment.	Standard No. 3	Required
20. Receivables Receivables from affiliated companies are disclosed.	Standard No. 5	Required
21. Shareholders' Equity When there is no cash option, dividends satisfied by the issue of par value shares are recorded by the issues at the greater of market and par value of the share.	—	Required
22. Shareholders' Equity General reserves are set up by charges to income.	—	Not Permitted
23. Shareholders' Equity Reserves are used by absorb charges which would otherwise be charges against income of current or future years.	—	Not Permitted

Exhibit 3 (cont'd)

Accounting concept or practice (Description below title)	Applicable IASC standard	Direction of movement
24. Subsequent Events Events or transactions occurring between the date of the balance sheet and the date of the auditors' report which may have a material effect on the financial position or results of operations being reported upon are disclosed or reflected in those financial statements.	Standard No. 10	Required
25. Income Taxes Provision for income taxes on the current period's profits is shown separately before determining net income.	Standard No. 5	Required
26. Income Taxes Accounting practices adhere strictly to tax requirements.	Standard No. 12*	Not Permitted
27. Consolidations Parent-company financial statements only are prepared for shareholders of a parent company.	Standard No. 3*	Not Permitted
28. Business Combinations In a business combination accounted for as a purchase, retained earnings of the acquired company prior to the combination are excluded from the retained earnings of the combined organization.	—	Required
29. Foreign Currency The basis for translating foreign currencies is disclosed.	Standard No. 1	Required

* With respect to practices 13, 14, 15, 16, 17, 26, and 27, the IASC standard listed prohibits the practice in question.

changing prices, the statement of changes in financial position, and research and development of activities are reflected in the list. Exhibit 3 also relates these international accounting practices to the applicable IASC standard. It was found that twenty out of the twenty-nine practices could be related to seven IASC standards. In every case, the direction of change was consistent with the position espoused by IASC. With respect to reporting on changing prices and accounting for research and development, it should be recalled that the position of IASC was in conflict with the U.S. position. This suggests a possible association between the U.S. position on an issue and subsequent harmonization. This link will be explored later in the paper. Thus, there is some evidence from Price Waterhouse, a source independent of IASC, that these standards have been reflected in an associated harmonization of international accounting practices in those topic areas.

National involvement in harmonization

In the final step of this analysis, the authors investigated which countries were involved in the observed recent movement toward harmonization. For each of the twenty-five accounting practices for which a significant movement toward harmonization occurred between 1975 and 1979, those countries which had been involved were identified and were then grouped using the characterization developed by Frank based on the similarity of accounting practices in use in 1973.[12] He characterized the thirty-seven countries in this study (plus Ethiopia) as belonging to one of the following models: the British Commonwealth (twelve countries), Latin America (nine countries), Central Europe (eight countries), and the United States (eight countries).

For example, with respect to the Going concern concept (number 1 as listed in exhibit 3), it was found that twenty countries moved in the direction of increased harmonization (requiring the practices), fourteen made no change, and three moved in the opposite direction (toward prohibiting it).[13] Of the twenty countries that moved toward harmonization, nine were from the British Commonwealth group, six were from the Latin American group, four were from the Central European group, and only one was from the U.S. group. This same pattern (countries identified with the U.S. group being much less active than those in the other groups) was typical of all twenty-five practices. The authors found that a majority of the British Commonwealth countries changed in the direction of increased harmonization for seventeen of twenty-five practices. Similarly, a majority of the Latin American and of Central European countries moved toward increased harmonization for twenty and fifteen of the twenty-five practices, respectively. On the other hand, a majority of the U.S. group participated in such a change for only three of the twenty-five practices. This suggests two possible explanations: the U.S. group countries were not interested in change, or the other countries were moving toward the position the U.S. group countries had already taken.

To distinguish between these alternative explanations, the position of the United States in 1975 on the twenty-five practices was examined. This analysis showed that of the seventeen practices the rest of the world required in 1979, the United States had already mandated fourteen of them, two had no application, and one was followed by a majority of firms in 1975. Similarly, of the eight practices that the rest of the world had moved toward prohibition in 1979, the United States had already prohibited seven, and one was followed by only a minority of firms in 1975.

This would tend to indicate that the United States enjoys a position of leadership in international accounting and that other countries tend to adopt the positions espoused by it. It confirms the observation made earlier on the pronouncements of the IASC and their relationships to U.S. pronouncements on the same topic. The inference of leadership by the United States is strengthened by the fact that harmonization was not detected on those issues on which the IASC's stand contradicted the U.S. position.

It is interesting to speculate on possible explanations underlying the apparent leadership role of the United States. Some insights into the nature of the standard-setting process are provided by examining the possible role of powerful groups in influencing decisions on accounting standards. This issue has drawn considerable attention in the United States where the actions of the APB and the FASB have been closely scrutinized. Horngren remarked that ". . . the setting of accounting standards is as much a product of political action as well as of flawless logic or empirical findings."[14] Solomons notes that "today, to judge from current discussions of the standard-setting process, accounting can no longer be thought of as non-political."[15] The Staff Study of the Subcommittee on Reports, Accounting, and Management of the United States Senate is replete with charges of corporate dominance of the standard-setting process.[16] Empirical investigations of the influence exerted on policy makers and of the rationale for such behavior on the part of lobbyists can be found in Rockness and Nikolai[17] and Watts and Zimmerman.[18]

In the international arena, there is no reason to suspect that the setting of accounting standards is any more a product of "flawless logic or empirical findings" than it is domestically in the United States. The pressure may be exerted more on the behalf of national accounting groups than from specific corporate or industry interests. These national accounting groups would be concerned with ensuring that the international accounting standard on a given issue varied as little as possible from the domestic standard on that issue. A national accounting group would lobby in this fashion in order to minimize the costs associated with changing to a new standard, or to avoid the stigma of noncompliance if it chooses instead to ignore the new international standard. One would expect the lobbying effort to be the greatest on the part of the accounting professions in those countries such as the United States which have devoted a great deal of effort and resources to developing an extensive and well-codified set of standards. These countries would have the most to lose if an international accounting standard was at variance with the domestically accepted accounting principle.

If the United States plays a leading role in IASC deliberations, then this suggests that rapid movement is not likely to occur in those standards which are the subject of heated controversy in the United States. Thus, in spite of the progress in accounting for the effect of changing prices in Europe, this topic has only just reached exposure draft form (Exposure Draft No. 17) with the IASC. This slow pace is also seen in the area of translating foreign currency. In the United States, the controversy surrounding FASB *Statement of Financial Accounting Standards No. 8*, "Accounting for the Translation of Foreign Currency Transactions and Foreign Financial Statements," caused that organization to issue a new exposure draft proposing changes from the existing requirements. Given the disagreement in the United States, it should not be surprising to find that no standard yet exists for this subject even though an exposure draft (No. 11) was issued in December 1977. Currently, efforts are being made to achieve a consensus on this subject by the professional accounting associations in the United States, Canada, and the United Kingdom.

Another implication of viewing the setting of standards as a political process is that governments, as well as the professional accounting organizations, would be expected to become involved. The European Economic Community (EEC), the United Nations, and the Organization for Economic Cooperation and Development are now taking an active role in developing international accounting standards. Directives issued by the EEC Council of Ministers are to be enacted into law by member countries, thus providing legal sanctions for the directives.

Summary and conclusions

The authors examined 131 accounting practices common to the 1973, 1975, and 1979 surveys of international accounting practices made by Price Waterhouse. Although in 1973 a majority of the thirty-seven countries in the sample were in agreement on mandating adherence to only eight of 131 practices, by 1979 agreement had increased to forty-nine practices. In further analysis of these forty-nine practices, it was found that a significant change in position had taken place for twenty-nine practices during the period 1973–1979, and for twenty-five practices during the period 1975–1979. Further, the topics on which IASC had issued pronouncements during the period 1973 to 1979 were related to the accounting practices on which the authors had detected harmonization. Harmonization was not detected on those issues on which the stand of IASC was in conflict with the stand of the United States. With respect to where harmonization had occurred, it was found that the United States and countries with similar accounting practices were not very active in making such changes. Most of the movement was due to changes made by countries from the British Commonwealth, Central Europe, and Latin America. Pursuing the possible reason for such behavior, the authors noted that the practices which the rest of the world had moved toward requiring (or prohibiting) by 1979 had been already required (or prohibited) in the United States in 1975.

In conclusion, it should be observed that the inference of causation is no easy task and that there are more dangers than rewards in such an endeavor. Nonetheless, the authors can state that the period of the IASC's existence

226

has coincided with a growing harmonization of accounting standards. This association between the two is strengthened by the fact that many of the topics on which the IASC has issued pronouncements are those on which the authors observe harmonization. Another conclusion to be drawn from this study is that the accounting practices in the United States seem to serve as a model for this harmonization process.

Acknowledgement

The authors express their appreciation to Thomas J. Linsmeier for his comments on an earlier draft of this paper.

Notes

1 Werner G. Frank, "An Empirical Analysis of International Accounting Practices," *Journal of Accounting Research* (Autumn 1979): 593–605; and R. D. Nair and Werner G. Frank, "The Impact of Disclosure and Measurement Practices on International Accounting Classifications," *Accounting Review* (July 1980): 426–50.

2 Nair and Frank, "Disclosure and Measurement Practices."

3 Joseph P. Cummings and Michael N. Chetkovich, "World Accounting Enters a New Era," *Journal of Accountancy* (April 1978): 52–61.

4 Lee Berton, "Arthur Young Professors' Roundtable: The International World of Accounting," *Journal of Accountancy* (August 1980): 74–79.

5 Deloitte Haskins & Sells, *International Accounting Standards Committee, Summary of Activities, January 1975–January 1980* (Deloitte Haskins & Sells, 1980).

6 The most recent survey the authors use describes the accounting practices in use as of January 1, 1979. Although IASC Statements 7 to 10 became effective for financial statements covering periods beginning on or after January 1, 1979, they were issued from two to fourteen months prior to this date. The authors feel that if the IASC does, in fact, influence accounting practices, it is reasonable to assume that firms would begin to move toward recommended practices as soon as the IASC statements are issued.

7 Frank, "International Accounting Practices."

8 Price Waterhouse International, *Accounting Principles and Reporting Practices* (Canada: Price Waterhouse, 1973); idem., *Accounting Principles and Reporting Practices* (Canada: Price Waterhouse, 1975); and idem., *International Survey of Accounting Principles and Reporting Practices* (Scarborough, Ontario: Butterworths, 1979).

9 A complete list of these practices is available from the authors.

10 Sidney Siegel, *Nonparametric Statistics for the Behavioral Sciences* (New York: McGraw-Hill Book Company, 1956).

11 Of these 131 practices, 39 had significant shifts in the period 1973 to 1979, but for 10 of these, the number of countries involved was less than nineteen; that is, the shift involved changes between the intermediate categories of Predominant practice, Minority practice, or No application.

12 Frank, "International Accounting Practices."

13 Consistent with the definition of harmonization used in the first part of this study, *movement toward harmonization* is defined as movement in the direction

taken by a majority of countries toward requiring (or prohibiting) a given accounting practice. For example, if a country moved from category 3, Minority practice, in 1975 to category 2, Predominant practice, in 1979, this was interpreted as a move in the direction of harmonization if a majority of countries required the use of this practice in 1979.

14 Charles T. Horngren, "The Marketing of Accounting Standards," *Journal of Accountancy* (October 1973): 61–66.

15 David Solomons, "The Politicization of Accounting," *Journal of Accountancy* (December 1978): 65–72.

16 U.S. Congress, Senate, Subcommittee on Reports, Accounting and Management of the Committee on Government Operations, *The Accounting Establishment: A Staff Study* (Metcalf Staff Report) (Washington, D.C.: Government Printing Office, 1976).

17 Howard O. Rockness and Loren A. Nikolai, "An Assessment of APB Voting Patterns," *Journal of Accounting Research* (Spring 1977): 154–67.

18 Ross L. Watts and Jerold L. Zimmerman, "Towards a Positive Theory of the Determination of Accounting Standards," *Accounting Review* (January 1978): 112–34.

41

THE INTERNATIONAL ACCOUNTING STANDARDS COMMITTEE

A performance evaluation

S. M. McKinnon and Paul Janell

Source: *International Journal of Accounting* (Spring 1984): 19–34.

The International Accounting Standards Committee (IASC) was established in 1973 by the professional accounting institutes of nine major countries in response to increasing calls for harmonization of worldwide accounting regulations. Since its inception, the IASC has expanded to include accountancy bodies in sixty-five countries. It has been acclaimed as the most successful and influential international body in achieving some degree of harmonization of standards. A review of the IASC, its objectives, and its achievements in order to evaluate the overall performance of the IASC in its first twelve years is appropriate.

This study analyzes the role of the IASC. After briefly commenting on the general desirability of harmonization, the study identifies the IASC objectives and analyzes three contemporary accounting issues in light of these objectives. The final step is an analysis of the role the IASC should play in consideration of its successes and failures.

Is harmonization desirable?

Much of the impetus for harmonization has focused on the need for comparative information in a world of expanding capital markets. Growing competition for both domestic and international financing has produced a seller's market for money, where the sellers have the power to demand additional information concerning potential investments. Differing standards present an obstacle to optimal economic resource allocation, and the necessity to accommodate differing accounting standards places a dual burden on the multinational executive concerned with financial reporting.

Since Jacob Kraayenhof's seminal paper on international harmonization,[1] few have questioned the desirability of harmonized standards. Most opponents have focused on the practical difficulties of achieving agreements among different countries, given the differences in background, tradition, needs of economic environments, and the inevitable challenge of uniformity to state sovereignty.

How effective has the IASC been?

The fact that harmonization itself can be assumed to be a worthwhile goal is not sufficient justification to conclude that the efforts of the IASC have been the best way to fulfill that goal. Critics of harmonization may be quite right when they state that complete international standardization is impossible. Since that objective is the essential premise of the IASC's existence, the IASC objectives should be analyzed in relation to what it has actually accomplished in its brief years of operation.

IASC objectives

The board of the IASC is charged with directing its major operations. The board has two representatives from the original founding members, plus two representatives from two additional member accounting organizations. The board issues exposure drafts (EDs) of proposed standards generally followed by the standards themselves. To take effect, a standard must be approved by a minimum of three-fourths of the committee membership. As of May 1985, IASC had issued over twenty Statements of International Accounting Standards, and numerous exposure drafts were outstanding.

The objectives of the IASC, as expressed in the agreement under which it was established, are ". . . to formulate and publish in the public interest, basic standards to be observed in the presentation of audited accounts and financial statements and to promote their worldwide acceptance and observance."[2] Several key points are expressed in this statement. The statement identifies two major goals: (1) to formulate standards, and (2) to promote their acceptance and observance. Within the first of these goals is the qualification to formulate basic rather than detailed standards. Paragraph 10 of the *Preface to Statement of International Accounting Standards*, published by the IASC in 1975, states:

> . . . it is the intention of the IASC . . . to concentrate on basic standards. It will therefore endeavor to confine the International Accounting Standards to essentials and not to make them so complex that they cannot be applied effectively on a worldwide basis . . .[3]

The second goal was further elaborated in an agreement by member accounting institutes to use their best endeavors to:

1. Ensure that published accounts comply with these standards or that there is disclosure of differences;
2. Persuade governments, securities markets, and the business community that published accounts should comply with these standards; and
3. Ensure that auditors report differences from these standards.[4]

Are these goals being met? In the next section, the authors examine three topics considered by the IASC: depreciation, the equity method, and foreign currency translation. Each is different in the points raised as to the effectiveness of the IASC, but none is a special case. These three subjects provide reasonable examples of the degree of acceptance of IASC standards throughout the world.

Depreciation

The standard on depreciation (IAS No. 4) was chosen because it was relatively noncontroversial and was one of the earliest standards issued, becoming effective January 1, 1977. IAS No. 4 is a prime example of the approach initially taken by the IASC to address those issues that would most likely be accepted first. Greater acceptance would be found for standards on which a consensus could be achieved among the members of the voting committee. Other countries would find adoption fairly easy, and the IASC would gain more influence and credibility as a standard-setting body.

This standard seems ideal for meeting the goal of setting basic general principles, yet the IASC initially fell into the trap of being too specific and narrow in its prescribed choices. The exposure draft chose the straight-line method as preferable and called for disclosure of any differences in income attributable to using a different method. This went beyond the requirements of any national professional body and was quickly eliminated.[5]

The final statement is general in its requirements, calling for depreciation of assets charged to income in a systematic fashion over the life of the asset. Depreciable cost is historical cost less estimated salvage. Disclosures of method, depreciation expense, and both the gross amount of the assets and the accumulated depreciation are mandated.

In analyzing the effect of IAS No. 4 on worldwide practice, two questions are important. First, does practice conform to the standards of the IASC? Second, has practice *changed* to reflect the new standard, or does practice conform for other reasons, such as existing local legislation? To help answer these questions, we referred to a study by Price Waterhouse International.[6] Sixty-four countries were surveyed, including thirty-three that are members of IASC. Practice in the surveyed countries on 267 reporting practices was classified into categories of acceptance, ranging from "Required" to "Not Permitted."[7]

These data cannot be used to measure conformity exactly, for many reasons. First, at least ten IASC member countries were not included in the study. Generalizations of practice in these countries cannot be drawn, for they include such diverse nations as Yugoslavia, Israel, Bangladesh, and Finland. Second, the survey covered practice as of January 1979, only two years after IASC No. 4, possibly not allowing enough time for the countries which may have been in the process of changing standards. Third, categories, such as "Required" and "Insisted Upon," always lead to arbitrary classifications by respondents who perceive the definitions of the groups in different ways. Despite these flaws, the study is valuable for providing a general overview of acceptance; it represents the most comprehensive collection of worldwide accounting practices available.

In all but five of the countries surveyed, depreciation charges to income are the predominant practice and the minority practice in those five. Of the IASC members surveyed, all except Jamaica and Portugal either require depreciation or insist upon it for an unqualified auditor's report; in these two countries, it is standard practice even though not mandatory. Quite obviously, the IASC tread on no toes by advocating depreciation charges. A slightly more stringent requirement of IASC No. 4 is the need to reflect salvage value in the estimated charges. Of the countries surveyed, only 37 percent require or insist on the consideration of salvage, even though another 16 percent indicate this as the predominant practice. (Actual figures are presented in exhibit 1.) The situation is slightly better for IASC member countries: 58 percent require or insist upon consideration of salvage, and an additional 12 percent say it is the majority practice.

These data may appear to give credence to the belief that IASC standards are being adopted in the member countries, but this assumption fails after an analysis of the source of the standards in the countries reporting high compliance. Exhibit 2 presents the analysis of countries by category and by

Exhibit 1 Countries Reflecting Salvage Value in Determining Depreciation Charge.

	Total survey		IASC members	
	Number	*Percent*	*Number*	*Percent*
Required	18	28	17	52
Insisted upon	6	9	2	6
Predominant practice	10	16	4	12
Minority practice	22	34	8	24
Rarely or not found	8	13	2	6
Total	64	100	33	100

Source: Table 58, Price Waterhouse Survey.

232

Exhibit 2 Consideration of Salvage — By Country.

ISAC members

Required	Trinidad and Tobago	Minority practice
Australia	United Kingdom	Belgium
Fiji	United States	Denmark
France	Zimbabwe/Rhodesia	Germany
Hong Kong		Norway
Ireland	Insisted upon	Philippines
Korea	Canada	Portugal
Malaysia	Jamaica	Spain
Mexico		Sweden
Netherlands	Predominant practice	
New Zealand	India	Rarely or none
Nigeria	Japan	Brazil
Pakistan	South Africa	Greece
Singapore	Zambia	

Other countries

Required	Jersey	Italy
Bahamas	Kenya	Malawi
	Nicaragua	Panama
Insisted upon	Taiwan	Paraguay
Bermuda		Switzerland
Botswana	Minority practice	Uruguay
Dominican Republic	Bolivia	
Venezuela	Chile	Rarely or none
	Colombia	Austria
Predominant practice	Costa Pica	Ivory Coast
Argentina	Ecuador	Morocco
El Salvador	Guatemala	Peru
	Honduras	Senegal
	Iran	Zaire

Source: Table 58, Price Waterhouse Survey.

membership in IASC. The most striking point of the IASC members reporting at least predominant practice is the number of recent former British colonies on the list. When they are removed, the only remaining nations are Japan, France, Korea, Mexico, the Netherlands, and the United States. The British established sophisticated accounting procedures throughout the empire years before the IASC was formed; eight of the former colonies cite IAS No. 4 as their authoritative source rather than credit the British systems installed years ago. Of the remaining nations, Japan, the Netherlands, and the United States take pride in their accounting independence; Korea and Mexico were influenced directly through trade ties with the United States; France, which credits the IASC standard, is actually strictly governed by its uniform Plan Comptable. Among those countries where consideration of salvage is a minority practice or not seen at all are eight European

233

countries; four are members of the European Economic Community (EEC). While IAS No. 4 was not enough to convince them to change their ways, these four, with Spain and Portugal, upon their entrance into the EEC in the 1980s, will need to consider salvage value when the EEC's Fourth Directive is incorporated into the national law. As for Brazil, with hyperinflation, one understands the reluctance to estimate future salvage value in terms of present dollars.

What does this exercise indicate of the depreciation standard? Simply based on this analysis, several points can be made:

1. The IASC succeeded in identifying and codifying standard practice in much of the world.
2. The IASC did not succeed in influencing practice in either its member countries or nonmember countries listed in the survey.
3. In this case, practice correlates somewhat to the IAS standard in terms of considering salvage value, but practice is based on previous standards.

The equity method

The equity method of accounting for minority-owned intercorporate investments is a much more controversial subject than the need to depreciate fixed assets. In the United Kingdom and United States, the equity method is required for investments where significant influence exists, generally defined as from the 20 to 50 percent ownership levels. Because the investor is considered to have such influence that dividend policy could be affected, dividends are considered as a return of capital, reducing the investment instead of increasing income. Profit or loss from the investment is counted as the ownership percentage of the associated company's profit or loss.

Practice in the United Kingdom and the United States is almost identical to the requirements of IAS No. 3, the statement on consolidations issued in 1976. This is not surprising, for the equity method is singularly suited to a reporting environment which emphasizes the investor. It attempts to measure the value of the investment, rather than only the immediate proceeds of the investment. This is also the controversial point as to its use. The equity method raises issues of the realization of profits and losses. Particularly in those countries where tax reporting is based on financial reporting, claiming profits and losses which have not been realized in a more concrete sense is not considered acceptable.

The equity method is a controversial topic, unlike depreciation. Its use has increased dramatically in the last ten years as more countries have accepted or legislated stricter requirements for financial relationships between companies. This is an area where the IASC has had a great opportunity to influence evolving practice. The Price Waterhouse (PW) study shows results

Exhibit 3 Countries Using the Equity Method for Significant Investments.

	Total survey		IASC members	
	Number	*Percent*	*Number*	*Percent*
Required	19	30	14	14
Insisted upon	1	2	0	0
Predominant practice	4	6	2	6
Minority practice	12	19	7	22
Rarely or not found	21	32	5	15
Not permitted	7	11	5	15
Total	64	100	33	100

Source: Table 103, Price Waterhouse Survey.

similar to the depreciation issue. A brief review of the percent of countries using the equity method is presented in exhibit 3. The same country-by-country analysis could be done as with the salvage issue.

Much more interesting analysis of this issue can be made by considering individual countries which have adopted the equity method within the past five years (or are in the process of adopting it).

The PW study lists Japan as an IASC member with minimal acceptance of the equity method. This is changing rapidly; in the years since the PW study was undertaken, the classification has probably reached "predominant practice." This is not in response to IAS No. 3 but to new securities legislation. The growth of the stock market in Japan has led to new and more detailed securities laws, one of which required consolidated statements after April 1, 1977. The same regulation called for the equity method for 20 to 50 percent investments but allowed an interim period during which companies can change from the cost method. The Japanese have stated that their primary impetus for changing standards is to conform to foreign securities markets' requirements.[8]

Germany is an entirely different case and a classic example of the influence of taxes on financial reporting. In Germany, use of the equity method is not allowed. However, Germany is included here as an example because, within the next five years, the equity method will be required procedure. This dramatic reversal will result from the implementation of the Seventh Company Law Directive of the EEC. The Seventh Directive requires use of the equity method when significant influence exists; therefore, Germany will need to change to a method of which many Germans have severe reservations.

Another EEC country changing its methods is Denmark, which traditionally had conformity between tax and financial reporting, but which has separated the two completely in the last decade. The PW study lists the equity method as rare in Denmark, but this is now inaccurate. Although the equity method is not yet required, its use is increasing, and in an interesting way. To cope with the problem of recognizing income, the Danes have modified the equity method, transferring the ownership percentage of profit and loss to a reserve account in owners' equity instead of the income statement. This does not conform to IAS No. 3 and will change when the Seventh Directive is implemented.

The last interesting example is Italy. The PW study lists Italy as a country where use of the equity method is rare. This is true, but it has existed, although it is not allowed for tax purposes. Many companies have voluntarily been presenting consolidated statements and using the equity method experimentally. No longer will this be voluntary. A move is under way by the new national stock exchange commission to require large listed companies to consolidate accounts. Most companies will probably follow rules advocated by the new accounting organization, ASSIREVI. These rules are quite openly based on U.K. and U.S. principles and include use of the equity method. The reason for this is the influence of the "Big 8" accounting firms in Italy, which began by auditing U.K. and U.S. subsidiaries, but whose work has expanded to include a large percentage of Italian firms.

In comparing the IASC and the equity method, we should make several points:

1. The IASC has succeeded in identifying and codifying practice which is predominant in investor-oriented countries and, since that is the growing trend, it has succeeded in advocating increasingly popular practice.
2. In countries where the equity method has recently been adopted, there are equally compelling reasons other than adherence to IASC No. 3. These reasons concern securities legislation, compliance with legal requirements imposed through community organizations such as the EEC, cooperation with trading partners, and the influence of the United Kingdom and United States.
3. The IASC has not greatly influenced either member or nonmember nations to adopt the equity method.

Foreign currency translation

The last area is the turbulent topic of foreign currency translation. A chronology of statements on foreign currency translation by the three major parties involved in the controversy is interesting. Without attempting to explain the major methods involved, the chronology of important events follows. Statement No. 8 by the Financial Accounting Standards Board

(FASB) in 1975 called for the use of the temporal method and immediate recognition of gains and losses on translation. This was bitterly opposed by companies which found their earnings shifting dramatically due to currency swings.

In 1978, the IASC issued ED 11, which was basically all things to all people. It allowed a choice between the temporal method and the closing rate method and allowed various alternatives as to recognition of translation gains and losses through both the income statement and direct movements to owners' equity. These choices were allowed even though the known preferred alternative of the majority of IASC members was the closing rate method. Why was the IASC hesitant to take a stand? Unlike depreciation, and even unlike the equity method, foreign currency translation is so emotionally charged that it actually renders the IASC somewhat powerless. The two major powers, the United Kingdom and the United States, were almost diametrically opposed in philosophy at that time, and any stand by the IASC would have been certain to contravene accepted practice in one of the two countries.

At approximately the same time, the Accounting Standards Committee (ASC) of the United Kingdom released ED 21 on the topic of accounting for foreign statement translation. Discussion leading to ED 21 was almost unanimously in favor of the closing rate method, yet the ED allowed the choice of either the temporal method or the closing rate method. Many British experts felt at the time that it would be difficult to adopt a method contrary to the U.S. method when the IASC was flexible enough to allow both.

The controversy continued, fueled by the decision of the FASB to re-evaluate foreign currency translation. A task force was established, and the IASC was represented at each meeting. Subsequently, the FASB issued Statement No. 52, requiring the current rate (closing rate) method in all but exceptional cases. The advocacy of the current rate method could be seen as a victory for the IASC in some ways. The extent of its influence is difficult to judge, however, for the major influence was obviously the American business community. The FASB has shown little inclination to do more than consider international standards briefly in setting U.S. standards.[9] No doubt the FASB was influenced somewhat because the major trading partners of the United States were strong proponents of the current rate method.

An analysis of the IASC role in the foreign currency issue is difficult because of the other factors involved. It is easy to state that the IASC exhibited weakness in its failure to issue a standard advocating the current rate method. Whether or not the IASC was influential behind the scenes is unknown. The FASB task force meetings and open hearings held on the subject indicate only cursory attention to international standards.

Impediments to IASC effectiveness

Earlier in this paper, the authors presented the aims of the member institutes' individual efforts to achieve the acceptance of IASC standards. The extent to which compliance has been achieved was categorized by the IASC into three areas in a discussion paper titled "Acceptance and Observance of International Accounting Standards."

1. Those countries where IASC standards are awarded the same status as domestic standards. (Mandatory compliance)
2. Those countries where accountancy bodies have declared support for IASC standards and advise disclosure of any areas where local standards differ from international standards. (Preferable compliance)
3. Those countries where no formal status of standards has been determined. (None or accidental compliance)

Few countries fit the first category, although the Bahamas, Figi, Malaysia, Nigeria, Pakistan, Singapore, Trinidad and Tobago, and Zimbabwe come very close. A number of countries, particularly those with long established standard-setting mechanisms, fit the second category. These include the United Kingdom, Canada, and, to a lesser extent, the United States. Many more countries comprise the latter category.

Lack of enforcement

A primary impediment to the IASC's effectiveness is its lack of enforcement powers. The IASC depends on voluntary compliance and the influence of the accounting institutes in each country to achieve incorporation of its recommendations into local standards. Despite the goals of these institutes, there is little evidence that much has been achieved.

In 1980, the Organization for Economic Cooperation and Development (OECD) published a survey of accounting practices in member countries.[10] The OECD lists among its members seventeen IASC members, comprising most of the "developed" world, and eight of the founding countries of the IASC. The survey included a question concerning the degree of flexibility existing in each country for accommodating recommendations on standards from international bodies. Of the eight IASC founders, only respondents from the United Kingdom and Ireland stated that IASC standards would be followed. Much more common were responses such as that of Germany: "International recommendations can be taken into account as far as they are compatible with existing legal provisions." Of the twenty OECD nations surveyed, fifteen expressed the view that international standards were often considered when local decisions were made, but that they were overridden by national concerns, particularly where accounting standards are actually enacted into law. Austria and Switzerland, nonmembers of IASC, claim no efforts to consider IASC standards, and France states that its national law goes beyond (and therefore includes) IASC standards, a debatable statement.

The IASC depends on others for its enforcement. Often these other parties are ineffectual in achieving compliance. Even in the United Kingdom, where the ASC has announced its intention to harmonize U.K. standards as far as possible with the IASC's statements, differences remain. A comparison of U.K. accounting practices with international standards produces a list of divergent requirements in at least seven of the first thirteen subjects addressed by the IASC.[11] In the United States, representation on the IASC is through the American Institute of Certified Public Accountants (AICPA) instead of the FASB. No longer does the AICPA have direct power over standard setting; therefore, it must attempt to influence adherence with international standards indirectly through opinions addressed to the FASB and the AICPA membership.

Other international bodies

An additional problem with setting international standards concerns the number of organizations which have decided to consider the subject. These groups represent diverse constituencies and include international organizations, such as the OECD and the United Nations (UN), and regional standard-setting groups such as the EEC.

The OECD and UN can be loosely typified as representing the "developed" and "developing" world, respectively. Each has recently compiled a code of behavior for multinational firms, including rules for reporting. Each must also rely on voluntary compliance. Their primary difference is their emphasis; standards applicable to industrialized nations are not necessarily appropriate for nations in the early stages of development.

In contrast, the EEC is not forced to rely on voluntary compliance. All member countries must pass national laws to include requirements complying with EEC company law directives, several of which include detailed accounting rules. Although regional in nature rather than worldwide, the EEC efforts are the most significant in terms of world harmonization because of the consensus required in choosing standards, the vast differences in the countries involved, and the agreement to make regional standards national law.

The combination of UN, OECD, IASC, and EEC efforts is often confusing and appears unnecessasry to many people. The IASC is hindered in not being the only recognized world authority, for how can there be more than one international standard?

Is there a better role for the IASC?

To answer this question, it is necessary to examine the present objectives of the IASC in comparison to the areas where they have been most and least effective. The two objectives were stated earlier as (1) to formulate basic standards and (2) to promote worldwide compliance with these standards.

In this paper, the case has been made that the IASC has had great difficulty in meeting the second objective. It has not been successful in either changing existing rules or in achieving compliance with new standards. It has been hindered by a lack of authority, a tendency to emphasize details, and questionable support from member nations intent on protecting local interests.

There are some areas, however, where the IASC has been influential. An examination of these areas provides a starting point to define a new role for the IASC more in keeping with the present stage of the international harmonization process, and which would be more realistic. The IASC has been effective in three major ways:

1. It has succeeded in identifying and codifying the most generally accepted principles in use in the developed nations of the world.
2. Its standards have provided a neutral source for countries in the process of standard setting.
3. The most effective way of influencing world harmonization has been through the IASC's ability to have its standards considered by other, more powerful groups.

The first point correlates closely to the first objective of the IASC: to formulate basic standards. To date, the standards have represented practice in the industrialized world with an emphasis on investor-oriented societies. The IASC should continue to codify the best of present practice in statement form but should expand this role to one which includes research as to how different standards are suitable to different reporting environments. Little work has been done in this area; the IASC could serve as a nonaffiliated clearinghouse for efforts to determine the best principles applicable to countries in different stages of development. This research should include the suitability of basic principles such as revenue recognition and matching to different political and industrial environments.

The second way in which IASC standards have proven to be effective has been as a reference for nations and companies needing neutral sources. Earlier, it was stated that many former British colonies refer to IASC standards rather than to U.K. standards as their source of practice. This is not a trivial role for the IASC to endorse for itself. Not all countries are as willing as Italy to adopt American or British standards openly as their own, yet many need an outside source to help legitimize choices of principles.

IASC standards should serve as basic models which local standard-setting bodies can use as benchmarks to evaluate existing practice. They should provide guidance in areas where local standards have not yet been formulated. A further need would be served by giving multinational corporations a reference point to deal with numerous divergent reporting requirements.

The IASC has been most effective when it has been able to obtain endorsements for its opinions by parties having greater enforcement powers. Although IASC standards are not recognized as law in many countries, they are endorsed by the International Federation of Stock Exchanges, which has the power to require adherence to IASC rules by companies listed on the major exchanges of the world.[12] The IASC lobbies to have its standards considered by the FASB and ASC, and its power to influence EEC law directives is considerable. This suggests that working toward the adoption of IASC standards should be secondary to working toward the incorporation of IASC principles into national standards. The IASC should assume the role of consultant to those groups which *do* have powers of enforcement.

Summary

This paper has examined the role of the IASC. Given the assumption that the harmonization of standards is a worthwhile goal, the IASC was evaluated in terms of its ability to date to achieve its stated objectives. This analysis leads to conclusions that the IASC has not succeeded in changing existing standards or setting new standards. It has succeeded in codifying generally accepted practice, in serving as a neutral source for standards, and in influencing groups with enforcement powers. These successes indicate that the IASC objectives should be changed to the following:

1. To serve as a research clearinghouse to study the effects of different principles in different reporting environments.
2. To provide a neutral model of possible standards for countries in the process of standard setting and for multinational firms dealing with divergent regulations.
3. To provide temporary standards to fill the void existing before local standards can be set.
4. To serve as a consulting body for organizations in the standard-setting process.
5. To channel efforts to influence harmonization to incorporation of IASC principles into local legislation rather than to adoption of IASC standards themselves.

The national differences preventing immediate worldwide harmonization of standards may disappear more quickly than many people think. The primary impetus will probably come from companies themselves. As more firms seek to raise funds in world securities markets, they will be forced to change standards to meet filing requirements. Such de facto harmonization may thus succeed in eliminating present barriers preventing worldwide cooperation. By providing a more research- and consulting-oriented role, the IASC will have a greater opportunity to influence the eventual content of international accounting standards.

Notes

1 Jacob Kraayenhof, "International Challenges for Accounting;" *Journal of Accountancy* (January 1959), 34–38.
2 George C. Watt, Richard M. Hammer, and Marianne Burge, *Accounting for the Multinational Corporation* (Financial Executives Research Foundation, 1977), 166–67.
3 International Accounting Standards Committee, *Preface to Statements of International Accounting Standards* (1974), par. 10.
4 Watt, Hammer, and Burge, *Multinational Corporation*.
5 International Accounting Standards Committee, "Accounting for Business Combinations," *Exposure Draft* (1976).
6 R. D. Fitzgerald, A. D. Stickler, and T. R. Watts, eds., *International Survey of Accounting Principles and Reporting Practices* (London: Price Waterhouse International and Butterworths, 1979).
7 In order of their level of acceptance, these categories are "Required," "Insisted Upon," "Predominant Practice," "Minority Practice," "Rarely or Not Found," "Not Accepted," and "Not Permitted."
8 Organization for Economic Cooperation and Development, *International Investment and Multinational Enterprises: Accounting Practices in OECD Member Countries* (1980), 194.
9 In early 1982, a vote was taken among the FASB and its constituency as to the most important problems requiring the board's consideration. The need for international standards ranked near the bottom on a list of over thirty subjects.
10 Organization for Economic Cooperation and Development, *International Investment*, 194.
11 Arthur Young International, "The United Kingdom," *World Business Reports* (AYI, 1981), 24, exhibit 9.
12 Fitzgerald, Stickler, and Watts, *International Survey*.

Additional references

Fantl, Irving L. "Case Against International Uniformity." *Management Accounting* (May 1971):13–16.
International Accounting Standards Committee. "Accounting for Business Combinations." *Statement of International Accounting Standards No. 3* (1977).
——. "Accounting for Depreciation." *Statement of International Accounting Standards No. 4* (1977).
——. "Foreign Currency Translation." *Exposure Draft* (1978).

42

"BOTTOM LINE COMPLIANCE" WITH THE IASC

A comparative analysis

Thomas G. Evans and Martin E. Taylor

Source: *International Journal of Accounting* (Fall 1982): 115–28.

Background

Introduction

The problem of diversity in national accounting principles has a long history. When nations emerged as distinct political units because of divergent environmental factors such as culture, language, and political and economic systems, the conditions encouraged each nation to establish accounting standards which tended to mirror the nation's diverse factors.[1] This is not surprising, since nations also prefer their own currency, customs, and laws. A comparison of the accounting standards in the major nations today reveals that differences continue to exist.

Although understandable, this current situation of national diversity in accounting principles is not necessarily optimal for the worldwide allocation of economic resources. Distinct national economies do exist, but now there is also a world economy in which trade, investment, and capital flow freely from country to country. National differences in accounting principles, however, impede this flow since resource allocation decisions are thought to be based on accounting information that is heterogeneous in nature.

A recent study by Scott found that one of the most important categories of accounting problems was that of international accounting standards.[2] Within this category, the most important perceived problem was that the lack of international accounting standards greatly diminished the usefulness of financial statements to users in countries other than that on whose accounting standards the statements are based.

This problem was recognized as early as the late 1950s by Kraayenhof who made a personal plea for an effort to reduce the diversity.[3] As it became increasingly apparent that national diversity existed and was not economically desirable, attention was focused on ways to remedy this situation. Two general views emerged.

One school of thought emphasized the justification for such differences.[4] An extension of this view held that the natural evolution of accounting principles within each nation would narrow alternatives and this would, internationally, also reduce the degree of diversity found from country to country. Other natural forces, such as the international competition for capital, would also work to reduce diversity. Evidence of this latter phenomena was found.[5] Today, as illustrated by the consultation of the Financial Accounting Standards Board (FASB) with other countries while considering changes in Statement of Financial Accounting Standard (SFAS) No. 8, informal efforts are still being made to reduce diversity.

The other (more dominant) view posits that formal action should be taken to reduce the diversity. Consistent with this view, a number (approximately ten) of accounting standard-setting bodies which claim international jurisdiction for their pronouncements have emerged in the last decade. The four main organizations are the International Accounting Standards Committee (IASC), the European Economic Community, the United Nations, and the International Federation of Accountants. Each has been active in issuing accounting and financial reporting rules which, if followed, would reduce the diversity and result in greater harmony in accounting principles from country to country. These current attempts at international harmonization, however, have created a number of related problems, especially with regard to the composition and authority of these standard-setting bodies. The failure of these agencies to coordinate their efforts has created problems of overlapping jurisdictions. Their productivity has created a bewildering array of new international accounting rules. For example, at last count, IASC has issued sixteen standards, has seven exposure drafts outstanding, and has authorized seven research projects. The question of the authority of these agencies is paramount, since almost all nations have retained their sovereignty to issue accounting standards.

The IASC

Given these developments, it is now appropriate to evaluate this approach to achieving greater harmonization of international financial accounting standards by standard-setting bodies. The evaluation should focus on the IASC, the premier international body and the most productive issuer of international accounting standards. It is also the only body issuing statements with a global rather than a regional orientation. So far, it has raised most of the important questions regarding international accounting standards.[6]

The IASC was formed in 1973 by leading accounting professional bodies in nine nations: Australia, Canada, France, Germany, Japan, Mexico, the Netherlands, the United Kingdom and Ireland, and the United States. It is important to note that nations are not members of the IASC; instead, professional accounting bodies within nations are members (for example, the American Institute of Certified Public Accountants, not the FASB, is the representative of the United States). The objective of the IASC is simply to issue international accounting standards to be followed in the presentation of audited financial statements. Currently, sixty-one national accounting bodies are members of the IASC. Each member is pledged to use its "best endeavors" to ensure that (1) accounting standards in its respective country conform to those of the IASC, (2) the independent auditors satisfy themselves that the financial statements comply with these standards or that the fact of noncompliance is disclosed in the financial statements, and (3) in the event of nondisclosure, reference to noncompliance is made in the audit report.[7]

The IASC follows a due process procedure similar to that of the FASB. Such procedures followed in developing international accounting standards are these:

- The Board selects an *agenda* of subjects to be studied.
- A Steering Committee, comprised of three members drawn from different countries, is appointed to develop an exposure draft on each subject.
- The exposure draft is submitted to the Board for approval.
- When approved by a *two-thirds vote of the Board*, the exposure draft is sent to professional accounting bodies and others for *comment*. The comment period, generally, is a minimum of four months.
- The Steering Committee reviews the comments and *drafts a final Standard*.
- A final Standard, when approved by at least three-quarters of the Board, is issued.[8]

In addition, the IASC should be the focus of any evaluation of the impact of international harmonization of financial accounting standards because it has the longest history of any other organization and because it is widely recognized as the main body for achieving success in international harmonization: "The work of the IASC is without doubt the most promising development so far [in international harmonization]. ...."[9] "... the IASC has been the most successful of any of the *large-scale* international efforts toward harmonizing accounting standards."[10] Concerning the IASC, it is particularly interesting that at least nine nations (Bahamas, Fiji, France, Malaysia, Nigeria, Pakistan, Singapore, Trinidad, and Zimbabwe Rhodesia) are reported to have accorded IASC standards the same status as domestic accounting standards.[11]

Research issues

The preceding events raise the following questions concerning the ISAC's performance to date:

1. Have IASC standards been accepted and followed by firms in member nations? This question of acceptance is critical to the whole issue of international harmonization by direct action through a formal agency, such as the IASC. The IASC has attempted to bridge this gap through its pledge of "best endeavors" by members. Has this approach worked? Are IASC standards really being followed in those countries? If not, then IASC standards will not achieve international harmonization.

2. What impact has the IASC had on the generally accepted accounting principles (GAAP) of developing countries? A special case for increased international harmonization can be made by asserting that the IASC directly benefits developing nations who lack a strong accounting profession and accounting infrastructure. If these nations can simply adopt IASC standards as their own GAAP, they will save themselves the effort and will also result in greater harmonization. The question then becomes whether the IASC has become the standard setter for those nations and how is it perceived in those nations. If the IASC is of benefit to those nations, how has this contributed to international harmonization?

3. How does the accounting profession (public accounting and industry) in developed nations, such as the United States, view the IASC and its standards? What are the perceptions of multinational firms which should be in compliance with IASC standards? This is a critical factor in the question of international harmonization and the IASC: lacking the formal authority to set accounting standards in member nations, has it been accorded the status it needs to obtain acceptance for its pronouncements?

Research methodology

This paper reports on the first phase of an investigation into these problems. To determine the impact of IASC standards on the financial reporting in member nations, financial reports were analyzed. The IASC has issued sixteen standards to date; five of the earlier ones were selected and used to check compliance in a sample of five IASC member nations. The standards and their effective dates are as follows:

IASC standard		*Effective date*
No. 2	"Valuation and Presentation of Inventories"	12/31/76
No. 3	"Consolidated Financial Statements"	12/31/77
No. 4	"Depreciation Accounting"	12/31/77
No. 6	"Accounting Responses to Changing Prices"	12/31/78
No. 7	"Statement of Changes in Financial Position"	12/31/79

Major provisions of IASC standards

The major provisions for each of the five standards selected are presented here.

IAS No. 2 — "Valuation and Presentation of Inventories." In the context of the historical cost system, (1) inventories should be valued at the lower of historical cost and net realizable value; (2) inventories should be segregated in balance sheets or in notes to the financial statements to show the amounts held in different categories (such as materials, work-in-process, and finished goods), and the accounting policies adopted for valuation, including the cost method used, should be disclosed.

IAS No. 3 — "Consolidated Financial Statements." Minority interest in the equity of consolidated companies, and in the profits and losses of such companies, should be shown separately in the consolidated statements and should not be included in the shareholders' equity or consolidated net income. IAS No. 3 prescribes the equity method of accounting for investments included in consolidated statements when the investor may exercise significant influence over the investee (that is, holds 20 percent or more of the voting stock), or the investee is a subsidiary not consolidated because its activities are so dissimilar from those of the parent as to make consolidated statements meaningless.

IAS No. 4 — "Depreciation Accounting." A depreciable asset should be depreciated on a systematic basis, and its cost should be allocated to each accounting period during its useful life. Disclosures for each major class of depreciable assets should include the following: the depreciation method, useful lives or depreciation rates, depreciation expense for the period, and gross depreciable assets and accumulated depreciation.

IAS No. 6 — "Accounting Responses to Changing Prices." Information that describes the procedures adopted to reflect the impact on the financial statements of specific price changes or changes in the general level of prices, or both, should be disclosed in the financial statements. If no procedures have been adopted, that fact should be disclosed.

IAS No. 7 — "Statement of Changes in Financial Position." This requires that a statement of changes in financial position be presented as a basic financial statement.

These earlier standards were selected since countries should have had ample time to adopt them. The countries selected to determine whether they are implementing IASC standards are France, Japan, the United Kingdom, the United States, and West Germany. All of these nations are founding members of the IASC. In addition, France is the only developed country that has reportedly accorded IASC standards the same status as domestic standards.

Methodology

To determine the impact of IASC standards on financial reporting in these nations, the published financial statements of a sample of large corporations in each country were examined to determine whether the major provisions of the five IASC pronouncements just listed are being followed. (See Appendix for a list of the firms included in the analysis.) The analysis concentrated on the consolidated financial statements. All of the Japanese and part of the French and West German statements were English-langnage versions.

In general, nine or ten financial statements were examined for each country and each IASC standard with a few minor exceptions. The only major exception was the case for Japan for 1975 when only four financial statements were available. For this reason, the case for Japan for 1975 was not considered in the analysis. Published financial statements were examined for each firm for the period 1975–1980. Since the earliest IASC standard was effective 31 December 1976, the current authors were able to discern whether a firm was following a certain financial accounting principle before its adoption by the IASC in a standard. The examination of the published financial statements for these nations in regard to the five IASC standards provided insight into whether these standards have had an impact on financial reporting in those nations and especially when that impact took place. In some cases, for example in the United Kingdom and the United States, it was expected that firms had followed certain reporting principles before their adoption by the IASC, and so the IASC has had no impact. However, in other nations, it was expected that the IASC has had an impact on financial reporting.

Analysis of findings

IASC No. 2, "Valuation and Presentation of Inventories"

The results of the analysis of compliance with IASC No. 2 is presented in exhibit 1. Part A concentrates on the valuation of inventories, indicating

248

Exhibit 1 Compliance with International Accounting Standard No. 2, "Valuation and Presentation of Inventories" (effective for fiscal year ending 12/31/1976).

Part A: Inventories should be valued at the lower of historical cost and net realizable value

Year	% compliance by country				
	France	Japan	U.K.	U.S.	W. Germany
1975	50	NA	78	44	38
1976*	22	33	80	50	67
1977	30	33	100	56	60
1978	40	33	100	50	60
1979	40	33	100	50	60
1980	30	33	100	40	60

Part B: Segregation of inventories by major categories

Year	% compliance by country				
	France	Japan	U.K.	U.S.	W. Germany
1975	50	NA	33	56	25
1976*	56	100	60	60	22
1977	50	100	100	56	90
1978	50	100	100	50	20
1979	50	100	100	60	20
1980	50	100	100	70	20

* Year of effect.

that prior to the issuance of IASC No. 2, the largest percentage of the U.K. firms in the sample were in compliance with this standard, and that the degree of compliance in the U.K. firms rose after the effective year (1976) to 100 percent and then stabilized. This can be explained by the fact that during this period, U.K. accounting standards were changed to conform to IASC No. 2. In each of the other cases, except for West Germany, the results were disappointing in that none followed the U.K. experience. Surprisingly, the case for the United States is "spotty," mainly due to the unacceptability of LIFO inventory valuation which is very popular in the United States. By the end of the period covered by the analysis, a majority of firms in the sample from West Germany and the United Kingdom were in compliance with IASC No. 2's inventory valuation procedure.

Part B concentrated on the presentation of details concerning inventory on the balance sheet. It is clear that the IASC standard had an impact in the United Kingdom, based on the sample of firms. Only in the United Kingdom is the compliance pattern demonstrated clearly, with a one-year lag period. An increase in the percentage of firms in compliance with this aspect of IASC No. 2 is evident in the United States, but otherwise the

Exhibit 2 Compliance with International Accounting Standard No. 3, "Consolidated Financial Statements" (effective for fiscal year ending 12/31/1977).

Part A: Disclosure of minority interest

Year   % compliance by country

	France	Japan	U.K.	U.S.	W. Germany
1975	80	NA	100	44	75
1976	78	22	100	50	78
1977*	80	22	100	56	80
1978	80	22	100	38	80
1979	80	22	100	50	80
1980	80	33	100	50	80

Part B: Use of equity method for firms in which between 20 percent and 50 percent of stock is owned

Year   % compliance by country

	France	Japan	U.K.	U.S.	W. Germany
1975	90	NA	44	67	0
1976	89	33	50	70	0
1977*	90	33	50	89	10
1978	90	33	56	75	10
1979	90	33	60	80	10
1980	90	33	60	80	10

* Year of effect.

results are disappointing from a compliance viewpoint. It should be noted here that when the financial statements examined referred to national legal requirements in regard to accounting methods, where the statements themselves did not give a clear evidence of compliance with the IASC standard, none was assumed.

IASC No. 3, "Consolidated Financial Statements"

The first part of exhibit 2 focuses on the disclosure of the minority interest in the sample firms. As the analysis shows, the IASC standard had no impact on U.K. firms in the sample, since they were fully in compliance before and after the effective date. Little impact was evident for Japan, West Germany, or France, and the record for the American firms is spotty. The wide difference in the degree of compliance with this IASC standard in 1976 regarding the disclosure of minority interest is interesting.

The use of the equity method of accounting for subsidiaries is presented in Part B of exhibit 2. As is obvious from the table based on the sample firms, the IASC standard has had no impact on the French, Japanese, and American statements. Only in the cases of the U.K. and West German

Exhibit 3 Compliance with International Accounting Standard No. 4, "Depreciation Accounting" (effective for fiscal year ending 12/31/1977).

Part A: Depreciable assets are depreciated using a systematic method

Year   *% compliance by country*

	France	Japan	U.K.	U.S.	W. Germany
1975	70	NA	100	100	62
1976	67	67	100	100	67
1977*	70	67	100	100	70
1978	70	56	100	100	70
1979	60	56	100	100	70
1980	60	67	100	100	70

Part B: Disclosure of depreciation details

Year   *% compliance by country*

	France	Japan	U.K.	U.S.	W. Germany
1975	10	NA	67	0	0
1976	0	11	60	10	11
1977*	10	11	50	11	0
1978	10	11	89	12	0
1979	10	11	100	30	0
1980	10	11	100	30	0

* Year of effect.

firms was marginal impact noted. In West Germany, the prevalent practice is the cost method.

IASC No. 4, "Depreciation Accounting"

Two aspects of depreciation accounting are shown in exhibit 3. The first concentrates on the use of a systematic depreciation method. The IASC standard has had no impact on any sample firms in the study. In general, a majority of firms in each of these cases were in compliance with this standard when it was issued.

A different situation existed, however, with regard to the disclosure of depreciation details, as shown in Part B of exhibit 3. When this standard became effective in 1977, the U.K. firms were the only ones near a majority in compliance with it. The overall low levels of compliance with this basic principle of disclosure is surprisingly evident for the period 1975–76. Dramatic improvement is evident only in the case of the U.K. firms, and it is also evident that the standard had no impact on France, Japan, and West Germany. An explanation for the low level of compliance of U.S. firms was a common deficiency concerning the disclosure of the useful lives or depreciation rates.

Exhibit 4 Compliance with International Accounting Standard No. 6, "Disclosure of Procedures to Reflect the Impact of Price Changes or Disclosure of the Fact That No Such Procedures Have Been Adopted" (effective for fiscal year ending 12/31/1978).

Year	% compliance by country				
	France	Japan	U.K.	U.S.	W. Germany
1975	0	NA	11	11	0
1976	0	0	10	80	0
1977	0	0	44	100	0
1978*	0	11	44	100	0
1979	0	0	60	100	0
1980	0	0	100	100	0

* Year of effect.

IASC No. 6, "Inflation Accounting Disclosures"

The results of the analysis of the disclosure of the impact of changing prices on the firms is presented in exhibit 4. As shown, the IASC standard had no impact in the case of France, West Germany, and the United States. Only in the case of the U.K. firms from 1978 through 1980 and for the Japanese firms in 1978 was there any evidence of an impact. U.S. compliance was affected by the Security and Exchange Commission's Accounting Series Release 190 passed in 1976 and FASB No. 33, effective in 1979. In the United Kingdom, Statement of Accounting Practice 16 on current-cost accounting was issued, effective for 1980. It is significant to note that only in the case of the latter two countries were any disclosures of the impact of inflation presented in the firm's annual reports by 1980.

IASC No. 7, "Statement of Changes in Financial Position"

Exhibit 5 shows the degree of compliance in the sample firms for the IASC standard requiring that a statement of changes in financial position be included as a basic financial statement. As shown by the analysis, this standard had no impact in any of the nations represented by firms in the sample: in no case did the percentage of compliance change. By 1980, a majority of U.K. and U.S. firms presented this statement; otherwise, it was not a majority practice.

Summary and conclusions

Mueller has noted that the IASC attempts to review procedures currently in use in countries around the world and then harmonize them by recommending a limited set of alternatives.[12] The IASC has no "real authority" to

Exhibit 5 Compliance with International Accounting Standard No. 7, "Statement of Changes in Financial Position" (effective for fiscal year ending 12/31/1979). Requires that a statement of changes in financial position be presented as a basic financial statement

Year	% compliance by country				
	France	Japan	U.K.	U.S.	W. Germany
1975	40	NA	89	100	11
1976	44	33	100	100	11
1977	40	33	100	100	10
1978	50	33	100	100	10
1979*	50	33	100	100	10
1980	50	33	100	100	10

* Year of effect.

implement its recommendations and must rely on the best efforts of its individual members which most often are not the accounting standard-setting bodies of those countries. The current study tends to indicate that the IASC has had very little impact on the accounting practices of the countries surveyed. Except for a few instances, a country following a particular method prior to the promulgation of an IASC standard continued to follow the same practice after the standard's issuance.

Notes

1 Financial Accounting Standards Board, "Objectives of Financial Reporting by Business Enterprises," *Statement of Financial Accounting Concepts No. 1* (Stamford, Conn.: FASB, 1978).

2 G. Scott and P. Troberg, *Eighty-eight International Accounting Problems in Rank Order of Importance — A DELPHI Evaluation* (Sarasota, Fla.: American Accounting Association, 1980).

3 Jacob Kraayenhof, "International Challenges for Accounting," *Journal of Accountancy* (January 1960).

4 Irving L. Fantl, "Case against International Uniformity," *Management Accounting* (May 1971).

5 Frederick Choi, "Multinational Financing and Accounting Harmony," *Management Accounting* (March 1974).

6 Thomas G. Evans, "Can American Accountants Serve Two Masters: FASB and IASC?" *CPA Journal* (January 1976).

7 International Accounting Standards Committee, *Preface to the Statements of International Accounting Standards* (London: IASC, 1974).

8 Deloitte, Haskins & Sells, *International Accounting Standards Committee* (D, H & S, 1981).

9 Frederick Choi and Gerhard Mueller, *An Introduction to Multinational Accounting* (Englewood Cliffs, N.J.: Prentice-Hall, 1978).

10 J. Arpan and Lee Radebaugh, *International Accounting and Multinational Enterprises* (Boston: Warren, Gorham, and Lamont, 1981).

11 R. Fitzgerald, A. Stickler, and T. Watts, eds., *International Survey of Accounting Principles and Reporting Practices* (Scarborough, Ontario, Canada: Price Waterhouse International, 1979).
12 Gerhard Mueller and L. Daley, "Accounting in the Arena of World Politics," *Journal of Accountancy* (February 1982).

Appendix. Firms included in sample

Country	Firm	Principal lines of business
France	Enterprise Minère et Chimique	Mining, chemicals
	Général Sucriere	Sugar
	Imetal	Mining, metallurgical products
	La Farge Copper	Cement, concrete, sanitary ware
	L'Oreal	Hair care, perfume, pharmaceuticals
	Sacilor	Steel
	Schneider	Heavy industry contractors, nuclear power plants, shipbuilding
	Thomson-CSF	Electronic equipment and components
	Union Laitiere Normande	Dairy products
Japan	Chizoda	Chemical engineering and construction
	Fuji Photo Film Co. Ltd.	Photographic film, cameras, magnetic tape
	Furakawa Electric	Electrical cable and wire
	Idemitsu Kosan Co. Ltd.	Oil products, chemicals, shipping
	Kubota	Agricultural machinery, pipe, building materials, industrial machinery
	Nippon Electric Co. Ltd.	Electronic products, data processing
	Sumitomo Metals	Steel, engineering
	Sumitomo Metal Mining	Metal mining and production
	Toyota Motor Co. Ltd.	Automobiles
United Kingdom	Allied Breweries	Alcoholic and nonalcoholic beverages, food
	Arthur Guiness Son & Co. Ltd.	Brewing, plastics, confections
	Cadbury Schweppes Ltd.	Confectionary, beverages
	Delta	Electrical equipment, metals, plumbing products
	General Electric Co. Ltd.	Manufacture of electrical and electronic products
	Grand Metropolitan Ltd.	Food, beverages, leisure
	ICL Ltd.	Computer systems
	RMC Group	Concrete
	Rolls-Royce Ltd.	Engineering, manufacturing
	The Welcome Foundation Ltd.	Pharmaceuticals, chemicals
United States	Amax	Mining, energy
	Avon	Cosmetics, jewelry
	Control Data Corp.	Computers, data processing equipment
	CPC International	Foods
	Exxon	Oil, energy
	General Tire	Tires, rubber
	Honeywell	Computers, control systems, electronics
	J. P. Stevens	Textiles
	Lockheed	Aircraft, aerospace, electronics
	W. R. Grace	Chemicals, energy, consumer products
West Germany	Babcock	Power generating equipment and engineering
	Bazer	Chemicals, rubber, pharmaceuticals
	Continental	Tires
	FAG	Bearings, machine parts
	Magirns-Dentz A.G.	Trucks, buses
	Metallgesellschaft	Metals, manufacturing, engineering, chemicals
	Sachs	Manufacturing, motors
	Schering A.G.	Pharmaceuticals, chemicals
	Thyssen	Steel, manufacturing
	Volkswagenwerk	Automobiles

43

GOODWILL ACCOUNTING IN SELECTED COUNTRIES AND THE HARMONIZATION OF INTERNATIONAL ACCOUNTING STANDARDS

Rudolf Brunovs and Robert J. Kirsch

Source: *Abacus* 27(2) (1991): 135–61.

Economic and financial markets interpenetrate and national economies are increasingly interdependent. This results in a growing need for comparability of accounting procedures internationally. Accounting for goodwill illustrates this phenomenon. By specifying the recommended asset treatment for purchased, positive goodwill, and the five-year amortization period, IASC has taken a significant step towards harmonization of goodwill accounting. As noted in the article, however, the implications for consolidated income may be quite drastic. This is especially so with respect to the implications of the revised IAS 22 (following IAS ED 32) for potential leveraged corporate buy-outs.

It is a truism that the world is witnessing the development of a global economy. Increasingly, companies expand the scope of their operations from domestic into international markets. Economic and financial markets interpenetrate and national economies are increasingly interdependent. In such an environment, there is a growing need for minimization of inconsistencies in accounting procedures from nation to nation in order to provide the users of accounting data with meaningful, comparable information. 'Consolidated financial statements obviously raise considerable problems if the parent company and each of its subsidiaries keep their accounts according to widely differing systems' (Organization for Economic Co-Operation and Development, 1986, p. 10). The international harmonization of accounting standards is a pressing issue.

Since 1904, when the First International Congress of Accountants was held in St Louis, a number of international accounting bodies have sought to increase comparability of accounting standards between countries, including such groups as the International Accounting Standards Committee (IASC), the European Community (EC) and the United Nations (UN).

To date, the International Accounting Standards Committee has issued thirty International Accounting Standards (IASs). The extent to which the IASC's standards are followed in a given nation depends upon whether the professional accounting body in that country has standard setting authority. Evans, Taylor and Holzmann (1985) identified three broad categories of compliance with IASs:

1. Countries with no formal national accounting standards. In some of them, their accounting bodies have declared that IASs are to be accorded the same status as domestic accounting standards;
2. Countries whose national standards are, with minor exceptions, generally compatible with IASs. These countries have not made compliance with IASs mandatory; and
3. Countries whose national standards are incompatible with IASs often due to provisions of those countries' commercial codes and tax laws.

In setting standards, the IASC has sought to develop a consensus, compromise or workable standard in order to maximize international support; thus, it has permitted free choices of alternative accounting treatments. However, the IASC has been hampered by the absence of an accounting theory, much less a universally accepted theory of accounting, in its efforts to harmonize differences in accounting across nations. Without such a theory, the removal of national accounting biases is difficult to envisage.

In 1986, in an effort to fill the void caused by the lack of an overarching theory to assist the IASC Board to develop future standards, an IASC Steering Committee was charged with the task of developing a conceptual framework for the preparation and presentation of financial statements. In March 1988, the full IASC Board approved the proposed exposure draft (ED); in May 1988, the IASC published *Framework for the Preparation and Presentation of Financial Statements*. The Board finalized the *Framework* in April 1989 for publication in July 1989.

On 1 January 1989, the IASC issued Exposure Draft 32, *Comparability of Financial Statements*, which proposed amendments to numerous International Accounting Standards, including IAS 22, *Accounting For Business Combinations*, which also governs the accounting for goodwill. The IASC sees the purpose of the proposed amendments as the first step in the process of improving IASs through 'the removal of free choices of accounting treatments presently permitted' (ED 32, para. 3). It may be regarded then as an important step in the international harmonization of accounting standards.

For the treatment of goodwill, that is, the difference between the cost of acquisition and fair values of net identifiable assets acquired, the IASC proposes:

1. That for positive goodwill any excess of cost over the fair value of net assets acquired be given asset recognition as goodwill on the consolidated balance sheet;
2. That goodwill be amortized to income on a systematic basis over its useful life; the amortization period should not exceed five years unless the company justifies and explains in the financial statements a longer useful life. The maximum useful life should not exceed twenty years; and
3. That, for negative goodwill, two treatments be permitted: (a) it should be allocated over individual non-monetary assets acquired in proportion to their fair values with any excess treated as deferred income and systematically amortized to income, over five years usually, but not to exceed twenty years; and (b) it may be treated as deferred income and amortized to income systematically, normally over five years, but not to exceed twenty years (ED 32, paras 164–75).

Thus, the proposed treatment for positive goodwill would eliminate one presently acceptable approach, the immediate adjustment of (write-off to) shareholder's interests. The proposed treatment for negative goodwill would still permit two approaches; however, in the first approach mentioned in 3(a) above, the term 'non-monetary assets' replaces the former term 'depreciable non-monetary assets'. For both positive and negative goodwill the proposed revisions specify a normal five-year amortization period, with a maximum twenty-year period for exceptional cases, in contrast to IAS 22 which is silent on the issue of the amortization period.

The proposed amended treatment of goodwill accounting would have a profound impact upon financial reporting in various countries and would result in significantly different reported results in consolidated financial statements if followed by those countries. Since the IASC does not have enforcement powers, national compliance would have to be voluntary and would require the support of national professional accounting bodies, standards setting boards (or commissions), and/or changes in national laws (Parker, 1988).

An indication of the magnitude of the issues involved can be obtained by examining in depth differences in treatment of goodwill accounting. This paper presents an analysis of the conceptual issues and develops numerical examples to demonstrate the impact of the differing accounting treatments of goodwill upon consolidated financial statements in selected countries.

The conceptual issues

Hughes (1982) identified commercial and legal references to goodwill as early as 1417. Goodwill has been the subject of accounting literature for in excess of 100 years. However, it was not until the proliferation of joint stock companies as separate entities that the debate over alternative accounting treatments for goodwill intensified. By the early 1900s three clear schools of thought had emerged. Hughes identified and classified the alternative accounting treatments as: (a) immediate write-off, (b) permanent retention as an asset, and (c) gradual reduction.

The immediate write-off to capital treatment is founded on the logic that goodwill is a permanent asset much like land, and to charge goodwill to revenue was as erroneous as to do so with land. However, in the case of goodwill the cost should not be retained permanently on the books so as to avoid possible future embarrassment to present owners if they decided to sell.

Support developed for the gradual reduction of goodwill by the use of 'reserve fund' accounting while maintaining the concept that goodwill was a permanent asset. A variation of the gradual reduction school of thought was the concept that goodwill was not external and that some provision should be made, even though based on an arbitrary estimate of the life.

In 1970 the Accounting Principles Board of the American Institute of Certified Public Accountants issued an accounting standard on goodwill, APB 7, *Intangible Assets*. This was the first such standard and was subject to much worldwide debate and analysis of its effects upon business combinations and financial reporting.

More recent years have seen the development of goodwill accounting standards by a number of accounting societies, institutes and other committees in various countries. These standards address the critical issues of initial recording, and subsequent treatment in the books of account, as well as financial statement presentation and footnote disclosure. Internationally, the discussion, analysis and criticism of goodwill issues continue. Arguments as to the validity of the very conceptual basis or rationale for the various accounting treatments of goodwill are equally matched by the pragmatic debate upon the impact on commerce of the alternatives.

While this debate is a healthy process, a company operating within one national boundary has, by virtue of national accounting standards, a reasonably prescriptive technique to follow. The following issue, however, does need examination. Does a multinational company which complies with the requirements of various national accounting standards covering goodwill distort its financial reporting to company shareholders?

The importance of this issue cannot be overstated. The success of the private enterprise system is largely dependent upon competitive markets. These are in turn dependent upon, among other things, adequate information to ensure the efficient allocation of scarce resources. With the globalization of business activities and the growth in size of corporations analysts external to the corporation need to have access to adequate and accurate financial information. In the case of a multinational corporation information contained in consolidated financial statements may be distorted by differences in accounting treatments in different countries in which its foreign subsidiaries are located. Not only is ongoing analysis of a single corporation made difficult, but comparative analysis of similar corporations is made less useful when the financial position and the earnings are influenced by differences in accounting standards depending upon the country of residency and countries of operation.

In considering the impact of goodwill accounting upon a multinational corporation, reference was made to the accounting standards that apply in the major English-speaking trading countries: Australia, Canada, Ireland, New Zealand, the United Kingdom, and the United States of America. They are listed in the Appendix, together with the identification of the accounting standard that applies, the name of the body or organization which issued the standard, and the effective beginning date for application of the standard. (In February 1990, the Accounting Standards Committee of the U.K. Consultative Committee of Accountancy Bodies issued Exposure Draft 47, *Accounting for Goodwill* [*Accountancy*, March 1990]. If adopted, ED47 would bring major changes to the treatment of both positive and negative goodwill in the United Kingdom and Ireland.) In its 1988 *Survey of the Use and Application of International Accounting Standards*, the IASC classified each of these nations as having a 'national requirement developed separately and [it] conforms in all material respects with IAS (22)'. Because IAS 22 permits alternative acceptable treatments of both positive and negative goodwill, individual nations may well conform 'in all material respects' with it and still differ markedly in their respective treatments of goodwill. Thus, there are a number of differences in the ways in which the major English-speaking countries account for goodwill.

The six key issues listed below were specifically reviewed as these matters represent the main areas of debate in the arena of goodwill accounting: (a) non-recognition of internally generated goodwill; (b) measurement of purchased goodwill; (c) amortization guidelines; (d) reassessment of carrying value of goodwill; (e) disclosure requirements in financial statements; and (f) treatment of excess of assets over purchase consideration. These key issues, along with the respective accounting treatments they receive in the countries examined, are summarized in Table 1 and are discussed below. In the paper the various national goodwill accounting treatments are compared and contrasted with the current IAS 22, and the effect of the

Table 1 Various national accounting standards covering goodwill (Comparative Analysis Matrix).

Issue	Australia	Canada	Ireland	New Zealand	U.K.	U.S.A.
Accounting for internally generated goodwill	No cost carry forward	Not specifically addressed	No cost carry forward	Not specifically addressed	No cost carry forward	No cost carry forward
Measurement of goodwill:						
Assign fair value to assets acquired	Yes	Yes	Yes	Yes	Yes	Yes
Assign fair value to identifiable and separable intangible assets	Yes	Yes	Yes	Not specifically addressed	Yes	Yes
Amortization:						
Basis	Systematic (not specified)	Straight-line method	Eliminate immediately against reserves[a] or amortize	Not specifically addressed	Eliminate immediately against reserves[a] or amortize	Systematic, usually straight-line basis
Period	Period of expected benefit	Estimated life	Useful economic life if amortized[a]	Not specifically addressed	Useful economic life if amortized[a]	Estimated life
Maximum period	20 years	40 years	Not specified	Not specifically addressed	Not specified[a]	40 years
Reassessment:						
Accounting	Loss charged against income	Loss charged either before extraordinary or as extraordinary item	Loss charged against income. Gain not allowed	Goodwill to be written down when permanently impaired	Loss charged against income. Gain not allowed	Gain/loss charged against income. Disclose reason for extraordinary

Table 1 (cont'd)

Issue	Australia	Canda	Ireland	New Zealand	U.K.	U.S.A.
Disclosure:						
Policy	Yes	No	Yes	No	Yes	Yes
Amortization period	No	Yes	Yes. Each major acquisition	No	Yes. Each major acquisition	Yes
Amortization expense	Yes	No	Yes	No	Yes	No
Cost on acquisition	No	No	Yes	No	Yes	No
Treatment of excess of assets over purchase consideration	Discount on acquisition reduces proportionately fair values of non-monetary assets. After zero remaining discount recognized as period income	Excess over cost assigned to identifiable non-monetary assets. Allocation is a matter of judgment	'Negative goodwill' credited directly to reserves[b]	Not specifically addressed	'Negative goodwill' credited directly to reserves[b]	Excess over cost assigned to non-current assets. After zero the remainder amortized systematically to income. Maximum 40 years

Note: Compiled by the authors from the goodwill accounting standards listed in the Appendix to this paper.

[a] Preferred treatment under SSAP 22 that would be eliminated under proposed terms of ED 47, which would allow only systematic amortization over a normal maximum period; under exceptional circumstances an absolute maximum of forty years would be permitted but causes of the long useful life must be disclosed.

[b] ED 47 would require that 'negative goodwill' be recorded on the balance sheet as a 'negative asset'.

proposed amendments to IAS 22 as they relate to goodwill accounting are discussed.

Non-recognition of internally generated goodwill

The Australian standard states that, despite the distinction frequently drawn between purchased goodwill and internally generated goodwill, the concept of goodwill is the same, regardless of how it is generated. It also adds that purchased goodwill can be valued on the basis of the amount paid for it, while internally generated goodwill is not usually capable of reliable measurement. The Australian standard cites the following reasons for not bringing internally generated goodwill to account: (a) the difficulty or impossibility of identifying the events or transactions which contribute to the overall goodwill and the extent to which they generate future benefits; and (b) the value of such benefits would not be capable of reliable measurement.

Not all the accounting standards reviewed specifically address the matter of internally generated goodwill. Reference to it does not appear in the Canadian or the International Standard. In the others, while the wording differs, the intent that internally generated goodwill should not be brought to account is clear. Thus, a conflict between the various standards does not exist in respect of this issue.

Measurement of purchased goodwill

The standards of all the English-speaking countries under study, using different wording, in essence state that purchased goodwill should be the difference between the purchase consideration and the fair value of net identifiable assets acquired.

Both the Australian and International standards define cost as purchase consideration plus incidental expenses. The reference to incidental expenses is not included in the other goodwill standards. While this may appear to be a minor difference, it begs the question as to the accounting treatment of a range of 'incidental' expenses (e.g., government stamp duties and taxes, legal fees, investigating independent accountants' costs and expert valuers' fees). These expenses would all be considered to be naturally attaching to the purchase transactions. However, the accounting treatment may differ between countries.

The other contentious area concerns the substance of the term 'fair value of identifiable net assets'. The standards of the United Kingdom and Ireland allow the creation of a provision for future losses or costs of reorganization among the items to be taken into account at the time of acquisition when arriving at the purchase price. (Given that the goodwill standards of the United Kingdom and Ireland are identical, they are collectively referred to hereafter as the United Kingdom standard.) Paragraph 14 of the U.K.

standard (as revised in 1989) states: 'When ascribing fair values to separable net assets at the time of acquisition, a provision may be needed in respect of items which were taken into account in arriving at the purchase price, that is, anticipated future losses or costs of re-organization'. The inclusion of such a provision among liabilities reduces the fair value of net identifiable assets and has the effect of correspondingly increasing the carrying value of goodwill. Note, however, that ED 47 is silent about provision for future losses or costs of reorganization at the time of determining the purchase price. However, ED 48, *Accounting for Acquisitions and Mergers*, issued in February 1990, would seem to retain the provision for costs of reorganization in acquistions. Paragraph 59 states that 'Adjustments made as provisions for reorganization costs should be identified' among the separate acquisition disclosures. ED 48 does not mention a provision for future losses. It would appear that, in future, U.K. companies will be permitted to continue to include provision for reorganization costs as part of the liabilities in the determination of the fair value of net identifiable assets. The omission of reference to provision for future losses (paras 58–63) would seem to imply their exclusion from the purchase price in future should ED 47 and ED 48 be adopted without modification in this regard.

The International standard takes a different viewpoint. While it recognizes that identifiable assets and liabilities acquired may include assets and liabilities not recorded in the financial statements of the acquired enterprises, paragraph 12 of that standard excludes the raising of provisions for future operating losses. This exclusion will be retained in the revised IAS 22.

The other standards do not specifically address this issue; however, their silence may be interpreted as not allowing the provision for future losses or costs of reorganization. The calculation of future losses would be, at best, very subjective. Clearly, the United Kingdom's allowance of this provision as part of the overall measurement of goodwill creates a significant difference between their standards and others. The costs of reorganization, while less subjective than provision for future losses, have a large degree of fluidity about the range of costs that could be incorporated as part of the overall cost of reorganization. The allocation of internal costs (e.g., in the area of management time) and recognition of the cost of inefficiencies of various resources during the reorganization would result in a variety of outcomes dependent upon the 'creativeness' of the accountant responsible for determining the cost.

While some standards referred to above have recognized the need for the inclusion of incidental expenses as part of the cost, they do not envisage the extent of cost allocation that is allowed in the United Kingdom standard by virtue of the inclusion of costs of reorganization. In the case of the United Kingdom the policy allows the bundling of reorganization costs associated with an acquisition with goodwill, whereas in the United States the costs of reorganization are charged against income. The alternative treatments result in a material difference between the reported earnings.

To compare the effects of two alternative techniques for measuring purchased goodwill (i.e., policies of the U.K. and the U.S.A.), the following numerical example is presented. The example highlights the impact of the alternative accounting techniques upon calculation of purchased goodwill. It also compares the financial consequences of three consolidation procedures: (a) separate consolidations based on the accounting policies of the United States; (b) the normal United Kingdom treatment, immediate write-off; and (c) the alternative permissible United Kingdom treatment, immediate write-off for one acquisition, and amortization for the other. And it considers the impact the proposed IAS 22 revisions would have if followed by each country. (ED 47, if adopted, would eliminate immediate write-off and require the capitalization and amortization of goodwill over its useful economic life, not exceeding twenty years except in rare circumstance. A maximum forty-year amortization period is specified [Preface, para.1.11].)

The model is based upon the following assumed data. At the beginning of 19X1, two companies, one in the United Kingdom and the other in the United States, with net assets (at fair value) of 100,000 each are purchased by B&K for a consideration of 200,000 each. Costs incidental to the purchase of each company (i.e., stamp duties, legal fees and expert reports) amounted to 10,000. At the time of the purchase it was estimated that the cost of reorganizing each business to eliminate an unprofitable segment would be 40,000. The numerical example concentrates on the purchased companies; other facets of B&K's operations are ignored. Also, to spotlight the impact of the differing accounting treatments, relative currency movements and tax considerations are not considered.

Schedule I presents the calculation of purchased goodwill according to the U.K. and U.S. standards, and it shows the impact IAS 22 revisions would have upon goodwill calculations. Presently the British practice of including costs of reorganization in the determination of purchased goodwill results in a 40,000 higher goodwill amount under the U.K. standard than under the U.S. standard. (This would also be the case should ED 47 be adopted without change.) The British practice of the immediate write-off of goodwill at acquisition means there would be no annual amortization charge; the U.S. maximum period of forty years results in an annual charge of 2,750. (Application of the ED 47 proposal would result in an annual charge of 7,500 with a normal twenty-year amortization period.) Following the revised IAS 22 would result in an annual 30,000 goodwill amortization charge in the United Kingdom, compared to 0 presently. The shorter amortization period would increase the U.S. charge to 22,000 annually, a 19,250 increase.

The example in Schedule II compares the goodwill consolidations at acquisition date according to the U.S. and U.K. standards, and contrasts

Schedule I Calculation of goodwill at date of purchase.

	Present practice		Following Revised IAS 22	
	U.S.A.	U.K.	U.S.A.	U.K.
Purchase consideration	200,000	200,000	200,000	200,000
Less: fair value of net identifiable assets (excluding reorganization costs)	100,000	100,000	100,000	100,000
	100,000	100,000	100,000	100,000
Plus:				
Incidental expenses Stamp duties Legal fees Experts' reports	10,000	10,000	10,000	10,000
Cost of reorganization	0	40,000	0	40,000
Good will	110,000	150,000	110,000	150,000
Annual amortization charge[a, b]	2,750	0	22,000	30,000

[a] Assumptions: United Kingdom: Goodwill written off at acquisition date; United States: forty-year effective life.
[b] If IAS 22 revisions are followed and goodwill is amortized over five years.

present practice with the impact of following IAS 22 revisions. Schedule III discloses the effect upon individual and consolidated Income Statements of present practice compared with the revised IAS 22. Schedule IV discloses the effect upon individual and consolidated balance sheets of present practice and the revised IAS 22. In each schedule, Consolidation A assumes that both financial statement preparers applied the standard applicable in the United States. Consolidation B assumes the normal U.K. practice, that is, inclusion of reorganization costs in goodwill and its immediate write-off against reserves for both companies purchased. Consolidation C reflects the result of consolidating according to the alternative permissible U.K. approach, that is, the immediate write-off of goodwill against reserves for the company acquired in the United Kingdom and the amortization of goodwill over forty years for the company acquired in the United States.

Schedule III discloses considerable variation in net income (loss) depending upon which national treatment (or mix thereof) is employed to account for reorganization charges and/or amortization charges. Adhering to the IAS 22 revisions and a five-year amortization period either replaces consolidated net income with a net loss or deepens the existing net loss in this numerical example (Schedule III). In reality, taking amortization of

Schedule II Comparative goodwill consolidations at acquisition date

	Consolidation A (U.S. standards): amortization over 40 years	Consolidation B (U.K. standards): immediate write-off	Consolidation C (U.K. standards): immediate and write-off amortization[a]
Purchase consideration	400,000	400,000	400,000
Less: fair value of net identifiable assets (excluding reorganization costs)	200,000	200,000	200,000
	200,000	200,000	200,000
Plus:			
Incidental expenses Stamp duties Legal fees Experts' reports	20,000	20,000	20,000
Cost of reorganization	0	80,000	80,000
Goodwill	220,000	300,000	300,000
Amortization charge presently (forty-year amortization assumed)	5,500	0	3,750
Amortization charge if IASS 22 revisions followed	44,000	60,000	60,000

[a] Amortization charged off against reserves for company acquired in the United Kingdom; goodwill amortized over forty years for company acquired in the United States.

goodwill to income over a shorter amortization period would significantly increase reported expenses and dampen net income. Also note the continuing influence of the U.K. practice of including the costs of reorganization in the determination of goodwill. The revised IAS 22 does not eliminate this difference in accounting practice, nor its effect.

In Schedule IV, the effect upon the net equity under the various consolidation procedures is primarily influenced by the amortization policy or the treatment of the total value of goodwill rather than the effect of the treatment of the cost of reorganization. Applying IAS 22, with the five-year amortization period, has a significant impact on the balance sheet. In the United Kingdom, the deficit in retained earnings when immediate write-off is used exclusively is eliminated; in the United States, net assets are significantly reduced. Matching the net income (loss) effects disclosed in Schedule III with the net equity positions in Schedule IV reveals significant

Schedule III Comparative financial models (Income Statement 19X1).

	U.S.A.		U.K. immediate write-off		Consolidation A (U.S. standards)		Consolidation B (U.K. standards): immediate write-off		Consolidation C (U.K. standards): immediate write-off and amortization[a]	
	Presently	Following Revised IAS 22	Presently	Following Revised IAS 22	Presently	Following Revised IAS 22	Presently	Following Revised IAS 22	Presently	Following Revised IAS 22
Sales	100,000	100,000	100,000	100,000	200,000	200,000	200,000	200,000	200,000	200,000
Cost of sales	(66,000)	(66,000)	(66,000)	(66,000)	(132,000)	(132,000)	(132,000)	(132,000)	(132,000)	(132,000)
Gross profit	34,000	34,000	34,000	34,000	68,000	68,000	68,000	68,000	68,000	68,000
Other expenses	(24,000)	(24,000)	(24,000)	(24,000)	(48,000)	(48,000)	(48,000)	(48,000)	(48,000)	(48,000)
Goodwill amortization	(2,750)	(22,000)	0	(30,000)	(5,500)	(44,000)	0	(60,000)	(3,750)	(60,000)
Cost of reorganization	(40,000)	(40,000)	0	0	(80,000)	(80,000)	0	0	0	0
Earnings (loss) before tax	(32,750)	(52,000)	10,000	(20,000)	(65,500)	(104,000)	20,000	(40,000)	(16,250)	(40,000)

[a] Goodwill charged off against reserves for company acquired in the United Kingdom; goodwill amortized over forty years for company acquired in the United States.

Schedule IV Balance sheets at 31 December 19X1.

Balance sheet	U.S.A.		U.K. immediate write-off		Consolidation A (U.S. standards)		Consolidation B (U.K. standards): immediate write-off		Consolidation C (U.K. standards): immediate write-off and amortization[a]	
	Presently	Following Revised IAS 22	Presently	Following Revised IAS 22	Presently	Following Revised IAS 22	Presently	Following Revised IAS 22	Presently	Following Revised IAS 22
Current assets	50,000	50,000	50,000	50,000	100,000	100,000	100,000	100,000	100,000	100,000
Property and plant	100,000	100,000	100,000	100,000	200,000	200,000	200,000	200,000	200,000	200,000
Goodwill	107,250	88,000	0	120,000	214,500	176,000	0	240,000	146,250	240,000
Total assets	257,250	238,000	150,000	270,000	514,500	476,000	300,000	540,000	446,250	540,000
Current liabilities	30,000	30,000	30,000	30,000	60,000	60,000	60,000	60,000	60,000	60,000
Loans	50,000	50,000	50,000	50,000	100,000	100,000	100,000	100,000	100,000	100,000
Total liabilities	80,000	80,000	80,000	80,000	160,000	160,000	160,000	160,000	160,000	160,000
Net assets	177,250	158,000	70,000	190,000	354,500	316,000	140,000	380,000	286,250	380,000
Equity	100,000	100,000	100,000	100,000	200,000	200,000	200,000	200,000	200,000	200,000
Retained earnings	77,250	58,000	(30,000)	90,000	154,500	116,000	(60,000)	180,000	86,250	180,000
Owner's equity	177,250	158,000	70,000	190,000	345,500	316,000	140,000	380,000	286,250	380,000
Earnings (loss) to net assets	(19)%	(33)%	14%	(11)%	(19)%	(33)%	(14)%	(11)%	6%	(11)%

[a] Goodwill charged off against reserves for company acquired in the United Kingdom; goodwill amortized over forty years for company acquired in the United States.

consequences for any measurement of earnings in relation to net assets. (Adoption by the U.K. and Ireland of ED 47 would eliminate differences attributable to immediate write-off of goodwill; however, it would not eliminate differences which arise from alternate treatments of reorganization costs, or from alternate amortization periods.)

Amortization guidelines

The accounting standards that specifically address the issue of goodwill make reference to the concept of 'useful life' as the basis for determining the amoritzation period and state that the cost should be amortized by systematic charge. While amortization of goodwill over its useful life accords with the concept of matching expense with revenue, there remains the practical difficulty of determining the useful life.

When dealing with unlimited term intangibles, the difficulty is in estimating the point in time at which their value will expire. Some of the standards set a maximum period for amortization. The maximum period specified, however, varies significantly from standard to standard. In the United States and Canada, forty years has been set. The Australian standard specifies twenty years as the maximum amortization period.

Given that there are many practical difficulties in assessing the useful life and that the concept of amortization still remains a highly controversial issue, it is not unlikely that many organizations would select the maximum period specified in the standards as the appropriate amortization period. In this event, the application of the amortization concept will not only vary significantly between countries, but its impact upon income statements could be material.

While the standards of Ireland and the United Kingdom allow the amortization of goodwill, they advocate that goodwill be eliminated immediately on acquisition by write-off directly against reserves. This treatment is not an option that is available in the other countries examined in spite of the International Accounting Standard (IAS 22) recognizing and supporting both concepts of immediate write-off and amortization. This alternative treatment is to be eliminated in the revised IAS 22. The U.K. standard does not preclude a company from using both immediate write-off treatment and amortization treatment in respect of the goodwill which relates to different acquisitions. In paragraph 11 of SSAP 22 (Revised), the U.K. standard states that 'there is no requirement . . . to select the same useful life for the goodwill arising on different acquisitions' since the factors which affect estimates of useful life of purchased goodwill are 'likely to vary according to the different acquisitions'. In Appendix 1, the standard specifies that 'it is inappropriate to indicate any maximum period [of economic useful life] in numerical terms'. The issue of the proper treatment of goodwill remains unsettled in the United Kingdom. Early in 1990, the Accounting Standards

Committee circulated an exposure draft to its members for a formal postal ballot. If approved, the draft will propose withdrawal of the option to eliminate goodwill against reserves. It will require amortization over its useful life, usually twenty years, longer in exceptional cases, with an absolute maximum of forty years (ED 47, Preface, para.1.11). Highly controversial, if adopted, ED 47 would cause major changes to the treatment of both positive and negative goodwill. The proposal, which could dramatically reduce the earnings of acquiring companies as goodwill would be now charged off against profit and loss, has brought immediate opposition from finance directors and some accounting firms (*Times* [London], 2 February 1990). Should the United Kingdom adopt this treatment, it would place it in closer conformance with the treatment advocated by the European Community's Fourth and Seventh Directives; these specify a maximum five-year amortization period. Article 37, paragraph 2 of the Fourth Directive states:

> The Member States may, however, permit companies to write goodwill off systematically over a limited period exceeding five years provided that this does not exceed the useful economic life and is disclosed in the notes on the accounts together with the supporting reasons therefore.

Appendix 1 of SSAP 22 (Revised) notes that the United Kingdom, in implementing the Fourth Directive, 'took advantage of the Member State option to permit amortization over a period exceeding five years, but not exceeding the useful economic life'. In this regard, the ASC proposal will not alter current amortization practice in the U.K.

In the case of New Zealand, paragraph 5.2(e) of its goodwill standard states: 'The amount attributed to goodwill should be shown separately on the balance sheet as an intangible asset, to the extent that it has not been amortized or written down'. This statement recognizes amortization; however, the standard does not specify that goodwill must be amortized. It is possible, therefore, to carry forward goodwill in the balance sheet at its original cost.

To illustrate the impact of the various goodwill amortization guidelines, the following numerical example has been developed and presented in Schedules V through VIII. The example emphasizes the effects upon consolidated financial statements of the different amortization policies in the six standard areas studied. To highlight the impacts of the different amortization policies, relative currency movements and taxes are ignored.

The model is based upon the following assumed data. At the beginning of 19X1, goodwill of 100,000 was purchased by K&B in each of the six different accounting areas. The goodwill was amortized in accordance with the respective accounting standards.

Schedule V Amortization calculation based upon various guidelines

Country	Calculation
Australia	$100,000 amortized over twenty years ($100,000 ÷ 20 = $5,000 per annum)
Canada	$100,000 amortized over forty years ($100,000 ÷ 40 = $2,500 per annum)
Ireland	$100,000 written off directly to retained earnings
New Zealand	$100,000 not amortized but carried at cost
United Kingdom	$100,000 written off directly to retained earnings
United States	$100,000 amortized over forty years ($100,000 ÷ 40 = $2,500 per annum)
Revised IAS 22	$100,000 amortized over five years ($100,000 ÷ 5 = $20,000 per annum)

Schedule V details the calculation of goodwill amortization for each goodwill acquisition under the separate accounting standards of Australia, Canada, Ireland, New Zealand, the United Kingdom and the United States. The impact upon earnings before tax of adoption of the various goodwill amortization policies is very significant. The comparative model results in a wide earnings range. When these earnings are expressed as either a return on investment or as a percentage of sales the variation is so significant that any meaningfulness contained in the data has been destroyed as demonstrated by Schedule VIII.

Schedule VI sets out the effect of amortization upon the income statements and balance sheets of an entity adopting the respective accounting standards of the countries listed in Schedule V above.

Schedule VII compares the effect of consolidating the income statements and balance sheets of the various countries referred to in Schedule V according to the United Kingdom's SSAP 22 (Revised) with a consolidation which adopts the goodwill accounting standard of the United States, and with one which adopts the revised IAS 22 standard.

Schedule VIII lists ratios derived from the earnings before tax for each of the six different accounting standard areas. In particular, it shows earnings as a percentage of sales and earnings as a return on investment (owners equity).

The consolidation of the income statement and balance sheet highlights the effect of consolidating the individual country's financial statements according to the Revised SSAP 22 of the United Kingdom compared with the consolidation based upon a uniform amortization policy, the present U.S. standard or the revised IAS 22 standard. Again, distortions have occurred in the income statement as well as in the carrying value of goodwill and its impact upon shareholders' equity in the balance sheet. From the information contained in the mixture of approaches permitted by SSAP 22,

Schedule VI Preconsolidation financial statements prepared according to various standards.

	Australia	Canada	Ireland	New Zealand	U.K.	U.S.A.
Income statement						
Sales	100,000	100,000	100,000	100,000	100,000	100,000
Cost of sales	(66,000)	(66,000)	(66,000)	(66,000)	(66,000)	(66,000)
Gross profit	34,000	34,000	34,000	34,000	34,000	34,000
Other expenses	(24,000)	(24,000)	(24,000)	(24,000)	(24,000)	(24,000)
Goodwill amortization	(5,000)	(2,500)	0	0	0	(2,500)
Earnings (loss) before tax	5,000	7,500	10,000	10,000	10,000	7,500
Balance sheet						
Current assets	50,000	50,000	50,000	50,000	50,000	50,000
Property and plant	100,000	100,000	100,000	100,000	100,000	100,000
Goodwill	95,000	97,500	0	100,000	0	97,500
Total assets	245,000	247,500	150,000	250,000	150,000	247,500
Current liabilities	30,000	30,000	30,000	30,000	30,000	30,000
Loans	50,000	50,000	50,000	50,000	50,000	50,000
Total liabilities	80,000	80,000	80,000	80,000	80,000	80,000
Net assets	165,000	167,500	70,000	170,000	70,000	167,500
Equity	100,000	100,000	100,000	100,000	100,000	100,000
Retained earnings	65,000	67,500	(30,000)	70,000	(30,000)	67,500
Owner's equity	165,000	167,500	70,000	170,000	70,000	167,500

Schedule VII Consolidated financial statements comparing results with U.K. standards, U.S. standards and revised IAS 22

	Six-country consolidation A (U.K. SSAP 22 Revised immediate write-off and amortization)[a]	Six-country consolidation B (U.S. standards)	Six-country consolidation C Six-(Revised IAS 22)
Income statement			
Sales	600,000	600,000	600,000
Cost of sales	(396,000)	(396,000)	(396,000)
Gross profit	204,000	204,000	204,000
Other expenses	(144,000)	(144,000)	(144,000)
Goodwill amortization	(15,000)	(15,000)	(120,000)
Earnings (loss) before tax	45,000	45,000	(60,000)
Balance sheet			
Current assets	300,000	300,000	300,000
Property and plant	600,000	600,000	600,000
Goodwill	385,000	585,000	480,000
Total assets	1,285,000	1,485,000	1,380,000
Current liabilities	180,000	180,000	180,000
Loans	300,000	300,000	300,000
Total liabilities	480,000	480,000	480,000
Net assets	805,000	1,005,000	900,000
Equity	600,000	600,000	600,000
Retained earnings	205,000	405,000	300,000
Owner's equity	805,000	1,005,000	900,000

[a] Goodwill charged off against reserves for companies acquired in the United Kingdom and Ireland; goodwill amortized over twenty years for companies acquired in Australia and New Zealand, and forty years for those acquired in Canada and the United States.

Schedule VIII Ratio calculations comparing impact of various goodwill standards on a country-by-country basis.

Country	Earnings as a percentage of sales	Earnings as a percentage of investment (owners' equity)
Australia	5.0	3.03
Canada	7.5	4.48
Ireland	10.0	14.29
New Zealand	10.0	5.88
United Kingdom	10.0	14.29
United States	7.5	4.48

an independent analyst would not be in a position to make allowance for the effects of aggregation of various goodwill accounting methods. Accordingly, the analyst and the public would not be properly informed as to the earnings or net asset position of such a multinational corporation. (Adoption of ED 47 would eliminate the mixture of approaches currently permitted by SSAP 22 and, therefore, would provide more meaningful earnings and net asset information.) Our example of the consolidation according to U.S. standards assumes that the amortization would be taken uniformly over forty years for consolidated statements. This need not necessarily be the case, in practice. In a telephone survey of fifteen U.S. MNCs conducted in February 1990, the authors spoke with fifteen managers at the vice-presidential level. Nine indicated that, for consolidation purposes, their companies would use a forty-year life for purchased goodwill, regardless of the local standards in foreign host countries. Five, however, indicated that they would not necessarily restate to amortization based upon a forty-year U.S. maximum if the local useful economic life estimates were reasonable, such as a twenty-year estimate for an Australian subsidiary. One indicated that the question did not apply to his company. Thus, in the U.S. case, it is possible to have consolidated statements with varying estimated useful lives combined. However, two U.S. corporate interviewees, whose companies had subsidiaries in the United Kingdom, indicated that the U.K. practice of immediate write-off of goodwill against reserves would require an adjustment to U.S. GAAP upon consolidation.

Reassessment of carrying value of goodwill

All standards require the write-down of carrying value of goodwill where there has been a permanent diminution in its value. The loss in value in all cases is to be charged against income; however, the charge can be treated as either an extraordinary item or an ordinary charge. Reference would then be made to the relevant accounting standard covering extraordinary

275

items to determine if the circumstances enable the loss to be classified as extraordinary.

The United States standard clearly envisages circumstances where, in spite of a few loss years, goodwill carrying value need not be adjusted. The U.S. Standard's paragraph 31 specifically states: 'A single loss year or even a few loss years together do not necessarily justify an extraordinary charge to income for all or a large part of the unamortized cost of intangible assets'.

While the above relates to permanent impairment in the value of unamortized goodwill, the standards also vary as to ability to extend the amortization period as a result of review of policy. This issue is not specifically addressed in the Canadian, New Zealand and International standards. The United Kingdom standard SSAP 22 specified that useful life may be shortened, but not extended. (ED 47 would permit as part of the required annual review of purchased goodwill carrying amounts either the extension or shortening of economic life estimates. Extension may be to only a maximum forty years from the date of acquisition. Sufficient information must be disclosed to explain such a long amortization period [Part 1, para.19].) The U.S. standard, however, states in paragraph 31 that in respect of subsequent review of amortization: 'if estimates are changed, the unamortized cost should be allocated to the increased or reduced number of remaining periods in the revised useful life, but not to exceed forty years after acquisition'.

Disclosure requirements in financial statements

The disclosure requirements in respect of the specific issues of policy, amortization period, amortization expense and cost of goodwill on acquisition were compared between applicable accounting standards. The results of the comparison are detailed in Table 1.

The requirements of the standards vary significantly. On one extreme the New Zealand standard does not specify any disclosure requirements in respect to these issues; on the other, the U.K. standard requires disclosure of all of the issues.

The lack of requirement to disclose specifically the period of amortization of goodwill is a significant matter where the Australian standard is out of step with the other countries. The Australian standard requires the disclosure of the goodwill amortization expense. However, this disclosure does not provide the more meaningful information, such as specifying the actual period or periods over which amortization takes place.

In respect of the amount of goodwill arising on acquisition only, the U.K. and the International standards require disclosure. In the case of the United Kingdom the information is required to be disclosed for each acquisition. Without this form of disclosure, the reader of the financial statements is required to estimate the cost by making a number of assumptions from the limited information available.

Treatment of excess of assets over purchase consideration

There exists great divergence between the standards as to the accounting treatment for the excess of assets over the purchase consideration. In most circumstances, the different treatments would result in significantly different outcomes. The extent of the effect, of course, depends entirely upon the mix of non-current assets versus the non-monetary assets. While many circumstances could be envisaged, the item with the greatest impact would be the value of inventory being a current asset of a non-monetary nature.

The U.S. standard requires the excess to be assigned to non-current assets (except long-term investments in marketable securities). The Canadian and Australian standards, however, specify that the excess be allocated to non-monetary assets.

The present International standard directs that the excess be allocated over individual depreciable non-monetary assets or treated as deferred income and recognized as income on a systematic basis; the proposed revised standard directs that the excess be allocated over all non-monetary assets, not just the depreciable ones, or treated as deferred income and amortized systematically to income.

The United Kingdom requires that 'negative goodwill' be credited directly to reserves. This treatment is consistent with their preferred treatment of goodwill as an immediate charge against reserves. (ED 47 would require that 'negative goodwill' be recorded on the balance sheet as a 'negative asset', under 'Provisions for liabilities and charges' or under 'Accrued and deferred income' [Part 1, para. 33]. This treatment does not agree with the IASC Definition of a liability and might place ED 47 in this area in conflict with the IASC's 'Framework'.)

It is interesting to note that in the case of New Zealand, the 1978 standard required that negative goodwill be credited to an undistributable reserve. This requirement of the standard was deleted in April 1984. However, it was not replaced with an alternative treatment and as a result the standard is silent on this issue.

Summary and conclusions

The above review of various national accounting standards has identified a number of inconsistent and conflicting guidelines. While some of the inconsistencies are minor and in all probability would not have a material impact upon consolidated financial statements, there are a number which profoundly influence the results and position of a corporation as disclosed by its financial statements.

The most significant of these is a conceptual difference which exists between the goodwill accounting standards issued in the United Kingdom and Ireland and those issued by the other bodies which were reviewed in this paper. The U.K. standard advocates that goodwill be eliminated immediately on acquisition by write-off directly against reserves, whereas the other countries require goodwill to be carried forward in the balance sheet and systematically amortized against income over the estimated useful life of the goodwill. This difference is not just an inconsistency, but rather represents the chasm of conceptual division as to the underlying question of what goodwill represents. The revised IAS 22, if followed by the United Kingdom and Ireland, would end this practice. (As noted above, ED 47 proposes to eliminate this option.)

Significant gains have been achieved by virtue of the codification of the accounting treatment of goodwill. Over the past decade numerous national accounting standards on goodwill have been issued to provide guidance and consistent treatment. However, as the goodwill accounting standard in the United Kingdom is the very antithesis of that in other countries, it is clear that no single theory has emerged which specifies a uniform accounting method for goodwill.

In Australia, where the goodwill standard was issued as recently as 1984, the debate over the appropriate accounting treatment is still current and widespread (*IASC News*, July 1989, p.8). Even though two major Australian accounting bodies jointly issued an accounting standard AAS 18, *Accounting for Goodwill* (effective as from April 1984), discussion of the issues continued, as did examples of non-compliance. The Australian standard was not uniformly complied with until ASRB 1013 was issued by the Accounting Standards Review Board. This standard, while identical to that of the two major accounting bodies, had the necessary legislative backing to ensure mandatory adoption as from financial years ended 30 June 1988.

In addition to the major conceptual difference referred to above, there are a number of specific procedural differences between the guidelines set out within the various accounting standards. The three issues which warrant further attention are: (a) treatment of the excess of assets over purchase consideration, (b) calculation of goodwill, and (c) amortization of goodwill. In this age of contested and competitive takeovers, the consideration paid for the purchase of a company or business generally appears to be at very high earnings multiples. The likely consequences of high earnings multiples is an excess of purchase consideration over assets acquired rather than the reverse. It is not very common for a corporation to purchase a company or a business and to pay less than the sum of the market value of the individual identifiable tangible assets.

The issues arising from the inconsistent guidance in the various national accounting standards as to the treatment of the excess of assets over purchase consideration are significant. However, the inconsistencies examined and documented in this paper have little relevance in the current market-place of mergers, acquisitions and hostile takeovers where a goodwill premium over net assets is generally paid.

Significant discrepancies exist between the accounting standards as to the acceptable method for the calculation of the amount of goodwill at acquisition date. A very material impact upon the financial statements arises from a difference between the U.K. and the U.S. goodwill standards. The United Kingdom specifically allows reorganization costs associated with an acquisition to be included in the determination of the fair value of net assets at acquisition. These costs will, as a consequence, form part of the cost of goodwill. A secondary, but not insignificant, difference between standards relates to the matter of incidental expenses associated with the acquisition. Some standards specify the inclusion of these expenses as part of the cost of acquisition while other standards are silent on this matter.

The inconsistency between standards in relation to the above issues has two financial reporting consequences. First, the U.K. standard provides the opportunity for inherently conservative calculations in the highly subjective area of estimating future reorganization costs to be incorporated in the calculation of goodwill on acquisition. This may result in the increase of goodwill which is to be immediately written-off directly against reserves. As a consequence costs and expenses which may in all other circumstances be charged against revenue in the income statement could be charged directly against reserves. Second, U.K. companies' future earnings are not penalized by amortization charges when the direct write-off approach is applied. On the other hand, those countries which require systematic amortization of goodwill over time may place resident companies at a competitive disadvantage in acquisition activity *vis à vis* U.K. companies since the non-U.K. companies must be concerned about the impact of future goodwill charges against future periods' earnings. Thus, non-U.K. companies may not be able to offer as much in competitive bidding. (As noted above, ED 47 would eliminate this option and thus place U.K. companies on a similar footing in this regard in the future.)

The standards applicable to goodwill generally specify that goodwill be amortized by a systematic method over its useful economic life. This guideline is an appropriate conceptual basis for calculating the amortization charge by providing the flexibility to the corporation so that it is responsive to the circumstances of the acquisition.

Recognizing the practical difficulty that arises in the highly subjective assessment of the economic life of goodwill, some of the standards also specify maximum allowable amortization periods. It is in this area that there exist considerable differences between the guidelines. They range from the proposed IASC guideline of five years to the U.S. and Canadian guidelines of forty years, with Australia somewhat in the middle with a maximum of twenty years.

A study of the correlation between the maximum amortization periods allowable by the standards and the amortization periods adopted by corporations does not form part of this paper. However, given the very subjective nature of the assessment of the economic useful life of goodwill, it would not be surprising if corporations, for ease of calculation, adopt the maximum allowable amortization period.

A more cynical view would suggest that a corporation may have a further incentive to adopt the maximum period for goodwill amortization. The income statement is recognized as the document which is given considerable emphasis in the assessment of performance by the external financial community. By increasing the amortization period to the maximum allowable, the reported earnings would not be as depressed over the medium term as would otherwise be the result.

German (1988, p. 71) considers leveraged buy-outs as one of the favourite means of buying and selling corporate America. He also identified one of a number of reasons for the popularity of the leveraged buy-out is that current shareholders receive a premium price for their equity. In accounting terms this premium would generally add to the goodwill figure arising on consolidation as the excess of the purchase consideration over the net assets at fair market value. It is self-evident that the higher the price that is bid in a competitive acquisition the greater the amount of premium and hence the greater the amount of goodwill.

With the high value of goodwill recorded in the consolidated financial statements of the acquiring company, management and/or directors must be under significant pressure to adopt the maximum allowable goodwill amortization period rather than undertake any specific useful life assessment which may result in a shorter period. An interesting future opportunity exists to compare the goodwill amortization periods adopted by acquiring corporations in leverage buy-out situations with those of U.S. corporations generally.

The effect of the selection of the goodwill amortization period is greatest upon the results reported in the income statement. If companies are adopting the maximum allowable period either as a matter of convenience or to reduce the impact of the charge against the income statement, then consolidation of financial statements prepared under various goodwill amortization approaches and/or useful life estimates may result in a distorted consolidated income statement.

The published financial statements of a company are used by many and varied external groups. The overall assessments of performance of individual companies are based, amongst other things, upon the key indicators provided by ratio analysis. In a number of analytical reviews, earnings is a critical number in the formula. It is critical both as a raw number and as a factor in a number of ratios.

If earnings can be significantly affected by both the calculation of goodwill and the amortization policy adopted, then the comparability of financial statements generally and the income statements in particular will be distorted. The extent of the distortion will largely depend upon the country of origin of the financial statements and the goodwill guidelines being followed.

In the case of multinational corporations, a difficulty will arise for the consolidation of financial statements of wholly and/or partly owned subsidiaries which operate in jurisdictions with varying goodwill accounting standards. Any consolidation of financial statements prepared under various approaches to goodwill and/or useful economic life estimates may render the consolidated financial statements less than meaningful.

Accounting for goodwill is a controversial and topical area. Its conceptual complexity is not, however, a jusitification for lack of uniformity in approach. It is vital that bodies such as the IASC act to resolve the parochial issues and take steps to further the establishment of a uniform international treatment for goodwill accounting.

The revisions to IAS 22 proposed in IASC ED 32 would reduce the differences in goodwill accounting from nation to nation if followed by IASC member nations. This would require affirmative action by the respective national professional accounting bodies, standard setting boards (or commissions), and/or national legislative bodies. By specifying the recommended asset treatment for purchased, positive goodwill, and the five-year amortization period, IASC has taken a significant step toward harmonization of goodwill accounting. As noted in our paper, however, the implications for consolidated net income may be quite drastic. If corporations in the United States or Canada have been routinely amortizing goodwill over forty years, and their respective accounting bodies mandate compliance with the IASC's recommended five-year normal amortization period, such corporations could find their reported net income streams replaced with net loss streams as a consequence of carrying much larger goodwill expense (as much as eight times as much) per annum to income.

The implications of the revised IAS 22 for potential corporate buyouts cannot be overlooked. The higher annual goodwill charges implied by IAS 22's five-year normal amortization period in countries permitting a longer period could drive down the amount in excess of fair value of net assets which purchasers would be willing to pay. In order to keep goodwill amortization charges to income as low as possible, purchasers are likely to pay less for purchased goodwill. Thus, purchase prices are likely to decline.

References

Accounting Standards Committee, *Accounting for Goodwill—SSAP 22 (Revised)*, ASC, July 1989.
——, Exposure Draft 47, *Accounting for Goodwill*, ASC, February 1990.

——, Exposure Draft 48, *Accounting for Acquisitions and Mergers*, ASC, February, 1990.

——, American Institute of Certified Public Accountants, Accounting Principles Board, *Opinions of the Accounting Principles Board No. 16—Business Combinations*, AICPA, 1970.

Australian Accounting Standards Review Board, ASRB 1013, *Accounting for Goodwill*, ASRB, 1988.

Canadian Institute of Chartered Accountants, *Business Combinations*, CICA, 1986.

German, J., 'LBO Accounting: Unveiling the Mystery of Carryover Basis', *Journal of Accountancy*, October 1988.

Hughes, H. P., Georgia State University Research Monograph No. 80, *Goodwill in Accounting: A History of the Issues and Problems*, College of Business Administration, 1982.

Institute of Chartered Accountants in Australia, Statement of Accounting Standards 18, *Accounting for Goodwill*, ICAA, 1984.

Institute of Chartered Accountants in England and Wales, Statement of Standard Accounting Practice No. 22, *Accounting for Goodwill*, ICAEW, 1984.

Institute of Chartered Accountants in Ireland, Statement of Standard Accounting Practice No. 22, *Accounting for Goodwill*, ICAI, 1984.

International Accounting Standards Committee, 'Australia: IASC Visit to Discuss E32', *IASC News*, July 1989.

——, Exposure Draft 32, *Comparability of Financial Statements: Proposed Amendments to International Accounting Standards, 2, 5, 8, 9, 11, 16, 17, 18, 19, 21, 22, 23 and 25*, IASC, 1989.

——, Exposure Draft 32, *Framework for the Preparation and Presentation of Financial Statements*, IASC, 1989.

——, International Accounting Standard 22, *Accounting for Business Combinations*, IASC, 1983.

——, *Survey of the Use and Application of International Accounting Standards*, IASC, 1988.

New Zealand Society of Accountants, Statement of Standard Accounting Practice No. 8, *Consolidated Financial Statements*, NZSA, 1984.

Organization for Economic Co-Operation and Development, *Harmonization of Accounting Standards: Achievements and Prospects*. OECD, 1986.

Parker, Robert H., 'Regulating Financial Reporting in the U.K., U.S.A., Australia and Canada', in C. W. Nobes and R. H. Parker (eds), *Issues in Multinational Accounting*, St. Martin's Press, 1988.

Appendix
Table of countries for which goodwill accounting standards were reviewed

Country	Title of applicable standard	Abbrevation	Effective beginning date	Standards setting organizations
Australia	Australian Accounting Standard,	AAS 18	April 1984	Australian Society of Accountants, The Institute of Chartered Accountants in Australia, and The Australian Accounting Standards Review Board
	Accounting for Goodwill	ASRB 1013	July 1988	
Canada	Accounting Recommendations, Business Combinations	AR 1580	April 1974	Canadian Institute of Chartered Accountants
Ireland	Statement of Standard Accounting Practice, Accounting for Goodwill	SSAP 22	January 1985	Institute of Chartered Accountants in Ireland
New Zealand	Statement of Standard Accounting Practice, Consolidated Financial Statements	ED 47	Proposed February 1990	New Zealand Society of Accountants
		B8	April 1978; amended April 1984	
United Kingdom	Statement of Standard Accounting Practice, Accounting for Goodwill	SSAP 22	January 1985; revised July 1989	The Accounting Standards Committee which consists of the six members of the Consultative Committee of Accounting Bodies.[1] The ASC is soon to be replaced by the Accounting Standards Board (ASB)
		ED 47	Proposed February 1990	
United States	Opinions of the Accounting Principles Board, Business Assets; Intangible Assets	APB 16	November 1970	American Institute of Certified Public Accountants
		APB 17	November 1970	
International Accounting Standards	Accounting for Business Combinations	IAS 22	November 1983	International Accounting Standards Committee
	Comparability of Financial Statements	ED 32	January 1989	International Accounting Standards Committee

[1] The six members are The Institute of Chartered Accountants in England and Wales, The Institute of Chartered Accountants of Scotland, The Institute of Chartered Accountants in Ireland, The Chartered Association of Certified Accountants, The Chartered Institute of Management Accountants, and The Chartered Institute of Public Finance and Accountancy.

44

PROFIT MEASUREMENT AND UK ACCOUNTING STANDARDS

A case of increasing disharmony in relation to US GAAP and IASs

P. Weetman, E. A. E. Jones,
C. A. Adams and S. J. Gray

Source: *Accounting and Business Research* 28(3) (1998): 189–208.

Abstract

UK accounting practice differs from International Accounting Standards (IASs) particularly with regard to amortisation of goodwill, provision for deferred taxation and the accounting treatment of pension costs. Under the core standards programme of the IASC the IASs have emerged closer to US practice. This paper evaluates the profit of those UK companies reporting to the Securities and Exchange Commission (SEC) in 1988 and 1994, spanning a period which saw the establishment of the ASB and the implementation of the IASC's comparability project. An increasing gap was found between the reported profit under UK accounting principles and that restated under US GAAP. The difference lay most frequently in accounting for goodwill, provision for deferral tax, and the accounting treatment of pension costs, with accounting for goodwill showing a particularly significant impact in 1994. Notwithstanding the introduction of FRS 10, an overall impression of increasing disharmony could continue to cause reconciliations to be required of UK companies seeking full listing on a US stock exchange, with consequent disadvantage relative to companies in other European countries seeking international capital in the US.

1. Introduction

A practical instance of the demand for harmonisation of accounting practices has been provided in the consultation between the International

Accounting Standards Committee (IASC) and the International Organisation of Securities Commissions (IOSCO). This has resulted in a target of revising the priority standards to IOSCO satisfaction by mid-1998, a project commonly referred to as 'the core standards programme' (IASC 1993a: 4). The divergence between UK accounting practice and International Accounting Standards (IASs) is noted in a number of areas (Keegan and King, 1996) but particularly with regard to the amortisation of goodwill, accounting for deferred taxation and the accounting treatment of pension costs and employee benefits.

A key element to gaining acceptance of the IASC core standards by IOSCO is participation by the US Securities and Exchange Commission (SEC), as a member body of IOSCO (IASC 1996b). The SEC imposes strict accounting requirements on foreign companies seeking a full listing on a US stock exchange. In particular, the SEC requires a report on form 20-F, a lengthy document which, in the case of UK companies as foreign registrants, includes a reconciliation of profit reported under UK accounting principles[1] to the profit figure which would have been reported under US GAAP. If in future the SEC accepts financial statements prepared under IASs then reconciliations will no longer be required where IASs are applied in full. However, if UK accounting standards remain different from IASs, there may well be a continuing requirement for reconciliations to be reported by UK companies while other companies enjoy exemption because they apply IASs in full.

In this context it is relevant to investigate the materiality of the differences in reported profit, as perceived by the US reader, of the profit and loss account stated under both US GAAP and UK accounting principles. Information is deemed to be material if it could influence users' decisions taken on the basis of the financial statements (ASB 1995: para. 2.7). The relative materiality of adjustments, indicated by this research, provides a benchmark against which to assess the likely impact of a continuing requirement to prepare reconciliations where there is a lack of compatibility with IASs. It is also relevant to consider relative magnitudes of material differences over the period in the early 1990s during which UK standards were being set under a new regime and the IASC was revising its standards.

A direct question regarding the future impact of non-compliance with IASs would be to seek quantification of *de facto* differences between profit reported under UK accounting principles and that reported under IASs. As UK companies do not provide such reconciliations, that would require a simulation or a speculative recalculation using information in the public domain. The reconciliations contained in form 20-F allow quantification of *de facto* differences between UK practices and US GAAP. The impact of UK practices which depart from IASs may be derived by comparing details of the various regulations.

Accordingly, the questions addressed in the paper are:

- what were the *de jure* differences between measurement practices under UK accounting principles as compared to those under US GAAP, during the period 1988 to 1994?
- what were the *de facto* differences in reported profits under UK accounting principles and US GAAP in 1988 and 1994, and what were the relative magnitudes of those differences?
- what implications do the quantified differences have for policy makers in setting UK standards, with particular regard to alignment with the IASs?

This paper evaluates the differences in profit measurement arising from reporting under both UK accounting principles and US GAAP at two points in time, namely 1988 and 1994. These dates have been chosen because the intervening period encompasses the change from the Accounting Standards Committee (ASC) to the Accounting Standards Board (ASB) in the UK and the implementation of the IASC's comparability project, but it predates the start of the IASC's core standards project. The paper estimates the extent to which the reported differences would remain if the core standards were accepted by the SEC but, at the same time, some UK standards were not aligned with the core standards. The paper also offers an evaluation of the extent of differences in reported profit during the early years of operation of the ASB.

Previous research analysing reports on form 20-F issued by companies, prior to the start of the IASC's comparability project (Weetman and Gray 1991), showed substantial differences when profit reported under UK accounting principles was compared with that under US GAAP. Since that time the pressures for international harmonisation have grown, most importantly across the major capital markets of the world. It is a matter for continuing debate as to whether investors can cope with accounting diversity. Choi and Levich (1991), interviewing stock market participants in the UK, US, Japan, Switzerland and Germany, found that about half the respondents felt that accounting diversity affected their decisions. Bhushan and Lessard (1992) found that, among US and UK-based international investment managers, uniform disclosure or harmomsation was seen as more important than quantitative reconciliation to US GAAP.

The purpose of this paper is to explore the extent to which there is greater or lesser diversity due to differences in reported profit as a result of differences between UK accounting principles and US GAAP. The next section draws on prior literature for factors creating pressure for international harmonisation of the paper. There follows in Section 3 a brief analysis of *de jure* differences in comparisons of UK accounting principles with US GAAP and with IASs. *De facto* differences between accounting practices under UK accounting principles and US GAAP are quantified using the 'index of comparability' measure described in Section 4 and applied to the sample as outlined in Section 5. The results are discussed in some detail in Section 6. Section 7 draws conclusions regarding the quantified differences and the policy implications.

2. Pressures for international harmonisation

International pressures for improvement in the comparability of accounting and information disclosure arise from the diverse interests and concerns of a wide range of participant groups and organisations around the world. Since the early 1970s, when the IASC was established, these pressures have grown at a rapid pace along with the development of stock markets internationally and especially those in emerging economies (IASC 1996b). While IASs issued during the 1970s and 1980s were recognised to have made a contribution towards international harmonisation, by the late 1980s the performance of the IASC was increasingly being questioned on account of the flexibility of the standards and continuing lack of comparability of financial statements across borders.

2.1 Involvement of IOSCO

An important development at this time was the interest of the IOSCO in the IASC's provision of mutually acceptable international accounting standards for use in multinational company security offerings and listings. IASC invited IOSCO to join its consultative group in 1987 (Wallace, 1990: 18–19). In 1988 a report of the Technical Committee of IOSCO concluded that differences in national accounting requirements presented a major impediment to multinational securities offerings and other foreign listings. The IASC and IOSCO agreed to work together to find a solution that would allow a company to list its securities in any foreign stock market on the basis of one set of financial statements conforming to IASs (Cairns, 1995: 57). The IASC responded in 1989 with the comparability project set out in the exposure draft E 32 *Comparability of Financial Statements* (IASC 1989). The proposals in E 32 were designed to eliminate most of the choices of accounting treatment then permitted under International Accounting Standards. IOSCO indicated that being seen to adopt a more uniform approach, as E 32 advocated, would enhance the credibility and acceptability of IASs by the international investment community.

The outcome of the comparability project proposals, refined by the *Statement of Intent* (IASC 1993b), was that 10 IASs were revised. These revisions included the elimination of some 20 permitted accounting treatments. Of relevance to this paper were the elimination of: the use of closing exchange rates when translating income statements; the expensing of development costs where specified criteria were met; and the immediate write-off to share-holders' interests of positive goodwill.

Subsequent to completion of the IASC's comparability project, IOSCO indicated that more work would be required (Cairns, 1995: 41) and pre-sented a list of core standards which it might be willing to accept provided the full programme of core standards could be completed successfully within a specified limit of time (IASC 1994: 13). In 1995 the Technical Committee of IOSCO agreed that successful completion of the IASC's work plan by the end of 1999 would mean that IASs would form a compre-hensive set of core standards. The Technical Committee would then be in a position to recommend endorsement of IASs for cross-border raising of capital and for listings in stock markets around the world. At the urg-ing of multinational companies and members of IOSCO, the Board of IASC brought forward the target date to March 1998 (IASC 1996a:1, 9–12).

2.2 US approach to IASs

A key player in the success of the IASC endeavour is the US. Both the SEC and the Financial Accounting Standards Board (FASB) have expressed sup-port for the objectives of the IASC's core standards programme. However, they have qualified this by stating that acceptance is dependent on IAS's constituting a comprehensive set of generally accepted accounting prin-ciples. The standards must also be of high quality and be rigorously interpreted and applied. The chairman of the FASB has been critical of the speed with which the IASC has carried out the core standards programme, question-ing whether this is compatible with high quality standards (IASC 1996b). The FASB has also identified more than 250 differences between IASs and FASB standards (FASB 1996, IASC 1996b). The IASC has pointed out that not all these differences relate to the core standards identified as priority matters but has confirmed that it will refer to the FASB's analysis as these standards are developed (IASC 1996b).

2.3 UK approach to IASs

Since 1990 the ASB, working within the European Directives, has refined and extended UK financial reporting requirements in ways which, in some measurement respects, have moved UK practice towards that of the US. At the same time measurement practices in the US have been developing further. Some of the most difficult and internationally contentious issues have only recently begun to be tackled by the ASB. In particular there are the issues of accounting for goodwill, deferred taxation and pension costs. This paper shows that in 1994 these remained the most frequent causes of reported difference in profit between UK accounting principles and US

GAAP. By the end of 1994 Financial Reporting Standards (FRSs) numbers one to six were in operation as mandatory requirements.

The chairman of the ASB has articulated the fear that if the IASC did not deliver the core standards within the agreed time scale then companies seeking US funding would switch to US GAAP and would probably not be interested thereafter in further changing to IASC standards (FRC 1996). Three possible strategies have been analysed by the chairman as a basis for reacting to the mounting pressure for harmonisation:

- adopt international standards for domestic purposes;
- develop domestic requirements without regard to international standards; or
- harmonise domestic requirements with international standards where possible.

Analysis of limitations and benefits lent support to the third of these and to the view that the ASB should depart from international consensus only when:

- there were particular legal or fiscal problems that dictated such a course; or
- the Board genuinely believed that the international approach was wrong and that an independent UK standard might point the way to an eventual improvement in international practice.

It was noted that the ASB had taken an independent course with regard to accounting for goodwill, and indicated the need for debate on accounting for deferred tax and accounting for pension costs (FRC, 1996: 42–46). This paper offers a contribution to that debate.

3. UK/US/IAS accounting differences

Accounting differences may be classified *de jure* by examining the regulations, or *de facto* by examining the practice.

3.1 De jure differences

Measurement practices of UK accounting which are not compatible with those of US GAAP are listed in Table 1. Panel (a) of Table 1 indicates the UK measurement practices which differ from both US GAAP and IASs. Panel (b) of Table 1 indicates the UK measurement practices which differ from US GAAP but are compatible with those of the IASs.

We provide later an evaluation of the UK/US differences in reported profit arising in total and for each item of Table 1 separately. If in future the

Table 1 Incompatibility of UK measurement practices with US GAAP and relation to IASs.

(a) Measurement practices where UK is not compatible with either US GAAP or IAS

Goodwill	UK SSAP 22 not compatible with either IAS 22 or US GAAP
Deferred taxation	UK SSAP 15 (revised) not compatible with either IAS 12 or US GAAP
Pension costs and post-retirement benefits other than pensions	SSAP 24 is not currently compatible with US GAAP and will not be compatible with the revised IAS (1998) which is closer to US GAAP
Capitalisation of development costs	SSAP 13 is permissive on capitalisation of development costs; IAS 21 is closer to US GAAP in prescribing conditions for capitalisation
Financial instruments	FRS 4 prohibits split accounting for mixed capital instruments
Consolidation policy	FRS 2 leaves little scope for exclusion of a subsidiary. IAS 27 allows exclusion. US definition of control is close to that of UK
Discontinued operations	FRS 3 differs from US definition. IAS policy remains under consideration

(b) Measurement practices where UK differs from US GAAP but is compatible with IAS

Valuation of property, plant and equipment	UK compatible with IAS 16. US GAAP does not permit revaluation
Borrowing costs	UK compatible with IAS 23. US GAAP has more specific rules
Foreign currency translation	UK compatible with IAS 21 where UK companies choose average rate for translating P&L account, but not compatible with US GAAP
Dividends payable	Dividends proposed may he accrued in UK or under IASs, not under US GAAP
Correction of fundamental errors resulting from accounting policy change	UK compatible with IAS 8 on fundamental errors; US GAAP requires effect of change in profit and loss account
Business combinations	UK compatible with IAS 22. US GAAP under APB 16 dictates that pooling of interest must be used where specific conditions are met. These conditions are not identical to those of FRS 6
Restructuring costs	Not dealt with in either UK standards or IAS. US GAAP has specific requirements
Revenue recognition	UK meets IAS 18 principles. US GAAP has more specific rules
Investments in marketable equity securities and debt securities	SSAP 19 consistent with IAS 25. US GAAP uses different classifications

---

Sources: See Appendix A.

SEC accepts financial statements prepared under IASs then, in principle, reconciliations will no longer be required of any company reporting under IASs. If, however, UK accounting standards remain different from IASs, there may well be a continuing requirement for reconciliations to be reported by UK companies in respect of those items in panel (a) of Table 1 (with the possible exception of accounting for goodwill under the new UK standard on intangibles). However the items in panel (b) of Table 1 would probably no longer be required.

An important change during the period which brought UK accounting closer to US GAAP was in respect of reporting extraordinary items, common in 1988 but virtually non-existent in 1994 as a result of the implementation of FRS 3 *Reporting financial performance* (ASB 1992a). Other evidence of movement towards US GAAP may be seen in aspects of UITF 6 *Accounting for post-retirement benefits other than pensions* (ASB 1992b) and in FRS 4 *Capital instruments* (ASB 1993), FRS 5 *Reporting the substances of transactions* (ASB 1994a) and FRS 6 *Acquisitions and mergers* (ASB 1994b). However, the US regulations on all these matters are more detailed. Situations remain where the UK practice under the new standards may not satisfy the US requirements entirely.

While these UK changes were bringing UK practices closer to US GAAP, new and amended US standards were widening the gap. In particular, the accounting treatment of deferred taxation was finally agreed in the form of SFAS 109; further SFASs appeared in relation to specific aspects of financial instruments; EITF guidance was issued on restructuring costs; and SFAS 115 provided a stricter approach to investments in marketable equity securities and debt securities.

Overall, from the detailed comparisons contained in Appendix A, it would appear that there was no significant *de jure* harmonisation of accounting measurement practices between UK accounting principles and US GAAP over the period 1988 to 1994 in the main areas of difference in policy and practice.

Analysis of differences in legislation gives no indication of how frequently such differences will be encountered in practice or how significant the differences may be in their impact on profit. The next section of the paper turns to the empirical evidence based on UK companies which report under US GAAP as well as under UK accounting principles.

3.2 De facto differences

De facto differences in UK and US accounting practices over the period 1986–1988 inclusive were analysed by Weetman and Gray (1991) using the reports of UK companies to the SEC on form 20-F. The availability of such data is confined to those UK companies which have a full listing on a US stock exchange. The advantage of the data lies in the detail of the reconciliation and the quality, being audited information prepared by the company. From a research perspective, each company provides a 'matched' set of data showing how the company's reported profit compares under each set of GAAP. This paper extends that matching by taking companies whose accounting information was available in both 1988 and 1994 (Appendix B).

4 The index of comparability as an indicator of harmonisation

Gray (1980) first used the 'index of conservatism' in comparing profit measurement practices of several countries. However, for the purposes of this paper, renaming the index as a measure of 'comparability' places clearer emphasis on relative accounting treatment without requiring a judgment as to which is more or less conservative. The index of comparability indicates the measurement impact of accounting differences and may therefore be distinguished from other indicators of harmonisation, such as H, I or C indices which quantify the incidence of accounting differences (van der Tas, 1988).

Gray's index has featured in a number of studies of comparative reported profit (Weetman and Gray 1990 and 1991, Adams *et al*, 1993, Cooke, 1993, Hellman, 1993, Weetman *et al*, 1993, Norton, 1995).

4.1 Formula for the index of comparability

Where UK reported profit is being compared to that reported under US GAAP, the index may be expressed by the formula:

$$1 - \left(\frac{\text{Profits}_{USA} - \text{Profits}_{UK}}{|\text{Profits}_{USA}|} \right)$$

The measure of profit used is the earnings for ordinary shareholders, after tax and after extraordinary items. The numerical value of the profit or loss in the US is chosen as the denominator because the reconciliation is a report addressed to investors who, it may be assumed, are accustomed to US GAAP and consequently will view the differences as departures from US profit or loss rather than departures from UK profit or loss. The use of US profit in the denominator also allows the index values to be used in inter-country comparisons. Profit is chosen for the denominator rather than a scale factor such as sales or market value, because the paper seeks to evaluate materiality as defined earlier.

Although there is no agreed guidance on materiality, auditors assessing materiality in relation to impact on users will make reference in their work to percentages. Audit practice (Grant Thornton, 1990, para 7.59) indicates a helpful guideline as being 5–10% of profit before taxation, and warns that a judgment based on turnover would not be appropriate in relation to, say, stock valuation. There is also a warning (para 7.63) that items should not be judged material by reasons of value where a small profit is turned into a small loss, or vice versa. This study provides information based on bands at 5% and 10% of profit.

The neutral value of 1.0 is used for consistency with prior literature. An index value greater than 1 means that the UK reported profit is greater than that reported under US GAAP (or a UK loss is not as large as a US loss). An index value less than 1 means that the UK reported profit is less than that reported under US GAAP (or a UK loss is larger than a US loss).

Because the reconciliations reported to the SEC contain considerable detail, it is also possible to present partial index values using the formula:

$$1 - \left(\frac{\text{partial adjustment}}{|\text{Profits}_{\text{USA}}|} \right)$$

These provide a relative measure of the contribution of each reconciling item. The neutral value is retained as 1.0 for consistency of interpretation. The indexes of partial adjustments add to the total index by the formula:

$$\text{Total index} = \sum_{1}^{n} adjustment_n - (n - 1)$$

4.2 Evaluation of the use of the index

It should be noted that the formula carries a disadvantage of reporting extreme index values if the US profit or loss is close to zero. Such occurrences are relatively rare in the data examined and do not seriously inhibit interpretation. The presence of such outliers has to be weighed against the attractiveness of the formula in having parallels in the accounting concept of 'materiality' which is usually judged in relation to profit. Such outliers cause comparable problems in practical interpretation of their impact on users of financial statements, and it has been suggested that materiality may not be judged on a relative value basis when profit is small or the item causes a change from a small profit to a small loss (Grant Thornton, 1990).

Use of the index to evaluate annual data may carry the risk of including in any particular year a short-term timing difference which reverses in the following year due to a difference in recognition criteria. An example might be a provision for a loss, where the timing of loss recognition follows different GAAP rules but the amount of the anticipated loss is the same under both systems. Each form 20-F gives scope for consideration of this aspect because it carries not only the results of the current year but also those of each of the two previous years for comparison. Scrutiny of the three-year comparisons within each 20-F reconciliation showed that only two specific reversals in reconciling items were observable in all the separate adjustments analysed.

As a further check, the data available over three years within each 20-F was aggregated in an attempt to provide a three-year total which would eliminate the potential influence of short-term reversals. The three-year aggregation indicated little evidence of matching items being eliminated in one year against another. It is not reported here in detail because there are difficulties in interpreting aggregation of a current year's profit with comparative data of previous periods. In particular, where a large adjusting item appears in one accounting period, with no reported figure for that line item in the other two years, aggregation of profit over the three-year period will effectively apply income smoothing to that item, leading to conclusions which would not be compatible with the principles of UK and US accounting. Furthermore, where there is a positive adjustment in one year and a negative adjustment in another year, these not being reversals of the same item, the resulting cancellation will again lead to misinterpretation of the significance of those reconciling items for reported annual profit.

One justification for concentrating on the annual result only is that this is the common practice of those who evaluate accounting information. Comments in analysts' reports and the press are largely based on annual results. The general consistency of results from one year to the next over a three-year analysis was shown previously for data in the 1980s (Weetman and Gray, 1991). In the course of the current analysis it was noted that, both at 1988 and 1994, a comparable number of adjusting items was reported for each of the two previous years, as compared with those reported for the current year at the date of the 20-F. This suggests that any one year may be taken as representative of the frequency and magnitude of adjustments.

5 Sample

The total number of UK companies providing a 20-F reconciliation was approximately 45 in each of 1994 and 1988. (There is no authoritative list available on a systematic basis; the information is deduced from listings provided by search agencies and from such sources as the web pages of the New York Stock Exchange.) This group is a sub set of a larger group of UK listed companies[2] (over 220 in 1994 compared with 162 reported by Weetman and Gray for 1988) whose shares are traded in the form of American Depositary Receipts (ADRs) in the US. The companies making use of the ADR facility are exempt from the 20-F filing requirement,[3] which is aimed primarily at those seeking to raise new capital on the US stock market.

Of the 41 UK companies listed in the Appendix to Weetman and Gray (1991) as reporting to the SEC in 1988, 25 reported to the SEC at December 1994, the remainder being unavailable because of intervening takeover or merger, cessation of the US listing and, in one case, a major change of activity, from manufacturing to licensing, in process during 1994 (Appendix B). In order to achieve a matching over the period of transition from Accounting Standards Committee to Accounting Standards Board, only those 25 are the subject of this analysis. The benefit of having a matched sample, albeit relatively small, lies in holding constant the nature of the business over the period of comparison.

As a further check on the constancy of the nature of the business, there was scrutiny of the section of each 20-F report containing the description of the business and the main business segments. None of these companies experienced a fundamental restructuring between the two dates used for the analysis. Three of the utilities had major plans in train but these had not become operational to a significant extent at the end of 1994. All companies reported sales to US customers which were, in the main, proportionately greater in 1994 than in 1988. This group of companies was active in expanding by acquisition rather than by organic growth.

There were changes in key financial indicators (taken from the UK information available on *Datastream*). For the group as a whole, the average level of gearing was higher in 1994, the average debt to equity ratio being 34.8% in 1988 and 44.1% in 1994. A higher level of gearing might be expected where companies active in acquisition were writing off goodwill against reserves, at a rate greater than the rate of expansion of net assets. However the average was distorted by extreme values and there were more companies by number having lower gearing in 1994. Net profit as a percentage of sales (10.0% in 1988 and 8.8% in 1994) and gross profit margin on sales (15.5% in 1988 and 13.7% in 1994) were both lower in 1994, and return on capital employed (18.7% in 1988 and 12.8% in 1994) was also lower. The gross profit margin was the only ratio showing a significant difference based on a Wilcoxon matched-pairs test. The paper does not claim to relate the impact of accounting policy differences to changes indicated by financial ratios. It is a matter for conjecture as to whether users of accounts would remember the financial condition of the company at an earlier period when noting the difference in reported profit under two different sets of accounting principles.

The years ended 31 December 1988 and 1994 are described in the paper as '1988' and '1994' for convenience. Where a company had a year-end other than 31 December, the closest year-end within six months either side was selected. Each company published a detailed quantitative reconciliation and also supporting narrative explanations of the accounting policy differences.

A technical detail relates to the number of adjustments labelled 'miscellaneous'. There was an increase in the number of items recorded in this category between 1988 and 1994. Although the average index value is closer to 1.0, reconciliations described as 'miscellaneous' or 'other' may have been a combination of larger adjustments which were offset against each other. Such items limit the refinement of the analysis of partial adjustments.

6 Results

This section presents the main causes of adjustment in the context of Table 1.

6.1 Main causes of adjustment

The numbers of reconciling adjustments made to reported profit are shown in Table 2, together with the relevant index of comparability measured as a mean and a median over the group as a whole. Each category in Table 2 represents a grouping of more than one type of adjustment or description within the category, so that the total adjustments presented by companies in their reconciliations (approximately 150 adjustments in each year) were significantly greater than the number of line items indicated in Table 2.

Table 2 Number of companies making each category of adjustment to profit, together with mean and median index of comparability for 1988 and 1994.

Nature of adjustment of profit	1988 Count	1988 Mean	1988 Median	1994 Count	1994 Mean	1994 Median
Overall	25	1.17	1.10	25	1.25	1.18
Goodwill	24	1.13	1.06	23	1.21	1.15
Deferred tax	22	1.06	1.01	23	1.00	1.00
Pensions/post-retirement benefits/insurance	10	1.01	1.01	19	1.02	1.02
Asset/expense	14	0.98	0.99	14	1.12	1.01
Historic cost/revalued asset	13	0.95	0.98	18	0.98	0.99
Intangibles	3	1.08	1.07	5	1.34	1.06
Restructuring	–	–	–	5	0.80	0.88
Foreign currency translation	5	1.00	1.01	4	0.94	0.99
Financial instruments	2	1.26	1.26	4	0.98	1.04
Leasing	2	1.05	1.05	4	1.16	1.15
Revenue recognition	3	1.02	1.00	3	0.95	0.99
Extraordinary items	12	0.95	1.05	–	–	–
Miscellaneous	5	1.01	1.03	13	0.98	1.01

The following outliers were excluded from calculation of the mean values of profit in respect of the 1994 data:
1. ICI Group plc (Overall index of comparability and partial index of comparability for pension costs and retirement benefits)
2. WPP Group plc (Overall index of comparability and partial index of comparability for amortisation of goodwill)

The overall index of comparability shows that in 1988 the adjustment to profit under UK accounting principles represented 16.8% of profit under US GAAP (index 1.1679), and by 1994 the difference had risen to 25.3% (index 1.2534). The skewness of the data is indicated by the median values, showing corresponding adjustments of 10.1% (index 1.013) in 1988 and 18.2% (index 1.819) in 1994. There is an apparently strong indication, under either the mean or the median, that harmonisation of measurement had moved in a negative direction over the period.

From Table 2 it may be seen that at both dates under consideration, four accounting issues (amortisation of goodwill, provision for deferred taxation, pension costs and the effect of fixed asset revaluation) caused the most frequent reporting of UK/US differences. Other items in those tables confirm the *de jure* differences itemised in Appendix A but their occurrence is less frequent.

The reason for a change in the number of companies showing an adjustment in Table 2 could be:

- the accounting policy difference did not exist in that year;
- the accounting policy difference existed but did not affect the company.

It would be desirable to eliminate the second explanation by reference to the company documentation but this is only occasionally achievable because the company may use the 'miscellaneous' category or may aggregate some groups of adjustments. Notwithstanding this limitation, the initial impression from Table 2 is that the differences which existed in 1988 remained in existence in 1994, augmented by new items such as the accounting treatment of restructuring costs. The adjustments for pension costs in 1988 were increased in 1994 primarily because of additional adjustments for post-retirement benefits. In some cases these are identified separately but in other cases they are aggregated. The only item to disappear between the two dates was extraordinary items.

6.2 Overall materiality of adjustments

The mean and median present convenient summary data for the group as a whole, but investors are more interested in the separate companies when they make investment decisions. Accordingly the findings are presented as distributions of adjustments in bands of materiality, shown in Tables 3 to 6. Comments are made in terms of adjustment to profit but could apply equally to adjustments to net loss. The results of tests of statistical significance relating to Tables 2 to 6 are set out in Table 7.

Turning first to the overall profit, Table 3 shows the distribution according to bands of profit difference which an accountant might describe as

Table 3 Frequency table of distribution of values of index of comparability for profit.

Level of materiality	Index values	1988	1994
Adjustment to UK profit is −10% or more of the amount of US profit	≤0.90	5	4
Adjustment to UK profit between −5% and −10% of the amount of US profit	0.91–0.94	1	1
Adjustment to UK profit within +/− 5% of US profit	0.95–1.04	3	2
Adjustment to UK profit is between +5% and +10% of the amount of US profit	1.05–1.09	3	1
Adjustment to UK profit is +10% or more of the amount of the US profit	≥1.10	13	17
Total		25	25
Range (excluding outliers): lowest value		0.65	0.75
highest value		1.79	2.76

The following outlying index values were eliminated before calculating the t-statistic presented in Table 7

Name:	Index value eliminated	Year	Cause
ICI Group plc	3.36	1994	Large pension expense adjustment
WPP Group plc	10.77	1994	Low US profit figure

'immaterial' or 'material' or 'potentially material' (i.e. differences less than 5%, more than 10% and a grey area between 5% and 10%). In the majority of cases for both years, UK profit was greater than US profit, with 13 companies in 1988 and 17 companies in 1994 showing differences greater than 10%.

Intuitively, Table 3 gives the impression of significant and growing differences in reported profit due to accounting policy differences. A single-sample t-test and a Wilcoxon test (Table 7a and Table 7b) confirmed that the overall index values for both 1988 and 1994 were significantly greater than 1.0. Two large outliers in 1994 were eliminated from the calculation of the t-statistic but not from the Wilcoxon test. A nonparametric paired test on the index values, comparing 1988 and 1994, indicated that the difference was statistically significant (Table 7c). Out of 25 companies, 16 had an index value in 1994 greater than that of 1988.

The principal factors contributing to the profit differences are now analysed in detail, using the classification of causes set out in Table 1, in order to quantify more specifically the causes of the differences.

6.3 Measurement practices where UK is not compatible with IAS or US GAAP

From Panel (a) of Table 1 there were seven items where UK measurement practices differed from those of US GAAP and IASs at the relevant dates. Comparing these with Table 2 only three occurred frequently (accounting for goodwill, deferred taxation and pension costs), two were found infrequently (capitalisation of development costs and financial instruments) and the other two were either not found (consolidation policy) or were not relevant to measurement of overall profit (discontinued operations). Accordingly the first three are presented here.

Accounting for goodwill

Table 2 reports in one line all the accounting consequences of the UK policy on accounting for goodwill being different from that of the US. This covers adjustments related to annual amortisation of goodwill and also adjustments on the sale of a business where a write-off may be necessary.

Table 4 shows the distribution of values of the partial index of comparability. The number of cases where the adjustment to UK profit was 10%

Table 4 Frequency table of distribution of values of partial index of comparability for amortisation of goodwill.

Level of materiality	Index values	1988	1994
Adjustment to UK profit is −10% or more of the amount of US profit	≤0.90	0	0
Adjustment to UK profit is between −5% and −10% of the amount of US profit	0.91–0.94	0	0
Adjustment to UK profit within +/− 5% of US profit	0.95–1.04	12	8
Adjustment to UK profit is between +5% and +10% of the mount of US profit	1.05–1.09	2	1
Adjustment to UK profit is + 10% or more of the amount of the US profit	≥1.10	10	14
Total		24	23
Range (excluding outliers): lowest value		1.00	0.95
highest value		1.78	2.30

The following outlying index values were eliminated before calculating the t-statistic presented in Table 7

Name:	Index value eliminated	Year	Cause
WPP Group plc	9.02	1994	Low US profit figure

or more of the value of US profit increased from 10 to 14 when comparing 1988 with 1994.

Tables 7a and 7b show that for each of the years 1988 and 1994 the index value was significantly greater than 1.0. The pairwise comparison of reported profits in 1988 and 1994 (Table 7c) showed a significant difference over the period, as would be expected intuitively from the increase in the mean and median values of the index. Of the 23 pairs examined, there were 16 companies where the partial index of comparability in 1994 was greater than in 1988, and seven companies where the partial index was less in 1994. However in the latter cases the index was relatively close to 1.0.

The increase in the index is not a surprise given the acquisitive nature of these companies, but it does indicate that for companies active in the takeover market there will be an increasing perception of penalty related to amortisation rather than writing-off to reserves. It is possible to see, in this increasingly material impact of the effect of amortisation of goodwill, a cause for the concern expressed among UK companies when it was proposed that amortisation should become the normal practice. (Such concerns are documented in the letters of comment received by the ASB on various discussion papers relating to the subject of accounting for goodwill and intangibles.) The adjustment for intangible fixed assets, where disclosed separately, appeared less frequently. In some cases there were indications that the goodwill adjustment included an element of amortisation of other intangibles.

Accounting for deferred taxation

The frequency table showing distribution of the partial index values (Table 5) confirms a clustering around the neutral value of 1.0 in both years.

From Table 2 it may be seen that the mean value of the partial index for 1988 was 1.06. The t test (Table 7) indicated this was significant at the 5% level, but the Wilcoxon test indicated significance only at the 10% level. In 1994 the partial index was close to 1.0 and not statistically significant. The deferred taxation adjustment was the second most frequently occurring but by 1994 had become, on the average, of insignificant impact on reported profit. From the 21 companies that permitted pairwise comparisons (Table 7c) there were 15 companies for which the index value for 1994 was less than that for 1988. Overall the decrease was significant at the 10% level but not at 5%.

Pension costs and post-retirement benefits

The frequency distribution (Table 6) confirms a clustering around the central value of 1.0. The index values for adjustments relating to pension costs and post retirement benefits ranged from 0.94 to 1.12. In 1994,

Table 5 Frequency table of distribution of values of partial index of comparability for deferred taxation adjustments.

Level of materiality	Index values	1988	1994
Adjustment to UK profit is −10% or more of the amount of US profit	≤0.90	1	5
Adjustment to UK profit is between −5% and −10% of the amount of US profit	0.91–0.94	1	2
Adjustment to UK profit within +/− 5% of US profit	0.95–1.04	12	10
Adjustment to UK profit is between +5% and + 10% of the amount of US profit	1.05–1.09	4	2
Adjustment to UK profit is +10% or more of the amount of the US profit	≥1.10	4	4
Total		22	23
Range lowest value		0.90	0.73
highest value		1.43	1.34

Table 6 Frequency table of distribution of values of partial index of comparability for pension costs and retirement benefits.

Level of materiality	Index values	1988	1994
Adjustment to UK profit is −10% or more of the amount of US profit	≤0.90	0	3
Adjustment to UK profit is between −5% and −10% of the amount of US profit	0.91–0.94	1	1
Adjustment to UK profit within +/− 5% of US profit	0.95–1.04	7	8
Adjustment to UK profit is between +5% and +10% of the amount of US profit	1.05–1.09	1	1
Adjustment to UK profit is + 10% or more of the amount of the US profit	≥1.10	1	6
Total		10	19
Range (excluding outliers): lowest value		0.94	0.72
highest value		1.12	1.22

The following outlying index values were eliminated before calculating the t-statistic presented in Table 7

Name:	Index value eliminated	Year	Cause
ICI Group plc	3.07	1994	Large pension expense adjustment

301

Table 7 Index of comparability for profit.

7a. Mean value and t-statistic

Year	N	Mean	St Dev	SE mean	t	P value
Profit 1988	25	1.17	0.33	0.07	2.55	*0.01
Profit 1994	†23	1.25	0.47	0.10	2.61	*0.01
Partial adjustments						
Goodwill 1988	24	1.13	0.18	0.04	3.57	*0.01
Goodwill 1994	††22	1.21	0.30	0.06	3.36	*0.00
Deferred tax 1988	22	1.06	0.14	0.03	2.17	*0.04
Deferred tax 1994	23	1.00	0.13	0.03	0.11	0.91
Pension costs 1988	10	1.01	0.05	0.02	0.79	0.45
Pension costs 1994	†††18	1.02	0.13	0.03	0.52	0.61

*Significant at 5% (1-tail test for profit and goodwill, 2-tail test for deferred tax and pension costs)
† For information on 2 outliers excluded from t-test, see Table 3
†† For information on the outlier excluded from t-test, see Table 4
††† For outlier excluded from t-test, see Table 6

7b. Actual median, Wilcoxon statistic and estimated median

	1988			1994		
Year	N	Median	Wilcoxon statistic	P value	N	Median	Wilcoxon statistic	P value
------	---	--------	--------------------	---------	---	--------	--------------------	---------
Profit	25	1.10	244.0	0.02	25	1.18	268.0	*0.00
Goodwill	24	1.06	300.0	0.00	23	1.15	268.0	*0.00
Deferred tax	22	1.01	184.5	0.06	23	1.00	135.0	0.94
Pension costs	10	1.01	33.0	0.61	18	1.02	106.0	0.38

(No outliers excluded)
*Significant at 5% (1-tail test for profit and goodwill, 2-tail test for deferred tax and pension costs)

7c. Wilcoxon matched-pairs signed-ranks test

Adjustment (94 vs 88 in pairs)	N	Mean rank +ve ranks	Mean rank +ve ranks	Cases with +ve ranks	Cases with −ve ranks	Ties	Z	2-tailed P
Total	25	14.81	9.78	16	9	0	−2.00	*0.05
Goodwill	23	13.94	7.57	16	7	0	−2.59	*0.01
Deferral tax	21	10.17	11.33	6	15	0	−1.89	0.06

*Significant at 5%

excluding the outlier, the range had spread further with index values ranging from 0.72 to 1.22 and there were nine companies in the zones of plus or minus 10% or more.

Table 7a shows that even in 1994, where the costs of post-retirement benefits had an effect in addition to pension costs, the mean value of the partial index was not significantly greater than 1.0. This was confirmed by the Wilcoxon test (Table 7b). Although pension costs and post-retirement benefits are a frequent cause of difference, there is no evidence of a material quantifiable difference overall. Investors would focus interest on the relatively infrequent large adjustments.

6.4 Measurement practices where the UK differs from US GAAP but is compatible with IASs

Panel (b) of Table 1 reveals nine items where UK measurement practices differ from US GAAP but are compatible with IASs. Comparing this list with Table 2 it may be seen that the most frequently occurring relates to valuation of tangible fixed assets. Accruing dividends payable has no impact on profit measurement and the remaining seven items are found relatively infrequently.

Valuation of property, plant and equipment (Table 2)

The additional depreciation due to asset revaluation caused UK reported profit to be lower than the US figure. There were 14 companies making this adjustment in each year. The partial index of comparability was 0.95 for 1988 and 0.98 for 1994. In neither year was the index significantly less than 1.0. The IASC permits revaluation of fixed assets as an allowed alternative. Accordingly, if the SEC were in future to accept accounting statements consistent with IASs, UK companies could continue to revalue fixed assets and yet not be required to report the difference.

Other items from Table 1, panel (b)

Compulsory capitalisation of interest under US GAAP (borrowing costs— Table 8) caused five companies to make adjustments in 1988 and six in 1994. Since the existing UK practice is compatible with the benchmark treatment of IAS 23, there would be no requirement for a reconciliation in this respect if the SEC accepted practices compatible with IASs.

In the case of foreign currency translation (Table 2), five companies made adjustments in 1998 and four in 1994. Of these, two companies at each date used the year end rate for revenues and expense. Other adjustments (three in 1988 and two in 1994) related to reversal of translation differences on disposal of a foreign currency investment. The impact was not material overall.

Restructuring as an adjustment (Table 2) appeared in 1994 but not in 1988. The five companies reporting this adjustment in 1994 showed that in all cases the UK profit was lower than the US profit because the US rule did not permit the expense which had been reported in the UK.

For revenue recognition (Table 2), the three cases encountered in each year comprised one case of the amortisation of a capital grant, when the US rule allowed a revenue item not reported in the UK, and two cases of sale and leaseback transactions when the US rule did not allow a revenue item recorded in the UK.

6.5 Items not dealt with specifically by IASs

Some adjustments between UK accounting principles and US GAAP were reported which are not covered by a specific IAS. These were lessor accounting and a collection of items related by issues of recognition as an asset or an expense. Lessor accounting differences caused two adjustments in 1988 and four adjustments in 1994. These are quite technical issues which have not yet been developed by the IASC. Table 8 summarises all situations

Table 8 Recognition of assets.

Nature of adjustment (*indicates that one or more of the adjustments reported has an index number less than 1.0)	1988	1994
UK asset with amortisation; US expense when incurred		
Deferred expenditure	–	1
Development costs	1	1*
Purchased R&D expenditure†	–	1
UK expense when incurred; US asset with amortisation		
Acquisition related items (UK debit may to P&L or to reserves)	1*	1
Amortisation of software development costs	1*	1
Program production and development	–	1*
Amortisation of favourable leaseback terms	1	1
Natural resources depletion	–	1
Timberlands depletion and reforestation	–	1
Replacement expenditure (infrastructure assets)	1*	1*
Interest capitalisation†	5*	6*
Loan origination fees and costs	2	2*
UK write-off against reserves; US asset with amortisation		
Amortisation of capital restructuring costs	–	1
Amortisation of convertible bond expenses	1	–
Amortisation of debt issue expenses	1	–
Amortisation of preference share issue costs	–	1
Convertible redeemable preference share issue costs	1	1

†Issues on which there is a specific IAS

encountered in the reconciliations where an item may be recognised as an asset in one country but as an expense in the other. Relatively few of these are covered by a specific IAS.

Three categories of recognition practice may be identified. One is that the UK reports an asset with amortisation while the US reports an expense. The second is that the UK reports an expense while the US reports an asset with amortisation. The third is that the UK reports a write-off against reserves while the US reports an asset with amortisation. What is perhaps surprising is the number of items where the US approach appears less prudent by reporting an asset and spreading the cost, rather than taking the approach of reporting an immediate expense. The quantified impact and direction of the adjustment depends on the date on which the expenditure was incurred. Accordingly there is no systematic direction of the quantified impact of the policy differences. The table gives some support to the proposition that income smoothing is a stronger feature of US accounting.

7. Summary and conclusions

Three questions were asked at the start of the paper:

- What were the *de jure* differences between measurement practices under UK accounting principles as compared to those under US GAAP, during the period 1988 to 1994?
- What were the *de facto* differences in reported profits under UK accounting principles and US GAAP in 1988 and 1994, and what were the relative magnitudes of those differences?
- What implications do the quantified differences have for policy makers in setting UK standards, with particular regard to alignment with the IASs?

The key findings of the study are as follows:

1. Between 1988 and 1994 the most significant element of *de jure* harmonisation was the virtual elimination of extraordinary items in UK reported profits, moving closer to the US position.

2. Between 1988 and 1994 the issue of new US standards increased the level of *de jure* disharmony in terms of the number of potential causes of difference. This was evidenced by the summaries of changes in regulation and by the increased number of categories of adjustments reported by the companies surveyed.

3. As regards *de facto* disharmony, in both 1988 and 1994 the UK reported profit was significantly greater than that under US GAAP. Between 1988 and 1994 the difference between UK and US reported profit increased and the change was statistically significant.

4. In respect of those situations where measurement practices in the UK are not compatible with either US GAAP or IASs (Panel (a) of Table 1), the partial index of comparability indicated that the impact of goodwill amortisation was significantly greater in 1994 than in 1988. The impact of deferred taxation was statistically significant in 1988, but not in 1994. The impact of pension costs and retirement benefit costs, although frequently occurring, was not statistically significant in either year. Capitalisation of development costs, adjustments in respect of financial instruments and matters related to consolidation policy and discontinued operations occurred relatively infrequently.

5. Other adjustments of interest in relation to the gap between UK and US reported profit were related to asset revaluation and to the distinction between assets and expenses. Both indicate a relative lack of conservatism in US income measurement, in terms of the lower depreciation charge under historical cost and of the instances where an item is amortised over a period, having been treated as an expense when incurred in the UK. Income smoothing is the most obvious explanation of the second observation. It would be possible for many of these UK practices to continue as acceptable within the bounds of IASC standards. The detail provided in this paper indicates the flexibility of measurement which may survive within a programme of global standard setting.

These research findings have relevance for both the FASB and the ASB in relation to accounting standards. However, generalisation from these results is limited because the companies included are all multinational companies of relatively large market capitalisation. Nevertheless, the financial statements presented by these companies in the UK purported to represent, at each date, a true and fair view of commercial reality. If the divergence from US GAAP increases there may be a perception for US readers that there is an increasing question mark over what represents that commercial reality. UK readers of the 20-F may also question the extent of the difference. The companies undertook essentially the same business at both dates, and so observers might question the credibility of accounting as a means of representing the activities of a business. It is pertinent to note that the UK companies listed in Appendix B are all high-profile organisations having an international presence commercially, and of necessity feature prominently in relation to the campaign to persuade the SEC to allow foreign registrants to follow IASs rather than FASB standards.

The FASB has pointed to an apparently alarming number of differences between US standards and IASs. This paper has shown that in terms of the concept of materiality it seems unlikely that many of these differences will have an impact on the reported profit of UK multinational companies. The FASB should perhaps distinguish materiality of impact on measurement from detailed aspects of disclosure.

306

In the UK context, the early years of the work of the ASB concentrated on domestic-oriented issues and by the 1994 reporting period had not significantly reduced the differences between UK and US reporting practices. In the same time period the FASB was issuing standards which were taking US practice further from UK practice. The consequence for UK companies seeking finance in the US market is that they have reported increasingly different profit figures under the two reporting regimes.

The findings of this paper contain a message for the work of the ASB in relation to the IASC work programme and in relation to the ASB's stated aim of ensuring that, through a process of regular communication, accounting standards are produced with due regard to international developments. The subject areas causing greatest difficulty are those where there is the most frequent need for an item of reconciliation and the differences are material in sufficient cases to attract continued interest. Furthermore, the differences (taken as a whole) are increasing over time. It is a matter for further investigation as to whether investors do in fact have 'coping mechanisms', in relation to accounting differences, which can cope with growing disparity.

With the introduction of the accounting standard FRS 10 (ASB 1997) relating to intangible fixed assets, it appears that the ASB may have overcome difficulties with the most significant item, namely accounting for goodwill. It is not yet clear though that US regulators would accept impairment reviews of long-lived intangibles if the impairment test of the UK and the IASs differs from that of the US. Irrespective of the goodwill debate, it seems possible however that, if the ASB bows to national pressure rather than moving towards international practice in the particular topics of accounting for deferred taxation and pension costs, reconciliations will continue to be required by the SEC of UK companies.

The research findings also raise a question as to the relationship between UK companies and the standard setters. It may be that the approach most suited after completion and acceptance of the IASC core standards project will be:

- International companies—Apply IASs
- Listed national companies—Potentially facing choice between IASs and UK standards
- Large unlisted nations companies—Apply UK standards
- Small national companies—Apply FRSSE (Financial Reporting Standards for Smaller Enterprises).

Such a solution would mean that only multinational and listed national companies would be likely to have a direct interest in matters of harmony or disharmony, while companies essentially having a domestic base would continue to take the guidance of standard setters in a national context.

Notes

1 This paper avoids the abbreviation 'UK GAAP' which is more broadly expressed as the all-encompassing 'generally accepted accounting principles' mentioned in UK company law (Companies Act 1985 s262 (3) and Coopers and Lybrand 1988: 2001) but which has been espoused as 'generally accepted accounting practice' in a popular text from the firm of Ernst & Young (Davies *et al*, 1997).

2 Weetman and Gray (1991) reported 162 in 1988. The *Depositary Receipts Universal Issuance Guide* 1997, available from Citibank, indicates a doubling of the total number of depositary receipt programmes between 1988 and 1994. The listings provided by Citibank include some 220 UK companies, covering most of the FTSE 100 and other major UK companies.

3 There are three levels of publicly traded ADR programmes. Levels One and Two expand an issuer's share base through broader distribution of existing shares, while Level Three facilitates raising capital by issuing new shares. At Level Three the issuers must comply with full SEC registration and reporting requirements for foreign registrants. (Source: Citibank, *Depositary Receipts Universal Issuance Guide 1997*).

Appendix A Key differences between US and UK accounting policies, period 1988 to 1994, and comparison with relevant aspects of IASs. UK is compatible with IASs except where bold highlighting indicates differences.

Item	US GAAP	UK accounting principles	IASs
Goodwill	APB 17: Capitalise and amortise over a maximum period of 40 years.	SSAP 20: Immediate write-off against reserves. Amortisation over useful economic life is permitted but rarely applied. **SSAP 22 not compatible with IAS, FRS 10 (1997) moves closer to IAS 22 in principle but differences remain in significant details which could affect measurement aspects.**	IAS 22 Amortisation over a period up to 20 years is the required treatment. The practice of permitting goodwill on acquisition to be set against shareholders' interests was discontinued following the comparability project (Issued 1993, superseding 1983 version).
Deferred taxation	1988: For foreign registrants the situation was in transition from APB 11 (which required the deferral method and full provision) to SFAS 96, issued in 1987 but with implementation postponed, requiring the liability method with provision. 1994: SFAS 109 (effective from 1992) requiring liability method with full provision.	SSAP 15 and Companies Act 1985 requiring the liability method with partial provision. **SSAP 15 (revised) (1978, 1985 1992) not compatible with the revised IAS 12.**	IAS 12 (issued 1979, reformatted 1995, revised Dec 1996) The 1996 revision satisfies the requirement of the core standards programme. It requires a liability method based on temporary differences and does not permit partial provision. The 1995 version required that the tax expense for the period should be calculated on the basis of 'tax effect accounting' using either the deferral or the liability method.
Pension costs	Throughout period: SFAS 87 and SFAS 88. Fundamental principle is to recognise the cost of an employee's pension over that employee's service period. The measurement rules are tightly defined and may be regarded as measuring 'current cost' of providing benefits. It is unlikely that SFAS 87 figures would precisely fulfil the requirements of SSAP 24.	SSAP 24, CA 85 and UITF 4. General principle is to recognise cost of providing pensions on a systematic and rational basis over the period during which the company benefits from the employee's services. The measurement rules allow flexibility within a principle of recognition of cost. It is unlikely that SSAP 24 figures would fulfil the requirements of SFAS 87. However, SSAP 24 (1988 amended 1992) is stated to comply with IAS 19.	IAS 19 (Issued 1983, revised 1993). Projected benefit valuation method is also allowed.

Appendix A (cont'd)

Item	US GAAP	UK accounting principles	IASs
Post-retirement benefits other than pensions	1994: SFAS 106 required businesses to estimate the total future cost of providing such benefits and recognise that cost as an expense as employees render service, rather than when benefits are paid. Requirements are similar to those of SFAS 87.	UITF 6 and SSAP 24. The principles to be applied are similar to those for pension costs and accordingly SSAP 24 is applicable. Companies which use the measurement rules of SFAS 106 will be deemed to satisfy SSAP 24 principles. It is possible that measurement using the greater flexibility of SSAP 24 would not meet SFAS 106 conditions.	IAS 19 (Issued 1983, revised 1993). Benchmark treatment for all retirements is to use an accrued benefit valuation method. Projected benefit valuation method is also allowed.
Extraordinary items	APB 30 and APB 16 Definitions unchanged throughout period.	1988: Definition in SSAP 6 superficially similar to that of US standards but more liberally applied in the UK. Consequently many items allowed as extraordinary in the UK were exceptional in the US. 1994: FRS 3 (issued 1992) emphasised the rarity of extraordinary items and effectively brought UK close to US.	IAS 8 Definitions of extraordinary items less rigorous than FRS 3. Disclosure required in income statement.
Valuation of property, plant and equipment	ARB 43 and APB 6 Require historical cost only.	CA 1985 permits valuation as an allowed alternative to historical cost. Depreciation must be based on revalued amount (SSAP 12).	IAS 16 Allows measurement subsequent to initial recognition (Issued 1993 superseding 1982) Benchmark treatment is historical cost, valuation is an allowed alternative.
Borrowing costs	SFAS 34 as amended by SFAS 42, SFAS 58 and SFAS 62 makes capitalisation compulsory for certain assets.	CA 1985 defines a fixed asset very generally, but no preferred treatment specified for borrowing costs. CA 1985 permits either capitalisation or write-off.	IAS 23 Benchmark treatment is that borrowing costs should be recognised as an expense in the period in which they occur. Allowed alternative permits capitalisation under specific conditions (Issued 1993 superseding 1984 version).

	US	UK	IAS
Foreign currency translation	FAS 52 requires that profit and loss account be translated at rate prevailing at time of recognition or at weighted average rate. For subsidiaries operating in hyper inflationary economics, temporal method is required.	SSAP 20 permits profit and loss account to be translated at average rate or at closing rate **SSAP 20 (1983) permits translation of income and expenses at either average rate or closing rate.** For subsidiaries operating in hyper inflationary countries, restate financial statements before translation.	IAS 21 Translate all assets and liabilities at the closing rate and income and expenses at exchange rate of date of transaction – average for the period is an acceptable approximation (Issued 1993 superseding 1983 version).
Capitalisation of development costs	SFAS 2, SFAS 68 and SFAS 86 require immediate write-off.	SSAP 13 and CA 1985 permit recognition of an asset where specific criteria are met, but choice of write-off is allowed. **SSAP 13 permits capitalisation under specific conditions but allows write-off.**	IAS 9 Requires capitalisation of development cost where specific conditions are met (Issued 1993 superseding 1978 version).
Dividends payable	Reg S-X: No provision for dividends undeclared at the year end.	CA 1985 Provision must be made for dividends relating to the financial year although not declared until after it ends.	IASs apply normal accruals requirements – UK practice is within the general principle of accruals.
Correction of fundamental errors resulting from accounting policy change	APB 20, SFAS 32 Cumulative effect of change to be shown as a separate item in profit and loss account. In certain circumstances restatement of prior year figures is allowed.	1988 SSAP 6 required adjustment to opening retained earnings and amendment of comparative information. 1994: FRS 3 continues this approach.	IAS 8 Benchmark treatment is to adjust the opening balance of retained earnings to take account of the cumulative effect on profit. Allowed alternative is to correct in the current period, giving sufficient additional information about the change (Issued 1993 superseding 1978 version).
Business combinations	APB 16 requires purchase method for acquisitions and pooling of interests method for uniting of interests. The two are not interchangeable and specific criteria apply to each.	1988: SSAP 14 and SSAP 23 taken together meant that acquisition (purchase) accounting and merger (pooling of interests) were not necessarily mutually exclusive. 1994: FRS 2 with SSAP 23 still in place but FRS 6 was issued in Sept 1994 (effective for accounting periods commencing on or after 23 December 1994) tightening the rules on merger accounting to be stricter than US rules for pooling of interests. FRS 6 generally consistent with IAS 22	IAS 22 Defines acquisition and uniting of interest. The comparability project tightened up the definition of uniting of interest (issued 1993, superseding 1983 version).

311

Appendix A (cont'd)

Item	US GAAP	UK accounting principles	IASs
Financial instruments	Considerable guidance in SFAS 52, SFAS 80, (relevant to 1988 and 1994 accounts) and SFAS 105, SFAS 107 and SFAS 114 (relevant to 1994 accounts).	Little authoritative guidance until FRS 4 was issued in December 1993 (effective for accounting periods ending on or after 22 June 1994). ASB issued exposure draft (1997) on disclosure aspects of financial instruments. **FRS4 (1993) prohibits 'split' accounting for capital instruments which have mixed debt and equity components.**	IAS 32 Primarily a disclosure standard. (Issued 1995) Measurement was taken as a separate project but 'split accounting' for capital instruments is required.
Restructuring costs	FAS 5 and Interpretation No 1 to APB 30 have generally resulted in restructuring costs being accrued. EITF guidance issued in 1994 was more restrictive than UK practice. Several specific standards exist in the US	Limited guidance in UK – some guidance in FRS 3 on provisions where there is a decision to terminate, but no specific standard.	No specific standard.
Revenue recognition		No specific guidance beyond the CA 85 – only subject to general requirement for prudence.	IS 18 Standard presents general principles. Revenue is recognised when it is probable that future economic benefits will flow to the enterprise and that these benefits can be measured reliably. (Issued 1993 superseding 1982 version).
Investments in marketable equity securities and debt securities	ARB 43 (applies to 1988 and 1994) plus SFAS 115 (applies to 1994 only). SFAS 115 requires an investment in debt or marketable equity securities to be classified as 'held-to-maturity', 'available-for-sale' or 'trading'. Accounting treatment depends on these categories rather than current/non-current classification.	CA 85 prescribes treatment based on classification as current or fixed. Current asset investments are normally stated at lower of cost and net market value. Under alternative accounting rules, current cost may be used. There are rules in UITF 5 for transfers from current assets to fixed assets. SSAP 19 (1981, 1992, 1994) requires revaluation of investment properties held as fixed assets. Current asset investments still under consideration; impairment under consideration.	IAS 25 current asset investments to be carried at market value or at the lower of cost and market value. Long-term assets to be carried at cost or revalued amount (Issued 1986, reformatted 1995) Project on impairment test was announced in June 1996 for general application to all intangible assets.

Consolidation policy	Definition of control is similar to, but not an exact match to UK definition	All subsidiary undertakings must be consolidated. FRS 2 (1992) leaves almost no scope for exclusion of a subsidiary. Definition of control differs and, particularly following FRS 5 may cause consolidation of subsidiaries and quasi-subsidiaries not permitted in US. Unlikely to affect the 1988 and 1994 accounts analysed here.	IAS 27 Defines control. Allows exclusion of subsidiary if specific conditions are met. (Issued 1989, reformatted 1995).
Discontinued operations	APB 30, AIN-APB 30, EITF 85–36 and EITF 90–16. Definition differs from UK definition.	FRS 3, SSAP 22 and UITF 3. Definition differs from US definition – but reconciliations of profit measurement are rarely affected because this is a matter for separate disclosure within the overall reported profit.	IAS 8 Definition linked to US definition but less rigorous, disclosures required but, in contrast to US approach, under IAS 8 discontinued operations are to be included in the profit or loss from ordinary activities (Issued 1993, superseding 1978 version).
Stocks inventory	US permits LIFO as well as FIFO.	SSAP 9 (1975, 1980, 1988) UK encourages FIFO (LIFO allowed by SSAP 9 but not allowed for tax purposes). Does not affect reconciliations since US accepts FIFO.	IAS 2 Requires lower of cost and net realisable value. FIFO is benchmark treatment, LIFO is allowed alternative (Issued 1993 superseding 1975 version).

Sources; various SSAPs, FRSs and SFASs plus Price Waterhouse (1994), *An Introduction to US GAAP* for position at 1994 and Joint Study (1995), *Financial Reporting in North America*, various IASs and Epstein and Mirza (1997)

Abbreviations
AICPA   American Institute of Certified Public Accountants
AIN   AICPA Accounting Interpretations
APB   Accounting Principles Board
ARB   Accounting Research Bulletin
CA 85   Companies Act 1985
ED   Exposure draft
EITF   Emerging Issues Task Force
FRS   Financial Reporting Standard
Reg S–X   Regulation S–X issued by the Securities and Exchange Commission
SFAS   Statement of Financial Accounting Standards
UITF   Urgent Issues Task Force
US GAAP   Generally Accepted Accounting Principles in the US

Appendix B List of UK companies analysed in this paper for comparison with Weetman and Gray (1991).

Firm	Year end for 1988 data	Year end for 1994 data
1 Attwoods plc	31.7.88	31.7.94
2 Barclays Bank plc	31.12.88	31.12.94
3 BET plc	1.4.89	1.4.95
4 BOC Group plc	30.9.88	30.9.94
5 British Airways plc	31.3.89	31.3.95
6 British Gas plc	31.3.89	31.12.94
7 British Petroleum plc	31.12.88	31.12.94
8 British Steel plc	1.4.89	1.4.95
9 British Telecommunications plc	31.3.89	31.3.95
10 Cadbury Schweppes plc	31.12.88	31.12.94
11 Carlton Communications plc	30.9.88	30.9.94
12 English China Clays plc	30.9.88	31.12.94
13 Glaxo Holdings plc	30.6.89	31.12.95*
14 Hanson plc	30.9.88	30.9.94
15 ICI Group plc	31.12.88	31.12.94
16 Midland Bank plc	31.12.88	31.12.94
17 National Westminster Bank plc	31.12.88	31.12.94
18 NFC plc	1.10.88	1.10.94
19 Reuters Holdings plc	31.12.88	31.12.94
20 Signet Group plc	28.1.89	28.1.95
21 The Royal Bank of Scotland plc	30.9.88	30.9.94
22 Tomkins plc	29.4.89	29.4.95
23 United News and Media plc	31.12.88	31.12.94
24 Waterford Wedgwood plc	31.12.88	31.12.94
25 WPP Group plc	31.12.88	31.12.94

*Glaxo Holdings plc changed its accounting date so that there was an 18-month accounting period to 31 December 1995.

List of UK companies reported in Weetman and Gray (1991) not available for this work

Beazer plc	Takeover
Blue Arrow plc	Takeover
Cambridge Instrument Co plc	Not obtained
Dixons Group plc	No US listing in 1994
Huntingdon International Holdings plc	No US listing in 1994
Jaguar plc	Takeover
LEP Group plc	No US listing in 1994
Lex Service plc	No US listing in 1994
Plessey plc	Takeover
Rodime plc	Major reorientation of activity occurring
Saatchi and Saatchi Co plc	No UK listing in 1994
Shell Transport and Trading Co plc	US standards applied
Unilever plc	1994 reconciliation includes Unilever N.V.
Ward White plc	Takeover
WCRS plc (Aegis plc in 1994)	No US listing in 1994
Wellcome plc	Merger with Glaxo

References

Accounting Standards Board (1992a). *FRS 3 Reporting financial performance.* London: ASB.

Accounting Standards Board (1992b). *UITF 6 Accounting for post-retirement benefits other than pensions.* London: ASB.

Accounting Standards Board (1993). *FRS 4 Capital instruments.* London: ASB.

Accounting Standards Board (1994a). *FRS 5 Reporting the substance of transactions.* London: ASB.

Accounting Standards Board (1994b). *FRS 6 Acquisitions and mergers.* London: ASB.

Accounting Standards Board (1995). *Exposure Draft: Statement of Principles.* London: ASB.

Accounting Standards Board (1997). *FRS 10 Goodwill and Intangible Assets.* London: ASB.

Adams, C. A., Weetman, P. and Gray, S. J. (1993). 'Reconciling national with international accounting standards'. *European Accounting Review*, 2(3): 471–494.

Bhushan, R. and Lessard, D. R. (1992). 'Coping with international accounting diversity: fund managers' views on disclosure, reconciliation and harmonization'. *Journal of International Financial Management and Accounting*, 4(2): 55–87.

Cairns, D. (1995). *A Guide to Applying International Accounting Standards.* London: Accountancy Books.

Choi, F. D. S. and Levich, R. M. (1991). 'Behavioural effects of international accounting diversity'. *Accounting Horizons*, (June): 1–13.

Cooke, T. E. (1993). 'The impact of accounting principles on profits: the US versus Japan'. *Accounting and Business Research* (Autumn): 460–476.

Coopers & Lybrand (1998). *The Coopers and Lybrand Manual of Accounting: The Guide to UK Accounting Law and Practice.* London: Accountancy Books.

Davies, M., Paterson, P. and Wilson, A. (1997). *UK GAAP* (fifth edition), London: Ernst & Young and Macmillan.

Epstein, B. J. and Mirza A. A. (1997). *IAS 97*, New York: John Wiley & Sons Inc.

Financial Accounting Standards Board (1996). *The IASC-US Comparison Project: a report on the similarities and differences between IASC standards and US GAAP.* Connecticut, USA: FASB.

Financial Reporting Council (1996). *Progress Report.* London: FRC.

Grant Thornton (1990). *Audit Manual.* London: Longman.

Gray, S. J. (1980). 'The impact of international accounting differences from a security-analysis perspective: some European evidence' *Journal of Accounting Research*, Spring.

Hellman, N. (1993). 'A comparative analysis of the impact of accounting differences and return on equity'. *European Accounting Review*, 3: 495–530.

International Accounting Standards Committee (1989). *Exposure draft E 32 Comparability of Financial Statements: Proposed Amendments to International Accounting Standards 2, 5, 8, 9, 11, 16, 17, 18, 19, 21, 22, 23 and 25.* London: IASC.

International Accounting Standards Committee (1993a). *IASC Insight*, December, IASC.

International Accounting Standards Committee (1993b). *Statement of Intent: Comparability of Financial Statements.* London: IASC.

315

International Accounting Standards Committee (1994). *IASC Insight*, December, London: IASC.

International Accounting Standards Committee (1996a). *IASC Insight*, July, London: IASC.

International Accounting Standards Committee (1996b). *Annual Review 1996*, section on Developments in the US. London: IASC.

Joint Study (1995). *Financial Reporting in North America.* A joint study undertaken by the Canadian Institute of Chartered Accountants, the Instituto Mexicano de Contadores Publicos, A. C. and the Financial Accounting Standards Board, assisted by KPMG Peat Marwick LLP and available from any one of the three participating professional bodies.

Keegan, M. and King, H. (1996). 'Together but different'. *Accountancy* (October): 130–131.

Norton, J. (1995). 'The impact of accounting practices on the measurement of profit and equity: Australia versus the United States'. Abacus, 3(3): 178–200.

Price Waterhouse (1994). *An Introduction to US GAAP*, London: Price Waterhouse.

van der Tas, L. G. (1988). 'Measuring harmonisatinn of financial reporting practice'. *Accounting and Business Research*, 18(70): 157–169.

Wallace, R. S. O. (1990). 'Survival strategies of a global organization: the case of the International Accounting Standards Committee'. *Accounting Horizon*: 1–22.

Weetman, P. and Gray, S. J. (1990). 'International financial analysis and comparative accounting performance: the impact of UK versus US accounting principles on earnings'. *Journal of International Financial Management and Accounting*, 2(2/3): 111–130.

Weetman, P. and Gray, S. J. (1991). 'A comparative international analysis of the impact of accounting principles on profits: the USA versus the UK, Sweden and The Netherlands'. *Accounting and Business Research*, 21(84): 363–379.

Weetman, P., Adams, C. A. and Gray, S. J. (1993). *Issues in International Accounting Harmonisation*, Research Report No 33. Chartered Association of Certified Accountants, 39 pp.